INTRODUCTION OF THE
REFORMATION INTO ENGLAND
EDWARD VI (1547–1553)

THE
REFORMATION IN ENGLAND
II

*INTRODUCTION OF THE
REFORMATION INTO ENGLAND
EDWARD VI (1547-1553)*

By

G. CONSTANT

Formerly Member of the French Historical Institute in Rome

Fellow of Liverpool University; Docteur-ès-Lettres;
Professor at the Institut Catholique, Paris

Translated by
E. I. WATKIN

NEW YORK
SHEED & WARD
1942

PRINTED IN THE UNITED STATES OF AMERICA
BY THE POLYGRAPHIC COMPANY OF AMERICA, N.Y.

PUBLISHERS' NOTE

From this English version some of the less
important Notes are excluded. For these the
French edition should be consulted.

CONTENTS

APPENDIX I: BIBLIOGRAPHY

CONTENTS

CHAPTER I

THE CHURCH OF ENGLAND AT THE ACCESSION OF EDWARD VI (1547)

Henry VIII's death and Edward VI's accession—The English Schism—
Anglican doctrine and discipline at Henry VIII's death—Two religious
parties in the government and on the episcopal bench—Henry VIII's
endeavour to secure an equal balance between them after his death.

HENRY VIII had reached his fifty-fifth year. He was no
longer the slim handsome prince whose gracious bearing
and good looks had been lauded to the skies by foreign
ambassadors. Gluttony had made him prematurely
stout and by now he had become enormous. His excessive and dropsical corpulence made him resemble some
gigantic clown. His head, bust and legs, as we see them
depicted in his latest pictures were hideously puffed
out.[1] His small but bright eyes had almost disappeared
beneath layers of fat and his thick and swollen lips over-
hung a too narrow mouth. Since a fall from his horse a
chronic ulcer in the leg had never healed and required
constant attention. The pain it caused was so acute that
it deprived him of speech and spread a deathly pallor
over his countenance. His temper and character were
affected by the agony.[2] For a long time past Catherine
Parr had been simply her husband's nurse.

The last hour approached. The doctors dared not
whisper the word of doom. For it was high treason

[1] See the portrait, taken from his psalter, preserved in the British Museum
and reproduced by Chamberlin (*The Private Character of Henry VIII*),
London, 1932.
[2] *Letters and Papers* XIV, Part 2, 142: XVI, 121, 311, 558, 589 *sq*.
Chamberlin, *op. cit.* 199–202, 212–215, 265, 267, 279 *sqq*. From contemporary memoirs and papers the author has made out Henry's Medical
Record from the age of sixteen till his death.

I

to predict the king's death. On Thursday, January 27, 1547, Sir Anthony Denny, the first gentleman of the bedchamber, plucked up courage to warn Henry and urge him to prepare for his last end. The king received his advice calmly and replied that the mercy of Christ could pardon his sins were they even worse than they had been.

When Denny asked him if he wished to open his soul to some discreet man, he replied that he would take a little sleep and then consider the matter. When he awoke he sent for Cranmer. The Archbishop reached the palace about midnight. He found the king speechless, almost unconscious. But when he asked him to give some sign of his trust in Jesus Christ, Henry rallied his failing strength for a last effort and squeezed his hand.[1] Thus died Henry VIII at two o'clock in the morning of Friday, January 28, 1547.[2] He had reigned thirty-seven years and nine months. In his Will he ordered that his body should be interred in the choir of St. George's chapel at Windsor. "And as for my body which when the soul is departed shall then remain but as a dead carcase and so return to the vile matter that it was made of . . . we would be content to have it buried in any place accustomed for Christian people, were it never so vile. For it is but ashes and to ashes it shall return again. Nevertheless, because we would be loathe in the reputation of the people to do injury to the dignity which we are unworthily called unto, we are content, also by these presents do ordain that our body be buried and enterred in the choir of our college of Windsor."[3]

There he rests, not in the magnificent monument of marble and bronze which Wolsey had prepared for him-

[1] Foxe, *Ecclesiastical Memorials*, ed. Townsend, V, 692; Strype, *Cranmer*, ed 1820, I, 179; Fuller, *Church History*, ed Brewer, III, 233, 234 *sqq.*
[2] The Earl of Sussex to his wife. Ellis, *Original Letters*, Series I, II, 137. The French Ambassador was not informed of the King's death until Jan 31. Lefèvre-Pontalis, *Correspondance politique de Odet de Selve* . . . Paris 1888, 104.
[3] Fuller (*Church History*, ed. Brewer, III, 214-229) has published the King's will in full. It is dated Dec. 30, 1546.

self and Henry had kept for his own burial after the
Cardinal's fall,[1] but in the tomb of his third wife, Jane
Seymour, in the centre of the choir between the stalls
and the altar. During the Civil War the tomb was stripped
of its ornaments which were sold cheap (1646). The
splendid mortuary chapel, begun by Henry VII, which
Henry VIII left orders to complete after his death, was
left unfinished for more than three centuries. To-day it
is dedicated to the memory of a Prince in whose veins no
Tudor Blood flowed.[2]

Two hundred and sixty-six years after his death, in
1813, Henry's tomb was opened. They found the king's
skeleton with a little beard remaining on the chin, also
that of Jane Seymour, and the remains of Charles I,
covered by a pall of black velvet, which had been
placed there hastily after his execution by a few faithful followers, and a still-born child of Queen Anne in
a mahogany box.[3] Henry VIII's funeral was conducted
on an imposing scale. For twelve days his body lay
in state on a magnificent catafalque adorned with
shields, banners and countless tapers, surrounded day
and night by thirty guards. On February 8, alms were
distributed to twenty-one thousand of the London poor.
The same evening the Office of the Dead was sung in all
the churches, while the bells tolled throughout the capital.
The following day a Requiem Mass was celebrated.
Six days later (February 14) the body was taken in state
to Windsor on an ornate funeral car on which a wax
effigy of the deceased was displayed in accordance with
an old custom which survived in England until the
beginning of the nineteenth century. The court followed
on horseback, their horses covered with black caparisons
trailing to the ground. The boughs of trees overhanging

[1] *Letters and Papers*, IV, Intro., p. DCXVIII. cf. Pote, *History of Windsor Castle*, 1749.
[2] Albert Prince Consort.
[3] Sir Henry Halford, *An Account of what Appeared on Opening the Coffin of King Charles the First*, London 1813. cf. Fuller, *Church History*, III, 236 *sq.*

the route had been cut back so that the funeral train, which was over four miles in length, might not be broken. At every village through which it passed the royal almoner distributed alms in accordance with the late king's last wishes. The night was spent at Sion where the coffin rested on a catafalque of wax, built in nine tiers, adorned with sumptuous blazons and bright with tapers. The following day it was borne to Windsor where it was solemnly received by the clergy of the Royal Chapel, Archbishop Cranmer and five other bishops. A catafalque of thirteen tiers had been erected in the Castle. The evening of the day when the body arrived, Vespers of the Dead were sung and the Vigils (Matins and Lauds). And the following day three Masses were celebrated, at the third of which the body was interred. This third Requiem Mass was solemnly sung by Gardiner, the Bishop of Winchester, who preached the funeral sermon and gave the absolutions before the corpse was lowered into Jane Seymour's vault.[1] To the intense displeasure of the Pope, Francis I had a solemn service performed at Notre Dame for the deceased monarch as though he had not died in schism. The brother of the French Ambassador to the Holy See, a de Rohan, sang the Mass, and three Cardinals, Givry, Sanguin and d'Armagnac assisted with a number of Bishops. It was proposed to do the same in Flanders. But the Emperor's ministers shrank from incurring the Pope's displeasure and a possible censure.

In accordance with the Acts of Succession of 1536 and 1543, and Henry's Will, Edward VI succeeded to the English throne. The Parliament had empowered the King in 1536 to settle the crown as he wished, but only in default of a lawful male heir.[2] Mary and Elizabeth

---

[1] Strype, *Ecclesiastical Memorials*, IV, 290; Wriothesley, *Chronicle*, I, 178, 181. cf. Lefèvre-Pontalis, *op. cit.*, 104 *sq.* (Letter of February 21, 1547).
[2] *Statutes of the Realm*, 28, Henry VIII, Cap. 7. That is to say the power to bequeath the crown was limited. Henry never possessed the power to debar from the succession Edward VI, the sole heir whose legitimacy

had been declared illegitimate after Catherine of Aragon and Anne Boleyn had been divorced. They could there-fore ascend the throne only with their father's consent.[1] In accordance with these principles Henry settled the crown upon his three children in the following order: Edward, Mary, Elizabeth, and subjected his daughters' rights to conditions whose non-fulfilment would invali-date them. The Parliament of 1543 recognised Jane Seymour's son Edward as Henry's successor.[2]

At Henry's death Edward VI was a child of nine and his minority would continue for nine years in conformity with custom and his father's will. On January 31, Parlia-ment acclaimed him in Westminster Hall while the heralds donned their scarlet robes to proclaim him in the city.[3] Everywhere abroad except at Rome Edward was recog-nised as Henry's successor. Paul III wrote to Charles V urging him to support the claim of Mary Tudor. Since he was born in schism Edward had no title to the throne. Catholics could recognise only the right of the daughter of Henry and Catherine. But the Emperor, threatened by the League of Schmalkalde, did not regard his internal position as sufficiently secure. He also feared that to intervene in England without the support of a strongly organised English party would prove a risky adventure and might cost Princess Mary her life. He therefore fol-lowed the example of his fellow monarchs and congratu-lated Edward on his accession.

On Quinquagesima Sunday, February 20, 1547, Edward VI after the customary procession from the Tower to Westminster was crowned "with the utmost

---

was beyond dispute. Parliament had preferred to leave the succession to Henry's choice rather than risk the civil war which might have broken out had Henry died in 1536 without the power to designate his successor.

[1] The Act of 1543 gave the right of succession to Mary and Elizabeth unless their father should exclude them which he did not do. The statute therefore did not repeal the statute which had declared both princesses illegitimate.

[2] *Statutes of the Realm*, 35, Henry VIII, Cap. 1.

[3] Wriothesley, *Chronicle*, Camden Society, I, 178.

rejoicing and solemnity" according to the traditional
ritual. A few details were however omitted in view of
his age and weak health. Moreover, in the opinion of
the Council "many points of the . . . old observances
. . . were such as by the laws of the realm at this present were not allowable."[1] Cranmer crowned the child
King. He greeted him as Christ's representative and
Vicar, a new Josiah called to reform the worship of God,
abolish idolatry, banish the Bishop of Rome and cleanse
the church of images. He added that the Coronation
ceremonies possessed no virtue in themselves and the
Prince would be just as much a King without them.[2]

The new spirit which in less than seven years would
revolutionise the schismatic church and profoundly
change Henry's work had already found utterance.

Though Henry VIII, once the friend of Leo X who
had given him the title of "Defender of the Faith", and
Luther's detested adversary, after twenty-four years of
filial obedience to the Holy See and wedlock with
Catherine of Aragon, had broken violently with Rome
for a divorce he could not lawfully obtain, he had
refused to go further. He and his kingdom were schismatic, not heretical. The Catholic creed remained the
Anglican creed, and Anglican discipline also remained
Catholic. Throughout his life the King clung to
orthodoxy and persecuted the adherents of the new
doctrines. If loyalty to the Pope was accounted treason,
attachment to the Reformation was heresy.[3]

It was Henry's constant care to preserve in his kingdom
the unity of religious belief which, like his contemporary
rulers, he regarded as the indispensable foundation of

---

[1] *Order for the Coronation of King Edward*, in Burnet, *op. cit.* V, 133–137.
Among other changes the King was presented to the people before taking
the oath to observe the laws and respect the liberties of the realm.
  In the opinion of Lingard, Hallam and Dixon, the alteration was
intended to get rid of the last vestiges of popular election.
[2] Strype, *Cranmer*, Bk. II, ch. I, ed. 1848, II, 7 *sqq.*
[3] See my earlier volume, *The English Reformation under Henry VIII.*
London 1934.

political unity. "Amongst other cures committed to this our princely office," he stated in his first confession of Faith, "we have always esteemed and thought . . . this to be the most chief, most ponderous and of most weight . . . that unity and concord in opinions, namely in such things as do concern our religion may increase and go forward and all occasion of dissent and discord touching the same be repressed and utterly extinguished."[1]

With this purpose he issued several doctrinal formulas, all of which sought, sometimes with the aid of the most ruthless sanctions, to impose a single belief and eliminate the elements of discord which were beginning to trouble the realm.

They were three in number. But the three are in fact but one, developed, explained and definitely stated in accordance with the circumstances and needs of the moment.

The First Confession of Faith, the Ten Articles of 1536, is the least explicit. The Bishops lacked the necessary time to examine, discuss and draw up at sufficient length the body of doctrine which the people were to be taught. Later, however, the Catholic belief was expounded more exactly; and the final Confession, *The Necessary Erudition of a Christian Man*, is the most orthodox and most complete formulary issued during Henry's reign.

What then was the teaching of the Church of England at this period upon the questions disputed between Protestants and Catholics? The first of these is the question of the Eucharist. Not only is this sacrament the most important in Christian worship, it was also in the sixteenth century the focus of controversy. The Ten Articles of 1536 affirm the Real Presence of Jesus Christ in the Eucharist: "under the form and figure of bread

---

[1] Wilkins, *Concilia*, III, 817; Strype, *Ecclesiastical Memorials*, I, 85; Cardwell, *Formularies of Faith . . . During the Reign of Henry VIII*, Oxford 1856, p. xv *sq.*; Burnet, *op. cit.*, IV, 272.

and wine is verily, substantially and really contained and comprehended the very selfsame Body and Blood of our Saviour Jesus Christ which was born of the Virgin Mary and suffered upon the Cross for our Redemption: and under the same form and figure of bread and wine the very selfsame Body and Blood of Christ is corporally, really and in the very substance exhibited, distributed and received unto and of all who receive the said sacrament." This is the Catholic dogma of the Real Presence which Luther retained, but Zwingli and Calvin denied. Luther differed from the Church as to the mode of this real presence. He did not accept Transubstantiation, the doctrine, that is to say, that the bread and wine are changed into Christ's Body and Blood. According to him the bread and wine co-exist with Christ's Body and Blood. His doctrine was termed concomitance or consubstantiation. If the Articles of 1536 are silent upon a point about which no controversy had as yet arisen in England, three years later (May 1539) the Six Articles affirm transubstantiation in the following terms: "In the most blessed Sacrament of the altar by the strength and efficacy of Christ's mighty word (it being spoken by the priest) is present really under the form of bread and wine the natural Body and Blood of our Saviour Jesus Christ conceived of the Virgin Mary, and after the consecration there remaineth no substance of bread or wine nor any other substance but the substance of Christ, God and Man."[1]

Fearful penalties enforce this dogma, not defined by the Council of Trent until twelve years later.[2] Its denial was punished by burning and confiscation of goods. Even abjuration did not save the culprit from the stake. For disbelieving it Anne Askew was burned, and one of the grounds on which Cromwell, lately Henry's all-powerful minister, was condemned was that he had favoured Eucharistic heresies.

[1] Wilkins, *Concilia Magnae Britanniae*, III, 848.
[2] On October 11, 1551, Session XIII, ch. 2.

As regards the Mass no change was made. Catholics hold that the Mass is a propitiatory sacrifice, not merely a thanksgiving. It is offered for the sins and needs of the living and the dead.[1] Luther denied its sacrificial character and held that its sole object is the communion of the faithful. The Mass profits only the communicant.[2] Consequently private Masses, those in which the priest alone communicates and Masses celebrated for the living and dead were condemned.[3]

So long as Henry lived the Mass strictly retained its orthodox significance. At the visitation of the monastic houses under Cromwell every priest was ordered to say Mass daily and pray for the King and Queen Anne.[4] At the London Conference of 1538 which sought to effect a doctrinal agreement between the Churches of Germany and England, the Lutherans condemned the English custom of private Masses though prepared to recognise public Masses.[5] On leaving London they addressed a long letter to the King (August 5) in which they stigmatised private Masses as "a perfidy of the Roman Anti-Christ".[6] Henry replied in person: "If private Masses are to be abolished on the ground that Thomas Aquinas, Gabriel and other doctors have taught as you affirm impious doctrines, the public Mass should be abolished for the same reason which nevertheless you retain and do not think should be abolished. The Mass," he argued, "is a true sacrifice. To deny it is to risk denying the real presence of Christ's Body and Blood in the Eucharist: and falling into the error of the Sacramen-

---

[1] Session XXII of the Council of Trent, September 17, 1562.

[2] This opinion was submitted to the Council of Trent which condemned it. The matter was discussed on July 19, 1562, and the following days.

[3] The Council of Trent later defined, "If anyone shall maintain that Masses in which the priest alone communicates are unlawful and therefore to be abolished let him be anathema." Session XXVII, September 17, 1562.

[4] Burnet, op. cit., Ed. Pocock, IV, 221 sq.

[5] Dixon, History of the Church, II, 4.

[6] The German theologians' Letter to Henry VIII, August 5, 1538. Burnet, op. cit., IV, 35.

tarians. Our enemies must not be given this opportunity to calumniate us."[1]

It was in vain that Melanchthon wrote to him in support of the German theologians.[2] The Six Articles of 1539 pronounced that "private Masses are agreeable to God's law." To maintain the contrary was punishable by confiscation of goods or imprisonment at the King's pleasure. Men were even brought to trial for not hearing Mass or not bowing at the Consecration. In 1537 Henry had twelve hundred Masses celebrated for the soul of Lady Jane Seymour his third wife, and in his Will he made provision for a large number to be celebrated for himself by the Dean and Canons of St. George's chapel at Windsor. He even founded Masses in perpetuity. This clause of his Will was suppressed by Somerset.[3]

Communion under both kinds was another subject of dispute between Catholics and Protestants. It had been the custom of the primitive Church. During the controversy with the Manichees it had even been regarded as a mark of orthodoxy.[4] It is still the usage of the Greek Church and other Oriental rites. Communion under one kind was equally ancient. In times of persecution the Eucharist was taken to the sick and the martyrs under the species of bread alone. The Liturgy of the Presanctified common to the Greek and Latin rites is confined to the species of bread. Reasons of a practical character, such as the danger of infection during an epidemic and fear of spilling the Precious Blood gradually made communion under one kind the universal practice.

[1] Henry VIII's reply to the German Delegates, August, 1538. Burnet, op. cit., IV, 380–384. It was drawn up with the assistance of Bishop Tunstall of Durham.

[2] Letter from Melanchthon to Henry VIII, April 1, 1539. Burnet, op. cit., IV, 347.

[3] Henry's Will can be found in Rymer, Foedera, ed. 1713, XV, 110 sqq., and in Fuller, op. cit., III, 214–229; cf. Burnet, op. cit., I, 548 sq.; Dixon, op. cit., I, 366; Pollard, England under Protector Somerset, p. 7; Blunt, The Reformation of the Church of England, II, 81.

[4] St. Leo the Great, 4th Sermon for Lent.

John Huss in the fifteenth century was the first to maintain that communion *sub utraque* is of obligation, that communion under one kind is mutilated and that the species of bread does not contain the Blood of Jesus Christ which is present only under the species of wine. His error caused the Council of Constance to forbid communion under both kinds as a practice which might henceforth imply an erroneous belief. A century later Luther after some hesitation espoused the opinion of Huss and ordered communion *sub utraque* which has been the usage of all Protestant Churches ever since.

At the London Conference of 1538 the German theologians laid stress on this point and in their letter to the King of August 5, they demanded as an essential condition of agreement the abolition of Communion under one kind.[1] In his reply[2] Henry defends its lawfulness. "We cannot believe you seriously hold that Communion must always be given to the people under both kinds, so remote is that opinion from the true meaning of Scripture."

A long catena of Scripture texts follows. The King then adduces practical reasons which have made communion under one kind universal and by appealing to the Mass of the Presanctified he proves that the usage exists in the Eastern as well as in the Western Church. Communion under one kind was therefore maintained so long as Henry lived. The Six Articles (Art. 2) declare that communion under both kinds is not necessary to salvation: "It is to be believed and not doubted of but that in the flesh under the form of bread is the very blood and with the blood under the form of wine is the very flesh as well apart as though they were both together."

Twenty-three years later the Council of Trent in its session of July 16, 1562, was to define "that we receive

[1] The German delegates' letter to Henry VIII, August 5, 1538. Burnet, *op. cit.*, IV, 352.
[2] Burnet, *op. cit.*, IV, 374 *sqq.*

no less under one kind than under both, since Christ is contained and received whole and entire under each."

The Eucharistic doctrine of the Church of England under Henry VIII was therefore strictly orthodox. All the doctrines which the Protestants denied, the Real Presence, Transubstantiation, the Mass as a propitiatory sacrifice, the sufficiency of Communion under one kind, are all formally professed in the various doctrinal statements and moreover in terms as precise as those which the Council of Trent was to employ a few years later. Their profession is enforced by heavy penalties, confiscation of goods, even imprisonment and death.

As regards the other Sacraments the official teaching was equally orthodox. In the first place their number of seven, rejected by the Protestants, was maintained.[1] The second Confession of Faith (1537) and the third (1543) enumerate them in the traditional order and explain them in the Catholic sense.

The Sacrament which next to the Eucharist aroused the most controversy in the sixteenth century was Penance. The Protestants rejected auricular confession. Henry VIII retained it. The Ten Articles of 1536 affirm that it is of Divine institution and the last of the Six Articles of 1539 declares that "auricular confession in use in the Church comes from God."

The penalty for maintaining the contrary was the confiscation of goods or imprisonment.

The Lutherans regarded Purgatory as a myth. This is how the Ten Articles speak of it: "The commandment of charity no less than the voice of Scripture prescribes that we should pray for the dead and have Masses said for the repose of their souls. As to the whereabouts of

---

[1] The Ten Articles of 1536 do not specify the number of sacraments and mention only three, Baptism, Penance, the Eucharist. But the remainder were not therefore abrogated. Formularies dealing with them had been prepared and actually signed by Cromwell, Cranmer, the bishops and theologians, as is proved by a document preserved in the archives of the chapter of Westminster. H. Jenkins, *The Remains of Th. Cranmer*, Oxford 1833, Vol. I, p. xv, n.i.

Purgatory and the nature of the suffering there, nothing was defined by Scripture and these questions were left to the wisdom of the Almighty."[1]

The Reformation had vigorously attacked various practices of Christian worship, for example the veneration of images and saints, and many liturgical ceremonies. In this matter also Henry's formularies remained in agreement with the traditional practice of the Church. On all these points the Ten Articles of 1536 spoke plainly.

The veneration of images in the Churches, above all those of Christ and Our Lady, was declared to be excellent. It was a way of raising our souls to things above the senses. The people must be instructed that any veneration paid to images is directed not to the material image but to God and His saints.[2]

The Saints must be venerated not with the worship due to God alone, but as Christ's elect, our forerunners, and intercessors with God. To invoke the saints is a most laudable practice. But no superstition must be admitted. Nor must we believe that God hears a Saint sooner than Jesus Christ.

Holy water, blest bread, the Candlemas candles, the veneration paid to the Cross on Good Friday, the blessing of the Font and such like ceremonies were continued and their spiritual meaning explained: "These customs, rites and ceremonies be not to be contemned and cast away but to be used and continued as things good and laudable to put us in remembrance of those spiritual things that they do signify; not suffering them to be forgotten or to be put in oblivion but renewing them in our memories from time to time. But none of those ceremonies have power to remit sin but only to stir and lift up our minds unto God by whom only our sins be forgiven."

What Luther most bitterly opposed in the Church's

[1] Only the indulgences granted "By the Bishop of Rome" were rejected, in consequence of the schism.

[2] Some images were certainly destroyed in Henry's reign. But the King had alleged particular superstitious practices as his reason for doing so.

discipline were religious vows and clerical celibacy. Article Four of the Six Articles forbade marriage to men and women who had taken a vow of chastity, and Article Three declares that priests may not marry after they have been ordained.[1] The Germans, however, at the conference of 1538 did their utmost to win the English to their views.[2] They pressed Henry to abolish the celibacy of the clergy, a relic, they maintained, of the papal abomination.[3] The following year Melanchthon wrote to the King to the same effect.[4] Henry was obdurate. Celibacy, he replied, is not contrary either to Scripture or the practice of the primitive church, whereas clerical marriage was forbidden by conciliar decrees. He appealed to the witness of the Fathers, from whose writings he made a selection of excerpts in his own handwriting.[5] On November 19, 1537, he enjoined the Bishops to make careful search for priests who had presumed to marry contrary to the practice of the Church of England and his royal will.

When the Six Articles became law, Cranmer himself was obliged to send his wife away for a time, though he was the King's friend and enjoyed his special protection. The Articles indeed even declared priests who did not separate from their wives felons; and priests who kept a concubine were to suffer a term of imprisonment and be deprived of their benefices and possessions. A relapse was felony.[6] The women themselves were subjected to similar penalties.

[1] Wilkins, *Concilia*, 848; Lords' Journal. Cf. Burnet, *op. cit.*, I, 415.
[2] Cf. Dixon, *op. cit.*, II, 4.
[3] The German theologians' letter to Henry VIII, August 5, 1538; Burnet, *op. cit.*, IV, 352.
[4] Melanchthon to Henry VIII, April 1539; Burnet, *op. cit.*, IV, 349.
[5] Henry VIII's reply to the German theologians, 1538. Burnet, *op. cit.*, IV, 384–392. Cf. Ibid., I, 420.
[6] Cases of felony must have been frequent. For the Parliament in 1540 mitigated the penalty, substituting for the death penalty confiscation of goods and deprivation of benefices. (Bill of July 16, 1540.) Even so it was found necessary to wink at breaches of the law, so great was the number of offenders.

That is to say when Henry VIII died the Church of England in her doctrine, liturgy and discipline conformed on all points, save papal supremacy, to the Roman Church and was opposed to the Reformed Churches.[1] Under Edward VI we shall see her depart from the former and approach the latter. Step by step she yielded to the Reformation on all the points we have just examined. The change was slow and moderate under Somerset, rapid and violent under Warwick. In less than seven years England passed from schism to heresy, from orthodoxy to Protestantism, professing doctrines which Henry's formularies pronounced heretical and punished with the severest penalties.

The change is difficult to understand until we remember that in Henry's reign the Church of England was divided by two conflicting parties. One of these strove to preserve orthodoxy, the other championed a more or less radical reformation. The former, though schismatic, desired to remain Catholic in doctrine, the latter had come under the influence of the new doctrines and tended to Protestantism. Both were represented on the episcopal bench and both had their adherents among the lower clergy. A small number of laity were active partisans of one party or the other.[2]

The orthodox came later to be known as Henricians or partisans of Henry. For in spite of their attachment to the Catholic faith they preferred to deny the authority of the Pope rather than disobey their King. Of their number were Gardiner Bishop of Winchester, Bonner Bishop of London, Heath Bishop of Worcester, Day Bishop of Chichester and Tunstall Bishop of Durham.

---

[1] For all this see chapter viii of my *English Reformation under Henry VIII*. Fr. M. E. C. Messenger (*The Reformation, the Mass and the Priesthood*, London 1936, I, Part III *passim*) claims to detect Protestant infiltrations into the doctrine promulgated under Henry VIII. I have replied to him in two articles published in the *Downside Review*, V, 54, 1936: (A.) *Formularies of Faith during the Reign of Henry VIII*. (B) *The Reformation, the Mass and the Priesthood*.

[2] For what follows, see Chapters VI and VII of my *Henry VIII*.

The orthodoxy of the Anglican Church under Henry VIII was largely due to the Henricians. In the discussions which preceded the issue of the doctrinal formularies they championed Catholic doctrine against the advanced party. The surviving records of these debates and their writings[1] prove their staunch allegiance to the old religion and the energy they displayed in its defence. All their arguments are in conformity with sound theology, a theology still uncontaminated by the new teachings. They opposed the advanced views of the hostile party.[2] They returned orthodox replies to the questions, often very bold, which Cranmer dared to submit to the Commissions entrusted with the revision of the Anglican creed.[3] They imparted a Catholic accent and character to the doctrinal formularies,[4] which were drawn up in accordance with their views and thus widened the gulf between their Church and the Reformed Churches. Gardiner whom we may regard as leader of the Henricians consistently opposed a doctrinal agreement with the Germans. The older Anglican historians ascribe to him the failure of the Wittenberg (1536) and London (1538) Conferences at which the Lutherans went to the limit of concession to win to their cause such a country as England. At that time he possessed the King's ear and consistently advised him to be content with a purely political alliance with the German Protestants. The King, he said, should remain master in his own house and not yield to the doctrinal demands of foreigners.

[1] See British Museum MS. Cleopatra E. V. 125. Burnet, *op. cit.*, IV, 400–405.

[2] When the Ten Articles of 1536 were being discussed they refuted on the nature and number of the Sacraments Alexander Alanus whom Cromwell had brought into the committee to defend the new doctrines. Alanus, better known as Aless, had come over from Flanders the previous year. Cf. Dixon, *op. cit.*, I, 144.

[3] The promulgation of the final Confession of faith (1543) was preceded by a questionnaire which betrayed Cranmer's Lutheran ideas. The Henricians' replies were unambiguously orthodox.

[4] Particularly to that of 1537: *The Godly and Pious Institution of a Christian Man*.

This language was best calculated to win Henry's assent. Cromwell, on the contrary, urged the King to unite with the Protestant League of Schmalkalde and Lutheranise the Church of England. The Henricians persistently opposed him and strove to undermine his power. The struggle became open and lasted almost a year. Cromwell seemed on the verge of triumph when he was suddenly arrested, sent to the Tower and beheaded (1540).[1] Cranmer, his supporter, remained however a member of the Council. Twice the Henricians attempted his downfall. He owed his safety to the King's special favour. The victory of the Moderates was the victory of orthodoxy. Already in 1539 the Act of Six Articles had been passed which, as I have said, enforced by extremely severe penalties belief in the articles of faith most bitterly attacked by the Protestants. It was the terror of the reforming party, who dubbed it "the whip with six strings," and it remained in force until the end of the reign. It was attributed to Gardiner and in his diocese of London Bonner enforced it with a rigour which made him unpopular.[2]

Anglicans call this period the Catholic reaction. Norfolk and Gardiner, old allies, held undisputed sway in the Royal Council. Wriothesley, formerly a supporter of Cromwell, changed his opinions, joined the Henricians and was rewarded with the Chancellorship.[3] The progress of the Reformation was completely checked. Barnes, Gerrard and Jerome were burned. Dr. Crome, who had hinted a doubt of Purgatory, was compelled to retract in open Council.[4] The Bishop of Worcester, Latimer, was imprisoned.[5] Shaxton, the Bishop of Salisbury, was

---

[1] See Chapter VI of my *Henry VIII*.

[2] For Bonner see R. S. Maitland, *Essays on the Reformation in England*. London, 1849, p. 376 *sqq.*, 406 *sqq.*; and for the VI Articles, ibid., 244–309; also my *Henry VIII*, Chapters VII and VIII.

[3] He replaced Audley who died in 1544 and had composed, together with Cromwell and Cranmer, a species of triumvirate.

[4] *Zurich Original Letters*, ed. H. Robinson, Parker Society, I, 212 and n. 1.

[5] Wriothesley, *Chronicle*, I, 167, 168.

tried, condemned and forced to recant (1546). The heretics were severely persecuted and continental Protestants compared Henry to Nero. Tyndale and Coverdale's translation of the New Testament, the works of Wycliffe, Frith, George Joy, Barnes, William Turner and Richard Tracy were burned.[1] To possess an Anabaptist book was punishable by a fine of five pounds. The Parliament of 1543 forbade women and common people to read the Bible even at home.[2] The Henricians had won. "You can now cross England from one end to the other, north to south, east to west," a Protestant wrote to Bullinger, "without meeting a single preacher who with pure heart and sincere faith seeks the glory of God. The King has banished them all." Even if this statement is exaggerated it at least conveys the impression generally received of this final period of Henry's reign.[3]

In opposition to this moderate or orthodox party was arrayed the advanced party which sought with equal energy to secure victory for its views and forward the Reformation.[4] At its head was the Archbishop of Canterbury, Cranmer, who, as Primate of England, had completed the Schism by passing judgment in the matter of the divorce in defiance of the Pope and in Henry's favour. He was followed by Latimer, Bishop of Worcester; Shaxton, Bishop of Salisbury; Barlow, Bishop of St. David's;[5] Holbeach, Bishop of Rochester; Goodrich, Bishop of Ely; the Bishops of Lincoln and Lichfield and some others. Cranmer's theological views were daring and would become still bolder. He and his party inclined

---

[1] In 1539 ordinances had been issued against heretical books. Wilkins, *Concilia*, III, 847; Strype, *Ecclesiastical Memorials*, I, 530.

[2] *Statutes of the Realm*, 34 and 35, Henry VIII, cap. 1.

[3] Richard Hilles to Bullinger, 1541, in *Zurich Original Letters*, I, 204. The entire letter is a lamentation over the position in England of anyone who supports the new doctrines. For the moderates or Henricians see my *Henry VIII*, Chapter VII.

[4] For this party see Chapter VI of my *Henry VIII*.

[5] Latimer and Shaxton resigned their sees in 1539, Barlow was Bishop of St David's from 1536 until 1548. He had been Bishop of St Asaph in 1536 and was Bishop of Bath and Wells from 1548 until 1553.

to Lutheranism and sought to introduce it into Anglican doctrine. When the Second Confession of faith was drawn up in 1537, Cranmer maintained at the preliminary discussion that Confirmation is not of Divine institution, that the chrism which the Church uses as the outward sign of this sacrament is nowhere mentioned in scripture and the sole value of the rite lies in the Bishop's prayer. Capon, the Bishop of Bangor, said that the sacrament was not instituted by Jesus Christ but by the Fathers of the Church. According to Barlow, Orders are not required to exercise the ministry of the Church; a cobbler, if appointed by the king, can be a Bishop without being consecrated. Hilsey, Rugg and Goodrich put forward similar opinions.

Cranmer secured the printing of the first official English Bible. It had been translated by two heretics, Tyndale and Miles Coverdale. He plotted more far-reaching changes. The all-powerful minister, Cromwell, who was to be accused of having been "the chief author of the novelties then introduced into religion" was his patron and shared his views. Already, under the pretext of superstitious abuse, many images had been destroyed, and the shrines of the saints profaned. He secretly encouraged heresy.[1] The Six Articles denoted the check of these bold designs. The advanced party fought hard to prevent its enactment (June 1539).[2] And when it became law, Cromwell and Cranmer took care to make it a dead letter. "The popish faction," the Lutheran Burchard wrote to Melanchthon (October 1539) "has not been able to establish the tyranny that it hoped for. The Act has been passed but not enforced."[3] Cromwell's fall was a fatal blow to the reformers, already weakened by the

[1] Cromwell was accused of favouring heretical preachers and opposing those who taught the traditional doctrines. Meriman, *Life and Letters of Cromwell*, Oxford 1902, I, 324, *Letters and Papers*, XV, 766.

[2] For Cromwell see the eleventh essay in S. A. Maitland's *Essays on the Reformation in England* referred to above; also A. D. Innes, *Ten Tudor Statesmen*, ed. 1934, where there is also a study of Cranmer; and my *Henry VIII*.

[3] Cf. Dixon, *op. cit.*, II, 117 *sqq.*

resignation of Latimer and Shaxton after the enactment of the Six Articles. Cranmer himself on two occasions narrowly escaped his foes. It was only the king's close friendship that saved his life and kept him in the Council. He and his supporters hardly raised their heads until the very end of the reign when some reforms were vaguely mooted. But Gardiner, then abroad on an embassy to Charles V, warned Henry that religious innovation would isolate England by driving the Emperor into the arms of the French,[1] and nothing was done. Cranmer, however, was not idle. In silence and retirement he prepared the reforms which would ripen and bear fruit under Edward VI. It was at this time that he composed the "Book of Homelies", the first Lutheran infiltration into the doctrine of the Church of England. He also drew up the scheme of a new code of canon law, the *Reformatio Legum Ecclesiasticarum* and in the field of liturgy two projects which in the next reign served as the foundation of the Book of Common Prayer.[2] During his reign Henry, by his intervention, kept the balance between the two parties. Indeed his personal authority was the balance which prevented the undisputed supremacy of either. At need he took severe measures. When the reforming party became too strong he sent its head Cromwell to the scaffold. When the orthodox seemed to hold undivided sway, Norfolk was sent to the Tower[3] and Gardiner was excluded from the royal presence.[4] As a result the Reformation in England stopped short at schism without becoming heresy but

---

[1] *Letters and Papers*, XIV, Part II, 149.

[2] See *Cranmer's Liturgical Projects, Edited from British Museum MS. Royal*, Bk. IV. With introduction, appendix, notes and indices by J. Wickham Legg. London, 1915.

[3] *Lords' Journal*, I, 287–289. It was even believed abroad that Charles V could have counted on the support of Norfolk and his son to restore Catholicism in England. See the passage from William Thomas's *Peregrine*, quoted by Froude; *The Reign of Edward VI*, ed. 1909, 14 n. 1.

[4] Gardiner himself says so. (*State Papers Henry VIII*, I, 884). The rumour even spread that he had followed his friend Norfolk to prison. (Hilles's letter dated January 26, 1547. *Zurich Original Letters*, ed. Robinson, Parker Society, 1846–7. See also ibid., 639.

did not return to the unity of the church. This is what has been called the Anglican *via media*. Henry called it pacification.[1] In fact it was merely a temporary compromise resting solely on the king's authority.

Henry sought to perpetuate after his death. a compromise difficult to preserve in such stormy times as the sixteenth century. He considered it was in the interest of the crown and country and was loath to admit that his work could be altered. A schismatic church was not unknown. Why should he not found one that would last? By his will he set up a government in which the conflicting forces acting with equal strength would, he expected, cancel each other out and thus produce a stable equilibrium. The orthodox would moderate the zeal of the reformers, the reformers check the reactionary aims of the orthodox. In this way his royal work would remain intact.

This idea, it is said,[2] governed Henry's choice of the men who were to rule after his death and govern the country during his son's minority. The reformers were represented by Cranmer, Hertford the future Protector, Russell[3], the Earl of Warwick, Denny[4] and Herbert;[5] the orthodox by Wriothesley,[6] Bishop Tunstall, and Browne.[7] The two Wottons,[8] William Paulet,[9] Paget[10]

[1] Gardiner to Cranmer in Strype, *Cranmer*, Vol. II. app. XXXV ed. Ecclesiastical History Society, 1848, II, 464.

[2] Cf. Froude, *The Reign of Edward VI*, ed. 1909, 1.

[3] Baron John Russell, Earl of Bedford, had been keeper of the. Privy Seal since 1542.

[4] Sir Anthony Denny, first gentleman of the bedchamber.

[5] Sir William Herbert who was created Earl of Pembroke.

[6] Lord Chancellor since 1544.

[7] Sir Anthony Browne, Gentleman of the Bedchamber. Seneschal of England from 1539 to 1548.

[8] Edward Wotton, treasurer of Calais, took part in the various commissions appointed to settle questions concerning Boulogne and the frontier. His brother, Dr. Nicholas Wotton, was Dean of Canterbury and York, ambassador extraordinary to the French court in 1546, ambassador from 1546 to 1549 and again from 1553 until 1557. He sat on a commission appointed to arrange the restitution of Boulogne before the date fixed.

[9] Baron St. John created Earl of Wiltshire and Marquis of Winchester.

[10] Sir William, later Baron Paget, chief secretary of State, and comptroller of the Royal Household.

and Sir Edward North, who had no very decided views, were intended to hold the balance between the two other groups, by inclining now to the one, now to the other. Henry had deliberately excluded those whose too dominant personality or too advanced views might endanger the balance of the two parties, for example, Gardiner whom Henry alone, so he averred,[1] could withstand, Bonner whose activity against the heretics had been inspired by a personal conviction no less strong than Gardiner's, and on the opposite side Lord Parr, the Queen's brother, and Lord Dorset, husband of the king's niece, who were both regarded as extreme partisans of the Reformation. Henry's calculations were to be speedily discredited by events and the balance destroyed to the advantage of the Reformers who ruled throughout the reign of Edward VI. Henceforward the history of the Reformation in England becomes practically identical with that of the two conflicting parties in the Church of England. During Edward's minority the party of reform seized power. Under Mary Tudor it was crushed by the Henricians now once more Catholics. With the advent of Elizabeth it regained power and made England definitively Protestant.

[1] Paget's words quoted by Foxe, *The Acts and Monuments*, ed. J. Pratt, London, VI, 163 *sq.* Cf. S. R. Maitland, *Essays on the Reformation in England*, London, 1849, 309–323, 328–329, 339 *sqq.*

CHAPTER II

PROTECTOR SOMERSET AND THE BEGINNING OF THE RELIGIOUS REVOLUTION (1547-1552)

Henry VIII's Will—Somerset's Coup d'État—The Protector's past history and character—His religious opinions—His manner of government—His government of the Church of England—The first alterations in religion.

HENRY VIII had appointed a body of testamentary executors to govern the kingdom during his son's minority in accordance with his wishes. His will was to be a rigid constitution limiting the powers of the members of the government and controlling their action. All must co-operate in the same work and none must dominate the rest.

This will[1] which set aside hereditary right and practically debarred the Scottish line from the succession, was later, to please the Stuarts, declared a forgery. Some historians have, in fact, doubted its authenticity.[2] The very year of the King's death his daughter Mary declared that she did not know whether it were genuine or forged.[3] Its origin is somewhat obscure. William Clerc mentions it in a list of documents validated by the king's stamp. Henry in his last illness some months before his death (August 31, 1546) had empowered Sir Anthony Denny, Sir John Gates and William Clerc[4] to affix this stamp to state papers. But the original of the will, kept

[1] The original is in the Record Office which also possesses an authentic copy. (Augmentations Books, 469.) There is another contemporary copy in the British Museum (MS. Stow, 576 f. 11). It has been printed by Fuller, *Church History*, ed. Brewer, 211-229; Bayly, *Life and Death of John Fisher*, 1655; Rymer, *Foedera*, ed. 1713; XV 110 *sqq.* and elsewhere.
[2] *A Brief Tractate of the Invalidation of Henry VIII's Will*, British Museum, Additional MS., 1714, no. 29, fol. 849.
[3] Van der Delft to Charles V, July 10, 1547; *Spanish Cal.*, IX, 123.
[4] The signature thus stamped was afterwards inked over.

at the Record Office, shows no trace of the stamp.[1]
At the beginning and the end it bears the King's auto-
graph signature.[2] Those who contest the authenticity of
the will argue that nothing proves the signature genuine.[3]
The obvious haste with which it is written, Gardiner's
exclusion from the list of executors, its production by
Lord Hertford, the suppression of certain clauses, all
these things prove, they argue, that it was fabricated by
Hertford himself, probably with Paget's connivance.
This view cannot be maintained. For the will was of no
service to Hertford's ambition. He is mentioned only in
the fifth place. His power is equal, not superior to that
of his colleagues. He enjoys no special prerogative as
the king's uncle. It would have been better for him had
no such document existed. Moreover, when he fell every
possible charge was trumped up against him. He was
not, however, accused of forging Henry's will but on the
contrary with violating it.[4] Moreover, Hertford must
have forged not only Henry's signature but also the
signatures of the ten witnesses. He produced the will
because Henry had entrusted it to him.[5] And the
suppressed clauses were concerned with the foundation
of Masses in perpetuity and contained nothing affecting
his personal interests. It remains to account for the
contradiction between William Clerc's statement that
the document was validated by the royal stamp and the

[1] Comparison with the long extract from the *Acts of the Privy Council*
(ed. Dasent, II, 39–41) proves that the will whose original is at the Record
Office is the document in the possession of the executors. The Council
decided that each should be furnished with a copy. One of these, Lord
Cobham's, is in the Record Office.

[2] Clerc expressly states that the will was signed at the beginning and
the end. In the judgment of experts the two signatures are not sufficiently uniform to have been made by the stamp and differ materially
from signatures made in this way.

[3] The text states, "Signed with our own hand"

[4] Despatch addressed to the ambassadors accusing Somerset, 1549.
Troubles Connected with the Prayer Book of 1549, Camden Soc., 113.

[5] He had the key of the room in which it was kept. He gave it up to
the Council. Hertford to the Privy Council, January 30, 1547. P. F.
Tytler, *England under the Reigns of Edward VI and Mary*, London, 1839, I,
18–19.

fact that it bears the king's signature. Either Clerc included by mistake, among the documents to which the stamp was appended, the will drawn up at the same period; or the validity of a document thus attested seemed dubious[1] and another copy signed by the king[2] was substituted for it.

While Henry lay on his deathbed the Earl of Hertford plotted with Paget in a neighbouring corridor to seize the reins of government when they fell from the king's hands.[3] Later they said the king had sent for them to give them his instructions.[4] Edward Seymour, Earl of Hertford, Lord Chamberlain of England and uncle of Edward VI had the royal will in his possession and proposed to violate its spirit, if not its letter, to gratify his ambition. Sir William Paget, chief secretary of state, was the king's most intimate confidant and as such the repository of his real or imaginary wishes. Had he not passed the last nights of Henry's life along with his sovereign in lengthy conversations with him?[5] He was typical of those Tudor functionaries "who smacked of the willow, not the oak".[6] With the same zeal he served Henry VIII, Edward VI, Mary and Elizabeth. His pliant character pleased Henry. Neither Wolsey nor Cromwell, wrote the French Ambassador, were on such intimate terms with the king or enjoyed such freedom of speech, as did Paget, at the end of his reign. His intimate friendship with Henry was so incontestable

[1] The statutes empowering Henry to bequeath the Crown required that the will should be signed by his hand. *Statutes of the Realm*, 28, Henry VIII, cap. 7, and 35, Henry VIII, cap. 1.

[2] A. Bailey, *Succession to the Crown*, 1879.

[3] Paget to Somerset, July 7, 1549. Strype, *Ecclesiastical Memorials*, II, Part II, 430.

[4] Van der Delft to Charles V, February 12, 1547. *Spanish Cal.*, IX, 30. Paget was careful to add that the other Councillors had been admitted to the royal chamber only at his request.

[5] Ibid.

[6] *Ortus Sum Ex Salice Non Ex Quercu.* Naunton *Fragmenta Regalia*, 95. This reply was given by William Paulet (1485–1572), Earl of Wiltshire and Marquis of Winchester to those who asked how he had survived so many revolutionary changes.

that at Edward's accession honours were distributed on
his mere statement that such had been the late king's
intention.[1] Unscrupulous and without definite religious
views, Paget was just the man Hertford required for his
schemes. Edward's uncle was not confronted by anyone
in a position to defeat his ambitious schemes. His most
dangerous rival, the Duke of Norfolk, was in the Tower.[2]
Surrey, the Duke's son,[3] had imprudently excited Henry's
jealousy, by displaying on his shield the royal arms side
by side with his own and by cherishing the hope that
his father might be Protector after the king's death. He
had even persuaded his sister—she is herself our informant
—to become Henry's mistress in order to promote the
interests of the Howards.[4] Henry remembered that
Norfolk had once been spoken of as a possible claimant
to the throne and that a marriage had been suggested
between the Earl of Surrey and Princess Mary. Father
and son were arrested. On January 13, 1547, Surrey was
found guilty of treason[5] and a week later beheaded. On
the 18th, a bill of attainder (for high treason) against the
Duke of Norfolk was introduced into Parliament. It was
passed on the 24th and on the 27th received the royal assent.[6]
Norfolk's execution was fixed for the following day. Henry's
death saved his life. But throughout Edward's reign he
was deprived of his titles and dignities.[7]

[1] *Acts of the Privy Council*, ed. Dasent, II, 12–22.

[2] Thomas Howard, third Duke of Norfolk, Lord Treasurer from 1522
to 1536, uncle of Anne Boleyn and Catherine Howard.

[3] Henry Howard, Earl of Surrey, Norfolk's eldest son, was one of the
best poets of the period. His works were published by Nott, *Works of
Surrey*, 1815–1816, 2 vols.

[4] He was tried by a special commission sitting in the Guildhall. For
his trial, see the Stow MS., 396 in the British Museum.

[5] Wriothesley in his *Chronicle* (I, 117) dates the condemnation January 17.
But other authorities date it the 21st.

[6] The royal assent was given by the stamp of which I have spoken
above. For this reason it was pronounced invalid in 1553 and Norfolk
restored to his titles and dignities without repealing the act of attainder.

[7] With a few others he was excluded from the act of pardon of 1547.
He remained a prisoner in the Tower. Cf. List of prisoners in the Tower
in October 1549. (Tytler, *op. cit.*, I, 268; also *Troubles Connected with the
Prayer Book of* 1549, Camden Soc., 124.)

Gardiner also could have opposed Hertford's schemes. But Henry had excluded him from the number of his executors. Hertford's path was thus clear.

His first step was to gain Paget's support by promising to follow his advice when he came into power in preference to any other.[1] The pair decided to keep the king's death secret for several days and make only part of the will public.[2] It was not until February 3 that Chancellor Wriothesley announced in Parliament the demise of the king with tears in his eyes and his voice choked with sobs.[3] He read a considerable part of the royal will and pronounced Parliament dissolved.[4]

Meanwhile Hertford had secured possession of the young king's person, fetching him from Hertfordshire. In his haste he even took with him the key of the coffer containing the will and Paget had to send an express messenger to recover it.[5]

On his return he had himself proclaimed Protector by Henry's executors. The moderate group raised no opposition. The two Wottons were abroad, one at Calais, the other in Paris. Sir Anthony Browne, well known for his orthodox opinions, accompanied the Earl on his journey to Hertford[6] to fetch the king, and from the outset approved the suggested Protectorate. The

[1] "You promised," Paget wrote to him in 1549, "the day when we agreed together to raise you to your present position before King Henry's death to follow mine advice in all your proceedings more than any other man's." Paget to Somerset, July 7, 1549; Strype, *Eccl. Memorials*, II, Part 2, 429 *sqq.* In 1549 Paget was ambassador at the Imperial court.

[2] The Earl of Hertford to Paget, January 29, 1547. Tytler, *England under the Reigns of Edward VI and Mary*, 15–16. The Imperial ambassador was not officially informed of the king's death until January 31. But he had been told of it as a strict secret on the 29th. During those days no letter was allowed to leave the country. Van der Delft to the Regent of the Netherlands, January 31, 1547, *Span. Cal.*, IX, 7.

[3] "The Chancellor wept so that he could hardly speak." *Lords' Journal.*

[4] Parliament had sat on the 29th, unaware that the king's decease had terminated its legal existence.

[5] Tytler, *op. cit.*, I, 18–19. Cf. Froude, *op. cit.*, 2. Edward and Elizabeth showed grief at the news of their father's death. Cf. Lord Herbert of Cherbury, *Life of Henry VIII*, in White Kennett, *Compleat History of England*, 1706, II, 27.

[6] Tytler, *op. cit.*, 16–17.

Bishop of Durham, Tunstall, was Hertford's personal friend and had been his colleague in administering the Scottish marches. Therefore, when the executors met in the Tower on the afternoon of January 31, it was only to ratify what had been already determined. They had tacitly admitted Hertford's claims two days earlier, by asking and following his opinion as to a general amnesty.[1] On that occasion he had already assumed the tone and authority of a Protector[2] and the rumour immediately spread that the government was in his hands.[3] Wriothesley alone protested and he accepted the decision of the majority. It was he, in fact, who as Lord Chancellor announced the Protector's nomination to the king and Lords.

The assembled executors, therefore, declared that: "it should be more than necessary, as well for the honour, surety and government of the royal person of the King . . . as for the more certain and assured order and direction of his affairs, that some special man of 'their' number and company should be preferred in name and place before others, to whom as to the state and head of the rest, all strangers and others might have access, and who for his virtue, wisdom and experience in things, were meet and able to be a special remembrancer and to keep a most certain account of all our proceedings, which otherwise could not choose within short time, but grow into much disorder and confusion. . . . We have therefore," they continued, "by virtue of the authority given unto us by the will and testament of our late sovereign Lord and Master for the doing of any act or acts that may tend to the honour and surety of our sovereign

[1] The pardon was granted, as Hertford wished, at Edward's accession. Besides Norfolk, the following persons were excluded from it: Cardinal Pole, Edward Courtenay, son of the Marquis of Exeter who was a prisoner in the Tower, Richard Pate, an exile, whom the Pope had made Bishop of Worcester, and two others, Fortescue and Throgmorton.

[2] The Earl of Hertford to the Council, January 30, 1547. Tytler, *op. cit.*, IX, 17.

[3] *Spanish Cal.*, IX, 8.

Lord that now is, or for the advancement of his affairs, given unto the Earl of Hertford his uncle, the first and chief place among us and also the name and title of the Protector of all the realms and dominions of the King's Majesty, and of the Governor of his most royal person; with this special and express condition that he shall not do any act but with the advice and consent of the rest of the executors in such manner order and form as in the said will of our late Sovereign Lord is appointed and prescribed."[1]

The declaration was subscribed by the thirteen executors. The next day, February 1, they swore to carry out the testament whose spirit, if not letter, they had just violated as regards one of its most fundamental dispositions. Then they waited upon Edward to inform him of the Protector's nomination to which he gave his assent. Chancellor Wriothesley informed the Lords, who "with one voice gave their assents to the same."[2]

Thus the Earl of Hertford was recognised as Protector of England.

Five days later (February 6) Hertford's supporters received their reward. Paget declared that Henry had intended to confer certain titles and dignities upon his executors and certain others and had been prevented from doing so only by his death.[3] To render his statement more credible he did not include himself in the list. On his testimony Wriothesley was created Earl of Southampton, Viscount Lisle Earl of Warwick and High Chamberlain in succession to Hertford, William Parr

---

[1] *Acts of the Privy Council*, ed. Dasent, II, 4–6. In his usual fashion Froude (*op. cit.*, 3–4) changes or omits certain phrases of the official text without warning the reader.

[2] *Acts of the Privy Council*, II, 8.

[3] We cannot be absolutely certain that these alleged intentions of Henry's were invented. Paget claimed two witnesses who were not in a position to contradict him, namely, Sir William Herbert and Sir Anthony Denny in whose presence, he said, the list of honours which the King intended to bestow had been read. Cf. Froude, *op. cit.*, 4–5.

Earl of Essex and the Queen's brother became Marquis of Northampton, Somerset's brother Sir Thomas Seymour received a peerage and the post of Lord High Admiral held hitherto by Warwick. Sir Richard Rich was created Baron Rich of Leeze (Leighs). But Russell and Paulet were kept waiting for their promised Earldoms.[1] The most influential courtiers were thus obviously rewarded for not having opposed the Protector and the favour of the remainder conciliated. Hertford himself was not passed over. He became Duke of Somerset, received the Barony of Seymour de Hache and succeeded Norfolk as Lord High Treasurer and Earl Marshal.

To spare the royal finances, all the new dignitaries refused the revenues attached to their titles which Henry, according to Paget, had intended to bestow.[2] They pointed out that the Emperor, a dubious friend of England, might declare war in order to subject the country once more to the yoke of the bishop of Rome. It would, therefore, be unwise to empty the treasury and impoverish the realm. Monastic plunder recompensed their disinterestedness.[3]

At this juncture an illegality in the exercise of his office cost Wriothesley, the only man who had opposed Somerset, his position and his influence. The king deprived him of his office as Lord Chancellor and fined him £4,000. Though a little later he was re-admitted to the Council, he no longer possessed his

[1] Seven courtiers, among them Sir Thomas Cheyne, Sir Thomas Arundell and Sir John Leger, did not receive the baronies which, according to Paget, Henry had intended to bestow upon them.

[2] For example, land to the value of 500 pounds sterling to Somerset's brother, to Somerset himself land to the value of £800 and a further £300 from the next vacant see. See the renunciation of these grants in the *Acts of the Privy Council*, II, 12, 22.

[3] Somerset took Glastonbury, Sion and its hospital, Holme and Wimborne in Dorsetshire and Tame which had just been annexed to the new see of Oxford. His brother, Lord Seymour, took Abingdon, Hales, Winchcombe and Bardsey; Warwick six priories, Calk, Hirst, Kilburn, Ludlow, Penkridge, Coombe and an annual income of some 500 pounds sterling from the revenues of Colchester Abbey; William Parr, Pipewell; and Wriothesley, Shaftesbury. Tanner, *Notitia Monastica*—sub locis.

former authority nor played the active part that he had formerly attempted to play. Thus, the most dangerous adversary that Somerset might have had to face in his schemes of religious innovation was removed from his path.

The last barrier which still separated Somerset from the supreme power was now to be crossed. Hitherto the government had acted on the authority of Henry's will. That is to say it derived its power, not from the regular commission of the reigning sovereign but from the abnormal authority of a dead monarch. All the officers of the Crown, therefore, not mentioned in the will, required confirmation by Edward VI to hold their positions. Accordingly the Lord Chancellor "to remove all occasion of doubt or controversy" received the great seal from the king's hands. The ambassadors on Hertford's advice renewed their credentials, and Cranmer and the other bishops sought confirmation of their spiritual jurisdiction.[1] The executors in turn raised the question of their authority. How far was it legitimate apart from confirmation by the new king? The difficulty came up even in the sphere of foreign politics. When negotiations were proceeding for a defensive alliance between France and England, Francis I raised the objection that when he attained his majority Edward might perhaps disavow a treaty concluded by a government which did not hold its authority from himself. To remove these scruples and dissipate all misunderstanding the Protector and his colleagues regularised the situation by asking the new king to confirm their authority. Edward did so on March 13, 1547.[2] He appointed at the same time twenty-six councillors, the fourteen executors and twelve

[1] *Acts of the Privy Council*, ed. Dasent, II, 6, 13, 27. Lefèvre-Pontalis, *op. cit.*, 98. The date of Cranmer's commission as recorded in his register was February 7. Strype, *Cranmer*, Book II, Chapter I. A solitary protest came from Gardiner, who was severely reprimanded by Paget. Paget to Gardiner, March 2, 1547. Tytler, *op. cit.*, 24; Froude, *op. cit.*, 6, n 4.

[2] *Acts of the Privy Council*, ed. Dasent, II, 64. The royal mandate was registered in its minutes a week later.

assistants.[1] But the Protector was at liberty to consult
only those whom he chose and even to increase the
number of councillors. He had received "full power and
authority to do, procure and execute . . . all and
every such thing and things, act and acts, which a Governor of the King's Person during his minority and a
Protector of his realms and dominions and subjects ought
to do, procure and execute, and also all and every
other thing . . . which to the office of a Governor of
a King of this realm during his minority or of a Protector
of his realms, dominions and subjects in any wise appertaineth,"[2] and he was bound only by his conscience.
His colleagues' authority was henceforward indisputable.
They had preferred to become the privy councillors of
the reigning sovereign rather than remain the executors
of a deceased monarch. But in taking the step they had
submitted to a master. Instead of executors whose advice
the Protector was bound to follow by the terms of his
office they were ordinary Councillors who had no veto
upon his acts and whom he was at liberty to consult or
not as he thought fit.

The *coup d'état* had been carried out. Nothing remained
of Henry's will. The obstacles to the rule of one man had
been swept away. The Protector was no longer *primus
inter pares*. He possessed the substance of power, royal
authority without the title and dignity. His place in
Parliament was on the throne itself, to the right of the
king.[3] The prayer with which he inaugurated his
government is that of a sovereign rather than a subject.
He terms himself the pastor of God's people, the executor
of Divine Justice, he prays for victory, wisdom and the
success of the great undertakings which God destines

---

[1] The complete list is in Pollard, *England under Protector Somerset*, 38.
The Privy Council was thus identical with Henry's with three exceptions.
Gardiner, Thirlby and Wriothesley were replaced by Thomas Seymour
of Sudeley, Sir Richard Southwell and Sir Edmund Peckham.

[2] *Acts of the Privy Council*, II, 69.

[3] The right was conferred by letters patent. Leman's *Calendar*, p. 3.

him to perform. In a letter to the French king he actually presumed to style himself "the brother of His Majesty". Francis I had to ask the English Ambassador to remind Somerset of his position.[1]

Edward Seymour, Earl of Hertford and Duke of Somerset was born in 1505. He was the son of Sir John Seymour of Wolf Hall in Wiltshire who served in the wars of Henry VII and Henry VIII as a simple "knight". His mother, the daughter of Sir Henry Wentworth of Nettlestead, reckoned among her ancestors the Clares, and the Cliffords, Hotspur and Edward III. In 1514, at the age of nine, he was a page of honour to Henry VIII's sister, Mary Tudor, at her marriage with the king of France, Louis XII, the widower of Anne of Brittany[2]. In his youth he won distinction on the field and it was in war that he served Henry best. At eighteen his valour and services in the French campaign of 1523 won him a knighthood at Roye (November 1). In March 1539 he fortified Calais and Guisnes. In 1543 he commanded the army which invaded Scotland.[3] The same year he played an important part in the capture of Boulogne, took command of the captured town and successfully defended it against the French[4]. He then returned to the Scottish frontier, and reinvaded Scotland in September 1545, burning and pillaging monasteries and castles.[5] The Royal Council recalled him and sent him back to Boulogne to repair the damage done by the excesses of Norfolk's son, the Earl of Surrey. A few months later peace was concluded and lasted till Henry's death.

---

[1] Strype, *Ecclesiastical Memorials*, IV, 311. Froude, *op. cit.*, 9.
[2] He studied at Oxford and Cambridge, *Athenae Oxon.* Ed. Bliss, I, 210. Cf. H. Cooper, *Athenae Cantabrigienses*, 1858-61, I, 107.
[3] Cf. *The late Expedition into Scotland*, London 1544.
[4] See Nott's preface to *Works of Surrey*, 1815-16. Lord Herbert of Cherbury, *Life and Reign of Henry VIII*, ed. 1719, 250.
[5] *State Papers*, V, 448-452. Cf. H. Robinson, *Zurich Original Letters*, Parker Society, 1846-7, I, 37.

Somerset, however, owed his advancement and fortune quite as much to his sister's marriage with Henry as to his prowess as a soldier. Jane Seymour married the king on May 30, 1536. A month later he received the title of Viscount Beauchamp of Hache and several manors in Wiltshire.[1] A year had scarcely passed before he was admitted to the Privy Council. Six days after the birth of the future Edward VI (October 12, 1537) the king made him Earl of Hertford. The Queen's premature death (October 24, 1537) was a blow to her brother's influence. But it did not prevent him from rising, though more slowly. In 1542 he was appointed Warden of the Scottish Marches[2] and Lord Chamberlain of England. It was at this time that he commanded the English forces in Scotland and France. In July, 1544, Henry made him lieutenant of the kingdom during his absence in France. Throughout the closing months of the reign he was engaged in a concealed struggle within the Privy Council for the predominance which under Edward would secure him the supreme power. Conqueror of the Scotch, the young king's uncle, he considered his title to the protectorate as sound as the Duke of Bedford's during the minority of Henry VI and the Duke of Gloucester's during Edward V's.

The Protector's character has been variously estimated, as historians have exclusively envisaged his good qualities or his defects. These, however, should not be considered apart.

Somerset was ambitious. This is sufficiently proved by the way in which he seized power at Henry's death. He was grasping like other noblemen and gentlemen of his time. Monastic spoils tripled his patrimony within a few years. Though the treasury was empty he built himself a magnificent palace whose materials were

---

[1] The King had already given him some in reward of his services. He had been seneschal to the king's natural son the Duke of Richmond (1525), and had accompanied Cardinal Wolsey on an embassy to France (1527).

[2] He did not go, and in December asked to be relieved of the post.

provided by an aisle of Saint Paul's and the Church of Saint John of Jerusalem.[1] In politics he was a man of ideas rather than a statesman. He was far-sighted but not clear-sighted. His intentions were good but he could not carry them into effect. On the other hand few statesmen were so moderate as he, and in the Tudor period he was an incomprehensible exception. His moderation was regarded as weakness. On the eve of the coup d'état which destroyed him, Paget warned him against it. "Your Grace would have far too much gentleness, which might have been avoided if your Grace would have followed my advice."[2]

Paget, however, was the most loyal supporter of his policy. What then must the other members of the Council have thought? John Mason declared a few years later that "the worst act that ever was done in our time was the general abolishing of the Act of Words by the Duke of Somerset."[3] This statute punished with death a word interpreted more or less correctly by an enemy or suborned witness. It had brought Fisher and More to the scaffold.

Somerset was generous to his rivals and political

[1] He had inherited an income of 2,400 pounds sterling. In 1547 it was doubled and during his protectorate was increased by a further 3,000 pounds. (To obtain the equivalent in modern currency these sums must be multiplied by about thirty.) Cf. Wiltshire, *Archaeological Magazine*, XV, 189; *Cartae Edwardi ducis Somerset*, and *Grants of the Forfeited Lands of Edward Duke of Somerset*, edited by Sir Thomas Philipps, London 1866. In a freak of vandalism Somerset had the aisle of Saint Paul's, containing a celebrated "Dance of Death", pulled down. The Church of Saint John of Jerusalem had been rebuilt on a magnificent scale by one of the last Priors. Cf. Stow, *General Chronicle of England*, (London 1615), and Heylyn's *Ecclesia Restaurata*, ed. 1849.

[2] Paget to Somerset, July 7, 1549. Strype, *Ecclesiastical Memorials*, II, Part 2, 429 *sqq.* "Would to God that at the first stir you had followed the matter hotly and caused justice to have been ministered in solemn fashion to the terror of others and then to have granted a pardon. But to have granted pardons out of course gave men occasion and courage to sin. . . . Take the liberty of such towns as have offended into the King's hands. . . . Give them no good words or make no promise in no wise."

[3] J. Mason to the Council. *State Papers*, Foreign, IV, 306. Quoted by Froude, *op. cit.*, 39. Mason was a member of the Privy Council under Warwick's administration.

adversaries and always continued on friendly terms with them. He had proposed to Norfolk a union between their families and on Henry's death he saved him from the block. Within a few weeks of Wriothesley's condemnation he was conversing confidentially and amicably with the former Chancellor to the astonishment of the French Ambassador. He soon restored him to the Council, remitted the fine of £4,000 and paid him the legacy bequeathed by Henry VIII. He took, indeed, severe measures against Mary Tudor and Gardiner to enforce their submission. But he did so in such fashion that when the Princess and Bishop came into power they contemplated restoring to his children the dignities and wealth of which Warwick had deprived them.[1] Mary had hardly been proclaimed Queen when she released from the Tower the Protector's widow whom she had always treated as her friend and whom she addressed as "My good Nan".[2] Gardiner was imprisoned. But Somerset sent him his own doctor and continued to treat him as an old friend. And later when Warwick wanted to deprive him of his see he refused. If the Protector was not guiltless of envy, he did not cherish hate. Those who were most hostile to his ideas preserved a genuine and lasting affection for his person. He won the people's heart and his popularity increased daily. His death, as we shall see, was mourned by the nation. He hated violence and brutality. He was the first to prohibit in England the barbarous custom of the duel which did not finally disappear until three centuries later. It was, he said, a practice which destroyed the body and soul of one of the parties. Therefore he prohibited "single combats whose motive is vainglory rather than justice." The regular and handsome features of Holbein's portrait in the possession of the Duke of North-

---

[1] They were dissuaded from doing so, we are told, by other councillors.
[2] Cf. Mary's letter to Lady Somerset, April 24, 1547. Tytler, *op. cit.*, I, 51.

umberland and the melancholy depicted on the countenance betray a refined and sensitive nature. The
forehead is tall and broad, the nose prominent and
straight, the beard and moustache long. The total
impression is that of a kindly and sympathetic character.

What were his religious opinions? There is good
evidence that already in Henry's reign he cherished
prudently a secret attachment to the reformed doctrines.
He was delighted at the announcement of Henry's
marriage to Anne of Cleves, which promised the English
Protestants more prosperous days. He had not, he
wrote, been more pleased by anything since the birth of
the young prince Edward.[1] In a dedication the reformer
Peter Martyr praises him for having favoured the truth
and glory of God in perilous times.[2] His wife was
accused of giving pecuniary support to the heretic Anne
Askew, burned in 1545. His advent to power was
immediately hailed by Protestant rejoicings. Richard
Hilles wrote from Strasbourg at the beginning of 1547
that Somerset "is well disposed towards the pious doctrine,
holds in abomination the stupid inventions of the Papists,
has never favoured the priests and is a great enemy of
the Bishop of Rome."[3] He seems to have favoured the
doctrines of Zwingli and of Calvin who corresponded with
him.[4] The Calvinist doctrine of predestination has been
detected in certain of his utterances.[5] On occasion he even
uses the language of a Puritan, for example, when in one of
his ordinances he recommends "parents to keep their

[1] Somerset to Henry VIII. *L. and P.*, XIV, Part 1, no. 1275.
[2] Dedication of P. Martyr's treatise to be found in the British Museum.
It is entitled, *Of the Sacrament of Thanksgiving, A Short Treatise of Peter
Martyr's Making.* The passage is quoted by Gasquet and Bishop, *Edward VI
and the Book of Common Prayer,* 158.
[3] Letters of January 26 and February, 1547. *Zurich Original Letters,*
Parker Society, I, 256, 258.
[4] See the Stowe MS., 155, fol. 9 in the British Museum. Cf. Dixon,
op. cit., II, 525.
[5] Preamble of act abolishing the statute of treasons in which he claims
to be "Elect" and chosen by God to rule. (1 Edward VI, cap. 13.)
Cf. Somerset's Prayer in Strype, *Ecclesiastical Memorials,* II, Part 2, 311,
312.

children from the evil and pernicious games of dicing,
carding, bowling, tennis, quoits, clusshes and the like.''[1]
But it is difficult from these few and vague indications
to form a precise notion of his religious beliefs. What is
certain is that in the Council he represented the advance-
guard of the Reformers and so long as he was in power
did much to promote the Reformation.

Somerset's temperamental moderation inspired a
method of government which was a complete novelty
in Tudor times. For violence and oppression he substituted liberty and toleration. It was against liberty that
Paget warned him on the eve of his fall,[2] and "liberty"
was the cry which he was accused of raising, when the
end came, to incite the citizens of London to rebellion.
"Nothing," he stated in the preamble to the act repealing
the Statute of Treasons, "being more godly, more sure,
more to be wished and desired betwixt a Prince the
Supreme Head and Ruler and the subjects whose governor
and head he is, than on the Prince's part great clemency
and indulgency and rather too much forgiveness and
remission of his royal power and just punishment, than
exact severity and justice to be showed, and on the
subjects' behalf that they should obey rather for the
necessity and love of a King and Prince than fear of his
strait and severe laws."[3]

This is the language of a man who attempted to break
the despotic yoke which the Tudors had imposed on
England and Thomas Cromwell had made still heavier.

His chief preoccupation was respect for constitutional
liberty. Never since the Wars of the Roses had Parliament exercised its power so freely. There was entire
freedom of debate. The Journal of the Commons begins
at this period. That of the Upper House often records
prolonged discussions, lively debates, the rejection of bills

[1] Calendar of Hatfield MSS., I, no. 234.
[2] Paget to Somerset, July 7, 1549. Strype, *Ecclesiastical Memorials*, II,
Part 2, 429–436.
[3] *Statutes of the Realm*, 2 Edward VI, cap. 12.

introduced by the Government.[1] Five Bishops, the Bishops
of London, Norwich, Hereford, Worcester and Chichester,
voted against the bill introducing Communion under both
kinds, eight[2] against the bill confiscating pious foundations
to the Crown, eight bishops, an Earl and two Barons
against the Act of Uniformity which imposed the Prayer
Book of 1549. The Protector's brother and Lord Dorset
opposed the statute confirming letters patent issued since
the beginning of the reign.[3] This was an action directly
hostile to the Government. In all these cases Somerset
displayed no rancour and did not attempt to deprive
his opponents of their positions.

Every member could express his opinion freely without
having to fear the Protector's vengeance. The immunity
of Parliament was inviolable. When the Act was passed
confiscating pious foundations the representatives of
Coventry and King's Lynn[4] stubbornly opposed the
measure and sought to win over their fellow members.
Their opposition was dealt with on lines not unknown
in modern British Parliaments. The Government
promised that if they gave way their constituencies would
be exempted from the operation of the statute. And the
promise was kept. Such an exemption would not have
been permitted by Henry VIII or Elizabeth who would
probably have summoned the recalcitrants before the
Council, or even sent them to the Tower.

So long as Somerset ruled, the Royal assent to a bill
passed by Parliament was never refused. He even
consulted Parliament on foreign policy, which neither
Henry nor Elizabeth nor the first Stuarts would ever do.[5]

[1] For example a bill to unite Trinity and Clare Colleges, Cambridge
(February 1549), and a bill to destroy parks. (March 1, 1549.)
[2] The same with the addition of Cranmer, Tunstall and Goodrich.
[3] Lords' Journal, December 10, 14 and 15, 1547.
[4] Christopher Varenne and Henry Porter of Coventry, Thomas Gawdy
and William Overend of King's Lynn.
[5] The Council wrote to Paget, at that time on an embassy to Charles V,
on July, 1549, "That the treaty on the king's part had been ratified by
Parliament." State Papers, Foreign, Edward VI, I, no. 180.

Even to-day Parliamentary control of foreign policy is very slight. Finally the elections were free and there is no sufficient proof that the Protector ever interfered with them.[1]

We must not, however, conclude that the Government exercised no influence or control over Parliament. In the Tudor period the majority of peers held office under the Crown. In Edward's first parliament a third of the members of the House of Commons either occupied a position at court or were related to some high official. A number of Privy Councillors also sat in this house and formed a channel of communication between the Protector and the members.[2] Even to-day forty to fifty government officials have seats in the Commons. From this we might conclude either that the Government controls Parliament or Parliament the Government. In fact both conclusions are true. There is a mutual control which makes for good government. Somerset however did not profit from this mutual relationship. For, as we shall see, the Upper House and the Privy Council were usually hostile to his policy.

The Protector could at least have made a purge of the Council which, as in the previous reign, was the axis of government. For Edward had empowered him to nominate Councillors at his pleasure. But from first to last he appointed only three new councillors and then to

[1] The letter addressed by the Government to several constituencies was despatched three years after Somerset's fall. As for the creation of constituencies with which he has been reproached (Hallam, *Constitutional History*, I, 45; Stubbs, *Constitutional History*, III, 487) we must observe that of the 22 new constituencies created in Edward's reign only seven were created by Somerset. Of these seven, five (Wigan, Liverpool, Peterborough, Retford and Westminster) were justified by the growth of their population. Their creation was a reform. The same is probably true of the two remaining constituencies, Hedon in Yorkshire, and Brackley in Northamptonshire, though we cannot be certain.

[2] The two secretaries, Sir William Paget and Sir William Petre; the speaker, John Baker, Chancellor of the Court of Augmentations; Sir Edward North; Sir Anthony Wingfield; Sir Anthony Browne; Armagil Wade, Clerk of the Privy Council.

fill vacancies made by death. And of these three, two took part in his overthrow.[1]

Somerset might also have selected from the Council his personal adherents and governed through a species of cabal. For Edward had given him the right to consult only those councillors "whom he chose."[2] In fact all the important measures taken during his government are subscribed by his avowed opponents. Many of the Council's acts bear the signature of only six councillors besides the Protector, and the six are always the same. But so far were they from being Somerset's creatures that four of them plotted his downfall.[3] As far as possible the Protector restricted the arbitrary exercise of the very extensive powers possessed by the Privy Council. Proclamations, that is royal ordinances, were not indeed abolished. At this period it would have been impossible to govern without them. But they no longer had the force of law—so that their infraction no longer involved the penalties attached to breaches of law. The Star Chamber, which was simply the Privy Council in its judicial capacity, exercised criminal jurisdiction throughout the realm. It functioned as a centralised police which maintained order and peace.[4] Later it became a byeword for tyranny. Somerset restrained its activity and mitigated its severity. Under Henry VIII the Star Chamber pronounced more than four sentences a month. Under Somerset this figure was reduced to one, whereas

---

[1] Wriothesley, the Earl of Shrewsbury and Sir Thomas Smith replaced Lord Seymour, Sir Anthony Browne and Sir Anthony Denny. The Secretary of State Thomas Smith, was the only partisan of Somerset's who remained faithful to him.

[2] *Acts of the Privy Council*, ed. Dasent, II, 64.

[3] William Paulet, Wriothesley, Wingfield, North. The six councillors who almost always signed the acts are Cranmer, Sir John (William Paulet), Northampton (Wriothesley), Sir Anthony Browne, Sir Anthony Wingfield and Sir Edward North.

[4] The Star Chamber was close to the dining hall of the Council. *Acts of the Privy Council*, II, 385. During the brief reign of Edward VI it took cognizance of some 2,500 cases. See Miss Cora Scofield, *Study of the Court of Star Chamber*, Chicago 1900; Leadam, *The Star Chamber*, Selden Soc., 1904.

under Warwick it rose to the unheard of maximum of eleven.[1] Trials for treason were rare—only eight during the whole Protectorate.[2] There is no instance of the intimidation of a jury. This was not the case when Warwick succeeded to power.[3] Finally the Protector repealed the horrible statute by which poisoners were thrown alive into boiling pitch. Alone among English rulers of the sixteenth century he made no use of torture nor even of the pillory still employed in the eighteenth century. His rule thus constituted a genuine progress towards liberty and humane government.

The Protector's liberalism and moderation left their stamp not only upon his government of the state but also upon his government of the Church of England as the representative of "the supreme head".

The word "quietness", which occurs in almost every ordinance concerning religion, reveals his desire for religious peace and his government anticipates the epoch of toleration which did not begin in England till centuries later.

The first act passed by his Parliament was the repeal of the statute which had brought to the scaffold or gallows all who refused to renounce the "Bishop of Rome" and recognise the king as "the supreme head". Statute after statute had swollen the number of treasonable acts till they had become almost innumerable. All the offences of High or Petty treason committed by words, writing or deeds which Henry VIII had created to rid himself of opponents were now, with but two exceptions, abolished. Somerset retained only those laid down by the statute of Edward III (1352).[4]

The Act of 1536 which made the denial of royal

---

[1] Cf. *Acts of the Privy Council*.

[2] Six of the Cornish rebels, Lord Seymour, and Sir William Sharington, Master of the Bristol mint.

[3] *State Papers*, Domestic, Addenda, Edward VI, III, 78.

[4] 1 Edward VI, cap. 12. It was treason to attempt to alter the order of succession established by Henry VIII.

supremacy treason was not indeed repealed. But it was
considerably modified. Though it was still treason to
maintain by "writings, books and publications" that
the king is not and cannot be the supreme head on earth
of the Church of England and Ireland, it was no longer
treason to affirm it in words—even in sermons. Nor
was the penalty any longer death. Under the new law,
Fisher and More would not have been beheaded. Moreover, a man could henceforward be accused, tried and
condemned for Treason, Petty Treason, and Misprision of
Treason, only on the evidence of two sufficient and legal
witnesses or on his own confession freely obtained. A
provision so novel marked a considerable progress towards
justice and legality. Further the right of asylum and
the privilege of Clergy were restored. The widows of
those condemned for treason could recover their dowry.
All accusations of treason must be brought within thirty
days if the crime were committed in England, within
six months, if committed abroad. The Preamble explained that the calmer and more settled reign of
Edward VI required less stern and rigorous laws than
the stormier reign which had preceded it.[1]

The repeal of the statute against treasons improved the
lot of Catholics. The repeal of the laws against heresy
gave freedom to the Protestants. Parliament repealed
"all statutes and laws respecting in any way religion
and opinions". Thus were repealed the statutes of
Richard II and Henry IV *De haeretico comburendo* which
condemned heretics to the stake, Henry VII's statute
against heretics and Lollards, the Six Articles of 1539,
and the statute which made it a penal offence to print,
sell or possess the Bible in English or books of religious
controversy, in short all statutes penalising religious
opinions.[2] By this measure Parliament did but ratify

[1] *Statutes of the Realm*, 1 Edward VI, cap. 12.
[2] *Statutes of the Realm, loc. cit.* There was complete freedom of the press
with the single reservation imposed in 1548 and still in force, that every
publication must bear the name and address of the printer and publisher.

the practice which Somerset had followed for ten months. Protestants and Catholics could live at peace. Under Henry VIII those who remained faithful to the Pope were guilty of treason, the Protestants of heresy. On July 30, 1540, at the same hour three priests were hanged as traitors for denying the royal supremacy, three Protestants burned for impugning Catholic doctrine.[1] Under Somerset rack and thumbscrew remained idle, the fires of Smithfield were extinct, the executioner's halter or axe was not once used for a religious crime.[2] After his fall persecution revived with renewed vigour and raged in England for many a long year under the Tudors and the Stuarts. Somerset, anticipating the future, tried to effect reforms and introduce liberties which would later be England's boast.

The beginning of the religious revolution effected during this reign was marked by the moderation and prudence of Somerset's rule and differed completely from the action taken under Warwick. The first changes were made slowly, even with hesitation. The Government though bent upon their introduction was equally determined to restrain the excessive zeal of the reformers which might discredit them.

In fact the repeal of the Six Articles and the statutes against heresy broke the dykes which had hitherto held back the deluge of reform. If the majority of Englishmen did not desire doctrinal change, it was the

---

[1] *The Chronicle of C. Wriothesley* (ed. W. D. Hamilton, Camden Soc., 1875), I, 120 sqq.

[2] Thomas Chamberlain urged the Council in 1551 to prevent Anabaptists from entering the country, "That it may not be said that England has become a haven of refuge for all unbelievers." Tytler, *op. cit.*, I, 380. There was no Catholic martyr under Somerset. We shall see how he treated the Henricians who refused to accept the religious changes imposed by the Government. He refused to deprive them of their sees as Warwick subsequently did. A few Anabaptists whose numbers had become formidable were condemned by the ecclesiastical courts in 1549 to bear a faggot at Saint Paul's Cross. This was the sole punishment inflicted. Joan Bocher was condemned for heresy in 1549 but it was Warwick who had her burned at Smithfield the following year. Cf. Strype, *Memorials of Cranmer*, ed. 1848, App. XXXIX, 488; J. Gairdner, *English Church*, 278 sqq.

reformers who showed energy and were active. And in every revolution the vocal and active few outweigh the peaceable and indifferent masses and draw them in their train. England, therefore, when Henry's heavy hand no longer restrained them became the prey of a violent agitation conducted by the propagandists of the new doctrine. The older clergy who were often ignorant of the prayers they recited and elementary truths of religion[1] could oppose no effective resistance to the rising tide of the Reformation. The younger clergy far from desiring to check it were carried away by it, captivated by the new opinions.[2]

Hence the object of the Protector's first injunctions was to restrain rather than encourage the zeal of the Reformers. He ordered the rector and churchwardens of St. Martin's in London to replace in their Church the images they had removed, and he fined them twenty pounds each. He forbade the ill-usage to which the clergy of the metropolis were subject at the hands of apprentices and grooms.[3] An inventory of church goods was drawn up to prevent their too frequent misappropriation by the nobility. The following year, January 1548, an ordinance reminded any who might be disposed to infringe it of the obligation to abstain in Lent and on every Friday and Saturday. Another of February 6 was aimed at "those who rashly attempt of their own singular wit and mind in some parish churches and otherwise, not only to persuade the people from the old and accustomed rites and ceremonies but themself bringeth in new and strange orders, every one in their church, according to their fantasies. Wherefore," the ordinance continued, "His Majesty strictly chargeth and commandeth that no manner person of what estate, order or

---

[1] See an extract from the record of the Gloucester visitation (1551) published by J. Gairdner in the *English Historical Review*, 1904, 98*sqq.*
[2] Cf. Blunt, *op. cit.*, II, 78, 84 *sqq.*
[3] Dasent, *Acts of the Privy Council*, 1547–1550, 25, 521. Cf. Strype, *Memorials of Cranmer*, App. XXXIV, ed. 1848, II, 458.

degree soever he be, of his private mind, will or fantasy do omit, leave down, change, alter or innovate any order, rite or ceremony commonly used and frequented in the Church of England and not commanded to be left down at any time in the reign of our late Sovereign Lord, His Highness' Father."[1]

As in Henry's reign no one could preach without a licence, and the Protector reserved to himself the power to grant licences (April 24, 1548).[2] Moreover the Privy Council forbade licensed preachers to stir up the people to any innovation or change not authorised by royal authority (May 13, 1548).[3] Some months later, on September 23, the Council observed that even licensed preachers had disobeyed this order and to put an end to all religious controversy withdrew all licences to preach until the Act of Uniformity should be passed, that is to say until the appearance of the Prayer Book of 1549 which would render Anglican worship uniform.[4]

The Protector's intention was not to prevent change but to avoid too hasty changes. He did not want changes introduced by the whim of individuals and the imprudent zeal of the most ardent reformers. To prevent disorder, confusion and excesses no change must be made without the express command of the king, that is to say the Council. And the royal command always justified itself by some practical motive which made the government appear rather to check than foster the movement of innovation. Somerset advanced with the utmost caution. At first he did nothing for which he could not invoke the

---

[1] Strype, *Ecclesiastical Memorials*, II, 12, 346, (cf. his *Memorials of Cranmer*, ed. 1848, II, 455 *sqq*); Wilkins, *Concilia*, IV, 21; Burnet, *op. cit.*, ed. Pocock, V, 188; Cardwell, *Documentary Annals*, I, 38, 42.

[2] Cardwell, *op. cit.*, I, 59. Cf. Heylyn, *Ecclesia Restaurata*, ed. Robertson, Cambridge 1849, I, 71 and n. 1; Strype, *Memorials of Cranmer*, ed. 1848, II, 449.

[3] The Council's letter dated May 13, 1548, was printed in London on the following June 1. Burnet, *op. cit.*, V, 193. (In consequence of a printer's error the date given is May 23 instead of 13); Cardwell, *Documentary Annals*, II, 63.

[4] Fuller, *op. cit.*, ed. 1845, IV, 31–34; Cardwell, *Documentary Annals*, I, 70. Cf. Strype, *Ecclesiastical Memorials*, II, Part 2, 346.

authority of Henry VIII. Between February 1547 and March 1548 he was content with renewing almost in identical terms, three injunctions of the late reign.

The first forbade candles in Churches except before the Blessed Sacrament and bade the faithful substitute alms for candles and pilgrimages. On October 27, 1549, Hooper could write to Bullinger that the English clergy "still retain their sacerdotal vestments and the candles before the altar".[1] The second ordered the parish priests to read to the people in English every Sunday and festival a chapter of the New Testament after the lessons of Matins and a chapter of the Old after Vespers. And the number of Latin lessons in the Divine Office was reduced.[2]

A third injunction abolished, on the pretext of public order, the procession around the Church and to the cemetery, to avoid, so it was said, quarrels about precedence and brawling among those who took part in it. It was to be replaced by an English Litany which the priest would chant kneeling in the middle of the church.[3]

In 1547 no important change was made. The young king devoutly received the ashes on Ash Wednesday. It was not until February 6 of the following year that a proclamation ambiguously worded declared that no priest should in future be liable to punishment for omitting the blessing of candles at Candlemas, and of palms on Palm Sunday, for dispensing with blessed bread and holy water, or ceasing to veil the Cross during

---

[1] *Zurich Original Letters*, Parker Soc, I, 72. See the "Injunctions" of, Edward VI in Cardwell, *Documentary Annals*, I, II, 17–19. They are summarised by Heylyn (*op. cit.*, I, 70 *sqq*). Cf. Cranmer's articles for the visitation of his diocese (1547–1548) in Cardwell, *op. cit.*, I, 50, 51, 52.

[2] See Edward VI's Injunctions, nos. 20 and 21 in Cardwell, *Documentary Annals*, I, 13. Cf. Cranmer's visitation articles just referred to, in Cardwell, *op. cit.*,. I, 54. In 1543 the Convocation of Canterbury had decreed the same, without however reducing the number of lessons. Cf. Blunt, *op. cit.*, II, 82 *sqq*.

[3] Cardwell, *Documentary Annals*, 14 *sqq*. Cf. Strype, *Memorials of Cranmer*, App. XXXIV, ed. 1848, II, 452–453 and 497. Wilkins, *Concilia*, IV, 3 *sqq*. Cranmer's visitation articles; Cardwell, *op. cit.*, I, 54.

Holy Week.[1] On January 18, Latimer had preached against these practices and on the 27th Cranmer had informed the Bishops that the Protector and the Privy Council wished to abolish the ashes, palms and Candlemas candles.[2] But the observance of Lent was continued and an act of Parliament passed shortly after appeared to enforce it.[3]

These first changes reveal the Protector's procedure. He does not order a change, he merely authorises it. No royal command is issued. The wishes of the government are indicated by the intermediary of the Primate. Somerset does not so much impose the reformation, as insinuate it slowly and without violent shocks. This procedure is peculiar to himself and demands notice.

It is equally exemplified by the proclamations about images. Somerset began by renewing Henry's former injunctions that any statue or picture liable to superstitious abuse should be removed.[4] But iconoclastic sentiment was so strong in certain districts that no distinction was made between what was and what was not superstitious. Therefore an injunction was issued ordering images not superstitiously abused to be replaced. During the Protector's absence in Scotland this injunction was suspended until his return (September 1547) "to avoid," it was alleged, "contention and strife among the people which the distinction between what was and what was not superstitious abuse might occasion." In fact these disputes occurred. They became so frequent, indeed so universal, that another injunction took the radical step of ordering

---

[1] Wilkins, *op. cit.*, IV, 121; Burnet, *op. cit.*, II, 129.

[2] Cardwell, *Documentary Annals*, I, 45. Cf. Cranmer's visitation articles, 1547–1548, ibid., I, 56. For Latimer's sermon see *Latimer's Sermons*, Parker Society, London 1858, 70 *sqq.*

[3] Wilkins, *op. cit.*, IV, 22; Heylyn, *op. cit.*, 71, 117 *sqq.*, 144; Cardwell, *op. cit.*, I, 38.

[4] Wilkins, *op. cit.*, IV, 3 *sqq.* ,Strype, *Memorials of Cranmer*, V, 235, App. XXXIV, ed. 1848, II, 445 *sqq.*, 449, 456; cf. ibid., 493, 502. See Heylyn, *op. cit.*, I, 71.

all images to be removed.[1] But it cannot have been strictly enforced. For Warwick immediately after his advent to power passed a bill through Parliament against the images and pictures which were still retained in the churches.[2]

The same procedure was followed as regards two books which received the Protector's authorisation at the beginning of his government, namely Erasmus's *Paraphrases of the New Testament* and Cranmer's *Book of Homilies*.[3]

Erasmus's *Paraphrases* was not a Lutheran book and it had been translated by Udall, the father of English comedy, in the reign of Henry VIII.[4] Princess Mary had taken part in the translation. Its authorisation did not therefore contravene the statutes lately passed which had forbidden Tyndale and Coverdale's New Testament as heretical. It appeared that a work of the previous reign whose earlier publication had been impossible, had now been published. Indeed one portion of the work had been dedicated to Henry VIII by Erasmus. The *Paraphrases*, however, cloaked beneath the story of Jesus and the Apostles a bitter satire on the Church of the sixteenth century. To put it in the hands of all readers indiscriminately by placing a copy in every church, as the Injunctions prescribed, could not fail to do considerable harm and was a dangerous step to take.[5]

---

[1] See Cranmer's *Mandatum ad Amovendas et Delendas Imagines* (February 24, 1548), in Cardwell's *Documentary Annals*, I, 47; Burnet *op. cit.*, V, 91, 1849, and Collier, *op. cit.*, Ed Lathbury, Vol. V. Cranmer simply passed on with his personal endorsement the Order of the Council of February 21 of the same year.

[2] 3 and 4 Edward VI., cap 10.

[3] Cf. Heylyn, *op. cit.*, 70, 73; Wilkins *Concilia*, IV, 3 *sqq.*; Strype, *Memorials of Cranmer*, App. XXXIV, ed. 1848, II, 447 *sqq.*; 458; cf. *Ibid.*, 496. Cranmer appealed to this order in his visitation articles (1547–8). Cardwell, *Documentary Annals*, I 52, 53.

[4] Nicholas Udall, headmaster of Eton from 1534 to 1541, was made a Canon of Windsor at Edward's accession and was headmaster of Westminster under Queen Mary. He had long adopted the opinions of the reformers. His name appears in 1528 in a list of Oxford men suspect of heresy. But he conformed to the religious views of the government with equal pliability under Henry, Edward and Mary.

[5] The *Paraphrases* are a translation of the Greek New Testament with accompanying notes. Not only was the English translation inaccurate but

Cranmer's *Book of Homelies* was also a work of the late reign. It had even been submitted to the Convocation of 1543 which probably refused its approbation.[1] In this case also it seemed that the Government merely continued what had been already begun, and that a book was published which had been already compiled in the late King's time. The ostensible object of the *Homelies* was to check the extravagance of ignorant preachers. But under colour of explaining certain articles of faith they introduced novel doctrines into the Anglican creed. On several points they ran counter to Henry's Confessions of Faith which, nevertheless, were still the official standard of doctrine. In the Homely on Good Works several rites and ceremonies are vigorously denounced as popish superstitions; for example, blessed bread, palms and candles. Justification, faith and good works, which had aroused in Germany controversies which had resounded throughout Christendom, were explained in the Lutheran fashion.[2] Bucer accordingly lavished praise on the *Homelies*. "I have received your Homelies," he wrote to the Church of England in imitation of St. Paul's manner of address. "I have received the sermons in which you piously exhort the people to read the Scriptures and expound with abundant knowledge the faith that makes us Christians and the justification wherein our entire salvation consists, also all the other principal points of religion. With what scrupulous accuracy you

---

many expressions and passages written before Luther had broached his heresy did not represent the later and wiser thought of Erasmus himself. Udall placed his translation under the patronage of Catherine Parr whose panegyric he writes in one of his prefaces. In the first he flatters the Protector.

[1] *L. and P.*, 1543, part I, n. 167.

[2] Justification is said to consist solely in the remission of sin and is effected by faith only without the participation of charity which, Gardiner said, is opposed to Scripture and the Fathers. Faith is confused with hope and in the work of salvation there is assigned to it a part which excludes good works. Cranmer's *Homelies* were printed by Grafton in July 1547; in the edition of 1549 they were redivided into thirty-two. Those on justification, faith and good works are to be found in Cranmer's works.

distinguish a living from a dead faith and define the works accomplished by those who are justified. Nothing of the old leaven will long survive among you whether in doctrine or in discipline. The work will be completed. The sacraments will be administered according to Christ's institution and held to be simple signs of grace."

In this way Protestant doctrine was discreetly insinuated into a creed which ostensibly remained inviolate.

Few changes were demanded so insistently by the Reformers as the abolition of clerical celibacy. Somerset granted their demand only with reluctance, gradually and incompletely. In November 1547, Convocation proposed that all canons and customs forbidding the marriage of priests or religious should be abolished. In consequence a bill was introduced into Parliament, enacting, not that priests might marry, but that married laymen might become priests and hold benefices.

This was, indeed, the custom of the primitive Church as it is still the custom of the Greek Church and even of the Uniats. It was in this form that Charles V and later his brother Ferdinand requested the Council of Trent and the Pope to permit a married clergy in Germany. The bill passed the Commons but reached the House of Lords too late (December 24, 1547).[1] The question was not brought up again till 1549. In that year an Act of Parliament repealed all enactments imposing lifelong celibacy, but apparently with regret and not without expressing some disapproval of the marriage it permitted. "Since it were not only better," said the Act, "for the estimation of priests and other ministers in the Church of God to live chaste, sole and separate from the company of women and the bond of marriage, but also thereby they might the better extend to the administration of the Gospel . . . it were most to be

---

[1] *Lords' Journal*, I, 311. Strype (*Ecclesiastical Memorials*, III, 20) says that the bill was not passed because it reached the Lords only two or three days before the close of the session.

wished that they would willingly and of themselves endeavour themself to a perpetual chastity."

That is to say the repeal of the laws against clerical marriage was not the recognition of a principle but a mere concession to human weakness, we might even say the choice of a lesser evil.[1] The statute, a mere toleration, was so humiliating for the married clergy and so contrary to the spirit of the Reformation that under Warwick the matter was reopened and another statute passed inspired by a completely different spirit.

Acts of Parliament and Royal Injunctions had been Henry's mode of procedure in ecclesiastical matters. Somerset's was the same. Convocation though it played a less active part than in the past, intervened in all the important steps. The clergy retained their right to judge and condemn heretics. In their hands were left the application of the penalties prescribed by the Act of Uniformity of 1549, whereas the Six Articles had given the task to the civil courts. Henry VIII had always claimed that the "Supreme Head" is the source of the bishops' spiritual jurisdiction. Therefore on his demise the bishops were obliged to ask his successor to confirm them in their office.[2] And the *congé d'élire* was a mere fiction. For a statute ordered the chapter to elect the royal candidate within twelve days, on the expiration of which period the king could appoint him directly.[3] For almost everything he did Somerset could appeal to the precedent of Henry VIII whose principles he applied. The first religious changes he made were moderate and slow though real. They were stamped with his own prudent caution Those which followed, though more radical, bore the same stamp, and this remained the distinguishing note of the earlier years of Edward VI.

---

[1] *Statutes of the Realm*, 2 and 3 Edward VI, cap. 21.
[2] *Acts of the Privy Council*, II, 13–14.
[3] Elizabeth restored the *congé d'élire*. It still exists giving the chapter the shadow of a power of which the Crown possesses the substance.

THE CHURCH OF ENGLAND ADVANCES ON THE ROAD TOWARDS LUTHERANISM. THE FIRST PRAYER BOOK (1549)

The Order of Communion (1548)—The first Book of Common Prayer (1549)—Its origin and contents—A comparison with other liturgical books of the period—It is brought into use.

WHEN Henry VIII died, the Church of England was schismatic. But she was still Catholic in doctrine and liturgy. Under Edward VI she gradually accepted the Reformation. This transformation, slow and moderate under Protector Somerset, became hasty and violent under Warwick. In religion as in politics the two parts of the reign differ and are in contrast. To the Protector's liberal system of government there corresponded a religious policy of toleration and compromise. His successor's government returned to absolutism and favoured a Protestantism increasingly radical. Somerset sought to conciliate the Henricians, who were struggling to preserve the old orthodoxy of the Church. Warwick threw them into prison and deprived them of their sees. The transformation of Anglican worship bore the mark of this double policy. The first Prayer Book is a product of the first period of Edward's reign, the second of the later.

The Eucharist, the centre of the Catholic religion, was the Reformers' main target. The most passionate controversies centred upon it.

It therefore attracted the special attention of the English reformers. The transformation of Anglican worship was pre-eminently a transformation of her Eucharistic worship.

At first no change was made. Henry's obsequies were conducted with the usual offices. Requiem Masses were celebrated in Latin according to the old rite. Gardiner himself, the leader of the Henricians, officiated at the funeral.[1] At his coronation Edward took the oath before the Blessed Sacrament exposed on the altar and heard the High Mass.[2] He heard another Mass at the opening of Parliament. The ambassador of Charles V assumed that it was no longer said at the palace. "Believe me," the Protector replied, "Mass is always said in the king's apartment. I give you my word of honour that this is so." He further assured the ambassador that "in the matter of religion nothing would be done against Almighty God," and that none of the recent injunctions proceeded from him, but had all been prepared by the deceased monarch.[3] On February 24, the Privy Council decided to execute the clause in Henry's will which provided for a large number of Masses for his soul to be said by the clergy of the royal chapel at Windsor. Four months later, on June 20, 1547, the Protector had a solemn Requiem celebrated with great pomp at Saint Paul's for Francis I who had died on May 31. In his *Annals* Stow relates that Cranmer pontificated, assisted by eight bishops using the Catholic rite. The following New Year's Day the king was present at a High Mass in his palace. In May 1548, the Protector authorised the elevation of the Host, though the ceremony had been abolished. And in June the imperial ambassador wrote to Prince Philip: "Since religious controversy has been forbidden, Mass is once more said in all churches."

[1] Cf. Strype, *Ecclesiastical Memorials*, Oxford ed. 1812–1824, IV, 290; Wriothesley *Chronicle* ed. Camden Society, London, 1875–77, I, 178, 181. *Correspondance Politique d'Odet de Selve* (ed. Lefèvre–Pontalis), Paris 1888, 104, letter of Feb. 21, 1547.
[2] Strype, *Memorials of Cranmer*, Book II, ch. I, ed. 1840, I, 204 and 264.
[3] Van der Delft to the Emperor, November 15 and December 5, 1547 *Sp. Cal.*, IX, 205, 218 *sq.*

Nevertheless the Protector, his brother and the Earl of Warwick had discontinued it in their houses for several months.[1]

The first statute passed by Parliament was directed against those who spoke irreverently of the "Sacrament of the altar".[2] Disobedience was punishable from May 1, 1548 by a fine and imprisonment. Accordingly a preacher named Hancock was fined ninety pounds by the Mayor of Salisbury[3] and two men, Hunt and Richard White by name, were imprisoned by Bishop Capon's Chancellor.[4] Shortly after (December 27, 1547) the Privy Council issued an order which reinforced the statute. It forbade discussions about the Eucharist and the teaching of any doctrine not explicitly stated in the Bible, until the king with the advice of his Council and the clergy had defined the doctrine of the Eucharist and declared what language might lawfully be used about it.[5] The Eucharist had, indeed, become the topic of arguments as frequent as they were violent and not confined to churches but as voluble in markets and breweries. "Already in every shop and hostelry, alehouse or other place of public resort nothing was to be heard but religious disputation. Not a gossiping old wife, not a dotard, not a sophist full of talk—but taught Holy Scripture having never

---

[1] Van der Delft to the Flemish Council of State, January 4, 1548, to Charles V, Nov. 15 and Dec. 5, 1547, Feb. 23 and May 16, 1548 and to the Infante Philip, June 15, 1548. *Sp. Cal.* 78 *sq.*, 205, 241, 253, 265 *sq.*, 273.

[2] *Statutes of the Realm*, (IV, London, 1819) I. Edward VI, cap. 1. *Sp. Cal.*, IX, 245.

[3] *Narratives of the Reformation*, ed. Nichols, London, 1860, 76 *sq.* Somerset remitted the penalty (*Ibid*) perhaps because the offence had been committed (Jan. 31, 1548) before the date fixed for the statute to come into operation.

[4] *Ibid.* 73 *sqq.*

[5] D. Wilkins, *Concilia*, London 1737, IV, 18; Strype, *Ecclesiastical Memorials*, II, ed. 1822, part 2, 340; Cardwell, *Documentary Annals*, ed. 1844, I, 34, The ordinance was confirmed by another of February 6 following (*Burnet, op. cit.*, ed. Pocock V, 188; Cardwell, *op. cit.*, I, 42) which expressly forbade any innovation or alteration whatsoever in the rites and ceremonies of the Church or preaching against them. This amounted to a restriction upon the freedom of the press. It was for this reason that Gardiner's and Tunstall's treatises on the Eucharist were printed abroad.

learned it."[1] Everywhere men debated the nature of the
Eucharistic Presence.[2] Sermons, books, tales, songs,
ballads and comedies ridiculed the Catholic doctrine.[3]
Nicknames were bestowed upon the Host, "Round
Robin", "Jack-in-the-Box."[4] Others made blasphemous
puns. They called "the sacrament of the altar", "the
sacrament of the halter". In the public pulpit preachers
termed the Blessed Sacrament an idol.[5] In a sermon
preached during Mass, Hancock maintained that it
was unlawful to kneel before the Host and offer It divine
worship. To do so was to commit a fearful sin of
idolatry. "It is an idol," he declared on several occasions, "not a God or a sacrament."[6]

In 1548 Gardiner's sermon[7] in defence of the Catholic
doctrine of the Eucharist led to the publication of a score
of pamphlets which were blasphemous lampoons rather
than serious controversy. Anthony Gilby's is typical:
"he had learnt," he said, "to speak plainly and call bread
bread. The Catholics on the other hand wanted a
carnal sacrifice, would have it that a piece of bread
became flesh and blood to be reverently worshipped,
that a paltry wafer was made God and man."[8] He calls
the Sacrament "the popish idol, the dumb God, the

---

[1] Sanders *De Origine ac Progressu Schismatis Anglicani Libri Tres.*
[2] Cf. Proclamation of Dec. 27, 1547 mentioned above; Ridley's Sermon
in Strype, *Ecclesiastical Memorials*, ed. above-mentioned, II, part 2, 340–341;
J. Foxe, *op. cit.*, V, 711.
[3] Act of Parliament above-mentioned.
[4] *Narratives of the Days of the Reformation*, ed. Nichols, London, 1859.
73–74. Cf. J. Gardiner, *Lollardy* II (1908), 313.
[5] Nichols, *Narratives of the Reformation*, 72–73 and 78. Hancock preached
to this effect at Christ Church in Hampshire and at Saint Thomas's,
Salisbury, in the presence of the chancellors of the Bishops of Winchester
and Salisbury.
[6] *Loc. Cit.*
[7] It was preached before the king and the Privy Council, June 29, 1548.
It is to be found in Foxe, *Acts and Monuments*, ed. above-mentioned, 1838,
VI, 87–93. In the majority of previous editions a portion of the sermon
had been omitted. Gardiner had also written in 1546 a treatise in defence
of the doctrine of the Eucharist against the Protestants. *Detection of the
Devil's Sophistry.*
[8] *An Answer to the Devilish Detection of S. Gardiner, Bishop of Winchester*, p. VI,
XVI.

poetical changeling." An anonymous pamphleteer in his
Lamentacyon against the City of London[1] exclaims: "thus
hath he changed the holy memory of Christ's death into
the worshipping of his God made of fine flour."

Such were the excesses which Parliament and the Privy
Council were obliged to repress and which enabled
Somerset to assume the role of a moderator by restraining
a movement which had been in part provoked by his
own liberalism. The ordinance of March warns subjects
against excessive zeal for reform and too great haste.
It bids them obey constituted authority, not their individual whims. At the same time it promises them a
measure of satisfaction. Innovations had already been
attempted.

The statute which forbade blasphemy against the
Blessed Sacrament introduced Communion under two
kinds. The conservative nature of the statute was to
compensate for the novelty it introduced. It was the
clergy in Convocation who first passed it on December 2,
1547, *nullo reclamante*. Cranmer had himself introduced
the measure on November 30.[2] The bill was then brought
into Parliament, which declared that it was in harmony
with the usage of the Apostles and the Primitive Church
for five centuries and more after the Ascension, that
the faithful should receive communion under both
kinds along with the priest.[3] The royal injunction of
December 27 simply confirmed the statute.[4] On March 8
following *The Order of the Communion*[5] appeared. It was a

---

[1] *The Lamentacyon Against the City of London for some Certain Great Vices
used therein*, 1548. Quoted by Gasquet and Bishop, *Edward VI and the Book
of Common Prayer*, London, 1890. 123.

[2] Strype, *Memorials of Cranmer*, Book II, Ch. 4, ed. 1848–1854, II, 37.
Wilkins, *Concilia*, IV, 16.

[3] *Statute of the Realm*, I Edward VI, cap, 1, art. 7. Gee and Hardy,
Documents Illustrative of the English Church, n. LXVII. (Cf. Strype, *Memorials
of Cranmer*, Book II, Ch. 4, ed. 1848, 40 *sq.*)

[4] Wilkins, *Concilia*, IV, 18; Strype, *Ecclesiastical Memorials*, II, Part 2,
340; *Memorials of Cranmer*, Book II, Ch. 4; ed. Cardwell, *Documentary
Annals of the Reformed Church of England*, I, 26.

[5] *The Order of the Communion*, 1548, printed by Richard Grafton.

little book of only ten pages, a copy of which every parish priest and curate must obtain by Easter (April 1) to follow in administering Communion.[1] When the attempts had been made at union with the Lutherans in 1538, the German delegates to the London conference, and later Melanchthon, had pressed for the adoption of communion *sub utraque* by the Church of England. But Henry had refused to yield, personally defending the practice of communion *sub una*.[2]

In itself communion under two kinds is not contrary to Catholic doctrine. It had been the practice of the primitive church. The Emperor Ferdinand I asked the Council of Trent and the Pope to sanction it for his dominions and in 1564 Pius IV made the concession for the German Empire. The practice survived in Austria until 1584 and in Bohemia until 1621, when the concession was withdrawn.

What was heretical was to hold that communion under both kinds is obligatory and that the Body and Blood of Christ are not contained together under either species. The act, however, expressly declared that by introducing communion *sub utraque* there was no condemnation of the alternative usage in churches outside the king's dominions. *The Order of the Communion* affirmed that every part of the Host contains the whole body of Jesus Christ. It is nowhere so much as hinted that communion under one kind is mutilated and incomplete or that communion under both kinds is necessary to salvation as John Huss and Luther had taught. Thus the Order did not even contradict the repealed statute of the Six Articles which

---

[1] Letter of the Council of March 13, 1548. Heylyn, *Ecclesia Restaurata* (1661), ed. Robertson for the Ecclesiastical History Society, Cambridge, 1849, I, 122. The letter addressed by the Council to the Bishops, accompanying the instruction is to be found in Wilkins, *op. cit.,* IV, II, in Foxe, *op. cit.*, ed. Pratt, V, 719, Heylyn, *op, cit.*, I, 120 and Cardwell, *Documentary Annals*, ed. 1844, XI, 72. Cf. Despatches of the Imperial Ambassador of February 27 and April 11, 1548 and March 19, 1549, *Sp. cal.*, IX, 261, 262, 350.

[2] Burnet, IV, 347, 352, 372 *sq.*

declared that communion under both kinds is not obligatory.

It is not easy to find in the *Order of the Communion* anything inconsistent with orthodox sacramental doctrine. The term "Spiritually" unnecessarily added to the words "To give us this Body and Blood" though not incorrect in itself, might indeed imply a doubt as to the Real Presence,[1] as also the phrases "Administer the *Bread*" and "Administer the *Wine.*" But they were corrected by the formula of administration which ran: "the Body given for you, the Blood shed for you."

In this way an attempt was made to satisfy the two conflicting views by combining them in ambiguous or even contradictory formulas which either party could invoke in support of its beliefs. The attempt expressed the spirit of conciliation which inspired Somerset's entire administration.

This conciliatory spirit was also displayed by an important innovation concerning not the Eucharist but Penance. The general confession, the Confiteor, which in accordance with Catholic usage preceded communion, might, it was declared, be substituted for auricular confession which, however, was by no means abolished. "Requiring such as shall be satisfied with a general confession, not to be offended with them that doth use to their further satisfying the auricular and secret confession to the priest, nor those also which think needful or convenient for the quietness of their own consciences particularly to open their sins to the priest, to be offended with them which are satisfied with their humble confession to God and the general confession to the Church."

This was to sanction both the Catholic and the

---

[1] This was in fact Cranmer's unavowed intention. In his reply to Gardiner's book on the Eucharist (1550) he maintained that there is no bodily reception of Our Lord in Communion and that the word "Spiritually" must be added or understood wherever the Prayer Book speaks of receiving the Body and Blood of Christ. *A Defence of the True and Catholic Doctrine of the Sacrament. Cranmer's Works*: ed. Parker Society, 1844–1846, 226 *sqq*.

Protestant practice.[1] Nothing shows more clearly the desire to combine conservatism with novelty, to change without destroying, and to please both the orthodox and the reformers by finding a formula sufficiently elastic to satisfy both.

The entire administration of the Communion must be in English. This was the first introduction of the vulgar tongue into the Anglican liturgy. The use of a language not understood by the faithful involves serious drawbacks, but a vernacular liturgy involves even more serious. Therefore the Western Church had refused to employ the vernacular for any part of her strictly liturgical services.[2] The Protestants on the contrary adopted it from the outset in preference to Latin. Therefore to administer communion in English was a step in the Protestant direction, as was also its administration under two kinds. The formulation of the Anglican liturgy was becoming Lutheran though its substance still remained Catholic.

The Protestants were delighted by this first advance towards the Reformation. Miles Coverdale sent Calvin the translation of *The Order of the Communion* a fortnight after its publication in England, convinced that Calvin would be pleased with it and find in it "the first fruits of true godliness."[3] It had indeed been modelled upon a Lutheran book, the *Pia Consultatio* of Hermann of Wied, Archbishop of Cologne, who, for attempting to introduce the Reformation into his archdiocese, had been condemned by Paul III and deposed by Charles V.[4] This famous *Consultatio*, largely Bucer's work,[5] had just been

[1] Moreover it implied that sacramental confession is not necessary.
[2] See Appendix II on the liturgical use of the vernacular.
[3] Coverdale to Calvin, Frankfort, March 26, 1548. *Zurich Original Letters*, I, 31.
[4] Strype, *Memorials of Cranmer*, II, 3–11, provides ample information about Cranmer's relations with Archbishop Hermann von Wied.
[5] Bucer was himself inspired by the Liturgy which Luther gave the Church of Nuremberg. Melanchthon also assisted in the compilation of Hermann's *Pia Consultatio*.

translated into English.[1] Moreover Cranmer corresponded with the Archbishop.[2] Richard Hilles compared the new Communion service to that used by the Churches of Nuremberg and Saxony.[3]

The Order of the Communion consists of two parts. The first contains exhortations to communion which were usually read after the Creed in place of a sermon.[4] The second part contains the new way of administering communion. Both parts have changed little since,[5] and *The Order of the Communion* of 1548 is still in use in the Church of England.[6]

Who composed it is not exactly known. But it was certainly the work of a group of ecclesiastics generally designated "The Windsor Committee." The Injunction of March 13 which accompanied the publication of the book says that it was drawn up by learned prelates after lengthy consultations and deliberations. John Foxe adds, on the authority of King Edward's diary, that these bishops met at Windsor Castle.[7] According to him they were seven in number[8] and were assisted by

[1] Three months before the Order of Communion. Cf. Strype, *Memorials of Cranmer*, Book II, Ch. 31, ed. 1848, I, 412.

[2] Strype, *op. cit.*, Book II, Ch. 31, ed. above-mentioned, I, 410 *sqq.*

[3] Cf. Pollard, *Thomas Cranmer*, London, 1904, 220.

[4] It was at this point that the exhortations are placed by the Prayer Book of 1549 (ed. Griffith Farran 196–198). In the 1552 Prayer Book (same ed. 163–166) they were placed after the collection for the poor (the offertory).

[5] In 1552 a new exhortation was added to the three of 1548 and the various Prayer Books change their order.

[6] For Communion in the Church of England see Rev. Darwell Stone, *The Holy Communion* in the *Oxford Library of Practical Theology*; Dr. H. M. Luckock, *The Divine Liturgy being the Order for Holy Communion Historically, Doctrinally and Devotionally set forth in Fifty Portions*; Rev. Meyrick, *The Doctrine of the Church of England on the Holy Communion*. Scudamore, *Notitia Eucharistica* and Procter, *History of the Prayer Book* may also be profitably consulted.

[7] Cf. Strype, *Memorials of Cranmer*, Book II, Ch. 4, ed. above-mentioned, I, 224; *A Commentary Explanatory Doctrinal and Historical of the Order for the Administration of the Holy Communion According to the Use of the Church of England.* 2nd ed., London 1876; Heylyn, *Ecclesia Restaurata*, ed., 1849, I, 118; Blunt, *The Reformation of the Church of England*, ed. 1892–1896, II, 90.

[8] Cranmer, Goodrich of Ely, Ridley of Rochester, Holbeach of Lincoln, Thomas Thirlby of Westminster, Skip of Hereford, Day of Chichester. Heylyn, *op. cit.*, I, 119; Blunt, *op. cit.*, II, 90; Dixon, *op. cit.*, II, 493 *sqq.*

six doctors of Divinity.[1] This committee, over which Archbishop Cranmer presided, served as a model for others
which met later to compose or revise the Reformed service
books.[2] Whatever its exact composition it undoubtedly
contained representatives of both the conflicting parties
whose respective views can be recognised in the Order.

The new communion service reveals more or less openly
the intention to change the Mass into a Communion,
as the phrase ran:[3] in other words to Lutheranise it.
For the Lutherans the Mass was not a sacrifice and its
sole purpose was the communion of the people. It
was celebrated only when there was a large congregation
of communicants. Already during the final months of
Henry's reign the advanced party was pressing for this
transformation of the Mass. Strype even states the
king commanded Cranmer to "pen a form for the alteration of the Mass into a Communion."[4] Edward's first
Parliament employed Lutheran language when it
spoke of "the Holy Communion commonly called the
Mass."[5] Cranmer and his supporters held that the
efficacy of the Lord's Supper is confined to its reception.[6]
This was the opinion of all the English Reformers. In
1547 Hooper wrote that the Eucharist was instituted
to be used as Communion and not as the Mass, the latter
being a blasphemy against God,[7] and that, in the time

---

[1] William May, Dean of St. Paul's; Richard Cox, Chancellor of Oxford
University, afterwards Bishop of Ely; John Taylor Dean, later Bishop of
Lincoln; Simon Heynes, Dean of Exeter; Thomas Robertson, Archdeacon
of Leicester, later Dean of Durham; John Redman, "Master" of Trinity
College, Cambridge. *Ibid.* The list is taken from Fuller (*Church History*,
1655, ed. Brewer, 1845, I, 388), but he gives it in connection not with the
Order of Communion of 1548 but the Prayer Book of 1549.

[2] Cf. Dixon, *op. cit.*, II, 493; Gasquet and Bishop, *op. cit.*, 94–95. It has
long been believed that there was a liturgical committee during the la ter
years of Henry's reign which Edward's did but continue. But the committee
of 1543 on which the belief was founded existed only on paper.

[3] The phrase "altering or turning the Mass into a Communion" dates
from the closing years of Henry VIII's reign.

[4] Strype, *Memorials of Cranmer*, Book I, Chapter XXX, ed. 1848, I, 311.

[5] *Statutes of the Realm*, 2 and 3, Edward I, cap. 1.

[6] Gasquet and Bishop, *op. cit.*, 86.

[7] Hooper, *Early Writings*, Parker Society, 139.

of Pope Gregory the Great, the Mass, as his Canon proves, was simply a Communion.[1] Similarly the anonymous author of the *Lamentacyon against the City of London*[2] complains that the Supper has been perverted from its primitive institution and changed into a vain and superstitious ceremony—the Mass.

We shall see how the Prayer Book satisfied the wishes of the Reformers. Already the Order of the Communion makes a concession to Lutheran doctrine when it condemns Communion at private Masses, Masses said on week-days. It restricts Communion to days on which the parish priest has announced its administration, Sundays or feasts, determined beforehand. This was a step towards the abolition of Masses without communicants, at which Cranmer was already aiming.[3] Nevertheless, the Mass still remained unchanged. The Order of the Communion did but add to it a short English service for the communion of the people which must follow the priest's communion. A rubric expressly forbids the change of any rite or ceremony of the Mass until further order should be taken. The Latin Mass according to the Sarum rite was still said and would continue to be said until June 1549, when the first Book of Common Prayer took its place. Cranmer himself, when he consecrated the new Bishop of St. David's, September 8, 1548, employed the Catholic ordinal.[4]

Mass for the dead continued. It was not abolished, as has sometimes been said, by the suppression of the chantries in 1547. This statute[5] simply renewed the statute passed in 1545 under Henry VIII.[6] But in the

[1] Hooper, *op, cit.*, 226.
[2] *The Lamentacyon against the City of London for some Certain Great Vices used Therein.* 1548.
[3] *Defence of the True and Catholic Doctrine of the Sacrament*, Parker Society's ed. of Cranmer's works, 349, *sqq*. Cf., Gasquet and Bishop, *Edward VI and the Book of Common Prayer*, 91.
[4] Strype, *Memorials of Cranmer*, Book II, Chapter IX, ed. above-mentioned, II, 105 *sqq*.
[5] *Statutes of the Realm*, (IV, 1819), 1, Edward VI, cap. 14. Cf., Heylyn, *op. cit.*, ed. above-mentioned, I, 123.
[6] Ibid., (III, 1817), 37, Henry VIII, cap. 4.

Six Articles Henry had affirmed that "the commandment of charity no less than the voice of Scripture
prescribes that we should pray for the dead and have
Masses said for the repose of their souls," and when
Dr. Crome maintained in a sermon that the act against
chantries implied the denial of Purgatory he was compelled to retract. The professed object of the statute
was purely material, to supply the deficit of the treasury
and found schools.[1] Cranmer, who held that the Mass
is not a propitiatory sacrifice, voted against the statute,[2]
whereas Gardiner gave it his approval.[3] Mass for the
dead remained, therefore, as lawful after the statute
as before it. Gardiner expressly said so in a sermon
preached before the king on June 29, 1548. "Ye would
say unto me: 'there be fewer Masses by putting away
the chantries.' So were there when abbeys were dissolved.
But this is no injury to the Mass. It consisteth not in
the number nor in the multitude but in the thing itself."[4]

Cranmer and his party were planning more far-
reaching reforms. *The Order of the Communion* had hardly
been finished[5] when the Archbishop drew up with his
own hand[6] a series of questions to which seventeen of

---

[1] Cf., *Acts of the Privy Council*, ed. Dasent, London, 1890–1899, II, 184–
186; Carlisle, *Endowed Grammar Schools*, 2 vols. London, 1818; *Lancashire,
Chantries*, ed. F. R. Raines, Chetham Society, 1862; Ashley, *Economic
History*, London, 1892, II, 139 *sqq.*; *Certificates of Chantry Commissioners*,
Surtees Society, Vol. XCI, 1894; Leach, *English Schools of the Reformation*,
Westminster, 1896; Pollard, *England under Protector Somerset*, London, 1900,
122 *sqq.* The Priests serving the chantries were indemnified by a pension,
Leach, *op. cit.*, 77.

[2] With him voted the Bishops of London, Ely, Norwich, Hereford,
Worcester, and Chichester. Cranmer voted for the bill in its final form.
The others persisted in their opposition.

[3] J. Foxe, *op. cit.*, VI, 87–93. Cf., Blunt, *op. cit.*, II, 141.

[4] J. Foxe, *op. cit.* VI, 89–90. Cf. Gasquet and Bishop, 82, n. 1.

[5] Cf., Jenkins, *Works of Cranmer*, II, 178; Dixon, *History of the Church
of England*, 1880, II, 476.

[6] The original is in the library of Corpus Christi College, Cambridge.
MS. 105, fols. 230–1. The questions and answers have been published in
Burnet's *History of the Reformation*, ed. Pocock, V, 197–218 from a manu-
script at Lambeth. Strype gives the questions alone in his *Memorials of
Cranmer*, Book II, Chapter IV. But the 1848 edition contains an appendix
(N. XXXVI, 475) in which the questions are followed by the answers.

the twenty-seven Bishops returned answers.[1] "Wherein consisteth the Mass by Christ's institution? What is the oblation and sacrifice of Christ in the Mass? Whether it be convenient that Masses satisfactory should continue (that is to say) priests hired to sing for souls departed?" The Henricians replied in the Catholic sense. Cranmer, on the contrary, Ridley of Rochester, Holbeach of Lincoln, and Barlow of St. David's,[2] also the theologians, Cox and Taylor, unambiguously espoused the Lutheran doctrine.[3]

We ought not to speak, they said, of an "oblation and sacrifice" of Christ in the Mass. These are incorrect terms. For the Mass is solely "a memorial, a representation" of the sacrifice of the Cross. In other words the Mass is not a sacrifice. Only the communicant, they add, participates in the fruits of the Mass. This amounts to denying that it is a propitiatory sacrifice, profitable to those for whom it is celebrated.[4] The Communion must, therefore, be retained but the Mass offered for the living and the dead, that is the Catholic Mass, abolished. (Answer to Questions 2 and 5).[5] This is the position taken up by the party of reform within a few months of Henry's death.[6] And its influence was so great, that theologians who had hitherto defended the orthodox doctrines, for example, Dr. Richard Smith, Professor

[1] Besides Cranmer they were the Archbishop of York and the Bishops of Durham, London, Hereford, Worcester, Chichester, Norwich, St. Asaph, Salisbury, Lincoln, Ely, Coventry and Lichfield, Carlisle, Rochester, Bristol, and St. David's. There is no evidence that the questions were sent to any other bishops. Gardiner was in prison.

[2] Holbeach and Barlow, however, differ from the rest by doctrinal distinctions of slight importance.

[3] Goodrich of Ely (1534–1554), the first Bishop consecrated by Cranmer after the schism took a cautious line. He appealed to the decision of authority and took care not to depart so far from the Catholic doctrine that he could not retract under Mary and keep his see. Cf., *Troubles Connected with the Prayer Book of* 1549, ed. Camden Society, London, 1884, 129.

[4] On this point Ridley was not so radical as Cranmer. He believed in the spiritual participation of all Christ's members "*in all godliness*".

[5] "I do not believe," Cranmer replied, "that satisfactory Masses should be continued." Holbeach and Dr. Cox dared not advise such a revolutionary change though they were favourable to it.

[6] Cf., Gasquet and Bishop, *op. cit.*, 85 *sqq.*

of Theology at Oxford, retracted them as erroneous, risking the necessity of a further retractation later. At the same time Hugh Latimer, the former Bishop of Worcester, preached at Paul's Cross: "This," he said, "is the mark at which the devil shooteth, to evacuate the Cross of Christ and to mangle the institution of the Lord's Supper. . . . Above these fifteen hundred years he hath been a doer, only purposing to evacuate Christ's death and to make it of small efficacy and virtue. For as Christ saith, according as the Serpent was lifted up in the wilderness: so would He Himself be exalted, that thereby as many as trusted in Him should have salvation: the devil would none of that. They would have us saved by a daily oblation propitiatory, by a sacrifice expiatory or remissory."[1] Hooper wrote that the private Mass is "wicked and devilish."[2] Lutheran pamphlets against the popish Mass were translated into English and circulated among the people.[3] Those of English origin were even more numerous[4] and all the courtiers carried about with them[5] a fashionable tract by a London physician: *John Bon and Master Parson*.[6]

That is to say at this juncture a powerful and virulent popular campaign was launched against the Mass similar to that carried on in Germany between 1521 and 1525. It would attain its goal and profoundly transform this essential portion of Christian worship.

It was the Book of Common Prayer issued in 1549 which changed the Mass for the first time.

[1] Latimer, *Sermons*, ed. Corrie, I, 72–73; ed. Watkins, I, 68.
[2] Hooper, *Early Writings*, ed. Parker Society, 226.
[3] For example Marcourt's, *Declaration of the Mass*, printed at Wittenberg and Luther's, *Disclosures of the Canon of the Popish Mass*.
[4] Between twenty and thirty are known, published in 1548. There were probably more. The press was free. It was not until August 13, 1549, that, as a result of the insurrections in the East and West, the Council decided that in future no book might be printed without a licence from a secretary of state or William Cecil (*Acts of the Privy Council*, 1547–1550, ed. Dasent, 312.)
[5] Gasquet and Bishop, *op. cit.*, 121.
[6] Reprinted by Pollard, *Tudor Tracts*, London, 1903, 159–169.

The Book of Common Prayer combines in one volume a Breviary, a Missal and a Ritual.[1] It is the liturgy of the Anglican Church. Revised in 1552, it is still in use. It derives from the Western and Oriental Liturgies and the more recent servicebooks of the German reformers. "A few things," according to Daniel the liturgiologist, "have been taken from various non-Roman rites, Eastern and Western, much from the Roman rite, and some things from the reformed servicebooks."

Under Henry VIII a Committee of theologians[2] had drawn up in 1540 a "Rationale of Rites and Ceremonies" which described the ancient rites and ceremonies of the Church and explained their historical and mystical meaning. Cranmer vigorously opposed its publication.[3] In 1543 a revision of the liturgical books was ordered;[4] but nothing was done under Henry beyond expunging the names of the Pope and St. Thomas of Canterbury, and correcting a few typographical mistakes.[5] But Cranmer spent the concluding years of Henry's reign compiling various servicebooks,[6] and he drew up several drafts which, though they were not made public in Henry's lifetime, served as the foundation of the first Prayer Book.[7] On the accession of Edward, the Convocation of 1547 asked him to produce them. But the

[1] The full title is The Book of the Common Prayer and Administration of the Sacramentes and other Rites and Ceremonies of the Churche after the Use of the Churche of England.

[2] It consisted of the Bishops of Bath, Ely, Salisbury, Chichester, Worcester and Landaff.

[3] It was published as an historical document by Collier (Church History, ed. Lathbury, VI, 102–122) from British Museum MS., Cleopatra, E, 5. in which a note is to be found in Gardiner's hand, and again in 1910 by C. S. Cobb in Vol. XVIII of the Alcuin Club Publications. According to Collier (loc. cit.), Cranmer prevented its adoption by convocation and Foxe in his Life of Cranmer adds that he refuted it. (Quoted by Strype, Memorials of Cranmer, Book X, Chapter XIX, ed. 1848–1854, I, 107).

[4] Wilkins, Concilia, III, 863.

[5] Gasquet and Bishop, op. cit., 4.

[6] A. F. Pollard, Thomas Cranmer, London, 1904, 213.

[7] Wood, Scottish Peerage, I, 330. Cf., C. W. Le Bas, Life of Cranmer, London, 1833. Two of Cranmer's drafts for a reformed breviary are preserved in the British Museum. See Appendix, III., Gasquet and Bishop, op. cit., App. IV.

Archbishop refused, probably because he did not consider that they had received their final shape.[1] It was not until September 1548 that the work was begun which gave the new Prayer Book its final form. It is usually ascribed to the Committee of Bishops, already referred to as the Windsor Committee.[2] Historians differ as to the names of its members. The lists they have consulted do not appear to derive from an authentic source.[3] Serious research has found no trace of a committee in the strict sense. It is, however, certain that a number of bishops met at Windsor,[4] and later as Cranmer's guests at Chertsey Abbey, and discussed the controversies then agitating men's minds. On their own admission[5] a draft of the new prayer book was laid before them.[6] But it does not appear that they had much share in its composition. One of them even complained that it was altered after receiving their approval. We lack, therefore, precise information as to the part they took in it and in what precisely their work of revision consisted.[7] It is certain that Cranmer had the principal share in the

[1] The Convocation of 1547 did not simply ask, as Dixon thinks, to see the Rationale. It asked for all the revisions of liturgical books made under Henry VIII, including, therefore, Cranmer's.

[2] No contemporary authority mentions any theologians as having been members of the committee along with the Bishops. (Cf., Gasquet, *op.cit.*, 178.) Nevertheless Somerset wrote to Cardinal Pole, June 4, 1549, that the Prayer Book had been examined both by the Bishops and other persons of good judgment fairly and impartially chosen. *Troubles Connected with the Prayer Book of* 1549. Camden Society, London, 1884, 10.

[3] Burnet's list of 24 bishops is fantastic. On the other hand Fuller's list (reproduced by Blunt, *The Reformation of the Church of England*, ed. 1892–1896, 90–91), which corresponds with the list of bishops who met at Chertsey Abbey in September 1548, (Strype, *Memorials of Cranmer*, Book II, Chapter IX, ed. 1848, II, 105), cannot have been invented. It is no longer in existence. It is also to be found in a Prayer Book of 1632 in the Bodleian.

[4] According to Strype, (*Eccl. Mem.*, II, Part I, 33), they met at Windsor in March, according to Heylyn, (*Ecclesia Restaurata*, on September 1). Cf., Cranmer's *Remains*, Parker Society, 1844–1846, 450.

[5] Made to the Parliament of 1549. *Certain Notes Touching the Disputations of the Bishops in this last Parliament Assembled of the Lord's Supper*. In Gasquet and Bishop, *op. cit.*, App. V passim.

[6] For this committee, see Gasquet and Bishop, *op. cit.*, Chapter IX and p. 180.

[7] Blunt, *op. cit.*, II, 91; Gasquet and Bishop, *op. cit.*, 180.

conception and composition of the Prayer Book,[1] and
that the presence of Henrician bishops and the desire
to secure their assent rendered the liturgical reform
more moderate, and to a very large extent explains the
compromise between the old service and the new and
the deliberate ambiguity of certain formulas.

As regards the Mass, the Reformers' principal object
was to destroy its sacrificial character, so vehemently
attacked by Luther, and as far as possible make it a
simple communion service. Cranmer already thought
what he would later say openly; that the Mass as such
must be abolished "for as much as in such Masses is
manifest wickedness and idolatry . . . all such popish
Masses are to be clearly taken away out of Christian
churches."[2]

The first step was to get rid of its old name; "*The
Supper of the Lord and the Holy Communion*, commonly
called the Mass" was its title in the Prayer Book. Cranmer
called the Missal simply the Book of the Communion.
After the publication of the Prayer Book, the only
designation of the Eucharist was the Holy Communion.[3]
Certain rubrics imply that the sole object of the Mass
is the communion of the people. One orders intending
communicants to give notice to the priest the previous
evening or in the morning at Matins of their intention
to communicate.[4] Another "prescribes that in chapels
annexed and all other places there shall be no celebration

[1] Gasquet and Bishop, *op. cit.*, 180; Pollard, *op. cit.*, 213, 215. Strype
says the Prayer Book passed through very few hands. Elsewhere he says,
"The Common Prayer Book and administration of the Sacraments by the
great care and study of the Archbishop was now finished." (Book II,
Chapter XII, ed. 1848, II, 137).

[2] *Defence of the True and Catholic Doctrine of the Sacrament*, Parker Society, ed.
of *Cranmer's Works*, 1844–1846, 349, 351. With several of the reforming
bishops he held that the sacrament of the altar had been ordained not
to be received by a single person for many, but by each for himself. (Strype,
Memorials of Cranmer, ed. 1848, App. XXXVI, p. 475.)

[3] *Troubles Connected with the Prayer Book of* 1549, (Camden Society, 128).

[4] *First Prayer Book*, ed. Griffith Farran (Browne, 193). The object of the
rule was practical: to let the priest know how much bread and wine he
must consecrate since the Sacrament was no longer reserved.

of the Lord's Supper except there be some to communicate with the priest;" a third that "in all cathedral
and collegiate churches there shall always some communicate with the priest that ministereth;"[1] and that
"the priest on the week-day shall forbear to celebrate
the Communion except he have some that will communicate with him."[2]

Every week, the Venetian Ambassador Barbaro reports,
one member of every family is expected to receive communion; certain merchants make light of the order
and send one of their servants in their place.[3]

The first part of the Mass from the Introit to the
Offertory was not substantially changed, for there
is nothing in it which clearly indicates the notion of
sacrifice. It is but the preparation for the more sacred
rites which should follow. For that reason in the primitive
Church even those not yet baptised could be present,
whence its name "the Mass of the Catechumens." The
Introit, Kyrie Eleison, Gloria in excelsis, Collect, Epistle,
Gospel and Creed follow in their traditional order.
Luther highly approved of all these prayers, as also of
the Preface, Sanctus and Agnus Dei because, he said,
they express praise and thanksgiving, not the notion of
sacrifice. In this first part of the Mass the Prayer Book
departed in a few points from the Sarum use on the
plea of returning to the primitive usage.[4] It suppressed
the prayers at the foot of the altar which formed no
part of the Mass of the Catechumens and which as late
as the eleventh and twelfth centuries were still said by
the priest on his way from the sacristy to the altar.

---

[1] *First Prayer Book*, 210.

[2] *Loc. cit.* Cf., Barbaro's Report of 1551, (Albèri, *Relazioni degli Ambasciatori Veneti*, Series I, Vol. II, 248).

[3] Ibid, Cranmer's Injunctions of 1550, (*Cranmer's Remains*, Parker Society,
1844–1846), and Hooper's of 1551, (*Later Writings*, 160), forbidding the
faithful to send a neighbour to communicate in their place, prove that the
practice was common.

[4] What is called ancient, he wrote to Queen Mary in 1555, is in reality
new and what is called new is ancient. *Cranmer's Remains*, Parker Society,
1844–1846, 450.

This eliminated the Confiteor which the Lutherans regarded as a preparation for the sacrifice. The Introit which was originally an entire psalm, but which about the eighth or ninth century had been reduced to two or three verses, was restored to its original form. The entire psalm was sung.[1] The Gradual and the Tract were omitted; and there was evidence of a desire to suppress the ceremonial which accompanies the reading of the Gospel.[2]

With the Offertory the sacrifice begins, the "Mass of the Faithful." At this point the spirit which inspired the new service became plainly visible. In the primitive Church the catechumens had left the church before the Offertory. The Prayer Book ordered that at the Offertory the communicants should approach the choir and the remainder of the congregation depart.[3] This amounted to treating the faithful who did not communicate like those not yet baptised and implied that they had no share in the Mass, which was thus essentially a Communion.

After the Creed, until the eleventh century the people offered the bread and wine for the sacrifice, a practice which survives in the Eastern Churches. Meanwhile, since the fourth century, the choir had chanted a psalm called therefore the Offertory. The priest then offered to God the bread and wine, the material of the Eucharistic sacrifice, thereby to separate them from common use and render them fitter for the transubstantiation they were to undergo. The words of the Offertory prayer were similar to those of the corresponding prayer in the Roman Missal: "Receive Holy Father, Almighty and Eternal God, this spotless host which I Thine unworthy

[1] Instead of adopting the Sarum introits the Prayer Book, with a single exception, deliberately selected others.

[2] After the creed one of three exhortations from the Order of Communion was read when there was no sermon. *First Prayer Book*, ed. above-mentioned, 196 *sqq.*

[3] *First Prayer Book*, ed. above-mentioned. 200.

servant offer to Thee who art my God living and true.
We offer Thee O Lord the chalice of salvation, beseeching
Thy Mercy that it may ascend as an odour of sweet
savour to the Presence of Thy Divine Majesty for our
salvation and the salvation of the whole world." The
celebrant concluded with the prayer known as the
Secret, asking God to accept the gifts offered upon the
altar. In the Middle Ages prayers of devotion were
added which amplify and develop this notion of oblation
and sacrifice, for example the *Suscipe Sancta Trinitas*.
The Prayer Book completely suppressed this part of the
Mass which constitutes a formal act of oblation.[1] The
celebrant simply placed the bread and wine on the altar
without any liturgical ceremony. The Offertory in the
papal Mass of the eighth century had indeed been no
more than this, the other prayers having been introduced
into Low Masses in the tenth and eleventh centuries.[2]
The mixture of water and wine, "the mixed chalice,"
one of the most ancient rites of the Mass, was however
retained.[3] The innovation was concealed by retaining
the external ceremonies, the popular usages, while
changing their purport and significance. Accordingly
the offering whose purpose had been to provide the
priest with the money necessary to purchase the bread
and wine for the sacrifice, a survival of the ancient
practice, was still made. But it was for the poor and the
term "offertory" acquired the sense of collection.[4] A
verse of Scripture on the fruits of almsgiving replaced the

---

[1] The Rubrics of the Sarum Missal already call the oblations "Sacrifices."
(Ed. Burntisland, 593 *sqq.*). This first oblation which Anglican writers call
the "lesser oblation," was restored, the ritualists maintain, in the last
revision of the Prayer Book (The Prayer Book of 1552 had only the word
"alms") by the words, "Mercifully to accept our alms and *oblations.*"
These latter words they contend, refer not to the pecuniary gifts ·of the
faithful, but to the elements of bread and wine placed on the altar.
Scudamore (*Notitia Eucharistica*, Chapter XII, sect. 2), considers that this
was not the intention of the revisers.

[2] *Prayer Book*, ed. above-mentioned, 200.

[3] *Loc. cit.*

[4] *Loc. cit.*

Secret.[1] Families who had been accustomed to offer the blessed bread, also a relic of the primitive usage, would give the equivalent to the curate for the expenses of the bread and wine needed for Holy Communion[2] and at least one of their members must communicate:[3] a change which also tended to substitute the notion of communion for that of sacrifice.[4] After the Preface[5] and the Sanctus, which were preserved, the Prayer Book reaches the principal part of the Mass, that which gives it its character and validity: the Canon.

The central and essential rite of the Canon is the consecration without which there would be neither Mass nor Communion. Therefore it is found in all Eucharistic rites which give it a significance in conformity with their doctrine. For many centuries the consecration had been surrounded by venerable prayers and rites which after a few changes made by Leo I and Gregory the Great, had remained practically invariable. Together they constituted the Canon. They were particularly odious to Luther, who condemned them for turning the Eucharist into a sacrifice.

The Prayer Book of 1549 dared not suppress them. It would have been too radical a change. The Henricians whose approval was sought would never have consented. The bishops who were asked to sanction the new Missal, had long been accustomed to the Canon. For Cranmer

---

[1] There are twenty-one verses, taken from St. Matthew, St. Luke, St. John, the Epistles to the Corinthians, Galatians, Timothy and Hebrews, Tobit, Proverbs and the Psalms. One or more is to be recited according to the length of the Offertory. *Prayer Book*, ed. above-mentioned, 192–200.

[2] Ibid, 200 and 210, Fourth rubric.

[3] Ibid, Fifth rubric.

[4] Many, it would seem, refused to make this offering for the elements and thus caused the Sunday celebration to be frequently omitted. On December 25, 1549, Warwick ordered the Bishops to summon the recalcitrants before them and overcome their obstinacy by suspension, excommunication and other ecclesiastical censures. *Troubles connected with the Prayer Book of* 1549. Camden Society, 128.

[5] The proper prefaces were reduced from ten to five, for Christmas, Easter, Ascension, Whitsun, and Trinity. Those for Christmas and Whitsun were entirely new and those for Ascension and the Trinity very considerably altered. *Prayer Book*, above-mentioned, 201.

himself, who had said Mass for more than thirty years, the prayers of the old Canon were closely bound up with the celebration of Divine Service and presented themselves spontaneously to his mind. He therefore retained them, but altered them in such a way as to get rid, as far as possible, of the idea of sacrifice, perhaps without complete success.[1] They were first stripped of their mysterious character by an order that they should be recited aloud or chanted, instead of being said in an inaudible voice.

Five prayers precede the consecration. In the first of these, the *Te igitur*, God is asked through Jesus Christ to accept and "bless these gifts, these offerings, these holy and spotless sacrifices" offered for the Catholic Church, the Pope, the Bishop and the faithful. The Prayer changed the words "gifts, offerings and sacrifices," which so clearly express the notion of sacrifice and oblation into "our prayers"—"We humbly beseech Thee most mercifully to receive these our prayers, which we offer unto Thy divine Majesty." The remainder of the prayer is similar to that in the Missal. There is a lengthy prayer for the King, the Royal Council, the bishops and other clergy.[2]

The *Hanc igitur oblationem* asks through the offering of the Mass, peace on earth and salvation hereafter: "We therefore beseech Thee, O Lord, favourably to accept this offering of our ministry, which is also the offering of Thy entire family." At this point the Prayer Book seems to refute the doctrine of the Canon, by affirming that the sacrifice of the Cross is unique, and

[1] Had not Somerset's entire administration been characterised by a spirit of compromise, Cranmer might perhaps have been able to get rid of the Canon in 1549. Wriothesley in fact relates that on May 12 of the previous year, when an anniversary service was held for Henry VIII, he sang a Mass in English from which the Canon was entirely absent. The astonishment of the people was great. Wriothesley *Chronicle*, ed. Camden Society, London, 1875–1877, II, 2.

[2] *First Prayer Book*, ed. above-mentioned, 202. The prayer reflects the attitude of the Reformers to the great ones of the earth, the state and the Church it was their ambition to reform.

that the Mass does not renew, but merely commemorates it. [1]

The same denial of the sacrifice of the Mass finds expression in the alteration of the prayer *Unde et memores* which immediately follows the consecration. "We offer," it runs, "to Thy supreme Majesty of Thy gifts bestowed on us, a pure victim, a holy victim, a spotless victim, the holy Bread of eternal life and the Cup of everlasting salvation." The idea of sacrifice could not be more plainly expressed. This is the corresponding formula of the Prayer Book: "Wherefore, O Heavenly Father, according to the institution of Thy dearly beloved Son, our Saviour Jesus Christ, we Thy humble servants do celebrate and make here, before Thy divine Majesty, with these Thy holy gifts, the memorial which He, Thy Son, hath willed us to make." [2] That is to say the Mass is a memorial service not a sacrifice.

The prayers which follow in the Canon state even more exactly and further develop the notion of sacrifice. They were therefore suppressed or completely transformed in the Prayer Book.

The first, the *Supra quae propitio*, brings the Mass into connection with three sacrifices of the Old Testament, which prefigure the sacrifice of Christ, those of Abel, Abraham and Melchisedech. The Prayer Book makes no allusion to them.

The *Supplices te rogamus*, which asks God to command that the victim present on the altar may be borne to the Divine Presence by the hands of His angel, is transformed as follows: "Command these our *prayers* and *supplications*, by the ministry of Thy Holy Angels, to be brought up into Thy holy tabernacle before the sight of Thy divine Majesty." Almost all the words of the old prayer are retained, but of its meaning nothing.

The oblation, which is frequently mentioned after the consecration, becomes in the Prayer Book exclusively

[1] *Prayer Book*, 203.   [2] *Prayer Book*, ed. above-mentioned, 203.

that of the Christian united with Jesus Christ, not of Christ Himself. The change eradicates the idea of sacrifice and substitutes that of communion. "And here we offer and present unto Thee, O Lord, our souls and bodies, to be a reasonable, holy, and lively sacrifice[1] unto Thee, humbly beseeching Thee . . . that whosoever shall be partaker of this Holy *Communion*, may worthily receive the most precious Body and Blood of Thy Son Jesus Christ."[2]

The last part of the Mass, that which follows the *Pater*, is wholly concerned with communion. It consists of preparatory prayers and thanksgivings. The Prayer Book closely follows the old Missal.[3] But it omits the fraction of the Host and the commixture of the species in the chalice, two ceremonies which in medieval symbolism suggested the idea of a victim. The office ends with the communion of the priest and people in conformity with the *Order of the Communion* of 1548 of which I have already spoken.[4]

The Prayer Book Mass, thus deprived of its sacrificial character,[5] and reduced to a simple service of praise

---

[1] The words are taken from the *Quam oblationem*, the prayer immediately preceding the consecration. But the meaning of that prayer is entirely different. "Which oblation do Thou O God, we beseech Thee, mercifully render in all things blessed, accepted, ratified, reasonable and acceptable."

[2] It is taken from the conclusion of the *Supplices te rogamus*, "That all those who partaking at this altar shall receive the most holy Body and Blood of Thy Son may be filled with every heavenly blessing and grace." But in Cranmer's mind the partaking of Christ's Body and Blood was totally different from that taught by the Catholic Church. It is spiritual not real. For the Prayer Book prayer, see p. 201 of the edition above-mentioned.

[3] The *Libera nos quaesumus* was omitted. This is simply an expansion of the *Libera nos a malo*, whence its name *embolismus*, development. The *Agnus Dei* is to be sung during the Communion. (*Prayer Book*, 206).

[4] After the people's Communion a verse of Scripture is to be sung. (A choice of 22 is provided. *Prayer Book*, 206–207). This verse, called in the Missal the Communion, the Prayer Book calls the Postcommunion, hitherto the name of the collect which followed. The invariable prayer preceding the final blessing is inspired by the Sarum prayer, *Qui me refecisti de Sacratissimo Corpore et Sanguine*. The office concludes with the blessing (Prayer Book, 208).

[5] The chasuble, the strictly sacerdotal vestment, was no longer required Its place could be taken by the cope worn by clerics in minor orders and

and thanksgiving, closely resembles Luther's, both his "Latin Mass" of 1523 and his "German Mass" of 1526. The debt is obvious. The changes made by Cranmer are those which Luther advised, the suppression of the prayers at the foot of the altar, the chanting of an entire Psalm at the Introit, the transformation of the Offertory into a collection for the poor, the separation made at the same point of the service between the communicants and the non-communicants, the omission after the *Pater* of the embolism, the fraction of the Host and the commixture of the species, and the final prayers are the same. Instead of praying, as hitherto, that the bread and wine may *become* Christ's Body and Blood, the new service prays that they may *be* His Body and Blood. The change seems to substitute the doctrine of concomitance for that of transubstantiation.[1] Even the words which at the Consecration relate the institution of the Supper, are similar to those of the Lutheran liturgy of Brandenburg-Nuremberg, the work of Osiander, Cranmer's uncle by marriage. Richard Hilles wrote to Bullinger from London on June 1, 1549: "We now have a celebration of the Eucharist uniform throughout the kingdom after the model of the Churches of Nuremberg and Saxony."[2]

The substance of the new service therefore, and the spirit which inspired it, were undoubtedly Lutheran. But in its formulation it was a compromise. Somerset

---

even by laymen. (Rubric 4 of the Prayer Book, 195). The signs of the cross made by the priest over the consecrated bread and wine were also omitted. It is true that the gestures of the priest during the service were left by a general rubric to the devotion of the individual. (Prayer Book, ed. above-mentioned, 268). But an Act of Parliament passed in 1549 ordered the order and form prescribed in the book to be strictly followed and nothing added.

[1] *Prayer Book*, 203. Therefore Thirlby Bishop of Westminster, protested against the change. Gasquet and Bishop, *op. cit.*, App. V, 404.

[2] *Zurich Original Letters*, I, 226. Hilles had lived many years in Strasbourg and was acquainted with the various Protestant services.

did not desire too hasty or too radical a reform. Moreover, it was necessary to win the assent of the moderates, or at least of some of them.[1] Therefore concessions were made.

The most important of these was the retention of the Canon, which Luther had called "a heap of filth" and the "abominable Canon." The Lutherans found fault with the Anglicans for keeping it.[2] It had indeed been expurgated, and the attempt made to remove from it every suggestion of sacrifice. Possibly, however, the attempt had not been completely successful. Here and there relics of the old formulas survived, which could be interpreted in the orthodox sense. For example, prayer was still offered for the living[3] and the dead.[4] This, as Gardiner argued later, implies the notion of a propitiatory sacrifice.[5] God was praised for having manifested His glory in the Saints and above all in the Blessed Virgin Mary, in the patriarchs, the prophets, the apostles and the martyrs. Surely then Mass could still be celebrated in their honour and to obtain their intercession, a practice which the Protestants condemned. Finally, in the Parliamentary debate preceding the adoption of the Prayer Book, the Henricians secured

[1] Cf., Gasquet and Bishop, op. cit., 177–178.

[2] Bucer, Scripta Anglicana, Bale, 1577, 371. The Lutherans also objected to the abolition of the elevation of the Host and Chalice.

[3] Prayer was offered for the King, the Council, the bishops, the clergy, and the entire Christian people.

[4] Much of the phraseology is taken from the Memento of the Dead in the Missal. But the commemoration is made before, not after the consecration. (Prayer Book, 203.) The funeral service provides for a celebration of Mass with proper Introit, Collect, Epistle and Gospel. (First Prayer Book, 256–258). All this will be removed from the later Prayer Books. In a lengthy injunction of 1547 (Wilkins, Concilia, IV, 3 sq.; Cardwell, Documentary Annals, ed. 1844, I, 21 sq.: Strype, Memorials of Cranmer, ed. 1848, II, 460), Somerset exhorts all the kings' subjects to pray for the dead. Later injunctions on the contrary (Burnet, op. cit., ed. Pocock, IV, 243; Cardwell, Documentary Annals, I, 76) forbid anyone to uphold the belief in purgatory and the invocation of saints.

[5] An Explication and Assertion of the True Catholique Fayth touchyng the Most Blessed Sacrament of the Aulter. Parker Society's, ed. of Cranmer's Works, 1844–1849. (In his reply to Gardiner Cranmer reprinted his adversary's entire treatise) p. 84 sqq.; ed. H. Jenkyns, III, 33 sqq.

an important modification of the final rubric of the
Communion service.[1] The words "Sacrament of the
Body" and "Sacrament of the Blood" were substituted
for the words "Sacrament of the bread" and "Sacrament
of the wine." Bishop Bonner strongly urged that at this
point in the service the words *bread* and *wine* were
heretical.[2] "You will find several things to censure in
the Supper," Dryander[3] wrote, when he sent the Prayer
Book to his master Bullinger, "for the language of the
book is in truth obscure and however one strives to give
it a plain interpretation, great absurdities are unavoidable.
The reason is that it was a long time before agreement
could be secured among the bishops."[4] The Communion
service of 1549 was but a stage on the road to the reform
which the Protestants had in view. It marks an intermediate phase.

The Breviary was also changed. Cranmer, who on
this point followed the example of more than one bishop
faithful to Rome, had composed two drafts of a reformed
Breviary between 1543 and 1548.[5] The first of these
refashioned the Sarum breviary on the model of the
Breviary which Cardinal Quiñones had dedicated to
Paul III in 1535.[6] The second is an intermediate stage
between the old office and the new to which it closely

[1] *First Prayer Book*, 206.
[2] Gasquet and Bishop, *op. cit.*, App. V, 406–407. Tunstall wrote his
De Veritate Corporis et Sanguinis D. N. I. C. in Eucharistia, published at Paris,
in 1554.
[3] His real name was Enzinas. He was Professor of Greek at Cambridge.
[4] *Zurich Original Letters*, Parker Society, 351.
[5] In 1543 Convocation and the king ordered a revision of the liturgical
books. Convocation asked Cranmer to produce the result of his revision,
which however he regarded as incomplete and withheld. In 1548 a new
office was adopted by the Chapel Royal. Cooper, *Annals of Cambridge*,
II, 18. This is probably the office mentioned in May 1548 by Wriothesley's
Chronicle, ed. Camden Society, II, 2.
[6] *Breviarium Romanum ex sacra potissimum scriptura et probatis sanctorum
historiis nuper confectum.* Rome, 1535. It was republished by Wickham Legg
from the Venice edition of the same year in 1888 and again in 1908.
Cardinal Quiñones was a Spanish Franciscan, a friend and confidant of
Clement VII and Paul II. His remodelling of the Roman Breviary was a
too revolutionary break with its past. Paul III gave it his approbation,

approximates.[1] Antiphons, responds, versicles and hymns
have disappeared from the Prayer Book of 1549.[2] The entire
Psalter, must be read through every month,[3] the Old
Testament, once a year and the New, three times.[4] The
Little Hours, Prime, Terce, Sext, None and Compline,
replaced by two lessons at Evensong, were abolished.
The office was divided into two parts corresponding to

---

but Paul IV refused to recognise it. Authorised for private recitation alone,
it was abolished by Pius V in 1568. It was very short.

A contemporary, Cornelius Schulting of Cologne noted its influence
on the Anglican office, and William Palmer, in his *Origines Liturgicæ*,
called attention to the likeness between the prefaces of Quiñones and
Cranmer. Gasquet and Bishop (*op. cit.*, App. III, 356-70) have printed
both prefaces in parallel columns, and when publishing Cranmer's first
liturgical draft (App. II, 317-352) have added notes showing its borrowings
from Quiñones' breviary. This draft, like Quiñones' breviary, shortened
the office, but retained its traditional division into eight parts (Matins,
Lauds, Prime, Terce, Sext, None, Vespers and Compline).

[1] The office is already divided into two parts, *Series Officii Matutini* and
Series Officii Vespertini. Compline and the four little hours have been
abolished. See Appendix III.

[2] "For this cause," the preface says, (*First Prayer Book*, 4), "be cut off
Anthems, Responds, Invitations and such like things as did break the
continual course of the reading of the Scripture." Cardinal Quiñones had
set the example of these excisions save for the hymns, which were retained
in Cranmer's second draft. There were twenty-six, of which six were taken
from the Sarum Breviary, and six from Josse Clichtowe's *Elucidatorium
Ecclesiasticum*, Paris, 1516 and Bale, 1519. When it was decided in 1543
to revise the service books, Henry VIII ordered all versicles and responds
to be expunged. Wilkins, *Concilia*, III, 863.

[3] In Quiñones' breviary it was recited weekly. In the *First Prayer Book*
the Psalms are divided between thirty days of the month. The Psalms
for the thirtieth day are repeated on the thirty-first when the month has
thirty-one days.

[4] Cranmer had already decided upon this arrangement in his second
draft. (See App. III). The Old Testament was read as the first lesson
once a year, with the exception, as the Preface says, of a few less edifying
chapters. The New Testament was read as a second lesson thrice a year,
except the Apocalypse from which only a few lessons were taken for certain
feasts. The great feasts had proper lessons. Quiñones' breviary also provided for reading almost the entire Bible in the course of the year. The
festivals of saints, retained even in the 1552 Prayer Book, were reduced to
the following: Conversion of Saint Paul, the Purification, St. Matthias, the
Annunciation, St. Mark, SS. Philip and James, St. Barnabas, the
Nativity of St. John Baptist, St. Peter, St. Mary Magdalen (omitted in 1552),
St. James, St. Bartholomew, St. Matthew, St. Michael, St. Luke, SS. Simon
and Jude, All Saints, St. Andrew, St. Thomas, St. John the Evangelist,
the Holy Innocents. The Convocation of 1543 had decided that all saints
not mentioned in Scripture should be excluded from the service books.
Wilkins, *Concilia*, III, 863.

the two chief divisions of the day: Matins[1] and Evensong.
They were almost equal in length.[2] In its general character, its general arrangement, and its reduction to
Matins and Evensong, the new office closely resembles
the contemporary Lutheran service.

The ritual displays the same resemblance to Lutheran
service books. About a third of the Baptismal office[3]
is taken from the Sarum ritual, but paragraphs or phrases
of Lutheran inspiration are scattered here and there.[4]
The remainder of the office when it is not an original
composition, is borrowed from Luther's ritual of 1524.[5]
The exorcism, anointing of the forehead and imposition
of the white garment or chrisom are retained.[6] These
ceremonies are no longer found in the Prayer Book
of 1552 or in Elizabeth's prayer book.[7]

When the infant has been baptised at home, the prescriptions of the ritual are intended not so much to
supply the ecclesiastical ceremonies omitted as to provide
proof that the baptism was valid. The exorcism and
unction are therefore omitted,[8] and the emphasis is laid

[1] Of Lauds only the *Benedictus* was retained and in Lent the *Benedicite*.
[2] At Matins after the *Pater* the *Domine labia* and the *Deus in adjutorium*
the *Venite* was recited. It was followed by the Psalms of the day with their
Glorias, the first lesson, the *Te Deum*, for which the *Benedicite* was substituted
in Lent, the second lesson, the *Benedictus*, the Creed, the paternoster,
versicles, suffrages for the king, clergy and people, and three collects, of
the day, for peace, and to obtain Divine Grace. At Evensong (Vespers)
the *Pater* and *Deus in adjutorium* were followed by the Psalms of the day,
the first lesson, the *Magnificat*, the second lesson, the *Nunc Dimittis*, and three
collects, of the day, for peace and against perils of the night. *First Prayer
Book*, 27–28. Cf., Dixon, *op. cit.*, III, 15 *sqq*.
[3] Some sixty-five or sixty-six lines out of some two hundred and forty.
[4] With the exception of an entire prayer taken from Luther's ritual.
The rubric ordering immersion, when the infant is healthy, follows the
Sarum ritual. *The First Prayer Book*, 221.
[5] Rather than Hermann's *Pia Consultatio*, as is sometimes said. The
Gospel from St. Matthew read over the infant in the Sarum ritual is
replaced by a corresponding passage from St. Mark (XV, 13–16) which
Luther had chosen.
[6] *The First Prayer Book*, 218, 219, 221. Oil for the anointing is no longer
blessed.
[7] The priest will, however, continue to make the sign of the cross on the
child's forehead.
[8] The imposition of the chrisom was retained.

upon the introductory rubrics,[1] enquiry from the parents,[2] and the certificate,[3] whose purpose is to make the baptism certain. All these prescriptions were plainly derived from Hermann von Wied's *Pia Consultatio* (1543).

The object of Confirmation, according to the Prayer Book of 1549, is not only to strengthen the Christian,[4] and give him the courage to confess his faith,[5] but above all that he should ratify by a public profession the promises made in his name at his baptism. This object, which the Prayer Book mentions first,[6] had no place in the old rite. It was inspired by the liturgy of the Lutheran churches, in which Confirmation is simply the final seal set upon the catechetical instruction.[7] The anointing with chrism was abolished, though it had hitherto been regarded as one of the distinctive signs of Confirmation, which was commonly called *Sacramentum Chrismatis*.[8] As among the Lutherans only the imposition of hands was retained.

Extreme Unction was retained: "If the sick man," the rubric declares, "desire to be anointed, then shall the priest anoint him upon the forehead or breast only, making the sign of the cross, saying thus, As with this visible oil thy body outwardly is anointed: so our heavenly Father Almighty God, grant of His infinite goodness, that thy soul inwardly may be anointed with the Holy Ghost who is the spirit of all strength, comfort, relief and gladness; and vouchsafe for His great mercy (if it be His blessed will) to restore unto thee thy bodily health

[1] *The First Prayer Book*, 225.
[2] Ibid., 226.
[3] Ibid., 224.
[4] *The First Prayer Book*, 228, rubric 3.
[5] Ibid., Rubric 4.
[6] Ibid., 228. A short catechism follows (229–231) which summarises the principal truths of faith which children should know before being confirmed.
[7] The final rubric of the Prayer Book (232) forbids any child to be admitted to Communion before it has been confirmed.
[8] The Bishop, however, continued to make the sign of the cross on the candidate's forehead saying: "I sign thee with the sign of the cross." *First Prayer Book*, 232.

and strength, to serve Him, and send thee release of all thy pains, troubles and diseases, both in body and in mind . . . and to pardon thee all thy sins and offences, committed by all thy bodily senses, passions and carnal affections. Who also vouchsafe mercifully to grant unto thee ghostly strength by His Holy Spirit to withstand and overcome all temptations and assaults of thine adversary that in no wise he prevail against thee."[1]

Though this prayer was new it expresses very well the effects which according to Catholic doctrine Extreme Unction produces on the soul and body. Auricular Confession, though no longer regarded as a Sacrament,[2] is a laudable practice sanctioned by a rubric of the Prayer Book. In the Visitation of the Sick the following words occur: "Here shall the sick person make a *special confession*, if he feel his conscience troubled with any weighty matter. After which confession the priest shall absolve him after this form: and the same form of absolution shall be used in all *private confessions*. 'Our Lord Jesus Christ who hath left power to His church to absolve all sinners which truly repent and believe in Him: of His great mercy forgive thee thine offences: and by His authority committed to me, I absolve thee from all thy sins, in the name of the Father and of the Son and of the Holy Ghost.' "[3]

At the London Conference of 1538 the Lutherans had admitted that Confession, though not of obligation, is a most excellent practice, "and must by all means be retained in the Church."[4]

---

[1] *First Prayer Book*, 245. This prayer, of which I have quoted only a part, is followed by Psalm xiii (Vulgate 12). *Usquequo Domine.*

[2] *The Book of Homilies* explicitly said so, as will also the 35th of Elizabeth's XXXIX articles.

[3] *First Prayer Book*, 243.

[4] Cranmer was of the Lutheran opinion that confession is not obligatory but most profitable. "Confession of sins called auricular and made privately to the ministers of the Church is most useful and profitable." *Cranmer's Works*, Parker Society, IV, 282–285. And in his catechism of 1548, which is a translation of a Lutheran catechism, he says, "Let the sinner confess his sins to a priest and ask from him, according to God's

The sacramentals were abolished. The Prayer Book does not mention them, and an appendix to the book "Of Ceremonies"[1] explains that many rites and ceremonies have been suppressed "because the great excess and multitude of them hath so increased in these latter days, that the burden of them was intolerable," and because "certain ceremonies . . . were so far abused, partly by the superstitious blindness of the rude and unlearned and partly by the unsatiable avarice of such as sought more their own lucre than the glory of God."[2]

Like the Lutheran liturgies, the entire service—the Divine Office, the Mass, the administration of the sacraments—was in the vulgar tongue. The Henricians had urged that the use of Latin should be retained,[3] and as late as 1548 Cranmer himself still thought the most sacred parts of the Mass should be said in Latin.

The Prayer Book of 1549 recast the old rites and ceremonies in accordance with the new ideas of the German reformation. Under pretext of restoring public worship to its primitive purity, it superimposed upon the old English liturgy that of the *Lutherans*, whose spirit inspired the entire work.

Commandment, absolution and comfort by the word of grace and forgiveness. And when the priest doth so, I must firmly believe that my sins are truly remitted." *Cranmer's Catechism*, edition of his works abovementioned, 202.

[1] *Prayer Book*, 266 sqq.

[2] The Observance of Ash Wednesday was retained and a long office provided. (*First Prayer Book*, 261–265). But the imposition of Ashes was abolished. The Lenten fast and the Friday abstinence were also retained. In 1551 the Venetian Ambassador wrote, "They eat fish on Fridays and Saturdays and in Lent . . . but in order not to follow the Roman usage they intend to substitute two other week-days for the Friday and Saturday." Albèri *Relazione degli Ambasciatori Veneti*. Series I, Vol. II, p. 245.

[3] In 1548 answers to a question proved that the Bishops were divided on the question of vernacular services. In spite of this in September 1555 Cranmer wrote to Queen Mary that at the Windsor conference all the Bishops were in favour of a vernacular service. *Cranmer's Remains*, Parker Society, 450. Ridley wrote to his chaplain to the same effect. *Ridley's Works*, Parker Society, 340.

The use of Latin, Greek and Hebrew for certain prayers was authorised at Oxford and Cambridge for purely educational reasons.

The Prayer Book of 1549 was not submitted to Convocation. Certain writers in the past have asserted the contrary.[1] But no modern historian agrees with them. Historians of the Reformation, such as Heylyn[2] and Fuller[3] who had the opportunity of consulting the records of the Convocation of Canterbury, burned in the Great Fire of London in 1666, do not mention any approval of the Prayer Book by the clergy.[4] Burnet[5] and Collier[6] are equally silent. W. Wake[7] states expressly that the approbation was not given. Strype, writing in 1723, was the first to affirm that "what divers learned divines had concluded upon was offered the convocation."[8] Dixon[9] and Gasquet[10] have so convincingly refuted the opinion of Strype and his followers that nothing further need be said. "Of the strange features of the change," Froude observes, "the strangest was, perhaps, that the official opinion of convocation was scarcely asked even in form. Parliament now discussed the faith of England, and laymen decided upon the doctrines which the clergy were compelled to teach."[11]

"The convocation of the clergy," adds the Anglican, Canon Dixon,[12] "had nothing to do with the first act for the uniformity of religion. Several pieces of legislation, indeed, during recent sessions had proceeded upon

[1] The editor of the *First Prayer Book* (edition above-mentioned), still affirms it but produces no evidence in support of his assertion.
[2] *Ecclesia Restaurata or the History of the Reformation*, London, 1661.
[3] *The Church History of Britain*, London, 1655.
[4] This is the more significant because Heylyn had to answer a writer who had maintained that the Anglican religion had been imposed upon the country purely by the authority of Parliament without any formal approbation by the clergy. See his argument in his *Ecclesia Vindicata or the Church of England Justified*, etc., London, 1657, 29–30, 79–84.
[5] *History of the Reformation*, London, 1669–1715.
[6] *Ecclesiastical History of Great Britain*, London, 1708–1714.
[7] *The State of the Church and Clergy of England in their Councils, Synods, Convocations, etc.*, App. VII, London, 1703.
[8] *Ecclesiastical Memorials*, II, 84.
[9] *History of the Church of England*, London, 1878–1899, III, 5.
[10] Gasquet and Bishop, *op. cit.*, Chapter X. *Convocation and the Prayer Book.*
[11] *The Reign of Edward VI*, ed. 1909, 86.
[12] *Op. cit.*, III, 5.

the suggestion of the clerical assembly; but neither the first Act for Uniformity nor any of the Acts that came thereafter, had any such origin. Laymen were the authors of those momentous measures. Laymen made the first English Book of Common Prayer into the schedule of a penal statute; and from the time that they first did so, with mournful consistency a penal statute accompanied every succeeding revision of a Book of Common Prayer. As little in the work itself, which was thus imposed on the nation, had the clergy originally any share. The empty records of convocation, the silence or ambiguity of other documents, at least permit the question to be raised whether the first Prayer Book of Edward the Sixth was ever submitted to the synods of the English Church. Evidence indeed had been adduced by several authorities to show that it was: but if the opposite conclusion be advanced, those who best favour the Church of England in the present day, may perhaps have less occasion to mourn than to rejoice that Uniformity, the invention of the sixteenth century, sought not the aid of synods."

If, however, the Prayer Book did not receive the sanction of Convocation it was submitted to the bishops.[1] To secure a measure of preliminary agreement about the new liturgy,[2] Somerset summoned a meeting of the bishops shortly after the injunction of September 23, 1548, which announced changes in the rites and ceremonies of the Church. It probably took place in October.[3] No agreement could be obtained about "the doctrine of the Supper." The debate turned principally

[1] In the course of the debate Somerset explicitly spoke of a consultation between the bishops to secure agreement. Gasquet and Bishop, *op. cit.*, App. V, 401.

[2] Hence his annoyance when Thirlby revealed to the House the dissension which existed in the episcopate. Gasquet and Bishop, *op. cit.*, App. V, 404.

[3] On the 29th of the month, Bucer wrote from Strasbourg to Bullinger that "The Government had called a synod of Bishops to deliberate on religion." *Zurich Original Letters*, Parker Society, 643.

on the Elevation, and therefore "adoration" of the Host abolished by the new Missal. Nevertheless, all the bishops, with the exception of Day of Chichester,[1] gave the Prayer Book their approval, attested by their signatures, in the hope and possibly on the promise of a further revision.[2] The Henricians, such as Tunstall, Heath, Bonner and Thirlby, did not intend by this to assent to the teaching of Cranmer and the advanced party. But they reluctantly subscribed a species of Interim in the interest of concord, to preserve the "Internal unity of the kingdom," threatened by intestine factions and foreign wars and they reserved the right to criticise certain parts of the book on the first opportunity.[3]

The opportunity soon arrived. On December 14, the Prayer Book was laid before Parliament. The debate in the House of Lords continued till the 18th. It was animated: "Members of the Commons flocked in large numbers into the galleries of the Upper House to listen to it",[4] and witness the difference of opinion which divided the bishops on questions of the gravest importance. The Bishop of Westminster complained that Parliament was invited to pronounce on matters on which the bishops could not agree.[5] The chief point in dispute was the Real Presence. Only three lay peers spoke:

[1] Heylyn (op. cit., I, 136) also says that Day refused his signature. His reasons were explained by Somerset at the opening of Parliament. (Gasquet and Bishop, op. cit., App. V, 404). Day objected that the Prayer Book abolished the use of chrism at confirmation, that in the prayer before the consecration it changed the words that they (the bread and wine) "May be made into that they may be," that it excised from the Missal the terms sacrifice and oblation.

[2] All this is proved by the speeches made by Somerset and Bishop Thirlby of Westminster in the course of the debate. Gasquet and Bishop, op. cit., App. V, 403-406.

[3] Thirlby's Reply to Somerset in Parliament. December 17, 1548. Gasquet and Bishop, op. cit., App. V, 404-405.

[4] Peter Martyr to Bucer, December 26, 1548, Zurich Original Letters, Parker Society, 469. Cf. Traheron to Bullinger the 31st of the same month. (Ibid., p. 323). Also John Isham to Bellingham quoted by Froude, op. cit., 1909, 88.

[5] Gasquet and Bishop, op. cit., App. V, 403.

Protector Somerset, who played the part of a moderator,[1] Warwick,[2] whose imperious language threatened opponents,[3] and the Secretary of State, Richard Smith, whose interruptions, often trivial, smacked of vulgarity and profanity.[4] Thirteen bishops declared in favour of the new liturgy,[5] ten against it.[6]

The debate was followed by a delay of three weeks before the Act of Uniformity was passed imposing the first Book of Common Prayer upon the country. The interval was utilised to make certain alterations in the book to secure for it an Episcopal majority. Somerset attached great importance to this, and it was undoubtedly he who pressed for compromise and concessions. So eager was he to obtain the approval of the bishops hostile to the Reformation, that he even attempted to secure the approbation of Reginald Pole, to whom he sent the new book.[7] The Act was passed on January 21,

[1] Gasquet and Bishop, op. cit., App. V, 404, 407, 423.
[2] A few months later the Earl of Warwick was to replace Somerset at the head of the Government.
[3] Ibid., 403, 418.
[4] Ibid., 399, 406, 422, 423, 424, 439.
[5] Cranmer, Holbeach of Lincoln, Goodrich of Ely, Ridley of Rochester, Barlow of Bath and Wells, Holgate of York, Chambers of Peterborough, Salcot of Sarum, Bush of Bristol, Sampson of Lichfield. To these ten we must add three Bishops absent from the debate: Ferrar of St. David's whose opinion is certain, King of Oxford, who had appointed Holbeach and Ridley as his procurators and Warton of St. Asaph represented by Goodrich and Salcot.
[6] Bonner of London, Tunstall of Durham, Heath of Worcester, Thirlby of Westminster, Rugg of Norwich, Aldrich of Carlisle, Skip of Hereford and Day of Chichester. To these eight we must add Gardiner who was in prison and John Bird of Chester who had appointed Bonner and Thirlby as his procurators. The vote of four other absentees is doubtful. Nothing is known of Wakeman of Gloucester. The Bishop of Llandaff, who had spoken against Cranmer during the debate, was not present at its conclusion. Voysey of Exeter arrived only after the vote had been taken; and the Bishop of Bangor had appointed Salcot, Thirlby and Bonner as his procurators.
Besides Appendix V in Gasquet and Bishop see for the entire debate Chapter VIII, of Part IV of Messenger's *The Reformation, the Mass and the Priesthood*. London, 1936-7.
[7] His long letter to Pole is to be found in Pocock, *Troubles Connected with the Prayer Book*, of 1549, p. vi, *sqq.* and Pole's reply to the effect that the rising of the West dispenses him from an examination of the Prayer Book. In *Venetian Cal.*, V, 241 *sqq.* Cf. *Messenger, op. cit.*, I, 420.

1549,[1] and received the Royal assent on March 14. It was
called the Act of Uniformity because it imposed a uniform
order of service to be observed in every detail in every
church throughout the realm. It abolished the old rites,
the local uses of Salisbury (Sarum), York, Lincoln,
Hereford, Bangor and all other local usages, that "now
from henceforth all the whole realm shall have but
one use."[2] The Prayer Book, it was asserted, had been
composed "with the assistance of the Holy Ghost and
the unanimous consent" of pious and learned bishops.

It must be used everywhere from the following Whit-
Sunday, June 9, 1549. Any priest who continued to
use the old rites[3] would be deprived for the first offence
of his benefices for a year, or undergo six months' imprisonment. A second offence would entail suspension
from his clerical functions, a third, imprisonment for
life. To ridicule the Prayer Book in songs or stage plays
was punishable by a fine of ten pounds or three months'
imprisonment for the first offence. For a second the fine
and term of imprisonment were doubled. A third involved confiscation of goods and imprisonment for life.[4]
The judges and local magistrates were required to apply
these sanctions and see that the statute was obeyed.

[1] *Statutes of the Realm*, 2 and 3. Edward VI, cap. 1. Cf. Collier, *op. cit.*,
ed. Lathbury, V, 295. See also *Lords' Journal; Journal of the House of
Commons Beginning in Anno Primo Regni Edwardi Sexti.*, 1875, Vol. I.

[2] "And besides the same, now of late much more diverse and sundry
formes and fashions have been used in the cathedrals and parish churches
of England and Wales." Somerset refrained from strictly enforcing the
law and abolishing at one blow every older form of service. Warwick was
uncompromising. He had hardly seized power before he sent a circular
letter to the Bishops ordering the thorough abolition of the Latin service
and the destruction of all the old service books. Royal letter to the Bishops,
December 25, 1550. *Troubles Connected with the Prayer Book of* 1549. Ed.
Pocock for the Camden Society, 127–128; Foxe, *op. cit.*, ed. Pratt, VI, 3;
Cardwell, *Documentary Annals*, I, 85, in which the royal letter is accompanied
by a letter from Cranmer to the clergy of his diocese demanding obedience
to its injunctions. February 14, 1550.

[3] The Second Act of Uniformity would render even passive opposition
to the new service punishable.

[4] *Statutes of the Realm*, 2 and 3. Edward VI, cap. 1. The laity were not
subjected to any penalty for absenting themselves from the services of their
parish church and attending some other church.

The bishops were also called upon to assist, and ecclesiastical censures which had been discarded as out of date, among them excommunication, were revived to enforce Uniformity. Royal injunctions commanded the clergy to suppress without delay the "popish Mass," all the rites, ceremonies and usages abolished by the Prayer Book and "all other abuses and superstitions."[1]

On June 24, 1549, the Council complained to Bishop Bonner that Low Masses were still being celebrated at St. Paul's, and moreover, according to an unauthorised rite, and on altars other than the High Altar, at which only one Mass a day might be celebrated.[2] And a month later (July 23) it censured him and the other bishops of his opinion (the Henricians) for their negligence, which was the reason why the new service was so unpopular in the country.[3] After Somerset's fall, the order was given to destroy all the old liturgical books. This order, confirmed and reinforced by a statute, produced an orgy of destructive vandalism deplored by more than one enlightened Anglican.[4]

The first Book of Common Prayer, in spite of its Lutheran tendencies, still retained too many Catholic features to satisfy the advanced reformers. Calvin reproached the Anglicans for clinging to things to which they have been accustomed. Their religious " conservatism " he regarded as puerile and frivolous.[5] " Some

---

[1] Among these abuses were mentioned the rosary, holy water, ashes, palms, candles, the Easter Sepulchre and Henry VIII's Six Articles. Burnet, *op. cit.*, ed. Pocock, V, 243, Cardwell, *Documentary Annals*, 1844, I, 74.

[2] An early service of Holy Communion was however permitted for the benefit of those prevented by their work from attending the later service. Foxe, *Acts and Monuments*, ed. Pratt, I, 723; Heylyn, *Ecclesia Restaurata*, ed. 1849, I, 154; Cardwell, *op. cit.*, I, 76.

[3] Foxe, *op. cit.*, ed. Pratt, V, 726; Cardwell, *op. cit.*, I, 78.

[4] Collier, *op. cit.*, ed. Lathbury, V, 360–362; Wood, *Historia et Antiquitates Universitatis Oxoniensis*, II, 106.

[5] "They love what they are accustomed to. This is futile and childish." Calvin to the Anglicans in Frankfort, February 15, 1555. *J. Calvini Opera*, ed. Baum, Cunitz, Reuss, in the *Corpus Reformatorum*, second series, XV Col. 394.

concessions," wrote Bucer and Fagius, referring to the new Prayer Book, "have been made out of respect for antiquity, and to spare the weakness of the present age. . . . They say that there is nothing superstitious in these things, and that they have been kept only for a time."[1]

The Prayer Book of 1549 was indeed to remain in use "only for a time." Within less than four years it was revised and recast, and everything plainly orthodox which remained was expunged. This, however, was not the work of Protector Somerset, whose fall closely followed the Act of Uniformity (October 1549). The first Prayer Book bore the stamp of the moderation and liberalism which distinguished the first part of Edward VI's reign and which were due to Somerset alone.

[1] Letter of April 26, 1549. *Zurich Original Letters*, Parker Society, 535–536.

CHAPTER IV

SOMERSET'S FALL (1549)

Foreign difficulties; war with Scotland and France. Internal troubles, social and religious unrest, risings in the East and West. Opposition of the Privy Council and Warwick's plot. The Protector's fall and pardon.

THE Protector had seized supreme power by a coup d'état. But would he prove strong enough to keep it? His position was difficult and insecure. Could not the Council which, with the king's consent, had raised him to the first rank, depose him from it with the same royal sanction? More than one member of the Council had witnessed his elevation with a jealous eye. Only seven had signed the letters patent which appointed him Protector.[1] Among the missing signatures was that of Warwick, the most influential Councillor after himself, and his secret enemy, the man who was destined to overthrow him. To preserve his work intact Henry VIII had done everything in his power to hamper the personal action of the government during his son's minority. The unprecedented statute of 1536 empowered the king, on reaching his twenty-fourth year, to annul all the measures taken in his name before that date.[2] This enactment undermined the Protector's authority and weakened his most weighty decisions.

Though his position was so weak, Somerset embarked on several undertakings, each of which required the absolute power of a Henry VIII. He attempted to reform

---

[1] Cf. Froude, *The Reign of Edward VI*, ed. 1909, 8. We must not exaggerate the significance of this. Lord Seymour's name is not on the list. Yet the Protector's brother recognised the Protectorate and confirmed his recognition in writing. Possibly the others did the same.

[2] The statute was amended by the first Parliament of Edward VI.

religion, alter the social conditions of the country, and
unite England and Scotland in a single kingdom. He
had, as Paget told him, "too many irons in the fire
at the same time."[1] His enemies could not fail to profit
by the difficulties in which so complicated a situation
involved him, to effect his overthrow.

The first project on which he embarked was the
annexation of Scotland. It was a legacy from preceding
reigns. Henry VII had married his daughter Margaret
to James IV. Henry VIII had attempted to conquer
Scotland, and had revived the obsolete claims to that
country which Edward I had put forward against Balliol.
He had defeated the Scots at Solway Moss (1542)[2] and
as the fruit of his victory had obtained from the Scottish
Parliament a promise of marriage between Mary Stuart
and the future Edward VI, then only five years old.
The promise seemed likely to realise the ambition of the
Tudors. At this period royal marriages were the usual
way of annexing a state. It was in this fashion that
France had acquired Brittany and a part of Burgundy,
and that Castile and Aragon had been united.

But France, whose interest it was to prevent any
increase in the power of her hereditary foe across the
channel, had never ceased to combat the English policy.
To the marriage between James IV and Margaret
Tudor, she had replied by a marriage between Mary of
Lorraine, now the Queen regent, and James V. The
suggested marriage between Mary Stuart and Edward she
broke off almost immediately. The Scots, infuriated by
Henry's claims to suzerainty, saw in the alliance with
France the safeguard of their independence, their sole
chance of liberty. They therefore broke the agreement
with England, and negotiated a marriage between their
young Queen and a French prince.[3] War followed

---

[1] Paget to Somerset, July 7, 1549. Strype, *Ecclesiastical Memorials*, II,
Part 2, p. 429 *sq.*
[2] Cf. Hamilton Papers, I, pp. lxxxiii-lxxxvi.
[3] L. and P., XVIII, *passim.*

(1545).[1] Henry died at peace with France,[2] but medita-
ting plans of vengeance and conquest against Scotland.[3]
All this past history doubtless influenced Somerset's
policy and drew him into a lengthy struggle against
Scotland and France.

The Protector had reason to fear that Scotland might
become for all practical purposes a French dependency.
Henry II had just succeeded to the French throne. As
Dauphin, he had always been the avowed enemy of the
English.[4] As king, he refused to ratify the defensive
alliance which Francis I had just concluded with Edward
VI,[5] and the English believed he was about to declare
war. On his Council, the Guises, protected by Diana
of Poitiers, were all powerful. Their sister Mary of
Lorraine was regent of Scotland. To uphold her against
the English was therefore to uphold the interests of the
family.[6] It had already been proposed to send Mary
Stuart to France, which could only be in view of her
marriage to a French prince.[7] French influence became
threatening and England, it would seem, was afraid of
being confronted in Scotland with a species of family
alliance.

Somerset decided to attack Scotland. He appealed
to the treaty of marriage between Edward VI and Mary
Stuart, approved by the Edinburgh Parliament in 1543.
It was, he said, the genuine expression of the nation's

---

[1] Cf. For the Scottish War, *Hamilton Papers*. And for the French *Spanish Calendar*, VII; L. and P., XIX, Part II, December, 1544, &c.

[2] Peace was concluded in June 1546. *State Papers*, ed. 1830–1851. I, 877–879, Lefèvre-Pontalis, *op. cit.*, 31–34; *Calais Papers*, No. 67 (I).

[3] See Despatch from Odet de Selve to Francis I, November 28, 1546, Lefèvre-Pontalis, *op. cit.*, 66, cf. Despatches of January 1 and January 15, 1547. Ibid., 78, 86. Also Despatch of January 25, ibid., 93.

[4] Cf. *Calais Papers*, No. 99 (I).

[5] It had been already signed by Henry VIII on his deathbed. Wotton had been ordered to receive Francis's Oath. *State Papers*, Foreign, I, 48. For this defensive league see the *Correspondance de Odet de Selve*. Ed. Lefèvre-Pontalis, 88, 104, 117, 123, 124.

[6] Lefèvre-Pontalis, *op. cit.*, XVII.

[7] The English Government was prepared to prevent the marriage at all costs. (Lefèvre-Pontalis, *op. cit.*, 161).

will. Mary of Lorraine and Cardinal Beaton were tools of the Guises, and had betrayed the true interests of Scotland.[1] This was the position which the Protector took up from the outset, and from which he never swerved. In his declaration of war he accused Arran and his fellow nobles of violating the solemn undertakings into which the Scottish Parliament had entered.[2] He repeated his accusations in the proclamations which his supporters spread throughout Scotland. When he crossed the frontier at the head of an invading army, he sent the Norroy King of Arms to Edinburgh "to enjoin the Queen and Council to deliver the young Queen to the Protector to be brought up with her husband, as a Queen of England, as he promises to do on his honour, failing which, he will use all means to bring it about by force."[3]

After his victory at Pinkie he released the Chancellor of Scotland, and treated his other prisoners of rank with great respect and consideration in the hope of winning them over to the English marriage and making them its advocates.[4] Finally, in January 1548, he addressed a letter to the people of Scotland in which he justified the invasion by the breach of the promise solemnly made. "All the world might testify," he says, "all other means not being able to do anything, after many other ways and remedies attempted: battle of us to be taken as an extreme refuge to attain right and reason among Christian men. If any man may rightfully make battle for his espouse and for to make peace: this

[1] The Cardinal, the soul of the Pro-French party in Scotland, had been assassinated in 1546, not altogether without Henry's complicity.

[2] *Acts of the Privy Council*, II, 115 *sqq*. James Hamilton, second Earl of Arran was governor of the Realm of Scotland (1542-1555) and First Duke of Châtellerault. (1549).

[3] *State Papers Scotland*, Edward VI, I, 53. For the projected marriage between Edward and Mary see *Spanish Calendar*, IX, 41, 161, 215, 234, 236, 491, 493, 525.

[4] See De Selve to the King of France, October 18, 1547 (Lefèvre-Pontalis), *op. cit.*, 221). Also *Memoire contenant les Articles proposés au Comte de Hontelay* (Huntley). Lefèvre-Pontalis, *op. cit.*, 268-269. Cf. pp. 224, 234.

is to make an end of all wars, to conclude an eternal and perpetual peace."[1]   Union was in the interest of both countries. For it would produce a permanent peace. "If it be lawful by God's law to fight in a good quarrell . . . we declare unto you . . . to be the King's Majesty's mind by our advice and counsel, not to conquer but to have in amity, not to win by force, but to conciliate by love, not to spoil and kill, but to save and keep, not to dissever and divorce, but to join in marriage, from high to low, both the realms, to make of one isle, one realm, in love, amity, concord, peace and charity. . . . We intend not to disherit your Queen, but to make her heirs inheritors also to England."[2] Indeed the union which the Protector proposed was not simply a union of two crowns. It was the complete fusion of both kingdoms in one political body. He proposed to abolish the names England and Scotland and subtitute for them "the Empire of Great Britain."[3] Somerset was more than a century in advance of his contemporaries. He wanted to attain this end without violence or recourse to arms, by the sheer force of persuasion. This was indeed typical of his character. "Most merciful God," he prayed when there was still some hope of preserving peace, "the Granter of all peace and quietness, the Giver of all good gifts, the Defender of all nations, who hast willed all men to be accounted as our neighbours, and commanded us to love them as ourself and not to hate our enemies·but

[1] This letter to the Scots was printed in London in 1548 in English and Latin. It was reprinted in 1872 by Murray for the Early English Text Society, "*An Epistle or Exhortation to Unitie and Peace sent from the Lord Protector to the Nobilitie . . . of Scotland.*"

[2] Ibid.

[3] Ibid., 241–242. He made the same proposal to the Earl of Huntley, the Chancellor of Scotland, who had been taken captive at Pinkie. "The names of Scotland and the Scotch and England and English will alike be abolished and the two peoples and kingdoms will be united in one empire that will always be named and called the Empire of Great Britain, and the ruling monarch the Emperor of Great Britain." *Memoire contenant les Articles proposés au Comte de Hontelay*, Lefèvre-Portalis, *op. cit.*, 269. Cf. Pollard, *The Elizabethans and the Empire.* 1921, 7.

rather to wish them, yea and also to do them good if we can: bow down thy holy and merciful eyes upon us . . . Give to us all desire of peace, unity and quietness and a speedy wearisomeness of all war, hostility and enmity . . . and especially have an eye to this small isle of Britain, and that which was begun by Thy great and infinite mercy and love to the unity and concord of both the nations that the Scottish men and we might for ever live hereafter in our love and amity. Knit into one nation, by the most happy and godly marriage of the King's Majesty our Soverign Lord and the young Scottish Queen whereunto promises and agreements hath been heretofore most firmly made by human order; Grant, O Lord, that the same might go forward and that our sons' sons and all our posterity hereafter, may feel the benefit and commodity of thy good gift of unity, granted in our days. Confound all those that worketh against it. . . . Put away from us all war and hostility, and if we be driven thereto, hold Thy holy and strong power and defence over us: be our garrison, our shield and buckler."[1] In the bidding prayers in every parish God must be entreated to grant "that the most joyful and perpetual peace and unity of this realm and Scotland may shortly be perfected and brought to pass by the most godly and happy marriage of the King's Majesty and the young Queen of Scotland."[2]

But to return to the position as it was in the early part of 1547. The truce between England and Scotland was still unbroken. The English and French fleets met near St. Andrew's[3] without a clash. But it did not last. On both sides preparations were being made for war.

[1] State Papers Domestic, Edward VI, II, No. 6. Jenkyns, Remains of Th. Cranmer. II, 186 note.
[2] Wilkins, Concilia, IV, 26. Jenkyns, Remains of Th. Cranmer, II, 186 sqq. Cf. Strype, Eccles. Mem., II, Part I, p. 46.
[3] Cardinal Beaton's assassins who had taken refuge in the castle of St. Andrew's were besieged by the Scotch, defended by the English. Cf. Kaulek, op. cit., 32, 41, 50–51, 54, 57–58, 65–67, 71, 74–75, 79, 110, 141–144, 153, 156. State Papers Scotland, Edward VI, I, No. 12.

And as de Selve observed, armaments ill assort with pacific professions.[1] The Scots encouraged by the fleet under Strozzi, commander of the French galleys, captured Langholm Castle held by the English,[2] refused to discuss the terms of peace offered by Somerset, in July 1547, and assembled on the frontier forces which the Protector regarded as a threat of invasion.[3] On their side the English had an army in readiness at Berwick, and it was to be supported by the fleet under Lord Clinton's command.[4] Somerset, after a final attempt at negotiations,[5] left London towards the end of August, 1547, and reached Newcastle on the 27th.[6] On September 4 he crossed the frontier, and on the 9th he won the celebrated victory of Pinkie, defeating with a force of 16,000 a Scottish army of 23,000 strongly entrenched on the river Esk.[7] A few days later, a solemn Te Deum with the English Litany was sung in every London church: on September 20 at St. Paul's, on the 21st in other churches. The victory was followed up during the concluding months of 1547 and the early months

[1] De Selve to the King of France, July 27, 1547. *Op. cit.*, p. 173.

[2] Kaulek, *op. cit.*, 157, 159, 162, 167, 175, 181, 194. Cf. Lefèvre-Pontalis *op. cit.*, 147, 158, 163, 168, 173. *State Papers, Domestic, Addenda* I, 24 (I).

[3] See De Selve to the King of France, July 27, 1547. Lefèvre-Pontalis, *op. cit.*, 173.

[4] De Selve to the King of France, July 27, 1547. Lefèvre-Pontalis, *op. cit.*, 173. The Earl of Warwick was in command of the army.

[5] See De Selve to the King of France, August 10, 1547. Lefèvre-Pontalis, *op. cit.*, 179–180.

[6] It was on August 22 or 23 that Somerset left London. (Cf. *Diurnal of Occurrents*, Bannatyne Club, p. 44). On the 21st he appointed his brother Thomas Seymour, Lieutenant and Captain general of the South in his absence. The conduct of ordinary business was left to the Council. *Acts of the Privy Council*. II, 115 *sqq.*

[7] For the victory of Pinkie or Musselburgh several contemporary accounts are available. Patten (an eye witness), *Expedicion into Scotland*, 1548, reprinted by Arber. *English Garner*, 1880 and incorporated by Froude into his *History of the Reign of Edward VI*, (ed. 1909, 30–33); an account by the Sieur de Berteville, a commander of the mercenaries in the English service published by the Bannatyne Club in 1825; accounts by the Earl of Huntley and Jean Ribaud, a citizen of Dieppe and a refugee in England, in de Selve's letter to the King of France of October 18, 1547, Lefèvre-Pontalis, *op. cit.*, 218–223. See also *Diurnal of Occurrents*, 44–45; J. Leslay, *History of Scotland*, 1578, ed. Bannatyne Club, 195–199.

of 1548 by fresh successes, which made the English masters
of the Eastern Lowlands and secured strong bases in
Scotland.[1]

As a skilful politician, Somerset combined the influence
of persuasion with that of arms. He tried, as has already
been said, to win over the most influential prisoners
taken at Pinkie, particularly Chancellor Huntley and
the Earl of Bothwell, and by active propaganda to gain
the Scottish nobility and gentry.[2] He sought to reassure
the Scottish people of his intentions. He pointed out the
danger to their freedom involved in marrying the young
queen to a French prince, and warned them against
"those vain fears and fantasies of expulsion of your
nation, of changing the laws, of making a conquest.
We seek not to take from you your laws nor customs" for
"in the realm of England diverse laws and customs be
according to the ancient usage of the parts thereof.
And likewise in France."[3] Scotland therefore would not
lose her independence.

Somerset was far from neglecting religious methods.
To convert the country to Protestantism would be to
win it to the cause of England, which the reformers
called "the good cause." The party in Scotland favourable to England had always been Protestant.[4] The
Protector accordingly cherished the hope of banish-
ing Catholicism from Scotland and thus getting rid
of the French influence. Abjurations were encouraged. The convert renounced the Bishop of Rome

[1] Cf. *State Papers Scotland*, I, 56; II, 47, 54, 57, 61, 67, III, 51, 53; IV,
2, 19; *State Papers, Domestic*, Edward VI, Addenda, I, 44–60; II, 17, 42,
59, 62; III, 7. *Hamilton Papers*, II.

[2] See De Selve to the King of France, October 19 and December 14,
1547. Lefèvre-Pontalis, *op. cit.*, 224 and 253. A Scot, James Harrison,
wrote a book in support of the English cause: "The godly and golden
Book for concorde of England and Scotland," reprinted by the Early
English Text Society in 1872. Cf. *State Papers, Scotland*, IV, 67 *sqq.*

[3] The Protector's *Epistle*, of January 1548, ed. Early English Text
Society, 1872.

[4] The Earl of Lennox, the Earl of Bothwell, the Earl of Glencairn,
Patrick, Master of Gray, and others.

at the same time as he gave his support to the marriage between Mary Stuart and the English King.[1] Wherever the English troops penetrated they were followed by the missionaries of the Reformation. The Bible was distributed among the people. The monasteries were dissolved and it was even proposed to distribute their goods among the nobles in order to eradicate Popery definitely from Scotland.[2] Protestantism made slow and silent progress in the country, and along with it the English cause. In 1549 the partisans of England were reckoned at forty or even fifty thousand.[3]

On his side Henry II did not remain idle. After Pinkie, in which no French troops took part, he sent ships and men. A company commanded by M. de la Chapelle disembarked at the close of December (1547) and, about the middle of the following June, an army of ten thousand men commanded by M. de Montalembert d'Essé crossed the Channel.[4] Several clashes occurred between the French and the English troops.

Nevertheless, England and France were not at war. The position was anomalous. Officially at peace, they fought on the territory of a third power. But this unstable peace could not be permanently maintained. The Protector still attempted to avoid an open rupture which would compel him to fight on two fronts at the same time. He proposed that the boundary of the Boulogne territory should be amicably settled, and the territory itself restored, before the date fixed by treaty. He

---

[1] *State Papers, Domestic*, Edward VI, Addenda, I, 45. See also *Memoire contenant les articles proposés au Comte de Hontelay*, Lefèvre-Pontalis, *op. cit.*, 269.

[2] *State Papers, Domestic*, Edward VI, Addenda I, 44, 45, 49, 50; II, 11. See also De Selve, Despatch of November 6, 1547 (Lefèvre-Pontalis, *op. cit.*, 234).

[3] Cf. *Complaynt of Scotland*, 1549, the work of a partisan of France, reprinted in 1872 by the Early English Text Society.

[4] Odet de Selve to the King of France, January 10, 1548. Lefèvre-Pontalis, *op. cit.*, 265. *State Papers, Domestic*, Edward VI, Addenda I, 61. Cf. Ibid., 62; Odet de Selve to the Constable of France, June 15, 1548 (Lefèvre-Pontalis, *op. cit.*, 379). *Spanish Calendar*, IX, 278, 288 *sq*, 295 *sqq.*, 308, 346, 369 *sq*.

dragged out the negotiations for months.[1] But when
in July Mary Stuart fled from Dumbarton to the French
fleet and was carried off to France and her espousals
with the Dauphin were announced, the rupture became
inevitable.[2] Nevertheless, it was postponed a year longer.
The declaration of war on August 8, 1549, did but
regularise a situation which had existed for many months.
The war issued in the defeat of the English, who retained
on the continent Calais alone. The treaty concluded
on March 24, 1550, restored Boulogne to France.

In Scotland the English were no more successful.
The marriage of Mary Stuart to the heir of the French
crown was a serious defeat for the policy of England.
It destroyed all hope of uniting the two countries and
tended to make Scotland a dependency of France and a
channel through which France could make her influence
felt in Ireland and thus surround England with a ring
of foes. The "encirclement" must be broken at all costs.
Somerset resolved to annex Scotland by force. Like
Henry VIII he revived Edward I's claim to suzerainty,[3]
and raising a body of German troops, he prepared for
another invasion in the following summer.[4]

But all his efforts were frustrated by internal troubles

[1] Lefèvre-Pontalis, *op. cit.* Cf. Pollard, *op. cit.*, 135–142. The negotiations
for the surrender of Boulogne begun in August 1548 became serious after
Pinkie, when the danger of a rupture between England and France
increased. Boulogne had been ceded to England by the treaty of 1546
(*State Papers*, ed. 1830–1851, I, 874, 879) and was to remain in English
hands for eight years, that is until 1554 when it was to be re-purchased
for 800,000 crowns.

[2] Odet de Selve to the King of France, July 31, 1548. Lefèvre-Pontalis,
op. cit., 418. In 1547 the Protector had determined to declare war if
Mary Stuart was sent to France. Cf. De Selve to the Constable, July 11,
1547. Lefèvre-Pontalis, *op. cit.*, 161. For Mary's voyage to France and
betrothal to the Dauphin, see *Spanish Calendar*, IX, 277, 290, 302 *sq.*, 313,
322, 326, 336, 361, 391, 509, 571 *sq.*, 574 *sq.*,; X, 26, 226, 298, 340.

[3] In September 1548, John Mason was ordered to collect proofs of this
alleged suzerainty. *Acts of the Privy Council*, II, 225. About this time was
published "An Epitome of the title that the King's Majesty of England
hath to the Soveraigntie of Scotlande." Reprinted in 1871 by the Early
English Text Society.

[4] Froude, *op. cit.*, ed. 1909, 96, 100. *State Papers, Domestic*, Addenda I,
III, No. 49.

and civil war. The disastrous result of the wars against France and Scotland was due to his fall.

The difficulties which confronted Somerset at home were no less complicated than those which he had to face abroad. Serious social problems hitherto unsolved pressed for solution. The wealth of a few rich men was disproportionately swollen whereas the poverty of the common people had become so great as to constitute a serious menace to public order. The country, as a contemporary wrote, "once renowned throughout Christendom as merry England, has lost its joy and merriment, and must be called sad and sorrowful England."[1]

The evil was due to several causes. One of these was the debasement of the coinage forced upon Henry by his depleted treasury.[2] He had inherited from his father no less than 1,800,000 pounds (in modern money thirty million pounds sterling). He bequeathed to his son a debt of a hundred thousand pounds. And Parliament had already paid his debts twice. The monastic spoils had been quickly squandered and he had lived on forced loans, free gifts (benevolences) and other financial makeshifts. Nor was his bankruptcy due solely to the extravagant and constantly increasing luxury of the Court and the cost of his wars. It was also, indeed principally, due to the progressive diminution of the crown revenues, a diminution which seriously hampered the government of the Tudors and their successors the Stuarts, and led James I and Charles I to impose the arbitrary taxation, which probably made it possible for Parliament to take up arms against the King and overthrow him by the revolution of 1649. The taxes (tenths, fifteenths, the subsidy, the royal right to provisionment) remained, indeed, the same

[1] Francis Trigge, *The Humble Petition of Two Sisters : the Church and the Commonwealth.* London, 1604.

[2] At his accession the expenses of the royal household were 11,000 pounds a year. In 1532 they had reached the sum of 19,000 and at the end of the reign were 28,000. Cf. Strype, *Ecclesiastical Memorials*, II, Part II, 156.

as before. But since the amount levied did not vary with the public wealth, the revenue they brought in continuously diminished, as the result of social changes, rising prices, and the importation of precious metals from America. By alienating a portion of the royal domain Henry VIII further impoverished the treasury.

To supply his needs he debased the coinage. In 1543 the alloy of the gold coins was a gramme and a half, and in 1546 a sixth. The alloy of the silver coins was a much larger proportion. In 1543 it varied from a third to a fifth. In 1545, owing to the cost of the war with France, it amounted to a half, and in 1546 to two-thirds of a silver coin.[1] Not only the purity but the weight of the coins was diminished. Twenty-eight sovereigns instead of 20 were minted from a pound of gold, and 48 instead of 45 shillings from a pound of silver. Gold fell to five times the value of silver.[2] In consequence it was so largely exported that it disappeared from England. The influx of Mexican and Peruvian silver into the continent produced a fatal depreciation of its normal value, and reduced still further the value of the English debased silver. The result was a dislocation of international trade, a rapid and excessive rise in prices, and the impoverishment of the working class, since in consequence of the agrarian crisis their wages did not rise correspondingly.[3] This agrarian crisis was in fact extremely grave, and was the most serious social problem which confronted the Protector. Its chief cause was the enclosure of lands, not their enclosure by material boundaries, but the eviction from them of large numbers of peasants who had lived hitherto on their produce.

Enclosure meant in the first place the accumulation of

[1] Cf. *State Papers, Domestic*, Edward VI, II, 10–12. Report by S. Harington, Master of the Bristol Mint.

[2] In 1543 it had fallen to ten times the value of silver.

[3] Cf. T. Rogers, *History of Agriculture and Prices in England*, III, and IV, Oxford, 1882.

many farms in the hands of a single landlord, that is to say the substitution of large for small scale farming, secondly the abolition by rich landowners of common rights of pasture, and finally the conversion of arable land into pasture. These three changes carried out simultaneously caused a rapid decline of agriculture in England.[1]

The system of large-scale farming involved the ruin of the peasantry. The yeomen or free farmers, who lived independently with their families and servants in their homesteads, were replaced by agricultural wage labourers, who had no longer a family or servants.[2] Their farms disappeared, absorbed in a single farm, the lord's, and the buildings erected by the former owners were abandoned and fell into ruin.[3] "They leave no ground," wrote Sir Thomas More, "for tillage; they enclose all in pastures; they throw down houses; they pluck down towns; and leave nothing standing but only the church, to make of it a sheephouse."[4] And a ballad ran,

[1] For the enclosures and the contemporary agrarian crisis see: *Six Ballads with Burdens*, ed. James Goodwin (Percy Society), 1844; *Ballads from Manuscripts*, ed. F. J. Furnivall, London, 1868; Thomas Lever, *Sermons*, ed. E. Arber, London, 1871; Th. Starkey, *Description of England in the Reign of King Henry VIII* (Early English Text Society), 1871; Th. Tusser, *Five Hundred Points of Good Husbandry* (London, 1557), ed. W. Payne and S. Herotage, 1878, or by Dorothy Hartley, 1931, or by E. V. Lucas, 1931; E. Prothero, *Pioneers and Progress of English Farming*, London, 1888; *Discourse of the Common Weal of the Realm of England*, ed. Elizabeth Lamond, Cambridge, 1893; W. J. Ashley, *English Economic History*, I, Part II, 1893; P. Cheyney, *Social Changes in England in the XVIth Century*, Philadelphia, 1895, with bibliography; J. S. Leadam, *Domesday of Inclosures* (Royal Historical Society), 2 vols., London, 1897; C. B. Lumsden, *The Dawn of Modern England*, London, 1910, Chapter XIII; Miss H. Bradley, *The Enclosures in England : An Economic Reconstruction*, New York, being Vol. 70, No. 2 of "Studies in History, Economical and Public Law"; W. R. Curtler, *The Enclosure and Redistribution of Our Land*, 1920. See Appendix 1B.

[2] The change increased the landlord's income by 12 per cent, according to Wolsey's commission of 1517.

[3] See a speech by the Lord Chancellor, John Russell, at the opening of Parliament, 1484. *Grants of Edward V*, Camden Society, p. xxxix *sqq.* Cf. Gairdner, *Richard III*, ed. 1878, 194. See also Tusser, *op. cit.*, 13, 142, 146.

[4] *Utopia*, Raphe Robinson's translation (1551), ed. King's Classics, Chatto and Windus, 1908.

"This sheep he is a wicked wight;
Man, woman and child he devoureth quite." [1]

The abolition of the right of pasture meant impoverishment for a large number of peasants, who had hitherto derived their subsistence from the free grazing of certain lands. "Where forty persons had their livings, now one man and his shepherd hath all." [2]

Finally the conversion of arable land into pasture gave the death-blow to agriculture. Lack of labour, the high price of meat, and above all the export of wool, at its height at this period, made the profit of pasture fifty per cent higher than that of growing crops. [3] Accordingly all landowners wanted to be sheep-farmers. One or two shepherds sufficed for land which had hitherto supported fifty labourers. The *Discourse of Common Weal* [4] complains of the general pauperisation produced by the change which made itself felt in every town except London. "More work for the labouring man, as well in the town as in the field: . . . more seldom where see ye the poor go begging from door unto door." [5]

The feudal system under which the land was a nursery of men responsible for the defence of the realm, had yielded to the modern system of commerce and competition for which the land is a source of wealth. It must bring in as high a rent as possible. Whatever the causes of this social and economic revolution, it produced profound and lasting discontent. It is not easy to estimate the extent of the crisis. But its echoes are to be found in More's *Utopia*, in the "Supplications"; [6]

[1] *Six Ballads with Burdens*, ed. J. Goodwin (Percy Society), 1877.
[2] *A Discourse of the Common Weal of this Realm of England*, ed. Eliz. Lamond, Cambridge, 1893, 15.
[3] Leadam (*Domesday of Inclosures*) comes to the conclusion that even this figure is too low.
[4] Edition, Eliz. Lamond, Cambridge, 1893, 15 *sqq.*
[5] Tusser, *op. cit.*, 142.
[6] *Four Supplications of the Commons*, published by Cowper together with the *Select Works of Crowley* (1550-1551), for the Early English Text Society, 1871 and 1872.

complaints,[1] sermons,[2] ballads,[3] and other contemporary productions,[4] in royal ordinances and in Acts of Parliament. "For the space of fifty years past and more" Holinshed's *Chronicle* observes, under the year 1520: "the nobles and gentlemen of England, being given to the grazing of cattle and the keeping of sheep had invented a mean how to encrease their yearly revenues, to the great decay and undoing of husbandmen of the land. For the said nobles and gentlemen after the manner of Numidians more studying how to increase pastures than to maintain tillage, began to decay husbandry, tacks[5] and tenements, and to convert arable ground into pasture, furnishing the same with beasts and sheep and also deer, inclosing the field with hedges, ditches and pales. . . . Hereof a threefold evil chanced to the commonwealth, as Polydor Virgil noteth. One for that thereby the number of husbandmen was sore diminished, the which the prince useth chiefly in his service for the wars—another, for that many towns and villages were left desolate and became ruinous: the third for that both wool and cloth and the flesh of all manner beasts used to be eaten was sold at far higher prices than was accustomed. These enormities at the first beginning being not redressed, grew in short space to such force and vigour by evil custom, that afterwards they gathered to such an united force, that hardly they could be remedied. Much like a disease

---

[1] H. Brinkelow, *Complaynt of Roderyck Mors unto the Parliament House of England, His Natural Country, for the Redress of Certain Wicked Laws, Evil Customs and Cruel Decrees* (1542), also *The Lamentation of a Christen agaynst the City of London made by Roderyck Mors* (1545), ed. J. Meadows Cowper for the Early English Text Society, 1874.

[2] Th. Lever's *Sermons*, ed. Arber, London, 1871; Latimer's *Sermons and Remains*, ed. G. C. Corrie, Parker Society, 2 vols; Gilpin, *Sermons in Gilpin's Life*, 1573.

[3] *Six Ballads with Burdens*, ed. J. Goodwin (Percy Society), 1844; *Ballads from Manuscripts* (Ballad Society), ed. Furnivall, London, 1868.

[4] *A Discourse of the Common Weal of England*, ed. Eliz. Lamond, Cambridge, 1893; Thomas Starkey, *Description of England in the Reign of King Henry VIII* (Early English Text Society, ed. Hentage and Cowper, 1871); Fitzherbert, *Book of Husbandrie;* Tusser, *Five Hundred Points of Good Husbandry* (London, 1557), ed. W. Payne and S. Herotage (English Dialect Society), 1878.

[5] Leaseholds of land. Trs. note.

which in the beginning with little pain to the patient and less labour to the surgeon may be cured; whereas the same by delay and negligence being suffered to putrify, becometh a desperate sore, and then are medicines nothing available and not to be applied.[1]

"There is another cause of stealing," More had written in 1516 in his *Utopia*, "which, as I suppose, is proper and peculiar to you Englishmen alone. . . . Forsooth your sheep, that were wont to be so meek and tame and so small eaters, now, as I hear say, be become so great devourers and so wild, that they eat up and swallow down the very men themselves. They consume, destroy, and devour whole fields, houses and cities. . . . Noblemen and gentlemen, yea and certain abbots, holy men, God wot, not contenting themselves with the yearly revenues and profits that were wont to grow to their forefathers and predecessors of their lands. . . . nothing profiting, yea much annoying the weal publique, leave no ground for tillage; they enclose all in pastures; they throw down houses; they pluck down towns; and leave nothing standing but the church, to make of it a sheephouse. And as though you lost no small quantity of ground by forests, chases, laundes and parks, these good holy men turn all dwelling-places and all glebe land into desolation and wilderness.

"Therefore that one covetous and unsatiable cormorant and very plague of his native country may compass about and inclose many thousand acres of ground together within one pale or hedge, the husbandmen be thrust out of their own . . . or by wrongs and injuries they be so wearied that they be compelled to sell all. By one means, therefore, or by other, either by hook or crook, they must needs depart away, poor, silly, wretched souls,—men, women, husbands, wives, fatherless children, widows, woeful mothers with their young babes and their whole household, small in substance and much in

[1] Edition of 1808, III, 659.

number, as husbandry requireth many hands: away they trudge, I say, out of their known and accustomed houses, finding no places to rest in. All their household stuff which is very little worth . . . they be constrained to sell it for a thing of naught, and when they have, wandering about, soon spent that, what can they else do but steal and then justly, God wot, be hanged or else go about a-begging. And then also they be cast in prison as vagabonds because they go about and work not; whom no man will set a-work, though they never so willingly offer themselves thereto."[1]

This was no exaggeration. This is the language which Somerset used thirty-two years later in his ordinance of June 1548: "The King's Majesty, the Lord Protector's Grace and the rest of his privy council, hath been advertised and put in remembrance as well by divers supplications and pitiful complaints of his Majesty's poor subjects, as also by other wise discreet men, having care to the good order of the realm, that of late by the enclosing of lands and arable grounds, in divers and sundry places of the Realm, many have been driven to extreme poverty and compelled to leave the places where they were born and to seek them livings in other countries with great misery and poverty insomuch that, whereas in time past, ten, twenty yea and in some places a hundred or two hundred Christen people hath been inhabiting and kept household to the bringing forth and nourishing of youth and to the replenishing and fulfilling of his Majesty's realm with faithful subjects, who might serve both Almighty God and the King's Majesty to the defence of this realm, now there is nothing kept but sheep and bullocks. All that land which heretofore was tilled and occupied with so many men, and did bring forth not only divers families in work and labour, but also capons, hens, chickens, small pigs and other such

[1] *Utopia*, ed. King's Classics, Chatto and Windus, 1908. Cf. Thomas Starkey., *op. cit.*, 97.

furniture of the markets, is now gotten by insatiable greediness of mind into one or two men's hands, and scarcely dwelled upon with one poor shepherd. So that the realm thereby is brought to a miraculous desolation; houses decayed, parishes diminished, the force of the realm weakened, and Christen people by the greedy covetousness of some were eaten up and devoured of brute beasts, and driven from their houses by sheep and bullocks."[1]

" The sheep he is a wicked wight;
Man, woman and child he devoureth quite.

.   .   .   .   .

Men were wont off sheep to feed;
Sheep now eat men on doubtful deed,"

sang the ballad.[2] And the chorus took up the refrain:

" The black sheep is a perilous beast;
Cujus contrarium falsum est."

The number of peasants and farm-hands thrown out of work is usually estimated at three hundred thousand, at least a tenth of the population.[3] Vagabondage assumed alarming proportions, and with it begging and theft. The severity and frequency of the statutes passed against vagrancy prove their ineffectiveness and the alarm of the ruling class. Under Henry VIII vagabonds were imprisoned, under Edward VI they were branded with a V (vagabond) on the chest and handed over as slaves for two years to those who had informed against them. Fed on bread and water they could be forced to work by harsh usage. If they fled, they were enslaved for life and branded with an S (slave) on the forehead and cheek.[4]

[1] British Museum, Lansdowne MS., 238 fol., 305 sqq., quoted by Pollard op. cit., 218.
[2] Six Ballads with Burdens, ed. J. Goodwin (Percy Society), 1844.
[3] Four Supplications, Early English Text Society, 98–101.
[4] Slavery was not uncommon in sixteenth-century England. See the detailed account of the emancipation of slaves belonging to the Earl of Derby in Elizabeth's reign in the Stanley Papers published by the Chetham Society.

A second flight was felony.[1] Thieves were hanged. But, as More had pointed out, what was the use of threatening those who did not work with severe penalties, when work became harder to secure every day? The lot of those who still found employment was scarcely less hard. Everything, as Thomas Starkey tells us, had become so dear that the labourer could not earn enough to live on. "Neither can poor labourers live with wages," said another writer.[2] For wages remained the same though the price of foodstuffs had tripled as a result of the agricultural crisis, the debasement of the coinage and the importation of precious metals.[3] "Victuals," wrote More, "be now in many places dearer. Yea, besides this, the price of wool is so risen that poor folk which were wont to work it and make cloth of it, be now able to buy none at all. . . . And this great dearth of victuals causeth every man to keep as little houses and as small hospitality as he possibly may, and to put away their servants: whither, I pray you, but a-begging?"[4] "A great number," wrote a bishop to Edward VI, "are so pined and famished by the reason of the great scarcity and dearth of all kinds of victuals, that the great sheep masters have brought into this noble realm, that they are become more like the slavery and peasantry of France than the ancient and godly yeomanry of England."[5]

[1] Act of 1547, *Statutes of the Realm*, I, Edward VI, cap. 3. It was repealed in 1550 but its re-enactment was suggested under Elizabeth. *Calendar of Hatfield*, MSS. I, No. 587. On the other hand the Act of 1547 ordered the parishes to make provision for parishioners too infirm to work, and a collection was taken for them every Sunday. For the miserable lot of the peasantry between 1530 and 1550 see Fr. Aydelotte, *Elisabethan Rogues and Vagabonds* (Vol. I of the *Oxford Historical and Literary Studies*, ed. Firth and Raleigh), Oxford, 1913.

[2] *Op. cit.*, ed. Cowper, 97. *A Discourse of the Common Weal of this Realm of England*. Ed. E. Lammond.

[3] The price of corn, mutton, beef, poultry and eggs was trebled during the first half of the sixteenth century.

[4] *Utopia*. Above-mentioned edition.

[5] Scory to Edward VI. Strype, *Ecclesiastical Memorials*, II, Part II, 482. Cf. *Causes of the Universal Dearth in England*, 1551. Tytler, *op. cit.*, I, 367–371.

Moreover, the decay of the farmers and yeomen emptied the schools and universities, which became the preserve of the wealthy. Those who still managed to keep their land, observes a contemporary Supplication,[1] were compelled to make their children work in the fields instead of sending them to school. It depleted the army, which drew its strength from the small freeholders, who were accustomed to military exercises, and whose equipment and pay were provided by their parish. "Shepherds are bad archers," remarks a contemporary writer.[2] The country no longer provided sufficient soldiers. Mercenaries had to be hired at considerable expense, a further drain upon the Treasury.[3]

The distress was thus universal. In one of its Supplications, the people beseech Henry to leave his son a State, not "an island of brute beasts of whom the stronger devour the weaker."

Somerset sought a remedy.

He began by reducing the expenditure of the Court,[4] which under his successor was to reach the unheard-of figure of £100,000. He improved the coinage which he made purer though reducing the weight, for the Treasury could not bear the cost of effecting a complete reform.[5]

The Protector devoted his chief attention to social reform. He attempted to check the agricultural revolution, which was profiting the rich at the expense of the common good. Henry VII and Henry VIII, who like the Yorkist monarchs, based their power on the commoners, had already taken the matter in hand.

---

[1] *Four Supplications*, Early English Text Society, 80.

[2] Crowley, *Four Supplications*, 100.

[3] The English troops both in Scotland and in France were badly paid in the reign of Edward. In consequence they mutinied and their officers entirely lost control of them. Soldiers pillaged the French and Flemish frontiers and the Council was obliged to apologise to the Emperor. Froude *op. cit.*, ed. 1909, 95 *sq.*

[4] He reduced it from £56,000 to £46,000.

[5] See Rudding, *Annals of the Coinage*, ed. 1840; Hawkins, *Silver Coins of England*, 1887, 289.

Two statutes against the first form of enclosure, large scale farming, "engrossing", had been passed in 1489 and 1515. In 1517 Wolsey despatched a Commission throughout the kingdom to discover those who had broken these statutes. On July 12, 1518, a royal decree annulled all enclosures made since 1485. And fresh ordinances were issued in 1526 and 1528.[1] In some places farms had been restored and pasture land given back to the plough. But by his attempt at reform, which was, moreover, largely unsuccessful, Wolsey had incurred the hostility of the rich without winning the gratitude of the poor. After his fall, preoccupations of a different nature absorbed the King's attention. The Cardinal's measures were not put into operation, and the evil grew unchecked.[2] The dissolution of the monasteries made it even worse. For many lords and gentlemen applied enclosure in its various forms to monastic lands, which had formerly employed much labour, and on which the poor had the right of pasture.[3]

The virulence of the evil gave birth to a group partly political, partly religious, which under Edward VI was composed of a number of theologians and politicians, for example, John Hales, Clerk of the Exchequer,[4] Bishop Latimer[5] and Thomas Lever.[6] This party desired to abolish the enclosures and revive agriculture. It took its stand upon the principle that a man is not born for

[1] Leadam, *Domesday of Inclosures*. Cf. Somerset's proclamation of June 1, 1548. British Mus. Lansdowne MS., 238 fol., 305 *sqq.*

[2] Wolsey did much for the poor as the poet Skelton, who certainly did not flatter the Cardinal, recognised. Cf. Fisher, Vol. V of *The Political History of England*. 223 *sqq.*

[3] Cf. Carte, *History of England*, III, 233; Davey, *Lady Jane Grey*, 195 *sqq.*

[4] For Hales see Lansdowne MS. 238, in the British Museum; Letter from Somerset to Hales, August 21, fol. 318–319; Hales's reply, August 30, 1548, fol. 319–321; letter from Hales to Warwick blaming him for his opposition to the measures against enclosure, fol. 321–325; Hales's defence against the charges brought against him, September 1, 1549, fol. 292–304; Hales's address to the jury, fol. 312–314.

[5] Latimer, *Sermons and Remains*, Parker Society, 1844. See especially his sermon "Of the Plough," 1549.

[6] Thomas Lever, *Sermons*, ed. Arber, 1871.

himself, but for the service first of God, then of the State. They were known as the Commonwealth Party.[1]

Their influence was due entirely to Somerset, who became their patron and on many points adopted their proposals and attempted to carry them out by legislation.

In the first year of the reign several measures of social reform were laid before Parliament. One of these secured farmers and tenants against arbitrary eviction by the landlord. Another sought to prevent the destruction of farms and throwing land out of cultivation.[2] A third provided for the education of poor children.[3] All these bills were thrown out by the Lords or the Commons.

Attempts at insurrection in several counties followed in the spring of 1548 and petitions were presented to the king (May 1548).[4] They decided Somerset to take action, though the entire Council did not share his views.[5] His first ordinance against the enclosures was issued on June 1, 1548.[6] It recalls the statutes of Henry VII and Henry VIII and puts them once more into force. A Commission of Enquiry, similar to that appointed by Wolsey in 1517, was charged to report all enclosures effected since 1485,[7] and discover who made the enclosures, at what time, the number of acres converted

[1] For this party see, *State Papers, Domestic*, Edward VI, VIII, No. 56. In the reign of Henry VIII it included both Catholics, Thomas More, Thomas Starkey, Thomas Lupset, and supporters of the Reformation such as Henry Brinkelow and Robert Crowley.

[2] *Commons' Journals*, December 17, 1547. *Lords' Journal*, November 12, 1547.

[3] *Commons' Journals*, November 8, 1547. Already in the previous reign Roderick Mors in his "Complaynt" had urged that every town should undertake the education of its poor children. He also proposed to devote the spoils of the monasteries to education.

[4] There was agitation in the counties of Hertford, Somerset, Gloucester, Wiltshire, Hampshire, Sussex, Surrey, Worcester and Essex. (John Hales's Defence, September 1, 1549, mentioned above. Cf. Wriothesley, *Chronicles*, II, 13).

[5] Cf. Tytler, *op. cit.*, I, 177 *sq.*, 183 *sq.*

[6] British Museum, *Lansdowne MS.*, 238, fol. 305–308.

[7] John Hales was a member of the commission and his letter of July 24, 1548, testifies to the satisfaction of the people who, when the Protector's intentions became known, "hoped that the iron age would be succeeded by the golden." Tytler, *op. cit.*, I, 113, 133.

into pasture, and the profit accruing, who owned more than 2,000 sheep or occupied more than two farms in the same place, and whether those who had received monastic land maintained a farm of adequate size with a sufficient number of labourers as the statute directed.[1] The purpose of this Commission was not the immediate punishment of offenders, but to secure the information necessary to draft the bills it was intended to lay before Parliament. These reform bills were introduced during the session which opened on November 8, 1548. Some were passed. One of these was a tax on sheep intended to prevent the conversion of arable land into pasture.[2] But it remained a dead letter.[3] To remedy the excessive increase in the price of food, middlemen were forbidden on pain of fine and imprisonment to sell at a price above that agreed upon between the vendors and themselves,[4] and since provision merchants combined to sell at extortionate prices, all such practices were forbidden. Finally, measures were adopted to compel producers and merchants to be more honest in the production and sale of their wares.[5]

But all the bills specifically directed against enclosure were rejected by Parliament. One of these compelled landowners to rebuild farms which had been allowed to fall into ruin, and maintain agriculture and employ the necessary labour. Another made it obligatory to raise two cows and a calf for every hundred sheep. A third forbade dealers to buy and sell the same live-stock without keeping it for a prescribed period. Its object was to

[1] The Commissioners' instructions are to be found in Strype, *Ecclesiastical Memorials*, II, Part II, 360 *sq.*

[2] *Statutes of the Realm*, 3 and 4, Edward VI, cap. 23. Cf. Tytler, *op. cit.*, 370.

[3] It was in fact provided in the act that it should not come into operation for three years, and before that period had elapsed, Somerset had fallen.

[4] *Statutes of the Realm*, 2 and 3, Edward VI, cap. 15. Cf. *Causes of the Universal Dearth in England*, 1551, Tytler, *op. cit.*, I, 367.

[5] Cf. Dowell, *History of Taxation*, ed. 2, I, 142. *The Causes of Dearth* was written by Hales. On it was based *A Discourse of the Common Weal of this Realm of England*. Published by Elizabeth Lamond, Cambridge, 1893 and 1929.

prevent a profiteering which injured the public.[1] The bill against the monopoly of farms was not even read,[2] and a majority threw out a bill which ordered the destruction of large private parks.

The Parliamentary opposition to the Protector's social reforms was intelligible enough. They adversely affected the interests of the Lords who composed the Upper House. And in the House of Commons, though some of the county members were genuine representatives of the common people, the members for the towns were either wealthy landowners or merchants who wished to become landowners, and they were as hostile to the proposed legislation as their colleagues of the Upper House. Both had been the first to break Henry VII and Henry VIII's statutes against the enclosures. How could they be expected to enact new statutes?[3]

In the country Somerset's commissioners had to face innumerable difficulties placed in their path by the landowners. They were deceived by false declarations and trickery of every kind.[4] Some of the Commissioners themselves were opposed to the reforms which they were charged to prepare.[5] And the general pardon granted by the Protector, at Hales's request, in order to avoid all appearance of punishing first breaches of the law, did but increase the number of delinquents.

The social reforms attempted by Somerset were thus doomed to failure. The people weary of their sufferings and enticed by false hopes, rose in rebellion. The revolt

[1] The three bills were drawn up by John Hales. See his defence of September 1, 1549. *Lansdowne MS.*, 238, fol. 292 *sqq.*; Tytler, *op. cit.*, I ,176.
[2] It is in the Record Office; *State Papers, Domestic,* Edward VI, V, 22.
[3] See *Complaynt of Roderyck Mors.* Early English Text Society, 12–13. Crowley, *Works,* passim.
[4] Some dug a furrow in a pasture to pretend that it was being ploughed. Others put one or two yoke of oxen among a flock of sheep and said their land was used for raising cattle. The poor farmers who had managed to survive were compelled by their landlord on pain of ejection to make false declarations to the commissioners. We learn of all these malpractices from John Hales's Defence.
[5] Latimer, *Sermons,* Parker Society, 247.

began in Somerset and Lincolnshire, where some large estates were plundered.[1] It spread inwards to Gloucestershire and Wiltshire, Oxfordshire and Buckinghamshire, and southward to Dorset. Kent was drawn into the movement. In June, Devon and Cornwall rose as one man. The commonalty of Norfolk seized Norwich and set up a species of republic. So great was the alarm in London, that a double guard watched the gates day and night, the bridges were broken and martial law proclaimed in the city. The government tottered. The troops were recalled from Scotland and France. The Protector's foreign policy was completely wrecked by a civil war.

The revolts of 1549, known as the risings of the East and West differed in character according to their place of origin. In the East the insurrection was due to social discontent. In the West dislike of the religious revolution played the chief part. The Norfolk rebels, the most dangerous of all, were by no means hostile to the religious innovations. They welcomed all the reforms carried out during the new reign and even desired more radical changes. In their camp on Mousehold Heath they named an old oak "the oak of reform" to emphasise their devotion to Protestantism. Beneath its shade they heard the new prayer book "Mass" and sang the English service. Two preachers holding Cranmer's licence, Mathew Parker and Robert Watson, preached to them. Their demands were exclusively social, with a tinge of Communism. Their leader was a Wymondham tanner, Robert Kett, who commanded a force of 16,000 men.[2]

It was otherwise in the West. Probably here also social grievances played their part in the movement.[3] But they were eclipsed by the religious grievances which

[1] Wriothesley, *Chronicle*, II, 13.

[2] See F. W. Russell, *Kett's Rebellion*, London, 1859, which is abundantly supplied with documents. The *Acts of the Privy Council*, 1550–1552 (p. 131) speak of the Eastern rebellion in September 1550.

[3] The leaders were a tailor named Underhill, Hegar, a journeyman, and Pounder, a shoemaker. Apart from the priests the rebels were of the same class as the Norfolk rebels.

gave the rebellion its special character.[1] Of the sixteen demands put forward by the rebels only one was social. All the others were concerned with religion. It was a religious innovation that first kindled the revolt. The Book of Common Prayer had been used for the first time on Whitsunday, June 9, 1549. The following day the people of Sampford Courtenay, in Devonshire, fifteen miles from Exeter, compelled their parson to say Mass according to the old rite. An eyewitness named Hooker, who is quoted in Holinshed's *Chronicle*, informs us that they made him put on his vestments and say Mass and the other services as of old. The rebels asked that no change should be made during the Royal minority, since the king was a child with no knowledge or will of his own.

In their reply to Somerset of July 15, 1549, they complain that a religion, two hundred years old, had been changed at the arbitrary whim of two or three, and that the bishops had not been consulted, but intimidated.[2] They advanced upon Crediton. The neighbouring parishes welcomed and joined the rising. It was in vain that the justices of the peace intervened. The gentry, who suffered from the enclosures, sympathised with the rebels. The movement spread. The neighbouring county of Cornwall, which resented the inventories taken in 1548, rose in arms.[3] When two gentlemen of the West country, sent to restore order, burned the barns, the rebels advanced upon Exeter and besieged it. Their number amounted to 10,000.[4]

[1] For the rising see Froude, Chapter III; Dixon, *op. cit.*, III, 45 *sqq*; and especially N. Pocock, *op. cit.*, which is a collection of documents taken from the Petyt MS.; Fr. Rose-Troupe, *The Western Rebellion of* 1549. *An Account of the Insurrections in Devonshire and Cornwall against Religious Innovations in the Reign of Edward VI*, London 1913. The author has drawn up a long list of mistaken readings in documents published by Pocock, and pointed out mistakes into which Pollard fell. Cf. my Appendix I.

[2] Pocock, *Troubles*, p. xix.

[3] Cf. Dixon, *op. cit.*, II, 504.

[4] Holinshed, *Chronicle*, 1022. John Vowell, better known as Hooker (1525–1601), an Exeter architect, has left us a detailed and vivid account of the siege of Exeter in 1549. Cf. John and James Wylie, *Report on the Records of the City of Exeter*, 1916.

In this home of the Poles and Montagues, the old
faith was still living.[1] The Act of Uniformity of 1549,
by altering the rites and ceremonies of the Church,
raised the people *en masse*. The innovations had aroused
their wrath. In the articles they sent up to the Council
to lay before the king,[2] they demanded the re-enactment of the Act of Six Articles, which so vigorously
maintained the Catholic doctrine of the Eucharist
(Article 2) and the retention of the Catholic Mass. "We
will have the Mass in Latin, as it was before, and celebrated by the priest without any man or woman communicating with him." (Article 3).

They thus protested against the abolition of private
Masses and the change of the Mass into a Communion
service. This innovation, which in the intention of the
reformers restricted the sacrifice to the reception of the
Victim and regarded the elements left unconsumed as
mere bread and wine, occasioned the rebels' demand
that the Eucharist be reserved and worshipped after the
Mass (Article 4). The latter must not be robbed of its
character as a propitiatory sacrifice. "We will have
every priest at the Mass pray, especially by name, for
the souls in purgatory, as our forefathers did." (Article 9).
Nor would they accept the use of the vulgar tongue:
"We will have the Mass in Latin"; nor communion under
two kinds. "We will have the sacrament of the altar
. . . delivered to the people . . . but in one kind."
(Articles 3 and 5).

The sacramentals and the old ceremonies must be
retained: "We will have holy bread and holy water

---

[1] The rebels asked that Cardinal Pole should be recalled to England
and be made a member of the Council. (Article 12). N. Pocock, *Troubles*,
180; Strype, *Memorials of Cranmer*, Book II, Chapter X, and Appendix XL.
Ed. 1848, II, 114, 116, 554.

[2] Strype, *Memorials of Cranmer*, Book II, Chapter III, ed. 1848, II, 113 *sqq.*
Tytler, *op. cit.*, I, 178. The articles are to be found in Appendix XL of
Strype; in Pocock's *Troubles*, in Froude, Chapter III; in Dixon and elsewhere. Holinshed in his *Chronicle* (p. 1009) gives a different version,
consisting of nine articles.

every Sunday, palms and ashes at the time accustomed, images to be set up again in every church and all other ancient ceremonies held heretofore by our Mother, Holy Church." (Article 7).

In short they rejected the Prayer Book. "We will not receive the new service, because it is but like a Christmas game. We will have our old service of matins, Mass, even-song and procession as it was before; and we the Cornishmen, whereof certain of us understand no English, utterly refuse the new English." (Article 8).[1]

They clung to the orthodox creed which Henry VIII had upheld against the reformers: "We will have the laws of our Soverign Lord King Henry VIII, concerning the Six Articles to be used again as in his time they were." (Article 2).

In general they adhered to the old Faith and admitted no departure from it. "We will have all the general councils and holy decrees of our forefathers observed, kept and performed and whosoever shall gainsay them, we hold them as heretics." (Article 1).

They even asked for monasteries "for devout persons who shall pray for the King and the Commonwealth." These could be partly restored by giving back half the proceeds obtained by their dissolution, and by the dissolution of the chantries, and by applying to the purpose the parochial collections for seven years. (Article 14).

Cranmer answered their demands by a lengthy lecture in which he treated them as ignoramuses: "When I first read your requests, O ignorant men of Devonshire and Cornwall, straitways came to my mind a request which James and John made unto Christ: to whom Christ answered 'You ask you know not what.' Simple and unlearned people you ask you wot not what . . . Is this the fashion of subjects to speak unto their Prince:

[1] They were so attached to the old service that, if tradition can be trusted, long after the reformation the breviary and missal were still used in Cornwall and Devonshire. Cf. Blunt, *op. cit.*, II, 95, note 8.

'We will have?' Was this manner of speech at any time
used of the subjects to their Prince, since the beginning
of the world? How be you bewitched by these false
papists! Why do you suffer them thus to abuse you by
their subtlety to make you condemn yourselves of heresy?
Why do you not send them unto the King's Majesty like
errant traitors as indeed they be? The first article is
nothing else but a clear subversion of the whole state and
laws of this realm. You will have all general councils
and decrees observed . . . and you will have the
Six Articles again. Let us compare the general councils
and decrees with the Six Articles and you shall see these
agree as well together as black and white. . . . The
whole that is done" (in the Mass) "should be an act of
the people and pertain to the people as well as to
the priest. And standeth it with reason that the
priest shall speak for you and in your name and
you answer him again in your own persons and
yet you understand never a word . . . oh superstition and idolatry how they prevail among you! The
very true heavenly bread of life . . . you refuse to
eat but only at Easter. And the cup of the most holy
Blood . . . you refuse utterly to drink of at any time.
Yet in the stead of these you will eat often of the un-
savoury and poisoned bread of the Bishop of Rome
and drink of his stinking puddles which he nameth holy
bread and holy water. . . . If it be a sufficient cause
for Cornwall to refuse the English service, because some
of you understand none English, a much greater cause
have they, both of Cornwall and Devonshire to refuse
utterly the late service for as much as fewer of them
know the Latin tongue, than they of Cornwall the
English. Tell me, I pray, if you can, whether there be a
Purgatory or no: and where or what it is. And if you
cannot tell, then I may tell you, that you ask you wot
not what."

The better to expose their ignorance and crush them

with the weight of his theological knowledge, Cranmer did not hesitate to appeal to Fathers and Councils, and the practice of the early church.[1]

He had sermons preached against the rebels, and the notes he supplied for them express sentiments no less violent. Employing scriptural language he treats the rebels as "*carnales*", carnal men, whose pretended wisdom is but earthly, sensual, and devilish (*terrena, animalis, diabolica*), and compares them with Dathan, Abiron, Absalom, Seba and other Old Testament rebels who were punished by God Himself. The devil is the instigator of their rebellion, as their deeds and words prove.[2] At the Archbishop's request, Peter Martyr and Bucer composed homilies for the clergy to use against the insurrection,[3] and at Somerset's, Nicolas Udal, the translator of Erasmus's *Paraphrases*, wrote an even longer reply to the insurgents' demands than Cranmer's, in which he speaks of them as ignorant fellows whose simplicty had been abused by evil-minded papists and rebellious leaders.[4]

Somerset himself, in the king's name addressed a remonstrance to the rebels (July 8, 1548). It was couched in language very different from Cranmer's, not harsh but paternal: "If ye our subjects, who by God's ordinance and your own oath do owe to us obedience, would hear us as readily according to your duties, as we of our princely clemency have taken and perused your supplication, we do not doubt but that ye would easily return to your old, quiet, and good order. . . . Ye do require things of us by a bill of supplication; but after what sort do ye come to your King to demand? With sword in

---

[1] Strype, *Memorials of Cranmer*, Appendix, ed., II, 502–562.

[2] "Sentences of Scripture against sedition." In Strype, *Memorials of Cranmer*, Appendix XLI, ed. 1848, II, 562. To avert God's wrath, of which the civil war was an open proof, the Archbishop advised prayer and penance, and he composed a prayer to that effect. Ibid., book II, Chapter X, 121.

[3] Strype, *op. cit.*, Book II, Chapter X, ed. 1848, II, 118 *sqq.*

[4] N. Pocock, *Troubles*, 141–193.

hand and in battle array. What manner is that to come
to your Prince? What other order would ye keep, if
the French or Scots should invade you?[1] Content yourselves good people. See our shires of Devonshire and
Cornwell well in order. See the corn and the fruits of
the earth, which God hath sent of His most great
clemency, whereby ye should be sustained in winter.
Do not with this rage and fury drive yourselves to the
sword, your wives and children to famine and hunger.
If anything be to be reformed in our laws, the Parliament is near at hand. . . . Ye object unto us, as
though these things were done, us not knowing. But we
do declare unto you that there was nothing but at our
consent and knowledge, nor nothing passes in Parliament
but our consent is at it. And for that, our Book of Orders of
the Church, we know nothing is in it but according to the
Scriptures and the word of God; and that we ourselves
in person, although as yet young in age, are able to justify
and prove, we trust, by scriptures and good learning
against whosoever will defend the contrary."[2]

Thus, even when confronted by insurrections, Somerset
did not abandon the liberal policy which more than one
critic blamed as weakness.[3] He did his utmost to restore
order by prudent and peaceable remonstrances. He
despatched to the insurgents men of their own counties
with orders to reprimand them gently, and bring them
to better sentiments by persuasion. And when he learned
that the Carews, whom he had sent to Devonshire for
this purpose, had committed acts of violence burning
barns, he reprimanded them sharply.[4] On several
occasions, even a few days before his fall, he advised

[1] To the charge of rebellion they replied that they had risen solely to
defend the king against those who held him in their power. Cf. Pocock,
op. cit., XVIII, *sqq.*
[2] Tytler, *op. cit.*, 178–182.
[3] Tytler, *op. cit.*, I, 177 *sq.*, 183.
[4] To bring the sporadic risings of the previous year to an end, Somerset
had employed the same method. Wriothesley, a native of Lincoln, was
despatched to pacify the East, and Carew was sent to the West Country

Lord Russell to show clemency to the rebels, and censured him for having confiscated their possessions and given them away.[1] Somerset almost sympathised with the Eastern rebels, who had been goaded into insurrection by the failure of his social reforms. He declared that the revolt was due to the cupidity of the noblemen and gentry, and that, when all is said, it is preferable to die in battle, than by starvation.[2] Though he forbade violent interference with the enclosures, he renewed his instructions to the Commissioners charged to find a remedy for the agricultural crisis.[3] On June 20, he promised a general pardon, if the rebels would return to their allegiance, and he treated with clemency those charged with complicity in it.[4]

Lord Paget wrote to him from Germany, indignant at such mildness. "Would to God that at the first stir you had caused justice to have been ministered in solemn fashion to the terror of others, and then to have granted a pardon. To have granted a pardon out of course . . . gave men occasion and courage to sin. In England the foot taketh upon him the part of the head, and the commons is become a king. . . . Take the liberty of such towns as have offended into the King's hands.

---

for the same purpose. (Pocock, *Troubles*, p. xvi, *sq.*). To justify their violent methods, they produced another instruction sent by the Privy Council. This proves how little the Protector's *entourage* understood or approved his method of conciliation. Cf. Holinshed, *Chronicle*, 1022; Dixon, *op. cit.*, III, 62, J. Gairdner, *English Church*, 268.

[1] Letter from the Council to Lord Russell instructing him to pardon the rebels, and blaming him for exceeding his instructions by punishing them. August 28 and September 10, 1549. Letter from Somerset to Lord Russell recommending mercy to the rebels, September 25, 1549. N. Pocock, *Troubles*, 65, 68, 74.

[2] This remark was made the 18th article in the accusation brought against him. See also articles 12, 15, 16, 17, 19, 22 in Pollard, *England*, 280 *sqq.*

[3] *State Papers, Domestic*, Edward VI, VIII, 33 and Addenda, III, 47. Two months later (July 1549) he made provision for the poor to obtain sureties in lawsuits against the rich.

[4] *State Papers, Domestic*, Edward VI, VII, 37. F. W. Russell, *Kett's Rebellion*, 95.

Attach . . . to the number of twenty or thirty of the
rankest knaves. Let six be hanged of the ripest of them
. . . the rest remain in prison. If Your Grace send
some of the doers away far from their wives to the north
or Boulogne.to be soldiers or pioneers, it would do well.
Give them no good words or make no promise in no wise."[1]

Exhortations and kind words were in fact insufficient.
Force was required to suppress a movement constantly
spreading. The mercenaries in English pay had to be
recalled from Scotland.[2] For a moment Somerset had
contemplated taking command of the troops sent to Norfolk. But fearing to alienate popular sympathies, he gave
the command to Warwick, his secret enemy. Warwick
defeated the rebels at the sanguinary battle of Dussindale
(August 27, 1549). Three hundred of the survivors were
hanged, amongst them Kett and his brother.[3]

The Western revolt was also suppressed. Lord Grey
took Exeter by assault on August 6, 1549, and gave up
the town to be pillaged by the mercenaries. On August
16, he crushed the rebels at the battle of Sampford
Courtenay. The leaders suffered at Tyburn the penalty
of treason. At Exeter a parish priest was hanged in his
canonicals from the steeple of his church, and martial
law struck terror into Devon and Cornwall.[4]

[1] Paget to Somerset July 7, 1549. Strype, *Ecclesiastical Memorials*, II, 432.
[2] These mercenaries were Spaniards, Italians, Flemings, and Germans,
and the majority of them were Catholics. On their return to the contiuent,
they sought absolution from the papal legate from the censure incurred
by their armed support of heretics. Cf. Dixon, *op. cit.*, 48, Note 3.
[3] Holinshed's *Chronicle* contains an account of the battle by an eye-
witness, which Froude has employed in Chapter III of his *Reign of
Edward VI*, ed. 1909, 128 and *sqq.* Warwick shewed clemency, but his
fellow commanders were pitiless in their reprisals. It was they who hanged
the survivors. For the Eastern rebellion and its suppression see, W. Russell,
op cit., abundantly documented; Tytler, *op. cit.*, I, 192 *sqq.*; Froude, *op. cit.*,
Chapter III, 121–130; Dixon, *op. cit.*, III, 80 *sqq.*
[4] *State Papers, Domestic*, Edward VI, I, 119, 21, 22. Cf. Dixon, *op. cit.*,
III, 52–80. Numerous details about the rising and its suppression are to
be found in Chapter III of Froude's *Edward VI*, ed. above-mentioned,
118–121. Pocock, *op. cit.*, 22–74, gives letters from the Council to Lord
Russell about the forces placed under his command, and the course he is
to pursue. July to September, 1549.

The civil war had its inevitable repercussion on the conduct of the wars in Scotland and France. The army which had been assembled to invade Scotland had to be employed against the rebel counties.[1] In France Henry II profited by the English difficulties to invade the district of Boulogne and capture several forts.[2]

The Royal Council took advantage of this opportunity to overthrow the Protector. For a long time it had been hostile to him, and Somerset could count upon only four or five members to support his policy.[3] Almost all the councillors were opposed to his social reforms, which ran counter to their personal interests. The Protector was therefore accused of issuing agricultural ordinances against the advice of the Council.[4] Warwick, who dominated the Council, had done his utmost to prevent the agrarian statutes being passed by Parliament and to hamper the Commissioners charged to enquire into the abuses of enclosure.[5] Several of his own estates contravened the law. He and his fellow councillors had watched with a jealous eye Somerset's power increase, and they chafed under his arrogant and domineering manner. Almost every councillor had a personal grievance against him. Warwick assembled the malcontents, and it was decided to strike a decisive blow. He had returned in triumph from the Eastern counties, where he had crushed the rebellion. He could count upon the support of the Lords, the gentlemen,

---

[1] State Papers, Domestic, Edward VI, Addenda III, 49.

[2] State Papers, Foreign, Edward VI, I, 195. Calais Papers, 173. Cf. Pocock, Troubles, pp. xviii and sqq.; Nichols, Literary Remains of Edward VI, 1857, I, 472; Foreign Calendar, 1547–1553, 72, 78.

[3] Paget who, as we have seen, did not hesitate to criticise Somerset; Cranmer; the two secretaries, Sir William Petre and Sir Thomas Smith, and Cecil who at the same time was on good terms with Warwick. (Cf. Tytler, 198, 201 sq.).

[4] Articles 14 and 15 of the formal charges against him. Somerset would be the victim of his agrarian law.

[5] John Hales blamed him for his opposition. (See his letter in the Lansdowne MS., 238, fol. 321–325). Warwick denounced Hales to the Council on the score of the agrarian laws. He also complained of the enclosure commissioners. (State Papers, Domestic, Edward VI, VII, 35).

the wealthy aldermen of the city and all who were alarmed by the Protector's social reforms, or had suffered loss through them. Somerset had alienated the upholders of the old faith by his love of innovation and his imprisonment of Bishops Gardiner and Bonner, and the reformers by his moderation. Warwick had scarcely arrived in London when he reached an understanding with Wriothesley, who disliked the reformation and bore a grudge against Somerset for his loss of the Chancellorship. The members of the Council hostile to Somerset met at their houses to concert plans. (September 1549).[1] The issue was speedily decided.

The Protector was at Hampton Court with the king and his handful of supporters, Archbishop Cranmer, Paget, Cecil, and the two secretaries, Sir William Petre and Sir Thomas Smith. It was not until October 4 that he got wind of the plot. He at once retired to Windsor, taking the king with him and addressed a proclamation to the people calling upon them "With all haste to repair, in most defensible array with harness and weapons to defend the King and his most entirely beloved uncle, the Lord Protector, against whom certain hath attempted a most dangerous conspiracy. And this to do in all possible haste."[2] At the same time Harry Seymour was ordered to raise troops, and Lord Russell and Sir William Herbert were summoned in haste to protect His Majesty.[3] The Council in London replied by ordering the sheriffs and justices of the peace, to resist the armed levy ordered by Somerset, who "abuses the King's Majesty's hand, stamp and

[1] The Protestants regarded Wriothesley as the principal agent of Somerset's fall. See J. G. Nichols, *Literary Remains of Edward VI*, 245 sq.

[2] Edward's letter of October 5, 1549, in Pocock, *Troubles*, 76 and Tytler, *op. cit.*, I, 205 (where it is dated October 1), Somerset's letter to the Earl of Shrewsbury of October 6 in Lodge, *Illustrations of British History in the Reigns of Henry VIII, Edward VI, Mary, Elizabeth, and James I*. London, 1838, I, 164.

[3] Royal proclamation signed by the king and Somerset. October 5, 1549. Letters of Somerset and the king to Russell and W. Herbert of October 5 and 6. Pocock, *Troubles*, 77–80, 82 sq.

signet . . . to levy the King's Majesty's subjects and
disturb the common peace of the realm . . . to no
small peril of the King's Majesty's person and the dis-
turbance of his Majesty's good and loving subjects,"[1]
by appealing for soldiers[2] and by an address to the
City.[3] The shopkeepers and wealthy merchants of the
capital, whole-hearted adversaries of Somerset's policy,
were his enemies' natural allies.

The Protector's last hope was Lord Russell's army
on its way home from the conquest of the Western
counties. Russell, to whom both parties addressed an
urgent appeal, favoured the Council. He refused Somerset's appeal, sent home the five or six thousand men in
full harness, who were preparing to march to Windsor,
and occupied himself in restoring order in Hampshire,
Wiltshire, Gloucester and Somerset, the Western Counties
and South Wales.[4] "It doth plainly appear unto us,"
he replied to the Protector, "that this great extremity
proceedeth only upon private causes between Your
Grace and them (the Lords of the Council). We therefore thought most convenient in the heat of this broil
to levy as great power as we may, as well for the surety
of the King's Majesty's person, as also for the preservation of the state of the realm which, this contention
enduring by factions between Your Grace and them,
may be in much peril and danger."[5] He placed himself
at the orders of the conspirators, and his name appeared
beside theirs at the foot of the proclamation denouncing

[1] Circular letter despatched by the Council in London to the sheriffs
and justices of the peace. October 8, 1549. Pocock, *op. cit.*, 92.
[2] The proclamation was withdrawn on October 11, "since the King's
person is now in safety and the Protector in safe custody." Pocock,
Troubles, 118. Cf. Stow's *Chronicle*, ed. 1631, 597.
[3] The Council's letter of October 6, 1549. Pocock, *Troubles*, 80.
[4] Lord Russell and Sir William Herbert to the Lords of the Council,
October 9, 1549. Tytler, *op. cit.*, 231 *sqq.*
[5] Lord Russell and Sir William Herbert to Somerset, October 8, 1549.
Tytler, *op. cit.*, I, 217 *sqq.*; Cf. Ibid., 233; Pocock, *Troubles*, 90. In their
letter of October 11, (*Troubles*, 112), they offer their services as mediators
between Somerset and the Council.

"the malice and evil government of Edward, duke of Somerset."[1]

Large numbers of peasants answered the Protector's appeal. But Somerset dared not embark upon a civil war. His character, of an almost feminine sensitiveness, quickly changed from confidence to panic. The succession of bad news speedily deprived him of heart. His enemies, informed of his changing moods, did not fail to take advantage of them to increase their demands. Protesting their loyalty to the king, they began by the complaint that Somerset governed without them,[2] and went on to inform the Councillors at Windsor of their intention to deprive him of his office.[3]

They soon proceeded to accuse them of keeping the king out of their reach and practically a prisoner in the hands of his servants, "strangers armed with his Majesty's own armour." These men were warned that they must answer for the King's safety with their lives. "If any ill come hereof, you can consider to whom it must be imputed. The example is very strange and perilous. And now my Lords if you tender the preservation of his Majesty and the State, join with us to that end'.[4]

Finally, they made a barely concealed threat, and demanded the surrender of the Duke, while offering a large reward to anyone who should inform against his supporters.[5] The defection of the secretary William Petre and Sir Philip Hoby, who had been sent to treat with Warwick, followed by that of his few adherents, with the exception of Sir Thomas Smith and Cecil,

[1] Pocock, *Troubles*, 95–102.

[2] Letter from the Council to the king, October 7, 1549. (Pocock, *Troubles*, 83; Burnet, V, 273).

[3] Letter from the Council in London to the Council at Windsor, October 7, 1549. Ellis, *Original Letters*, Series I, Vol. II, 166; Pocock, *Troubles*, 86.

[4] Letter from the Council in London to the Council at Windsor, October 9, 1549. Burnet, V, 280; Ellis, *op. cit.*, II, 169; Pocock, *op. cit.*, 104. The reply of Paget, Cranmer and Smith is dated the following day. Tytler, *op. cit.*, 223.

[5] The Council in London to Lord Paget, October 10, 1549. Ellis, *op. cit.*, II, 174 *sq.* Proclamation by the Council in London, October 10, 1549. Pocock, *Troubles*, 108.

destroyed the last shreds of the Protector's courage. On October 7 he made an offer to Warwick of surrender, "if any reasonable conditions and offers would take place," which he would explain himself to the king.[1] The councillors in London assured him "of their faiths and honours that they do not intend nor will hurt in any case, the person of my Lord Duke, nor take away any of his lands or goods but do intend to preserve his honour." He suddenly veered round to an exaggerated confidence and dismissed his guard. On the 10th he made no resistance when Sir Anthony Wingfield arrested him and imprisoned him in the Beauchamp Tower of Windsor Castle.[2]

Four days later, in spite of Warwick's fair promises, he was taken to the Tower of London with six of his friends, and an inventory of his possessions was drawn up.[3]

The Council was received by the king who had never been fond of his uncle.[4] It had not neglected to obtain the support of the Princesses Mary and Elizabeth and to win over the Emperor to its side. Its triumph was complete[5].

Foreign wars, domestic troubles, rebellions, opposition to his measures of social reform, his intereference with private interests had made possible or actually brought about the Protector's fall. With it ended the first part of the reign. As regards England's religious history the second part was marked by a different character from that which the years of Somerset's rule displayed.

[1] The Protector to the Council, October 7, 1549. Pocock, *Troubles*, 88; Tytler, *op. cit.*, 214 *sqq.* Articles presented to His Majesty by the Protector the same day. Ellis, *op. cit.*, II, 173, Note; Burnet, V, 275.

[2] Declaration by Sir Hoby, as the representative of the Council in London to the Council at Windsor. Tytler, *op. cit.*, I, 238 *sqq.* See Ellis, *Original Letters*, Series I, Vol. II, p. 173 *sqq.*, where the Council's letter to William Paget ordering Somerset's arrest may be found.

[3] This inventory signed on behalf of the king (Pocock, *Troubles*, 123, Froude, *op. cit.*, Chapter III) includes monastic spoils; silver acticles, church ornaments, "lead, stones, stuffs of great value from Sion, Reading and Glastonbury."

[4] See his letter of October 8 in Pocock, *Troubles*, 102.

[5] Details bearing on Somerset's fall may be found in the despatches of the Imperial Ambassador, Van der Delft, of September, November and December, 1549. (*Spanish Calendar*, IX, 445, 449, 453-455, 456-463, 469, 477).

CHAPTER V

WARWICK AND THE PROGRESS OF THE RELIGIOUS REVOLUTION

John Dudley, Earl of Warwick and Duke of Northumberland—His character—His jealousy of Somerset—He procures Somerset's second fall, condemnation and death (October 1551–January 1552)—His religious policy—Rapid progress of Protestantism.

JOHN DUDLEY, Viscount de Lisle (1542), soon to be created Duke of Northumberland, who had overthrown the Protector, was a brilliant soldier, a clever diplomat, and an accomplished man of the world. In 1546 he was employed on a successful embassy to Francis I. When the French attempted an invasion in 1545, he commanded the English fleet at Spithead, and engaged the French galleys off Shoreham.[1] He was second in command at the Battle of Pinkie (September 10, 1547), and was Lord High Admiral under Henry VIII (1543–1547). He became Lord Chamberlain at Edward's accession, handing over his position of Admiral to the Protector's brother, Thomas Seymour.[2] Brave and apparently good natured and generous, his contemporaries called him, not without some reason, a second Alcibiades.[3]

The son of a father beheaded for taking part in a plot against Henry VIII, he was a born intriguer; and it was a conspiracy which finally brought him like his father to the block. Prudent, silent, cunning, completely self-controlled, an accomplished disciple of Machiavelli,

[1] *State Papers*, I, 794, 816.
[2] Cf. Lefèvre-Pontalis, *op. cit.*, 102, 104, 106.
[3] Bishop Ponet gives him this name in his *Short Treatise of Politike Power* of 1556.

he successfully concealed his motives and designs from his contemporaries; and the historian experiences the utmost difficulty in unravelling them. Few were more skilful in achieving their aims. Richard Morison, the English ambassador to Charles V, said of him that he had always two alternative plans in his head, one of which was certain to succeed, however events should turn out. It was typical of such a schemer that he rid himself of his enemies under plausible pretexts, which concealed his real motives.[1] Energetic, determined, unprincipled, a hypocrite and a double dealer, he was one of the cleverest and most unscrupulous party leaders who have ever employed their country's resources and wealth for their private interest. No one was better fitted to continue and complete the religious revolution, which Somerset had begun with moderation and a certain timidity. Until he was certain of victory, Warwick avoided any open conflict with the Protector. While apparently deferring to his wishes, he had always been his secret enemy. He would remain so to the end, and would not rest till he had accomplished Somerset's death. But he proceeded warily, to make success absolutely certain. To have destroyed Somerset straight away would have been dangerous. In more than one quarter the Protector found open sympathy. Warwick judged it prudent to take this into account. He therefore decided to release his rival on condition he signed thirty-one articles of accusation.[2] To secure the ratification of Parliament the articles were altered, and differ in

[1] For example when Thomas Stukely (died 1578), a supporter of Somerset, informed him of a hostile intrigue of Henry II, he believed the information, but imprisoned Stukely, telling the French king, who denied the plot, that he had done so to prove his confidence in the king. He treated W. Paget in the same way.

[2] The articles have been published by Sir John Hayward, (*Life and Reign of King Edward the Sixth*, 1630, p. 308), G. Burnet (*History of the Reformation*, ed. Pocock, V, 283, with some changes in the order of the text and omissions), J. Foxe (VI, 290 *sqq.*, cf. p. 748), Thomas Carte (*History of England*, 1747-1755, ed. Oxford, 1851, III, 242), and other historians. They are in Harleian MS., 353 (fol. 78 *sqq.*) in the British Museum.

important respects from the charges originally brought against the Protector.[1] They are little more than a vote of censure. The first ten censure him for doing what the letters patent of March 13, 1547, signed by the King and Council, empowered him to do, namely consult and appoint councillors[2] at his pleasure, and take any action which a Guardian of the king and a Protector is entitled to take. His accusers appealed to the declaration of January 31, 1547,[3] which raised Somerset to the Protectorate "with this special and express condition" that he "shall not do any act but with the advice and consent of the rest of the executors," ignoring the fact that it had been annulled by the Royal mandate of the following March 31.

The Council's real grievances against the Duke were his desire for social reforms, his attempts to combat enclosure, and prevent the ruin of agriculture and the peasantry, his sympathy with those who had been reduced to destitution by the greed of the rich, and the mildness he displayed towards them, when the refusal of the proposed reforms had goaded them into revolt. He was, indeed, charged with having said openly that the nobles and gentlemen "were the only causes of the dearth of things whereby the people rose and did reform things themselves" (Article 10), with having issued contrary to the Council's advice "proclamations concerning enclosures whereby the common people hath made divers insurrections" (Article 11), with having appointed commissions of enquiry into the enclosures (Article 12), with having been too slow in taking steps to crush the insurgents (Article 13), with having encouraged them "by giving to them divers sums of" his "own money" (Article 14), with having issued ordinances

---

[1] Cf. Minute of the despatch to the ambassadors denouncing Somerset. *Troubles Connected with the Prayer Book of* 1549, 113–118.

[2] *Acts of the Privy Council*, II, 64. They were inscribed in the minutes of the Council on March 21.

[3] Ibid., II, 4–6.

forbidding them to be sought out and brought to trial (Article 15), with having said that he understood their position and that it was the avarice of the great Lords that had driven them into rebellion (Article 16), with having declared that since "the Lords of the Parliament were loth to incline them to reformation of enclosures and other things, therefore the people have good cause to reform the things themselves" (Article 17), with having written to the nobles "to speak fair to the rebels and to handle them gently" (Article 20), and finally with having released a number of them (Article 3).[1]

The concluding articles censure the Duke for the manner in which he had sought to defend himself against Warwick's plot, as though the chief culprit were not the plotter himself.[2]

Like Wolsey before him,[3] Somerset submitted and signed the thirty-one articles (December 23, 1549). In return he was merely imprisoned and his goods were not confiscated. A few months later, on February 6, 1550, he was released from the Tower on payment of a surety of 10,000 pounds. Twelve days later Edward remitted it entirely. On April 10 he was readmitted to the Council and made Earl Marshal of England. On the 27th all his possessions were restored of which the king had not disposed during his imprisonment.[4] On May 14 he was appointed a gentleman of the bed-chamber.[5] At the same time the marriage of his daughter Anne to Warwick's eldest son (June 3, 1550) seemed to

[1] Cf. *State Papers, Domestic*, Edward VI, VIII, 56.

[2] Article 20 accused the Protector of neglecting the defences of Boulogne, Ambleteuse and Blackness, though the Council at that very moment was allowing the enemy to seize several fortresses both in France and in Scotland.

[3] The Cardinal admitted that he had violated the statute of *Praemunire* by exercising his legatine authority, though it had been sanctioned by the king.

[4] "It was agreed by the whole Council that the King's Majesty should be moved for the restitution of the Duke of Somerset unto all his goods, his debts and his leases yet ungiven." Extract from the minutes of the Council. *Troubles Connected with the Prayer Book of 1549*, p. 139.

[5] Cf. *Spanish Calendar*, X, 7 *sqq.*, 11 *sqq.*; 28, 62 *sqq.*, 72, 109; Tytler, I, 298.

put the seal upon the reconciliation of the two, who did not pass a single day without seeing each other.[1]

But the reconciliation could not last. Somerset was an obstacle to Warwick's ambitious schemes and must be put out of the way. Since the king's health was obviously becoming worse, Warwick may have already conceived the design of altering the succession to the throne to the profit of his family. In any case he was soon made anxious by his rival's recovery of influence. On his restoration to the Council, Somerset vigorously opposed the policy of weakness abroad and violence at home, which his successor had inaugurated. The Western rebels were treated with the utmost severity, the Henricians and Mary Tudor were persecuted, and the enclosures, far from being abolished, were protected by statutes which made it felony to resist them.[2] But the government concluded a humiliating peace with Scotland and France. Boulogne was restored to France, four years before the date fixed by the treaty of 1546, and for half the indemnity then agreed upon, on payment of 400,000 gold crowns. Edward VI was to wed Elizabeth of France, Henry II's daughter.[3] Scotland was evacuated and the Council gave its approval to Mary Stuart's marriage with the Dauphin, which defeated the projects

---

[1] Cf. *Spanish Calendar*, X, 87, 98, 109.

[2] It was felony for twelve persons to assemble to demolish an enclosure, treason, if forty assembled for the same purpose. Any tenant who failed to oppose such gatherings was to forfeit his lease in perpetuity. If he took part in them, he was guilty of felony. To assemble with the object of reducing the price of corn was also made a felony. (*Statutes of the Realm*, 3 and 4, Edward VI, cap. 5). The statutes of Henry VII and Henry VIII against enclosure were repealed, and the latter might be carried out practically without restriction. (Ibid., 3 and 4, Edward VI, cap. 3). The taxes on sheep and on woollen stuffs were abolished (Ibid., 3 and 4, Edward VI, cap. 23) and replaced by the payment of the "Fee farms" from which Somerset had released the poor peasants. (Ibid., 3 and 4, Edward VI, cap. 18). In 1551 a farmer was imprisoned and put to death for having presented to the Star Chamber a petition against certain persons who had destroyed his corn, (Tytler, I, 271-273). According to Tytler there would not appear to have been any trial other than the investigation of the petition.

[3] Tytler, I, 261. This was vetoed by Somerset. *Spanish Calendar*, X, 227.

of the Tudors, and might prove a serious danger to
England, as indeed Elizabeth would discover in the
early years of her reign. The fleet, built at great expense
by Henry VIII and carefully kept up by Somerset,
was reduced. The fortifications of Calais, Guisnes and
the Scottish border were neglected and the garrisons of
the strongholds diminished.[1] At every point this policy
reversed Somerset's. He could not, therefore, give it his
approval. His criticisms offended Warwick. But the
moderate members of the Council—Paget, the Earl of
Arundel, Lord Grey of Wilton, supported him. The
report spread that the Council was divided, that its
two chiefs were no longer agreed. It was to no purpose
that the Councillors made a public show of complete
harmony, and at feasts and public banquets, lavished
on one another flatteries and tokens of affection. The
air was thick with rumours of plot and counterplot.
Though Warwick courted popularity, the crowd received
him with hostile murmurs. Somerset, on the other hand,
was placed on May 10, 1551, at the head of the counties
of Buckingham and Berks, the Earl of Derby's son sought
his daughter's hand, and his party, insufficiently crushed,
seemed to be reviving.[2] Before the adjournment (February 1550), the question of restoring the Protectorate
to him had been raised in the Commons, and the suggestion was repeated the following session. Warwick,
however, possessed the King's ear.

"Every day," wrote the Imperial Ambassador, "his
power increases at Somerset's expense. Nothing of
importance is done without his advice, and if he is
obliged to keep his chamber, the entire Council often
waits upon him. His system of government is despotism.
He fills government offices and positions of profit with

---

[1] *Acts of the Privy Council*, II, 43–44, 47, 100, 194, 209, 225, 364.
[2] Despatches from Jehan Scheyfve to the Emperor, April 9 and 21,
May 12 and June, 1551. *Spanish Calendar*, X, 262 *sqq.*, 280, 291 *sqq.*, 300
sqq. Cf. Letter from Simon Renard to Charles V, Paris, April 28, 1551,
Ibid., 285.

his creatures."[1] He, therefore, hastened the execution of his design. Profiting by an illness which kept the Duke in his palace, he confined to his house Somerset's most faithful supporter, William Paget, on a pretext remote from the true reason.[2] At the same time he had himself created Duke of Northumberland and bestowed honours on his friends. Dorset became Duke of Suffolk, William Paulet (already Earl of Wiltshire) Marquis of Winchester, Sir William Herbert, Earl of Pembroke. Knighthoods were conferred on Cecil, who had abandoned Somerset's party, Henry Sydney, who had just married Warwick's daughter (March 1551), Henry Dudley, his brother, and Henry Neville. The lesser fry had to be content with plunder from the bishoprics.[3]

The very day Warwick was created Duke of Northumberland (October 11), the Council ordered an investigation into Somerset's debt to the Crown. Rendered suspicious, the Duke questioned Cecil, whose reply was cold and evasive. Three days later Somerset was arrested and sent to the Tower. Next day he was joined in the Tower by his most influential supporters: William Paget, the Earl of Arundel, and Lord Grey of Wilton.[4] This step

[1] Despatches from Jehan Scheyfve, June and July 6, 1551. *Spanish Calendar*, X, 301, 325.

[2] When Charles V complained to the Council that the promise made to Princess Mary during Somerset's protectorate, that she should be permitted her Mass, had not been kept, Paget denied that it had been made. Thereupon Warwick wrote to the Emperor on October 16 that Paget had been imprisoned for doubting the Emperor's word. (*State Papers, Foreign*, Edward VI, No. 461). William Paulet had also refused to believe the Emperor's word and he was at liberty. But Paget's membership of the Council would have embarrassed Warwick.

[3] The Bishop of Winchester, John Ponet, was ordered on September 27, 1551, to bestow various properties of his see on Sir John Gates, Andrew Dudley, another brother of Warwick's, Sir Philip Hoby and others. British Museum, Royal Ms., 18c., XXIV, fol., 135; Collier, *Ecclesiastical History of Great Britain*, ed. Lathbury, 1852, IX, 298.

[4] Tytler gives a list (II, 37) of prisoners arrested as accomplices or supporters of Somerset. Cf. *Spanish Calendar*, X, 393, 407 *sqq.*, 425. For Somerset's arrest see despatches from Jehan Scheyfve to the Emperor, October 10, 18, 26, 1551, a letter from the regent of the Netherlands of October 26, and of the Emperor, November 24. Ibid., X, 381, 384–386, 387–393, 396 *sqq.*

removed from the Council all who might have defended him. To prevent a rising of the people false reports were circulated, and Parliament, which should have met on November 4, was prorogued.[1] It only remained to trump up some plausible charges against Somerset. The year before, to arm himself against his rival, Warwick had caused Parliament to pass a statute unparalleled in English history even in the reigns of Charles I and James II. It was made treason to assemble twelve persons with intent "to murder, kill, slay or imprison any of the King's Privy Council, or unlawfully to alter or change any laws made or established for religion by authority of Parliament, or any other laws or estates of this realm, if they or any of them, notwithstanding a proclamation to retire, remain or continue together by the space of one whole hour after such proclamation. And if any person or persons by open word or deed shall procure, move or stir any other person or persons to arise and make any traitorous or rebellious assembly, . . . every person so procuring, moving or stirring any other shall be decreed and adjudged a felon."[2] The Council thus secured the same protection as the King himself. It was for a breach of this statute, repealed after his execution, that the former Protector was condemned.

Sir Thomas Palmer, a brave soldier, but an unprincipled man and a personal enemy of Somerset,[3] and a man named Crane, who had squandered his fortune, accused the Duke of inciting the people to revolt on Saint George's Day (April 23). It was on this charge that Somerset had been arrested.[4] Torture, whose

---

[1] It did not meet between February, 1550, and the morrow of Somerset's execution, January 23, 1552.

[2] *Statutes of the Realm*, 3 and 4, Edward VI, cap. 5.

[3] A sixteenth century hand has written into Edward the Sixth's *Journal* at the place where the king mentions Palmer (October 1551): "A man who hated the Duke and was hated by him." Cf. Burnet, II, 304 *sqq.*, 307, 316; V, 50 *sqq.*, 57, 77; *Calendar of State Papers, Domestic*, 1547–1580, 36.

[4] Sir Thomas Palmer's accusation was made on October 3. It was kept secret several days and is mentioned only in Edward's *Journal*. (October 7–19, 1551). *Literary Remains*, (Roxburghe Club); Burnet, V, 50–52.

employment he had abolished, was revived against him, in the attempt to extort a confession from the prisoner.[1] And since at this period it was an easy matter for the Crown to exert pressure upon juries, the sheriffs of the City of London and the counties of Middlesex and Kent were ordered to summon grand juries and obtain from them bills against Somerset (November 16, 1551). These bills charged him with two offences. He was accused of plotting with others on more than one occasion to "arrest and imprison" the Duke of Northumberland, the Marquis of Northampton, William Parr the Earl of Pembroke, and Sir William Herbert, and of inciting the citizens of London to revolt to the sound of drum and trumpets and the cry of Freedom, Freedom.[2] These charges unconfirmed by any contemporary chronicle,[3] made it possible to condemn Somerset in virtue of the Statute above mentioned. "It has proved impossible to convince the people," wrote the Imperial Ambassador on October 26, 1551,[4] "that the charges brought against him are true. Everyone is convinced that he is an innocent man against whom a charge of plotting has been trumped up, and for no other reason than Warwick's baseness and his fear of the Protector." On December 1, 1551, Somerset faced

---

Crane's accusation was brought on October 26, (Ibid.,) and is the only accusation still extant. (*Crane's Information Against the Duke of Somerset and the Earl of Arundel*; Tytler, *op. cit.*, II, 38–41; *State Papers, Domestic*, XIII, No. 65). Crane's deposition and the Earl of Arundel's confession (*Confession of the Earl of Arundel*; Tytler, II, 43–45), are the sole documents at our disposal from which to judge of Somerset's trial.

[1] On November 5 the Council authorised the employment of torture in the investigation of the charges. *Acts of the Privy Council*, III, 407.

[2] *Baga de Secretis. Fourth Report of the Deputy-Keeper of the Records.* App. II.

[3] The Chronicles or Diaries written at this time by citizens of London say nothing whatever of the incitements to revolt, accompanied by the sounding of drums and trumpets with which Somerset was charged. There is no mention of them in Wriothesley's *Chronicle*, the *Greyfriars' Chronicle*, *Narratives of the Reformation*, Edward's *Journal*, Grafton's *Chronicle*, or contemporary letters. (*Zurich Original Letters*, Parker Society and Ellis, *Original Letters*).

[4] *Spanish Calendar*, X, 388.

his judges. For fear of a popular demonstration in his
favour he was taken to Westminster at five in the morning
and by water. The Court had been carefully packed.
Only twenty-five temporal peers out of forty-seven
had been summoned and among them were Somerset's
most bitter enemies: Warwick, the Duke of Suffolk,
Henry Grey, the Marquis of Northampton, and William
Paulet, who on November 28 had been appointed grand
seneschal to preside at the trial.[1] Somerset was not
confronted with any witness except Lord Strange, a
youth of about eighteen[2], and he brought forward
several well-grounded objections to his accusers' credibil-
ity. He denied everything.[3] A long debate ensued
among the peers who finally acquitted the accused of
treason, but were induced by Warwick's supporters to
find him guilty of felony. It made no difference to his
enemies. Felony as well as treason was punishable by
death.[4]

[1] William Paulet to Lord Clinton, December 2, 1551. Tytler, II, 64.
[2] He deposed merely that the Duke had employed him as an intermediary to marry the king to one of his daughters and to be informed of
what passed in the Council. And Somerset denied the allegations on
oath. Letter above-mentioned from W. Paulet to Lord Clinton of December
2, 1551. Cf. *Spanish Calendar*, X, 406.
[3] That Somerset had confessed nothing in prison Warwick complained
bitterly to the lieutenant of the Tower, Sir Philip Hoby and he ordered
him to strip Somerset of his Garter and the Collar of the order. The
story that Somerset thanked the Lords for their judgment and asked
pardon, set down in Edward's *Journal*, is contradicted by the report spread
by Warwick himself after Somerset's execution to the effect, that he had
been put to death, because he had refused to ask pardon.
[4] The penalty of the former was beheading, of the latter hanging.
The trial, the debate, and Somerset's reply to the charges are reported
in full detail by J. Scheyfve in his French despatches of December 10,
1551. (*Spanish Calendar*, X, 405-409). The letter of December 2 frequently
reproduced, from W. Paulet to Lord Clinton is much shorter. The letter
sent to Lord Clinton the same day by the members of the Council with
the object of justifying the condemnation to the French Court, follows the
same lines. (*Calendar of State Papers, Foreign*, 1547-1553, 200; cf. ibid.,
185, 187, 192, 195). Jean Ulmer sent an account to Bullinger two days
later. (*Zurich Original Letters*, I, 439 *sqq*. Cf. Burnet, III, 364 *sqq*), probably
presenting Warwick's version of the affair for the benefit of the continental
Protestants. Edward's *Journal* (December 1551), can but repeat Warwick's
story, who to destroy Somerset, must have deceived the young king and
blackened his uncle. All his rival's friends had been removed from court.
Edward, only fourteen years old, was not present at the trial and knew of it

In a trial of this kind there could be no question of justice. It is impossible to be at once a judge and an interested party. But the acts of which Somerset was accused were directed against Warwick's supporters, and it was they who ordered his arrest, collected the evidence against him, examined the witnesses and exchanged the rôle of prosecutors for that of judges. Anyone who gave evidence against Somerset, even though himself implicated in the plot, was at once released and sometimes even admitted to Warwick's favour. Those on the other hand who denied it were sent to the gallows or the block. Like Somerset himself they maintained their innocence on the scaffold itself.

When Somerset left Westminster, the Tower axe was not borne in front of him, a sign that he had not been found guilty of treason. The people, who in large numbers waited outside the hall to learn the issue of the trial and had cried from time to time "God save the Duke," believed that he had been acquitted. Shouts of joy were raised and the huzzas of the crowd could be heard beyond Charing Cross. Men flung their caps into the air. The entire route was loud with acclamations. In some places the bells were rung and bonfires lit in honour of the "good Duke".[1] When the people learned their mistake, a gloomy silence succeeded to their shouts of joy.

No one, however, expected Somerset's execution. But his rivals' calumnies had poisoned the young king's mind against him. "The king is said to be troubled and sad on account of his uncle's imprisonment," the

---

only what the Protector's enemies told him. We may consult Tytler, II, 1–75; Lingard, *History of England*, fifth ed., 1848–1851; J. A. Froude, *The Reign of Edward the Sixth*, Chapter V; A. F. Pollard, *England under Protector Somerset*, 1900, 288 *sqq.*; also Vol. VI of his *Political History of England*, 1910, 61–66.

[1] John Stow, *Annals*, ed. 1631, 606; Wriothesley, *Chronicle*, II, 63; letter from Jean Ulmer to Bullinger; *Zurich Original Letters*, Vol. XII, 439 *sq. Acts of the Privy Council*, III, 462.

Imperial Ambassador had reported on October 26.[1] "But I know from a reliable source that evil reports have so prejudiced him against his uncle that he does not grieve at his fate." Moreover, Warwick held the Council in his hands. He had no time to lose. For Parliament would meet on January 23. On the 18th among "certain points of weighty matters to be immediately concluded on by the council", Edward wrote with his own hand: "the matter for confederates of the Duke of Somerset to be considered as appertaineth to our surety and the quietness of the realm that *by this punishment* example may be shown to others." The note has been altered by erasures and interlineations, and made to run: "the matter *for the Duke of Somerset and his* confederates to be considered . . . that by this punishment *and execution* according to the laws, example may be shown to others."[2]

Thus Edward's order to try Somerset's accomplices became an order to execute his uncle. The influence to which the alteration was due is easy to guess, though the hand which executed it cannot be discovered with certainty. The following day the Council, of whose proceedings no record remains, decided upon the immediate execution of the former Protector. It took place on January 22, 1552. It was kept secret and fixed for eight in the morning, an order being given that no one might leave his house before ten.[3] In spite of these precautions the crowd thronged Tower Hill when Somerset mounted the scaffold, where by Royal command decapitation awaited him in place of the ignominious

[1] *Spanish Calendar*, 389 *sq.*

[2] Tytler, *op. cit.*, II, 69; Pollard, *op. cit.*, 307. The document is in the British Museum among the Cotton MSS. Vespasian F. XIII, fol. 171. It is endorsed: "These remembrances within were delivered by the King's Majesty to his Privy Council, the Monday being the 19th of January, 1551 (1552). A° 5 of his Majesty's reign." In his *Journal* Edward simply mentions without a touch of feeling Somerset's execution, "Between eight and nine in the morning".

[3] H. Robinson, *Zurich Original Letters*, Parker Society, II, 731, 732; *Spanish Calendar*, X, 444, 445, 452.

punishment of hanging. The Duke wore the rich and ornate dress which he used to wear at court functions. He knelt down, made a brief prayer, then rose to his feet. Addressing the people he protested his innocence and declared his submission to the law which had condemned him. "Masters and good fellows," he said, "I am come hither to die, but a true and faithful man as any was unto the King's Majesty and to his realm. But I am condemned by a law whereto I am subject as we all, and therefore to show obedience I am content to die, . . . for the which I do thank God, taking it for a singular benefit, as even might have come to me otherwise. For as I am a man, I have deserved at God's hand many deaths; and it has pleased His goodness whereas He might have taken me suddenly, that I should neither have known Him nor myself, thus now to visit me and call me with this present death, as you do see, when I have had time to remember and acknowledge Him and to know also myself, for the which I do thank Him most heartily."[1] The royal chaplain who accompanied him, spoke to him in a low voice. Whereupon he added: "My friends more I have to say to you concerning religion: I have been always, being in authority, a furtherer of it to the glory of God to the uttermost of my power, whereof I am nothing sorry, but rather have cause and do rejoice most gladly that I have so done."[2] Somerset was still speaking when Sir Anthony Browne was seen galloping towards the scaffold. The people thought he was bringing the royal pardon and began to exclaim: "Pardon, Pardon. God save the King." And they threw their caps and cloaks in the air.

"The good Duke," an eyewitness relates[3] "standing

---

[1] He had written in prison a preface to a manual of devotion entitled: *Spiritual and Precious Pearle*, which ran into many editions. Cf. Hazlitt, *Bibliographical Handbook.*

[2] H. Ellis, *Original Letters*, 2nd. series, II, 215–216; Foxe, VI, 293 *sqq.*; *Spanish Calendar*, X, 452 *sqq.*

[3] Ellis has published the account in his *Original Letters. Loc. cit.*

upright with his hat in hand signed to the crowd to approach and said, 'There is no such thing, good people; there is no such thing. It is the ordinance of God thus to die, wherewith we must be content. Let us now pray together for the King's Majesty, to whose Grace I have always been a faithful, true and most loving subject, desirous always of his most prosperous success in all his affairs, and ever glad of the furtherance and helping forward of the commonwealth of this realm'."

To which they all replied, "Yea", three times. Then muttering, "Lord Jesus, save me", the Duke laid his head on the fatal block. Many rushed to the scaffold to dip a handkerchief in the blood of a man regarded as a martyr to their cause. Throughout the day large crowds thronged to the scene of execution, lamenting the Duke's death and speaking about it at length.[1]

Thus died the Duke of Somerset. When Parliament met on the following day, the 23rd, it was faced with a *fait accompli*. But it showed its disapproval by repealing the clause in the statute under which Somerset had suffered and enacting that in future the two witnesses required to support a criminal charge must be confronted with the accused.[2] But Warwick was henceforward omnipotent. To make the king forget Somerset and to win his affection he gave him a liberty he had not hitherto enjoyed.[3] The Council was almost entirely composed of his supporters and he increased their number. Master of the Council, he made himself completely independent of it by persuading the Councillors

---

[1] Other accounts of Somerset's death are to be found in Stow's *Annales*, in a long letter from Bourgoyne to Calvin; *Zurich Original Letters*. Parker Society, Vol. 12, 731–737, in Wriothesley's *Chronicle*, II, 165, in Foxe VI, 293 *sqq.*, (cf. ibid., 262 *sqq.*), and in the despatch of Jehan Scheyfve of February 12, 1552, *Spanish Calendar*, X, 452 *sqq.* Cf. Collier, *op. cit.*, V, 432–445.; Burnet II, 305–317, 327 *sq.*; H. Soames, *The History of the Reformation of the Church of England*, London, 1826–1828, III, 679; Froude, *The Reign of Edward VI*, Chapter V.

[2] *Statutes of the Realm*, 5 and 6, Edward VI, cap. 11.

[3] J. Scheyfve to Charles V, January 14, 1552. *Spanish Calendar*, X, 437 *sq.*

to agree that in future the Royal signature would
suffice on all state papers which had hitherto required
the signature of six members of the Council.[1] Every
ordinance drawn up in his absence must be submitted
to him for his correction, and must then be issued without
further examination.[2] He almost regarded himself as
raised above the law. Without the title of Protector he
possessed all a Protector's authority, indeed even more.
He employed his power to promote the Reformation and
carry further the religious revolution in England, to the
bitter disappointment of those who had expected him
to restore Catholicism and with this hope had supported
his party against the Protector.[3] In a letter the Emperor
spoke, alluding to Warwick, of "certain people who now
possess great credit in England and once showed a desire
to restore religion to its original condition with the sole
object of gaining this credit".[4] Princess Mary alone had
seen clearly. "The Earl of Warwick," she had told the
Imperial Ambassador in 1550, "is the most inconstant
man in the realm. The plot against the Protector is
inspired solely by envy and ambition. The Protector's
accusers are as guilty as he is, since all he did was done
with their advice and consent. You will see that no good
will come of all this. It is God's punishment and the
beginning of our woes. That is why I want to leave
the country."[5]

When his government began, no one knew whether
Warwick would favour the Reformation or orthodoxy.
To overthrow Somerset he had made use of the orthodox
party, which expected its reward. Wriothesley and the
Earl of Arundel were already among the six peers
entrusted with the charge of the king's person. Richard

---

[1] *Acts of the Privy Council*, III, 411, 416.
[2] *Acts of the Privy Council*, III, 125.
[3] *Spanish Calendar*, IX, p. ix, liv, 476 *sqq.*, 489; X, VIII *sqq.*, 397.
[4] Charles V to J. Scheyfve, November 24, 1551. *Spanish Calendar*, X, 397.
[5] Van der Delft to Charles V, January 14, 1550. *Spanish Calendar*, X, 6.

Southwell had once more become an active member of the Council. The two Henrician bishops, Bonner and Gardiner, who were imprisoned in the Tower for their opposition to the religious changes already made, awaited their speedy release and congratulated the Council on overthrowing the Protector.[1] At Oxford, Mass was once more celebrated. Here and there the Latin service was reintroduced with blessed bread, holy water and the other ceremonies of the Church.[2] On every side it was whispered that the religious legislation of the reign was about to be repealed and the old rites and ceremonies restored together with the Mass. So likely did a reaction appear that Charles V thought himself in a position to require the restoration of the Catholic religion as the condition of an alliance. Had not his ambassador in London wanted to assist Warwick against Somerset in the moral certainty that the state of religion would be improved?[3]

The Protestants on their part feared a change and were beginning to take alarm. "Those cruel beasts, the Roman Catholics," one of them wrote,[4] "are once more triumphant. They are rejoicing at the Protector's fall, the ruin of the Gospel, and the restoration of their darling, the Mass." "The Papists," another wrote,[5] "are hoping and striving with all their might for their kingdom. If they win, it won't be long before I am despatched to my native country and my Father in heaven."

[1] Van der Delft had informed the Emperor that it was rumoured that they would be released. *Spanish Calendar*, IX, 458.

[2] Stumphius to Bullinger, *Zurich Original Letters*, Parker Society, II, 464. Oxford clung persistently to Catholicism. Cambridge had from the outset declared in favour of Protestantism. Letter from the Privy Council to the Bishops, December 25, 1550. Pocock, *Troubles*, 127; Burnet, V, 287.

[3] Thomas Cheyney to the Council. Strype, *Ecclesiastical Memorials*, III. Van der Delft to the Emperor, London, September 23, 1549. *Spanish Calendar*, IX, 455.

[4] Stumphius to Bullinger, *Zurich Original Letters*, Parker Society, II, 464.

[5] Letter from Hooper of November 7, *Zurich Original Letters*, Parker Society, I, 70.

It was reported at Basle that Bucer and other reformers had been arrested at the same time as Somerset, and that his fall would be the ruin of the Reformation. The Protestants attributed his overthrow to the Papists, who, it was said, had cunningly entangled him in their snares.[1] Warwick's personal sympathies were with orthodoxy, and on the scaffold he confessed that he had always believed the Catholic faith, though a few months before, he had boasted that he had been a Protestant for twenty years.[2] But with him ambition dominated every other consideration. He favoured the side which he thought would best assist his advancement and the advancement of his family. As the result of his education the young king was a devoted adherent of the Reformation. The Protestants regarded him as a new Josiah. "No study," wrote Bucer on June 15, 1550, "so arouses the King's enthusiasm as the study of Scripture. He reads ten chapters of the Bible daily with the utmost attention."[3] Warwick thought it wise to win royal favour and pursue the course on which the youthful Edward had embarked with such zeal. Moreover, if he had favoured the orthodox and the moderates, the Duke of Norfolk and Gardiner would have been released from the Tower and would have opposed his supremacy. The Shrewsburys, Oxfords, Derbys, and Rutlands, in short all the ancient peerage would have reappeared in public life, and his armorial bearings, new beside theirs, would have lost their lustre. The wiser course was to throw himself into the revolution and lead it. He did so.

The war waged by France against Charles V, in 1551 and 1552, and the Emperor's domestic difficulties,

---

[1] *Zurich Original Letters*, XII, 464; Nichols, *Literary Remains of Edward VI*, (Roxburghe Club), 1857, II, 247.

[2] H. Ellis, *Original Letters*, 2nd series, II, 246. Northumberland's speech on the scaffold is in the British Museum, Royal MS. 12 A. xxvi. His letter to Cecil of December 7, 1552, in which he professes his Protestant faith, is in Tytler, II, 148 *sqq.*

[3] Cf. Carte, *History of England*, III, 244.

left him free to act as he pleased, without any risk of foreign intervention.

He began by ridding himself of the Henricians of whom he had made use to overthrow Somerset, but whose services he no longer needed. He broke them like useless tools. They disappeared quietly, how we hardly know. In February 1550, Wriothesley was removed from the list of Privy Councillors. He died the following July 30, of grief, it was said.[1] The Earl of Arundel deprived of his position as Chamberlain, was confined to his house and fined £12,000 on some vague charge.[2] Sir Richard Southwell was sent to the Tower.[3] The Henrician bishops who had been expecting their release remained in prison. They were deprived of their sees, which were filled by extreme Protestants.

Warwick decisively espoused the Protestant cause. Already a proclamation had denied the rumours that the Mass and "popish ceremonies" would be restored, and had ordered anyone who spread them to be arrested and punished. It promised an even more thoroughgoing reform *Ad ampliandam Dei gloriam et ad progressum verbi ejus*.[4] The Protestant lamentations speedily gave way to shouts of joy. Warwick was extolled to the skies. Bale compared him to Moses, others to Joshua. Hooper called him "the most faithful and courageous servant of Christ", the mainstay of the Reformation, "the most holy and fearless instrument of God's word".[5]

Bullinger entered into correspondence with him and

---

[1] Wriothesley, *Chronicle*, II, 41; Ponet, *Treatise of Politike Power*, III.

[2] According to Edward's *Journal* he had broken bolts and bars at Westminister and given away materials which were the property of the Crown.

[3] He was charged with spreading seditious reports. (Cf. Burnet, II, 260, V, 12). For the disgrace of Somerset's supporters see the letter from the Council in ed. Lodge, *Illustrations of British History*, 1838, I, 170 *sqq.*

[4] Proclamation of October 8, 1550, mentioned above.

[5] *Zurich Original Letters*, Parker Society, I, 82. Hooper adds, "Had it not been fo his striving for me in the cause of Christ, I should have been hanged five months ago, when the Duke of Somerset was in grave difficulties", ibid., 83.

with Suffolk, whose daughter, Lady Jane Grey, was to be Queen for a few days after Edward's death.[1] The continental reformers indeed regarded Warwick and Suffolk, his tool, as "the most shining lights of the Church of England", "the terror and dismay of the Roman bishops, who alone have done more for the reformation of the Church than all the rest of the Council".[2] The Protestants had now nothing but censure for Somerset's lukewarmness, the cause, they said, of his downfall. Under Warwick the Reformation did in fact make rapid strides. In three years the country witnessed more religious changes than it had experienced in the twenty years since Wolsey fell.[3] A deeper gulf was dug between the Catholic and the Anglican Churches. The doctrine of the latter was lowered to the level of the reformed churches of the continent.

The liberalism which had marked Somerset's government was completely absent from its successor. The Council exercised its authority unchecked at the expense of the liberty of the subject and the principles of the Constitution. Words spoken against Northumberland, or his supporters were punished with the utmost severity. Torture, the pillory, and mutilation were revived. The Statute of Treasons which Somerset had repealed was re-enacted by Warwick, who even added to its list of treasonable offences.[4]

The Catholic and the orthodox were once more persecuted. Sir Anthony Browne was imprisoned for hearing Mass. John Boxall, who became Secretary of State under Mary, William Rastel, More's nephew and the publisher of his works, Nicholas Harpsfield, who wrote on Henry VIII's divorce, and Richard Smith, a professor of theology,

---

[1] *Zurich Original Letters*, XII, 453, 454, 455, 457.
[2] Jean Ulmer to Bullinger, May 25, 1550. *Zurich Original Letters*, XII, 399.
[3] Cf. *Social England*, III, 171, in which the author mistakenly attributes these changes to Somerset.
[4] *Statutes of the Realm*, 3 and 4, Edward VI, cap. 5, cap. 17.

vice-chancellor of Oxford and a well-known controversial writer, were obliged to seek refuge on the Continent.[1] Thomas Watson, Gardiner's chaplain, who under Mary became Bishop of Lincoln, was summoned before the Council on December 4, 1550 and imprisoned. Another of Gardiner's chaplains, John Seton, underwent the same fate. Those who objected to the new English Mass and refused to go to communion were imprisoned or fined.[2] The Anabaptists were not treated more mildly. The fires of Smithfield were rekindled. For this reason Foxe calls Warwick a "cruel butcher". On April 24, 1551, a surgeon, George van Paris, was burned[3], and a few days later Joan Bocher for maintaining that although Christ was born of the Virgin Mary, He had not taken her flesh. Joan did not spare her judges, whose views changed as the years passed. "It is a goodly thing," she told them, "to consider your ignorance. It was not long ago you burnt Anne Askew for a piece of bread, and yet came yourselves soon after to believe and profess the same doctrine for which you burned her. And now forsooth you will needs burn me for a piece of flesh, and in the end you will come to believe this also, when you have read the scriptures and understood them."[4]

Hitherto, as the King's sister, Mary Tudor had been suffered to practise her Catholic religion in peace. Wherever she went her chaplains accompanied her. More

---

[1] See *Zurich Original Letters*, XII, 478 *sqq.*; Burnet, II, 195 *sqq.*; 280 *sqq.*; V, 5, 313; Strype, *Memorials of Cranmer*, ed. 1854, II, 48, 49, 77, 80 *sqq.*, 155–162, 167 *sqq.*, 308, 321, 325, 483–488; III, 106, 213, 736, 738; *Ecclesiastical Memorials*, II, 63; J. Foxe, VI, 35, 39 *sqq.*, 65, 298, 461, 469; VII, III; Collier, V, 186 *sqq.*, 416.

[2] See Wood, *Athenae Oxon.* Ed. Bliss, 386–389. Cf. Strype, *Memorials of Cranmer*, I, 289; III, 106. The fine was usually 40 pounds sterling, 500 gold pounds in our money. Cf. Blunt, *op. cit.*, II, 71.

[3] Foxe, *op. cit.*, VI, 699; Strype, *Cranmer's Memorials*, ed. 1848, II, 100; Heylyn, *Ecclesia Restaurata*, ed. 1849, I, 185 *sqq.* He had denied the divinity of Christ.

[4] Cf. *Acts of the Privy Council*, 1550–1552, 15, 19; *Hutchinson Works*, Parker Society, p. iii–v; *Literary Remains of Edward VI*, p. ccvi, ccxi; *Latimer Remains*, ed. 1845, 114; Burnet, II, 203 *sq.*; V, 17, 246 *sqq.*; Foxe, V, 699; Strype, *Memorials of Cranmer*, ed. 1848, II, 98 *sqq.*; Heylyn, *op. cit*, I, 185–188; N. Pocock, *Troubles*, 139.

than one person in the neighbourhood heard Mass with
her and her household. She would rather die, she had
declared, than conform to the new services. As the
result of the Emperor's repeated insistence, Somerset had
been holding out hopes of letters patent exempting the
Princess from the operation of the law, when he fell
from power.[1] Henceforward the Princess was constantly
harassed by the Council, and received severe and repeated
orders accompanied by threats. To escape she would
have accepted the hand of the Infante Don Luis of Por-
tugal. But no dowry was allowed her.[2] Then she thought
of fleeing to the continent. After some opposition
Charles V finally agreed. The ambassador Van der
Delft with his secretary Duboys disguised as corn merchants
on two occasions tried to get her away to Flanders.
But the disturbed state of the country and the Princess's
hesitations at the last moment, made the attempt fail.
Van der Delft died in the chagrin of a failure very dangerous to Mary, June 1550.[3] As Warwick's power grew
the persecution increased. One of Mary's chaplains, for
saying Mass in her absence, was compelled to fly. He
was caught and sent to the Tower. To the Imperial

[1] The Emperor to Van der Delft, January 25, May 10, July 26, September
2, 1549. Mary to the Emperor, April 3, 1549. Van der Delft to the
Emperor, May 28, July 19, August 13, September 15, 1549. *Spanish
Calendar*, IX, 330, 360, 375, 382, 407 *sqq.*, 419, 430, 441, 444 *sqq.*, 447.
Letter from Mary to the Privy Council and the Council's reply, June 22
and 24, 1549. Letter from Mary to Somerset, and the Council, June 27,
1549. Letter from Edward to his sister, January 24, 1550 in Foxe, ed.
Pratt, VI, 7–11. Cranmer and Ridley, according to Foxe, advised the
King to grant his sister's wish in consideration of the Emperor and the
danger which the kingdom would incur from the loss of his friendship.

[2] The Emperor to Van der Delft, July 26 and November 27, 1549.
Spanish Calendar, IX, 411 *sqq.*, 479. Van der Delft to the Emperor, January
14, March 8, April 22, 1550. Ibid., X, 6, 41, 67.

[3] Van der Delft to the Emperor, March 17, May 2, June 6, 1550. Mary
of Hungary, Regent of the Netherlands, to M. d'Ecke, June 13, 1550.
Charles V to Mary of Hungary, June 21 and 25, 1550. Jean Duboys:
report on his attempt. July 1550. Conversation between the French
Ambassador Sebastien de l'Aubespine and the President of the Imperial
Council of State, July 28, 1550. The Emperor to Mary of Hungary,
July 29, 1550. Granvella to the same, August 16, 1550. *Spanish Calendar*,
X, 47, 80–86, 94–96, 107, 111, 117, 124–135, 144, 146, 156.

Ambassador and the Princess, the Council denied that it had ever promised to respect Mary's beliefs, which had merely been tolerated for a time, in regard for her weakness of mind and in the hope that she would yield to gentle treatment. "You were at first time," Edward wrote to her, "when the law was made, borne withal, not because you should disobey the law, but that, by our lenity and love showed you might learn to obey it. We made a difference of you from our other subjects, not for that all others should follow our laws and you only gainstand them, but that you might be brought as far forward by love, as others were by duty."

Mary was even summoned to court and twenty-five members of the Privy Council remonstrated with her on her serious misconduct. She replied that though ready to give her life for her King her soul belonged to God. Three gentlemen, and after them three peers, among them the Chancellor Lord Rich, waited upon her during the following month to warn her she must no longer have Mass said. When the Imperial Ambassador intervened, the King replied that his sister was as much bound by the law as his other subjects. Nevertheless, fear of difficulties with the Emperor, who had complained to the English Ambassador Sir R. Morison, prevented Warwick from pressing his demands too far. And at the end of the reign, Mary still kept one or two chaplains—though on the Emperor's advice, she refrained from surrounding her worship with any provocative external solemnity.[1]

[1] Jean Scheyfve to Charles V, August 3, 1550. The regent of the Netherlands to Scheyfve, August 11, 1550. Edward VI to his sister, January 28, 1551. J. Duboys to the Regent of the Netherlands, February 13, 1551. Mary to the Same, February 22, 1551. J. Scheyfve to the Same, March 1, 1551. The Emperor to J. Scheyfve, March 7 and 17, 1551. J. Scheyfve to the Emperor, April 6. Mary to the Privy Council, May 2, 1551. The Council's reply, May 6. The Emperor to Scheyfve from the Netherlands, October 14, 1551. J. Scheyfve to the Emperor, December 15, 1551. *Spanish Calendar*, X, 150 *sqq.*, 154 *sqq.*, 205–212, 220–223, 224, 230–237, 239, 247 *sqq.*, 317, 356–364, 383 *sqq.* Foxe (VI, 11) had already published Edward's letter of January 28, 1551, but dated January 24, 1550, Mary's letter to the Council of May 2, 1551 and the Council's reply of May 6,

Thus, Sanders concludes, "throughout this calamitous time, the royal virgin was never deprived of the consoling presence of the Saving Victim".

The reforms which had been carried out with moderation under Somerset's rule, were imposed by Warwick in a violent and uncompromising fashion. The Bishops were ordered to enquire among many other things into the way in which the new Prayer Book was used, whether it was criticised, whether ceremonies and practices which had been abolished were still retained, whether Mass was said in private houses, whether labourers refused to work on the suppressed feasts.[1]

The Protector had scarcely fallen from power when Parliament passed an Act ordering the disuse and destruction of all the liturgical books in use before the Prayer Book of 1549, with the single exception of Henry VIII's Prymer.[2] Somerset had carefully refrained from going too fast and destroying whatever had existed before, at a single blow. Warwick showed no such moderation. He sent the Bishops[3] a circular in which he ordered them "to put away all vain expectation of having the public service, the administration of the sacraments, and other rites and ceremonies again in the Latin tongue, which were but a preferring of ignorance to knowledge, and darkness to light, and a preparation to bring in papistry and superstition again. We have thought good to require

---

(p. 18 *sqq.*), and other letters from Mary, Edward and the Council, also verbal instructions about the Catholic worship continued by the Princess. (Ibid., 12 to 14.)

[1] Wilkins, *Concilia*, IV, 60; Cardwell, *Documentary Annals of the Reformed Church of England; Being a Collection of Injunctions, Declarations, Orders, Articles of Inquiry*, &c., Oxford, 1844, I, 93–96.

[2] *Statutes of the Realm*, 3 and 4, Edward VI, cap. 10. For the old service books see Ch. Wordsworth and H. Littlehales, *The Old Service Books of the English Church*, 1904.

[3] Letter sent to the Bishops in the King's name, December 25, 1550. (N. Pocock, *Troubles*, 127 *sqq.*; Strype, *Eccles. Mem.*, ed. Oxford, 1822, II, 329–334.) It is dated November 25, 1550. But it does not appear to have been sent before the Act of Parliament was passed a month later. (*Statutes of the Realm*, 3 and 4, Edward VI, cap. 10.) Cranmer's letter to his clergy is in fact dated February 14, 1551. (Strype, *Mem. of Cranmer*, II, 577–581.)

you, and do straitly command and charge you that ye, immediately upon the receipt hereof, do command the Dean and Prebendaries of your cathedral church, the Parson, Vicar or curate, and churchwardens in every parish within your diocese, to bring and deliver to you or your deputy . . . all antiphoners, missals, grails, processionals, manuals, legends, pies, porteouses, journals and ordinals after the use of Sarum, Lincoln, Bangor, Hereford, or any other private use . . . and that ye take the same into your hands or into the hands of your deputy, and then so deface and abolish that they never hereafter may serve either any such use as they were first provided for, or be at any time a let (hindrance) to that godly and uniform order which by a common consent is now set forth." As a result of this fanatical prescription of the old service books, many precious books and richly illuminated manuscripts were destroyed at Oxford, which had nothing superstitious about them except the red letters, the historian of the University observes, on the title-page or in headings, or perhaps geometrical patterns after the Byzantine style, on account of which they were treated as works of magic. Books of theological controversy, in particular the writings of the schoolmen, were torn to pieces. Merton College, New College and Balliol were the worst sufferers from this vandalism. Dr. Cox, Edward's tutor and Chancellor of the University, was chiefly responsible for it. For this reason he was called the "cancellor".[1]

From service books the reformers turned their attention to images. Somerset's injunctions had been mitigated by a measure of toleration and he had not enforced them rigorously. On January 25, 1551, in the teeth of vigorous opposition by bishops and lay peers, Warwick carried through Parliament a statute which ordered the destruction of all statues and paintings still preserved in

[1] Cf. Wilkins, *Concilia*, 1737, IV, 60; E. Cardwell, *Documentary Annals*, Oxford, 1844; Collier, V, 360 *sqq.*, 417.

the churches, "provided that the act shall not extend
to any image or picture set or graven upon any tomb
. . . only for a monument of any king, prince, noble-
man or other dead person which hath not been commonly
reputed or taken for a saint."[1]

Distinction was no longer made between a superstitious
and a legitimate employment of images. The magnificent
windows at New College, Oxford were on the verge of
being broken because they depicted Saints. They were
saved only by pleading the extreme poverty of the college
and by a promise to replace them as soon as the college
could afford to reglaze the windows.

Along with their works of art the churches were stripped
of their costly ornaments. They were an easy prey. In
December 1547 Somerset had ordered an inventory of
Church ornaments to be made, to save them from the
greed of certain wealthy men and prevent their alienation
and sale.[2] Warwick seized them all. On March 3, 1551,
he appointed a commission "to take into the King's hands
such church plate as remaineth to be employed unto his
Highness' use.[3] All the gold and silver plate in the
churches, the jewels, the sacerdotal vestments, and
the furniture were set down in the inventory. Edward's
commissioners, particularly after the beginning of
1552—travelled up and down the shires and took
good care to make the pillage profitable. Their work
was interrupted only by the King's death. The
inventories are preserved in the national archives
and many of them have been published.[4] Presently

---

[1] Statutes of the Realm, 3 and 4, Edward VI, cap. 10. Cf. Grey Friars'
Chronicle, 55; Collier, V, 361 sqq. Six bishops and eight lords voted against
the bill on the final reading.

[2] Acts of the Privy Council, II, 535 sqq. They record four instances in which
Somerset, in virtue of this decision of the Council, restored to churches
objects which had been taken from them. Ibid., II, 39, 520, 539. Cf.
Pollard, op. cit., 270.

[3] Acts of the Privy Council, III, 228.

[4] A list of these publications scattered among books, periodicals and
pamphlets can be found in F. de Mély and Bishop, Bibliographie Générale
des Inventaires Imprimés, Paris, 1892–1895, I, 235–278. Since then more

the Treasury took its toll. Almost all gold or silver objects were confiscated, candelabra, candlesticks, crosses, bells large and small, cruets, chrismatories, pyxes, monstrances and the sacred vessels. Rich ornaments and banners, costly chasubles and copes, embroideries among them embroidered antipendia, cloth of gold and cloth of silver, tapestries of Arras work, carpets, cushions, precious stones, objects of wrought iron or embossed copper, all these were gathered up by what Dixon has termed, this "terrible sweep". The plunder was sold to fill his Majesty's empty coffers. The commissioners were instructed to leave, as a gift, such was the insulting phrase, an alb or two, one or two ornaments and a surplice "for the good administration of the Communion" and the simplified service. After the session of 1553, his ambassador informed Charles V[1] that the king on his own authority had appointed commissioners to take any ornaments, silver, and sacred vessels still remaining in the churches, leaving nothing but a chalice or cup. Greedy laymen bought for small sums, if the private plunderer had not forestalled the Treasury, the wealth accumulated by the art and piety of centuries. Many altar cloths were made into hangings or cushions, others into curtains. Former copes covered tables and beds, and more than one chalice was drained by tipplers in hall or inn. Occasionally the

---

inventories have been published by the Alcuin Club: S. C. Thomas and T. Crib, *Edwardian Inventories for Huntingdon*, 1906; F. C. Ecles and J. E. Brown, *Edwardian Inventories for Buckinghamshire*, 1906; the same *Edwardian Inventories for Bedfordshire*; Beatrix F. Cresswell, *Edwardian Inventories of the City and County of Exeter*, 1916. See also *Inventory of Church Goods*, Surtees Society, xcvii, Durham, 1897; E. Pocock, *English Church Furniture in Lincolnshire*, 1866, 212-237, 243-247; E. Nightingale, *Church Plate of Dorset*, (Salisbury, 1889) of *Wilts*, (Loc. cit., 1891); A. Trollope, *An Inventory of the Church Plate of Leicestershire*, Leicester, 1890, 2 vols. T. North has published inventories of the Church bells of Leicestershire (Leicester, 1876), Northampton (1878), Rutland (1880), Lincoln (1882), Bedford (London 1883), and Herts (1887). Inventories and sales of plate or bells are recorded here and there in the *Acts of the Privy Council*, III, 104, 109, 148, 154, 228, 263, 467.

[1] Despatch of J. Scheyfve, April 28, 1553. *Span. Cal.*, XI, 36.

foreigner took advantage of this sale of the national inheritance. For example, Valentia and Saragossa preserve rich ornaments once belonging to Saint Paul's.[1] "Twenty thousand ounces of silver, worth 20,000 ducats, have been stored at St. Paul's," wrote the imperial ambassador three weeks before the king's death.[2] The London churches, in particular Westminster Abbey famous for the splendour of its coronations and funerals, were so thoroughly pillaged that the majority lacked the ornaments necessary for the Rogation procession. The country churches are still suffering, from the spoliation which then befell them.[3] *The Victoria History of the Counties of England*, a standard county history in process of publication, ascribes to the pillages of Edward's reign the emptiness of the churches in several counties, transformed as they have been into mausoleums, and stripped of their rich furnishings and ornaments. According to Strype, the "odious work" displeased Cranmer. "But this being somewhat an odious work, he (Cranmer) was not very forward to enter upon, especially because he thought whatsoever he and the other commissioners should recover, would be but swallowed up by the Duke of Northumberland and his friends, and the King be little the better."

In fact, "although some profit was raised to the King's exchequer," Heylyn observes,[4] "yet the far greater part of the prey came into other hands. By the avariciousness of this King's ministers, the royal import was so retrenched that it was scarce able to find work enough for the Court Exchequer." "All this income," Fuller

[1] Richard Ford, *Handbook for Travellers in Spain*, 1845; I, 440; II, 959.
[2] *Spanish Calendar*, XI, 51.
[3] Fuller, IV, 105, Note; Dixon, III, 452.
[4] J. G. Nichols, *The Diary of Henry Machyn*, 1550–1563. Camden Society, 1848, 34; the Same, *Chronicle of the Grey Friars of London*, Camden Society, 1852, p. 71; Heylyn, I, 281–287; Fuller, IV, 96–103, where, as also in Heylyn, the instructions to the Royal commissioners of 1552 may be found. Burnet, II, 360 *sqq.*; V, 69 (Edward's *Journal*). Strype, *Ecclesiastical Memorials*, IV, 15, 69; *Memorials of Cranmer*, II, 89 *sqq.*, 411; III, 699; Collier, V, 494–497; Dixon, III, 447–455.

remarks, "rather stayed the stomach than satisfied the hunger of the King's Exchequer."[1]

Pious foundations were surrendered to its maw. For centuries these had been multiplied by the desire of Catholics to be released as soon as possible from the Purgatorial flames. Chantries, chapels without cure of souls (*sine cura animarum*), collegiate churches had been endowed with lands and income to insure the dead annual Obits or more frequent Masses. To provide for the cost of the war against Scotland and France, the Parliament of 1545 had already placed at Henry's disposal for his life, the endowments of all these foundations, on the pretext that they were being employed contrary to the donors' intentions. Henry however had spared them.[2] Edward's first Parliament, though not without vigorous opposition, surrendered them to the king, on the plea that the belief in Purgatory and in the satisfactory value of Masses was superstitious.[3] According to Heylyn and Collier, 2,374 chantries and 90 colleges, none of the latter belonging to either University, were dissolved in virtue of this statute. Fuller, however, merely says their number was very large and unknown. At Saint Paul's alone there were 47 chantries; and Saint Stephen's Westminster, from its endowment of 1,085 pounds, supported 38 clerics, among them 13 Canons and 13 Vicars.[4] *Nemo scit*, God alone knows, Fuller adds, the amount of the money which poured into the treasury as the fruit of dissolution. The state, however, was obliged to give pensions to the clergy thus cut adrift.[5]

[1] *The Church History of Britain*, IV, 103.

[2] *Statutes of the Realm*, 37, Henry VIII, cap. 4. The first assault upon these possessions held in mortmain was delivered in 1532 followed by a further attack in 1536 (Ibid., 23, Henry VIII, cap. 10, 27, Henry VIII, cap. 10). After the passing of the Act of 1545, a visitation of the chantries was decided upon. Burnet, V, 222.

[3] Ibid., I, Edward VI, cap. 14; Gee and Hardy, *Documents of English Church History*, No. lxviii; *Spanish Calendar*, X, 230.

[4] Cf. Heylyn, I, 103 *sqq.* He is followed by Collier, V, 227, 256; Fuller, III, 469 *sqq.*, 477 *sqq.*

[5] *Statutes of the Realm*, I, Edward VI, cap. 14, section II. The pension was to cease, if the beneficiary received a benefice bringing in a higher income. (Sec. XI.)

The act envisaged the foundation and endowment of schools. In reality, as James Gairdner observes, following A. F. Leach, very little was spent for this purpose. The foundation of certain schools and hospitals already in existence has been erroneously attributed to Edward. "Amid the more pressing interests of the day, the heavy taxation of the people and the greed and covetousness of great men, educational institutions undoubtedly fared badly."[1]

Somerset had confiscated £50,000 belonging to the chantries, and spent it on the defence of the realm. Warwick gave their endowments or sold them for a small sum to his creatures. His friends Lord Darcy and Sir John Gates were among a large number who enriched themselves in a fashion as sudden as it was scandalous.[2]

"The courtiers," Fuller writes,[3] "were more rapacious to catch and voracious to swallow these chantries than abbey lands . . . knowing this was the last dish of the last course; and after chantries, as after cheese, nothing to be expected." Thus, as before when the monasteries were suppressed, it was the noblemen and the courtiers who derived the most profit from the pillage.

Three commissions, appointed respectively March 3, 1551, May 6, 1552, and January 16, 1553, were charged to confiscate and dissolve the pious foundations throughout the kingdom "to pay my debts" as Edward remarks

---

[1] J. Gairdner, *The English Church in the Sixteenth Century*, 1904, 314 *sqq*. Cf. Maitland, *History of London*; A. F. Leach, *English Schools at the Reformation*, 1896; the Review in the *Times Literary Supplement* (March 2, 1933, p. 141) of H. W. Saunders's *Norwich Grammar School*; G. E. Hodgson, *Unpublished Documents relating to the Suppression of Yorkshire Chantries*. A thesis for Edinburgh University, 1930. Leach gives "Specimens of Edwardian Spoliation", (p. 114 *sqq*.), and in Part II of his "Documents", (122 *sqq*.), the instructions given to the various commissions appointed to liquidate the chantries. Bath school, which continued a wealthy Benedictine priory, was indeed lavishly endowed by Edward VI. But the town appropriated the greater part of the royal grant and even refused to provide scholarships. See Mrs. K. E. Symons, *The Grammar School of King Edward VI, Bath*, Bath, 1934.

[2] *Acts of the Privy Council*, III, passim; Strype, *Ecclesiastical Memorials*, IV, 16 *sqq*.; cf. ibid., III, 461, 480. Dixon, 276 *sq*. gives in a note a list of church property granted to various gentlemen.

[3] *Op. cit.*, 478.

in his Journal.[1] It meant the impoverishment of the Church of England and her clergy, as Anglican historians sadly point out.[2] Already Calvin had written to Somerset on July 25, 1551, urging him "to put things in order".[3] "The stipends of the clergy," he says, "are so alienated and squandered that there is not sufficient to maintain good men fit to exercise the office of true pastors. Ignorant priests are therefore appointed. . . . Those who to-day are profiting from church goods suffer no detriment, if the pastors receive a sufficient living. . . . Indeed they will benefit by making provision for this. For they cannot prosper, if they defraud God's people of their spiritual pasture, by depriving the churches of good pastors." Even Archbishop Cranmer, though so pliant and so submissive to the authority of the civil ruler, protested and opposed the spoliation Warwick had determined to carry out. Employing the Henricians' argument, he said that the government should wait until the king attained his majority and could decide himself how he would dispose of the wealth of the Church.[4] "I have heard," Ridley wrote, "that Cranmer" was "in high displeasure for repugning . . . against the late spoil of the church goods, taken away only by commandment of the higher powers without any law or order of justice."[5] The protest, as the Imperial Ambassador observes,[6]

[1] Cf. Edward's *Journal*, Burney, V, 34, 48; British Museum, Add. MS., 5498, fol. 40; ed. Lodge, *Illustrations of British History*, 1838, I, 149 *sq.* The reports of the chantry commissioners appointed under the act of 1547 are preserved in the Record Office (M. S. Giuseppe, *A Guide to the Manuscripts preserved in the Public Record Office*, London, 1923–1924, I, 140–141). Those for Wales, Somerset, Gloucestershire and Shropshire have been printed (C. Read, *Infra Cit.*, Nos. 1500 and 4296a), also for Kent (*Kent Chantries*, edited by A. Hussey for the Kent Archaeological Society, 2 vols., 1932 and 1936).
[2] Heylyn, I, 126 *sq.*; Collier, V, 188 *sq.*, 228 *sq.*, 256 *sq.*; Dixon, III, 276 *sq.*, 455 *sq.*
[3] Strype, *Memorials of Cranmer*, II, 655. App. lviii.
[4] *Morice's Anecdotes of Archbishop Cranmer*, in J. G. Nichols, *Narratives of the Reformation*, Camden Society, 1859, p. 247; Heylyn, I, 103; Burnet, II, 101; Collier, V, 226.
[5] *Piteous Lamentation* in *Works of N. Ridley*, ed. Parker Society, 1841, p. 59.
[6] *Sp. Cal.*, X, 389, 453, 591, 593; XI, 33.

cost Cranmer his influence at Court. Bishop Latimer, though his zeal for the Reformation made him violent against the clergy, complained that large numbers of churchmen were destitute, though it was incumbent upon the laity and the king to provide for their subsistence. He knew, he tells us, an important and commercial town whose population was very wealthy, in which the priest's stipend was not more than 12 or 14 marks a year. How, he asked, could he buy books or offer his neighbour a drink? All the money went elsewhere. "To consider," he preached, "what hath been plucked from abbeys, college chantries, it is marvel no more to be bestowed upon this holy office of Salvation. Every man scrapeth and getteth together for his bodily house, but the soul's health is neglected. I think verily there are a great many, which if the minister should have no living but at their appointment, he would not have clouting leather to piece his shoes with." And addressing the profiteers of the pillage he exclaimed: "My lords . . . all such proceedings . . . do intend plainly to make the yeomanry slavery and the clergy shavery. We of the clergy had too much, but that is taken away and we have too little".[1] "Many clergymen," Burnet adds, "were carpenters and tailors and some kept alehouses".[2] Bucer himself in his *De Regno Christi* warns Edward against "men greedy for the goods of the Church, who hope that when they have once been confiscated, no one will devote himself to the cure of souls."[3] And the danger of this was the greater since celibacy having been

[1] *The Sermons and Life of Hugh Latimer some time Bishop of Worcester.* Ed. John Watkins, London, 1858, I, 94, 274, 288. Cf. Heylyn, I, 126.

[2] *Op. cit.*, II, 340.

[3] Book II, cap. iv, quoted by Gasquet and Bishop, (*Edward VI and the Book of Common Prayer*, 1890, p. 300 *sqq.*) and A. F. Pollard (*Thomas Cranmer*, 1904, 227 *sqq.*), Dixon (III, 2).

See Burnet, I, 531; II, 43, 101, 137; V, 6; Heylyn, I, 74, 126; Fuller, Book VI, section 6, ed. 1845, III, 466–480; Collier, V, 146, 147, 226–228, 238, 256 *sqq.*; Dixon, II, 280, 379, 381, 460, 500 *sqq.*; III, 108, 126, 263 *sqq.*, 276, 455.

abolished, priests and curates had now families to support.[1]

In one of the sermons from which I have quoted, Latimer says, "For mine own part I have no cause to complain for, I thank God and the King, I have sufficient." Cranmer, however, the Primate of England, wrote to William Cecil on July 21, 1552, "I fear stark beggary. For I took not half so much care for living when I was a scholar of Cambridge as I do at this present. For although I have now much revenue, yet have I much more to do withal. . . . If I knew any Bishop that were covetous, I would surely admonish him. But I know none, but all beggars, except it be one" (Holgate, Archbishop of York) "and yet I dare well say, he is not very rich."[2] In fact after the parochial endowments, the episcopal revenues had tempted the cupidity of Warwick and his government. Every new bishop was obliged on his nomination to surrender a manor or two belonging to his see. When Ridley was translated from Rochester to London (1550) he surrendered a number of estates and houses, the property of his new see, and in a letter to Cecil of September 6, 1551, he informs him that the royal officials are literally plundering his woods and forests.[3] When, in 1551, Ponet succeeded Gardiner as Bishop of Winchester, he was obliged to surrender to the Crown all the possessions of his see in exchange for a yearly income of 2,000 marks. Hooper did the same when he became Bishop of Worcester in 1552. And his former see, Gloucester, was suppressed and replaced by an archdeaconry to facilitate the confiscation of its endowments.[4] When sees fell vacant it was an excellent

[1] *Statutes of the Realm*, 2 and 3, Edward VI, cap. 21; 5 and 6, Edward VI cap. 12. Cf. Heylyn, I, 139–143, 268.
[2] *Latimer's Sermons*, ed. above-mentioned, 194; *The Remains of Thomas Cranmer*, ed. H. Jenkyns, Oxford, 1833, I, 351 or *Cranmer's Works*, ed. Parker Society, II, 437, or Strype, *Memorials of Cranmer*, App. No. 67 (ed. 1848, III, 673). For Holgate, see ed. Lodge, *op. cit.*, I, 153 Note.
[3] P. Fr. Tytler, *op. cit.*, I, 431.
[4] Strype, *Ecclesiastical Memorials*, II, 526; Burnet, II, 341.

opportunity to plunder their revenues. A vacancy in the see of Lincoln from August 1551 to June 1552, made possible, Collier informs us, "a fearful pillage," which left the new bishop but a single manor, that of Buckden, with a few small estates.[1] Burnet mentions other instances and concludes: "In all the vacancies of sees, there were a great many of their best lands taken from them: and the sees that before had been profusely enriched, were now brought to so low a condition, that it was scarce possible for the bishops to subsist: and yet if what was so taken from them had been converted to good uses, to the bettering the condition of the poor clergy over England, it had been some mitigation of so heinous a robbery; but these lands were snatched up by every hungry courtier who found this the easiest way to be satisfied in their pretensions."[2]

The see of Westminster was suppressed (1552). It had already been impoverished by the avarice of the courtiers. What remained of its possessions was used to repair Saint Paul's, which was in a serious state of dilapidation. This, it would seem, is the origin of the expression "robbing Peter to pay Paul."[3]

Certain bishops were accused of lukewarmness towards the Reformation. To keep their sees they were obliged to compound with those in power. Salcot of Salisbury, for example, surrendered to certain of Warwick's favourites, advantageous leases of his farms and manors. Sampson of Lichfield and Coventry divested himself of a large part of the possessions of his see to allow William Paget to create a barony for himself with them. Kitchen of Llandaff alienated almost all the estate of his wealthy see and let the remainder for a modest rental.

More than one bishop, under compulsion, or to win the favour of his temporary masters, surrendered episcopal possessions to some powerful lord. In 1550 Aldrich of

---

[1] Heylyn, I, 275 *sqq.*; Collier, V, 488.　　[2] Burnet, *op. cit.*, II, 341 *sqq.*
[3] Collier, V, 257; Dixon, III, 441.

Carlisle sold to Lord Clinton, Earl of Lincoln, the lord-ships of Horncastle, Nethercompton, Overcompton, Marning, Ashby, Conesby, Haltam, Thimelby, Boughton, Morley, Enderby, and Moram. Shortly after he gave up to him an annual rent of £200, paid by the Bishop of Hereford for his town house in London. Holbeach, "that zealous apostle of the Gospel" as Strype calls him, alienated forty-four properties of his bishopric of Lincoln. John Voysey, Bishop of Exeter, administered the pos-sessions of his see so well, that whereas their value on his appointment was more than £1,565, his successor received no more than £500.[1] Bucer, in his *De Regno Dei*, raised a cry of alarm: "A bishop should consider what a hideous sacrilege it is to impoverish churches in return for a few personal favours and to alienate their possessions to any purpose other than the service of God."[2]

To silence the protests audible here and there among the clergy, Warwick, speaking in Parliament, expressed his indignation against those who dared to denounce the pillage in their sermons, and warned the bishops to put a stop to it. It was, he said, a scandalous attitude, calculated to foment disorder and sedition.[3]

One use made of these possessions of the Church was to reward Warwick's supporters, and confirm their allegiance to him. They glutted their greed with them. The Earl of Bedford, John Russell, with an accomplice named Downing, secured five estates, the last remnants of the see of Gloucester. Sir William Herbert, Earl of Pembroke, added to his possessions numerous estates belonging to the see of Durham and Saint Dunstan's Church in London. Sir Philip Hoby took Evesham Abbey from the see of

[1] Strype, *Ecclesiastical Memorials*, II, 217, 232, 272, 277, 361.
[2] In his commentary on the Decalogue he says: "Cursed be every man who sacrilegiously robs God and His Churches of what has been dedicated to the maintenance of holy and faithful ministers of religion, for schools or the poor."
[3] Despatch of the Imperial Ambassador, J. Scheyfve, April 10, 1553. *Sp. Cal.*, XI, 33.

Worcester to carve out an estate for himself. The Earl of Westmorland, a man of very ill repute but a creature of Warwick's, received the Garter from the king and five manors. Sir Thomas Palmer and Sir Anthony Wingfield shared between them a number of plundered estates and houses.[1] From Strype, Thomas Tanner, the State Papers at the Record Office and manuscripts in the British Museum, an entire series of lists could be compiled of grants made by the king in the latter part of his reign from the possessions of churches and hospitals, and what yet remained of the monastic booty taken by his father.[2] At the same time the prebends of cathedrals and collegiate churches, food for the lesser nobility, were bestowed on gentlemen who had no intention of taking orders.[3]

Warwick did not forget his own pocket. "He is always short of money," the Imperial Ambassador had remarked as early as 1550.[4] "So much is required to satisfy his taste for luxury and display. He has therefore taken to visiting the less compliant prelates to see what he can extract from them." He laid hands on the manors of Feckenham, Bromsgrove and King's Norton in Worcestershire and other estates too many to enumerate. He dreamed of taking in the North the place hitherto occupied by the wealthy family of the Percys, whose influence had greatly declined in the last reign, and

[1] No. lxvii of Collier's *Documents* (IX, 295 *sqq.*), consists of "alienations of Church property under Edward VI, chiefly the property of episcopal sees." See also Strype, *Ecclesiastical Memorials*, IV, 32, 74 *sqq.*, 107, 115, 236, 238. Lodge (*Illustr. of Brit. Hist.*, I, 158 n.) says that Warwick considerably enriched with church spoils Sir Thomas Gargrave, President of the Council of the North.

[2] Strype, *Eccl. Mem.*, IV, 32, 75, 105, 115, 236; Tanner, *Notitia Monastica*, 1695, gives a list of "gifts of monasteries and hospitals, anno 7, Edward VI." Record Office, Vol. XIX of *State Papers, Domestic*, Edward VI, with a full index of names. (Cf. *Calendar of State Papers, Domestic*, 1547–1580, 53), and No. 600, *Calendar and Indexes, Court of Excheq. Augm. Off. Class. Deeds of Purchase and Exchange.* British Museum Cotton MSS. Julius B ix; Galba B xi, 39; Vespasian F xiii, 177.

[3] Strype, *Eccl. Mem.*, II, 280, 283. Cf. Burnet, II, 44 *sqq.*

[4] Van der Delft to Charles V, March 8, 1550, *Sp. Cal.*, X, 43.

carving out for himself in Northumberland a species
of county palatinate. The see of Durham, one of
the wealthiest in England, whose occupant had the
title of Earl Palatine, was suppressed. Parliament
had indeed decided to employ its possessions in creating
two sees, the one at Durham, the other at Newcastle.
But in May 1553, the King erected the domain of the
see into a county palatine, which he bestowed on Warwick
who had already taken possession of the Bishop of Durham's London palace. Edward's death a few weeks later,
frustrated the Duke's ambition and saved the bishopric,
which Mary soon re-established at Durham.[1] "They
were beginning to gnaw and devour the last bones,"
wrote the Anglican bishop Godwin at the opening of the
seventeenth century[2] "when God to punish all this
sacrilegious robbery took from the world the young
king so full of promise."

The episcopal historian Burnet writing a century and
a quarter after the event, deplores the pillage, and in
doing so is the mouthpiece of the entire Anglican clergy.
"A fourth prejudice" (against the Reformation) he
wrote on September 10, 1680,[3] "is raised from the
great invasions which were then made upon the church
lands and things dedicated to pious uses; which is a

---

[1] *Journal of the Lords*, 442; *Statutes of the Realm*, IV, 226; Fr. Godwin,
De Praesulibus Angliae Commentarius, 1616, Prov. Ebor., 139; Heylyn, I,
287–291; Fuller, IV, 103 *sqq.*; Strype, *Eccl. Mem.*, II, 395; the same, *The
History of the Life and Acts of Ed. Grindal*, ed. 1821, 10 *sqq.*; Collier, V, 492
sqq.; VI, 71; Dixon, III, 506, 511, 535; Tytler, II, 315 *sqq.*, 373. Burnet,
(II, 359) appealing to the Act of Parliament, combats the account of
Warwick's action given by earlier writers. But he contradicts himself a
few lines later on, when he admits that in May 1553, the domains of the
see were transformed into a county palatine which the King bestowed upon
the Duke. Moreover, J. S. Brewer refutes him in a note to his edition of
Fuller (Oxford 1845, IV, 104). In October 1552 (Tytler, II, 142 *sqq.*),
Warwick wrote to Cecil that when the two new bishoprics of Durham and
Newcastle had been endowed, the remainder of the lands of the old see of
Durham would more than bring the Crown an annual revenue of at least
£2,000. What followed shows what he meant by the Crown. Cf. Lodge,
op. cit., I, 155 Note.

[2] *Loc. cit.*

[3] Preface to the second part of his *History of the Reformation*, published in
1681, ed. Pocock, II, 12 *sqq.* Cf. Collier, 188 *sqq.*

thing hated by men of all religions and branded with the odious names of *sacrilege* and *robbing of God*; so that the spoils of religious houses and churches seem to have been the secret motives that at first drew in, and still engage, so many to the Reformation." Then reminding his readers that in every religion he who has the cure of souls should be set free from secular scares and assured of his subsistence, he continues, "A decent maintenance of the clergy is of natural right and that it is not better looked to is a public reproach to the whole nation. This is as high a contempt of religion and the gospel as any can be, and is one of those things for which this nation has much to answer to God: that now in one hundred and twenty years' time so little has been done by public authority for the redress of such a crying oppression. . . . Some hundreds of parishes in England pay not ten pounds a year to their pastors, and perhaps some thousands not fifty. This is to be numbered among those crying sins that . are bringing down vengeance on us, since by this many souls are left to perish, because it is not possible to provide them with able and faithful shepherds. . . . I pray God to inspire and direct his Majesty and his two houses of Parliament effectually to remove this just and, for ought I know, only great scandal of our English reformation."

Having laid hands on the bishoprics and their possessions, Warwick proceeded to annex the bishops by appointing men who would be his creatures. Already Edward's first Parliament had obliterated the last vestige of ecclesiastical liberty by substituting for the *congé d'élire*, preserved by Henry VIII, simple letters patent, which, as Dixon remarks, made a bishop a "kind of ecclesiastical sheriff."[1] The bishops had, indeed, twice attempted in

---

[1] *Statutes of the Realm*, I, Edward VI, cap. 2. Cf. Heylyn, I, 104 *sqq.*, Burnet, II, 76 *sqq.*, 362 *sqq.*, Collier, V, 220 *sqq.*; IX, 244 *sqq.*, where the sum is given, payable by each bishop to the king or his officials for his nomination and consecration. It might be as much as £33; Dixon, II, 458; III, 186, 197, 214, 254.

Parliament to recover something of their jurisdiction, which was being increasingly swallowed up by the temporal power. But Parliament, which disliked and distrusted the spirituality, had on each occasion refused their request.[1] Warwick intended to make the bishops his tools. Since it served his ends to promote the Reformation, he raised to the episcopate men who, a few years before, would have been burned as heretics. There was the satirist Bale for instance. His language was more daring than suitable to a churchman, and he had been obliged in the last reign to seek refuge abroad. But in his *Expostulation with a Frantic* he had compared Warwick with Moses; and Warwick made him an Irish Bishop (1551). Bale was a married man, and as he said, "no Mass merchant," but an indefatigable preacher, disliked, as also was his wife, by his clergy and people. On Mary's accession he lost no time "in shaking off the dust of his feet" against the city of Ossory, comparing himself with Saint Paul. Miles Coverdale, who had been compelled to find safety at Hamburg[2] while his translation of the Bible was publicly burned (1546)—replaced at Exeter the nonagenarian Voysey (August 14, 1551). He was married to Elisabeth Macheson whose sister collaborated in the first translation of the Bible into Danish. He was very unpopular with his flock; and Queen Mary imprisoned him. The King of Denmark's intervention obtained his release.[3] To "stimulate" Cranmer's blunted zeal Warwick wanted to place in the see of Rochester the Scottish Calvinist John Knox, who had been involved in the successful

---

[1] Collier, V, 362.

[2] See his *Vocation of John Bale to the Bishopric of Ossory in Ireland: His Persecutions in the Same and Final Deliverance.* Rome at the sign of St. Peter, December 1553. Cf. J. G. Nichols, *Narratives of the Days of the Reformation*, P. XVI, 61, 287, 315.

[3] For Coverdale, see Hooker, *Bishops of Exeter*, 1584; *Mem. of Coverdale*, 1838; Strype, *Memorials of Cranmer*, II, 347, 363, 371; III, 24, 38, 343; J. G. Nichols, *op. cit.*, 295; J. Gairdner, *Lollardy and the Reformation*, 1908–1913, II, 249–260, 271–277, 461; III, 249, 255 *sqq.*: IV, 25 *sqq.*, 338.

plot to murder Cardinal Beaton and had been sent to the French galleys. That he might rave the more comfortably against "the idolatry of the Mass", Warwick had appointed him preacher at Berwick and Newcastle, and a royal chaplain, and had presented him to a London living.[1] Hooper also was never weary of fulminating against the Blessed Sacrament, that idol, as he called it, and "this God made of fine flour." He was made Bishop first of Gloucester (1550–1552) then of Worcester (1552–1553). This strange bishop was a former monk who having embraced Calvinism, had to fly abroad and remain abroad till Henry's death. On his return to England he became the leader of a small but noisy group of reformers on the extreme left, who objected to the pomp of episcopal functions and desired to free the liturgy and public worship of every vestige of ceremony and reduce it to the most severe simplicity, destroying "candles, sacerdotal vestments, crosses, and altars, that legacy of Satan." He refused at first the bishopric of Gloucester because he regarded the oath of allegiance to the King as impious. Nor would he wear the episcopal vestments which he called "Aaronic" relics of "Jewish bondage". It was in vain that Archbishop Cranmer, Bucer, and Peter Martyr pleaded with him. To persuade him, the government sent him to prison. There he reflected that it would be as well to put an end to the vexatious "tragedy", and that he ought to give way for the good of the Church. He therefore allowed himself to be consecrated, his conscience meanwhile secretly protesting against the impiety of the ceremonial (March 8, 1551). "From that

[1] See in Tytler (II, 142), his letter of October 28, 1552, in which he urges that Knox should be appointed bishop "to be a whetstone to quicken and sharp the Bishop of Canterbury." Cf., ibid., I, 295 Note; Heylyn, II, 120, 178–182, 297, 318 *sq.*, 324, 326; Fuller, IV, 217; Burnet, II, 294, 544; Strype, *Memorials of Cranmer*, II, Chapter 17 and App. xli. (Peter Martyr's reply to Hooper); Collier, 154 *sq.*; Dixon, II, 326–330, 475–481, 485–487, 491; *Original Letters from Zurich Archives*, ed. Parker Soc.; Lorimer, *John Knox and the Church of England*, 1875; James Stalker, *John Knox, His Idea and Ideals*, 1904.

time his influence with the council increased daily."[1]
He took advantage of it to plunder the churches and
their wealth—to cleanse them, he called it, "from the
idols of Baal" and "the devil's wares".[2]

The same vandalistic fanaticism inspired Ridley, whom
Warwick translated from Rochester to London, to throw
out onto the rubbish heap London's shrines, sacred
sculpture and tomb-stones. "When churches were thus
treated," says an Anglican writer, "by those who should
have been especially their guardians, it is not surprising
that their sacred character was altogether lost sight of
by the multitude."[3]

John Ponet, who married the wife of a butcher in her
husband's lifetime, and then publicly divorced her in
St. Paul's, was raised at the age of thirty-five to the see
of Rochester (1550), and from Rochester was translated
to Winchester (1551). In his usual fashion Burnet accuses
Sanders of inventing this story of the marriage and divorce.
"This story," he says "is a forgery". But its truth is
attested by two contemporary documents, the *Grey Friars'
Chronicle* and Machyn's *Diary*. And Ponet's conduct, they
tell us, was all the more scandalous because at the time of
the divorce he was Bishop of Winchester and had to pay
the butcher a pension. Nevertheless, he remarried a few
weeks later before a crowd of parishioners—*coram multitudine
parochianorum*—as the Croydon marriage register records.[4]

[1] Micronius to Bullinger, March 9, 1552. *Zurich Original Letters*, XII,
580. Cf. 588.
[2] See C. H. Smyth, *Cranmer and the Reformation under Edward VI*, Cambridge, 1926, 95–105, 194 *sq*., 202, 220, 276 *sq*.; J. Gairdner, Bishop
Hooper's *Visitation of Gloucester in Engl. Hist. Review*, Vol. XIX (1904),
98–121; G. Baskerville, *Elections to Convocation in the Diocese of Gloucester
under Bishop Hooper* (shows the effect upon the clergy of the religious changes).
Ibid., Vol. XLIV, (1929), 1–32.
[3] J. H. Blunt, *The Reformation of the Church of England*, 1892–1896, II,
98 *sq*., 157–160, 399, 407–410. Cf. C. Hardwick, *Hist. of the Christian
Church*, ed. Stubbs, 1872, 199; *Zurich Original Letters*, XII, 712; *J. Calvini
Opera*, ed. Baum, Cunitz, Reuss, p. xiii, col. 625–630 (Utenhove to Calvin,
August 23, 1550); Strype, *Cranmer*, II, 205–224, 258, 627 *sqq*., 663 C. J. G.
Nichols, *op. cit*, 158, 264 *sqq*. Albèri Series, II, 249.
[4] Burnet, *An Appendix Concerning some of the Errors and Falsehoods in
Sander's Book of the English Schism*, Pocock's ed. of *The History of the Reforma-*

With such bishops the Reformation could not fail to make rapid progress. This, in fact, was Warwick's intention. But was his action motived by a genuine religious conviction? No, the historian A. F. Pollard replies.[1] To make the country fanatically Protestant by a radical reformation would debar the Catholic Mary from the throne, open a way for his own family to ascend it, and insure his wealth and power in the next reign. The ardent zeal of the new Moses cloaked the unbridled ambition of an adventurer.

---

tion, V, 603; *Chronicle of the Grey Friars of London,* July 27, 1551, ed. Nichols, 70; *The Diary of Henry Machyn,* same date, ed. Nichols, 8. 320.

[1] *Thomas Cranmer,* 1904, 276. After an interview with Warwick, Knox was perspicacious enough to detect his selfish ambition. See his *Admonition to the Professors of the Truth in England,* 53. Cf. Tytler (II, 154 *sqq.*), where a letter from Northumberland to Cecil of January 3, 1553, is given which Tytler calls "a masterpiece of hypocrisy".

CHAPTER VI

THE CHURCH OF ENGLAND TURNS TOWARDS CALVINISM
THE SECOND PRAYER BOOK (1552).

Projects for a more thoroughgoing reform—The men who refashioned the Prayer Book of 1549—The Second Prayer Book (1552)—The English Ordinal of 1550–1552 and the validity of Anglican Orders.

UNDER Somerset's successor, Warwick (October 1549–July 1553) the Reformation made rapid progress in England. In three years, the country witnessed more religious changes than in the twenty years since Wolsey's fall. Anglican doctrine was reduced to the level of continental Protestantism.

As we have seen,[1] the Book of Common Prayer represented a compromise between Catholic and Protestant doctrine. Theologians of such different views and character had taken part in its composition that its doctrine had become sufficiently flexible to be accepted by men of conflicting beliefs. Protector Somerset had aimed at a system of uniform worship whose vague and non-committal formulas would win the assent of the largest possible number. These formulas were couched in such terms that Gardiner, the leader of the Henricians, could state in writing that the book "was godly and Christian";[2] that as regards the Eucharist "the true faith of this holy mystery . . . in the Book of Common Prayer is well termed, not distant

[1] Chapter III.
[2] This was one of the articles he signed in 1550 when questioned in the Tower about the Prayer Book. Cf. Gasquet and Bishop *op. cit.*, 278, *Gardiner's Long Matter* in Foxe, *op. cit.*, VI, 113 *sq.*; Muller, *Stephen Gardiner and the Tudor Reaction*, London, 1926, 187 *sq.*

from the Catholic faith in my judgment,"[1] and that he would, therefore, use and cause it to be used everywhere in his diocese.[2]

"The ceremonies," Sanders wrote, "and the form of administering the Holy Eucharist drawn up in this first assembly of the estates of the realm, scarcely differed from those observed in the celebration of the Catholic Mass. This was done that the people might not think anything of the latter had been removed or cut away, but should believe that what had formerly been read in Latin was now being read in English. Therefore, at first the Canon of the Mass was almost verbally translated. Even the signs of the cross made in blessing, were retained; those, I mean, made by the celebrant alone."

This policy of compromise was not that of the new government. The first Prayer Book was certainly Lutheran in its tendency. But after Somerset's fall the Anglican Church was hurried beyond Lutheranism towards the more radical views of the Swiss reformers. The Prayer Book of 1549 was, therefore, doomed.

From its first publication it had been violently attacked by the advanced Protestants. Traheron, alluding to the semi-Catholic compromise, exclaimed, "These fools of bishops have made a fine recantation."[3] Dryander complained that "certain ceremonies are useless, perhaps harmful, at least if they are not given an innocent interpretation," that the book spoke of the Lord's Supper "in very obscure" language not always easy to understand in the Protestant sense, and that "ambiguous

---

[1] *An Explication and Assertion of the True Catholique Fayth, Touchyng the Moost Blessed Sacrament of the Aulter with Confutacion of a Booke written against the Same,* Rouen, 1551, ed. in Cranmer's *Works,* 1841, 92; ed. Jenkyns, 171. It was a reply to Cranmer's book published the previous year: *A Defence of the True and Catholic Doctrine of the Sacrament of the Body and Blood of our Saviour Christ.*

[2] This is what Gardiner wrote to the Privy Council, Heylyn, *op. cit.,* I, 209; Strype, *Memorials of Cranmer,* Book II, Chaper XIX. Cf. Muller, *Stephen Gardiner,* 187 sq.

[3] Traheron to Bullinger, *Zurich Original Letters,* I, 323.

and cunning language is intolerable in religion."[1]
Bucer and Fagius censured as superstitious the sacerdotal
vestments, the use of candles at the Communion service,
the commemoration of the dead, and the use of chrism
at baptism.[2] Calvin condemned as "manifest abuses
. . . prayer for the dead, and pleading before God the
intercession of the saints".[3] Hooper, a royal chaplain,
said that the Prayer Book was "manifestly defective, of
dubious meaning, and in some points plainly impious."[4]
On December 27, 1549, he wrote to his friend, Bullinger,
"The public celebration of the Supper is far removed
from Our Lord's order and institution. Though administered under two kinds, it is celebrated in some
places thrice daily. The sacerdotal vestments are retained[5] and the candles before the altar. . . . Moreover,
that Popery may not disappear, the priests, though forbidden any longer to use Latin, continue the tone and
fashion of chanting to which they have hitherto been
accustomed."[6]

Preaching before the king in Lent, 1550, Hooper
urged that the Prayer Book should be revised. It was
a book, in Calvin's words, "full of tolerable absurdities,"
"tolerable things to be born with for the weak's sake
awhile."[7] "Great shame it is," he adds, "for a noble
King, emperor or magistrate, contrary unto God's
word, to detain and keep from the devil or his minister
any of their goods or treasure as the candles, vestments,
crosses, altars."[8] "As ye have taken the Mass from the
people," he exclaimed on another occasion, "so take

---

[1] Dryander to his master, Bullinger, ibid., 350–351.
[2] Letter from Bucer and Fagius to their colleagues at Strasbourg. Written
from Lambeth Palace, April 26, 1549, ibid., 535–536.
[3] Calvin to Edward VI, *Zurich Original Letters*, I, 707.
[4] *Zurich Original Letters*, I, 332–333.
[5] *Zurich Original Letters*, I, 72.
[6] Calvin to the English Protestants at Frankfort, February 15, 1555.
Calvini. Opera, ed. Baum, Cunitz and Reuss, Vol. XIV, col. 394.
[7] Hooper, *Works*, I, 479.
[8] Ibid., I, 534.

from them her feathers, also the altar vestments and such like as apparelled her."[1]

It was after these violent diatribes against the Book of Common Prayer that Hooper, who prided himself on professing, together with Cranmer, the Eucharistic doctrine of the Swiss reformers,[2] received from Warwick the see of Gloucester. Bishop Ponet also preached before the young King (March 1550) that the antiquity of a ceremony or rite does not justify its preservation. That our ancestors have done anything is no reason why we should do it. By this reason, if our forefathers denied Christ, we must also deny Christ.[3]

Though he was more moderate than his colleagues, and though the Prayer Book was his own work, Cranmer was not altogether satisfied with it. The concessions for which Somerset had asked, had prevented him from introducing into it his new sacramental belief.[4] Influenced by the foreign Protestants, he desired more radical changes, and regarded the first Prayer Book as but a "stage" on the road of reform. He imparted his views to Bucer, Peter Martyr, Fagius, Dryander, Emanuele Tremellio[5] and certain French Protestants, at a meeting held at Lambeth Palace in April 1549. The relics of Catholicism in the book, he informed them, "were only for a time, and lest excessive changes should repel the people who had not yet learned to know Jesus Christ and embrace His religion."[6] At the close of 1550 he proposed to Convocation the revision of certain parts of the Book.[7] Calvin, moreover, stimulated the Arch-

[1] *Early Writings*, Parker Society, 440.
[2] *Zurich Original Letters*, I, 71.
[3] *A Notable Sermon*, London, 1550, fol. 2.
[4] In his *Answer of* 1551 to Gardiner's book on the Eucharist, he attempts to show that the 1549 Prayer Book is in harmony with his views, but obviously he does so under compulsion and to meet the exigencies of controversy.
[5] Or Tremelius of Ferrara.
[6] Letter from Bucer and Fagius, Lambeth Palace, April 26, 1549. *Zurich Original Letters*, I, 536.
[7] Festivals to be kept or abolished, the formula for administering communion. Heylyn is our authority for this. (*Op. cit.*, I, 227.)

bishop's zeal urging him to make an end of compromise, and tergiversation, and dig up the roots of Popish Superstition. "The exalted position which you occupy," he wrote, "fixes the eyes of all upon you. The people will follow your lead or remain inert under the cloak of your lukewarmness. Had you led the attack boldly, three years ago,[1] superstition would have been destroyed with less labour and conflict. Do not slumber at ease. Do not imagine you have reached the goal. . . . To speak plainly, I fear that so many autumns wasted in procrastination may be followed by an eternal winter. I fear you may die with the knowledge that you delayed too long and have left everything in confusion. Though foreign superstitions have been corrected, there still remains in the ground many vigorous shoots and more than one parasite. I mean the many relics of popery."[2] Cranmer promised to follow Calvin's advice. "We shall reform the Anglican Church to the utmost of our power, and take care to correct her doctrines and usages in accordance with the rule of Holy Scripture."[3]

---

[1] This allusion to the Prayer Book of 1549 enables us to date Calvin's letter to 1551.

[2] J. Calvini, *Opera*, ed. Baum, Cunitz, Reuss, XIII, 682–683. Cf. 312, a letter of April or May 1551. Cf. Strype, *Memorials of Cranmer*, Book II, Chapter XXV. See also Calvin's letter to Somerset, July 25, 1551, ibid., App. LVIII, ed. 1848, 654.

The Scot Alexander Aless, professor of theology at Leipzig, had published in 1551, a Latin translation of the Prayer Book, in which he strove to adapt it to the taste of the Calvinists as well as the Lutherans. The numerous alterations made in his unfaithful translation are deliberate, the result of this intention. To please the Calvinists he cut out all mention of anointing in baptism and the visitation of the sick. To please the Lutherans he used their terminology, even borrowing the formula of the *Pia Consultatio* for the absolution before communion. (See Proctor *History of the Prayer Book*, 65.) He even tried to please Charles V, who had authorised the translation. He made use of Catholic phrases which had been banished from the Prayer Book, for example "Officium Missae", "Ad Introitum Missae" and translated "congregatio" "congregation" by "Ecclesia. Dixon, *op. cit.*, III, Note on pp. 295–297.

[3] Cranmer to Calvin, Lambeth, October 5, 1551. Cf. Calvini, *Opera*. Ed. Baum, p. 14, col. 370. Cf. Strype, *Memorials of Cranmer*, Book II, Chapter XXV.

In his diocese of London, Ridley[1] anticipated Cranmer's secret hopes, and publicly professed his desire for more thoroughgoing reforms. His instructions for the visitation of his diocese, issued on May 5, 1550, are concerned not so much with enforcing the Prayer Book introduced the year before, as with effecting openly or covertly more radical changes. "No minister" may "counterfeit the Popish Mass as to kiss the Lord's table, washing his fingers at any time in the Communion, blessing his eyes with the paten or sudary, or crossing his head with the paten, shifting of the book from one place to another, laying down and licking the chalice of the Communion, holding up his fingers hands or thumbs joined towards his temples, breathing upon the bread or chalice; shewing the Sacrament openly before the distribution of the Communion; ringing of sacring bells, or setting any light upon the Lord's board at any time."[2] Moreover, Ridley led the destruction and the vandalism. Unsupported by any statute or royal injunction, on his own authority he ordered the altars to be replaced by tables. "Whereas in divers places" his instructions of 1550 continue,[3] "some use the Lord's board after the form of a table and some as an altar, whereby dissension is perceived to arise among the unlearned: therefore, wishing a godly unity to be observed in all our diocese; and for that the form of a table may more move and turn the simple from the old superstitious opinion of the Popish Mass to the right use of the Lord's Supper, we exhort the curates, churchwardens and questmen here present to erect and set up the Lord's board after the form of an honest table, decently covered, in such place of the quire or chancel as shall be thought most meet by their

[1] He was translated from Rochester, of which see he had been Bishop from 1547 to 1550.
[2] Wilkins, *Concilia*, Vol. IV; Cardwell, *Synodalia*, Oxford, 1842, Vol. I, 94. On April 19, 1550, Ridley ordered the candles on the altar to be extinguished before he entered the choir. *Chronicle of the Grey Friars of London*, ed. Camden Society, 1859, p. 66.
[3] Wilkins and Cardwell, *loc. cit.*

discretion and agreement, so that the minister with the
communicants may have their places separated from the
rest of the people; and to take down and abolish all other
by-altars or tables." Ridley thus anticipated the
Prayer Book of 1552, which would abolish the altars
in every church throughout the kingdom. With the
altar was bound up the idea of sacrifice, of a victim,
which the reformers wished at all cost to eliminate
from the Mass, whereas the table symbolized only
communion, the participation of the faithful in the
Eucharistic banquet.[1] To replace the altar by the
table was to substitute, even in its external setting,
Holy Communion for the sacrifice of the Mass. Hooper
said that "the altars of Baal" must be "overturned."[2]
"As long as the altars remain," he preached, "both
the ignorant people and the ignorant, evil persuaded
priest will dream always of sacrifice."[3]

Ridley enforced precept by example. During the night
of St. Barnabas, June 11, 1550,[4] he demolished the
high altar at St. Paul's, and at the foot of the steps set
up a table in front of a large curtain hung across the
choir.[5] During Whit-week, Wriothesley relates in his
chronicle, the altars were removed from all the London
churches, and a table placed in the choir for the Communion service.[6]

[1] One of the reasons given by the Council in their order to the Bishops
to demolish the altars (November 24, 1550) was that since there were
no more sacrifices, there was no further need of altars. Cf. Heylyn, *op. cit.*,
I, 205 *sqq.*
[2] Hooper to Bullinger, November 27, 1550. *Zurich Original Letters*,
Parker Society, I, 79.
[3] Sermon on Jonas, *Early Writings*, 448. Cf. Heylyn, *op. cit.*, I, 201.
[4] To defend Ridley from the charge of illegality, Heylyn (*op. cit.*, I, 207)
says that he did this on St. Barnabas Day 1551. Collier follows him in this,
and Foxe also affirms that he did not demolish the altars until after the
injunction of November 1550. But these statements are refuted by the
Grey Friars' Chronicle.
[5] *Grey Friars' Chronicle*, Camden Society, 67.
[6] Wriothesley, *Chronicle*, ed. Camden Society, 1875, II, 41. Already in
March, according to Hooper, many altars had been demolished in London.
Hooper to Bullinger, March 27, 1550. *Zurich Original Letters*, Parker Society,
I, 79.

Far from forbidding this unauthorised innovation, Warwick gave it his support and encouragement.[1] A month later[2] he ordered the High Sheriff of Essex[3] to follow Ridley's example. On November 24 a letter from the Council ordered every Bishop to substitute tables for altars, "to have all occasions of contention taken away which many times groweth by these and suchlike diversities."[4]

To justify the innovation some reasons were adduced, possibly from Ridley's pen, and it was argued that the exchange was not in conflict with the Prayer Book of 1549, which "calleth the thing whereupon the Lord's Supper is ministered indifferently a table and an altar."

Thus the signal was given for a war against altars, for what an Anglican historian has termed their universal and lamentable destruction.[5] No respect was paid to their age or artistic beauty. When at the close of 1550 Thirlby reached his new diocese of Norwich, he found it stripped of altars.[6] And the following year the Venetian ambassador Barbaro reports that the English "still use bells and organs, but have no more altars or crosses."[7] Thus the pun of a Swiss student at Oxford, Jean Ulmer, *"arae factae sunt harae,"* was verified.[8] The

---

[1] Together with Ridley he had been a member of the Commission which the previous year, May 1549, had demolished six altars at Jesus College, Cambridge. Cooper, *Annals of Cambridge*, II, 28.

[2] On July 15, according to Edward's *Journal*, on the 22nd, according to the minutes of the Council.

[3] Sir John Gates.

[4] Heylyn, *op. cit.*, I, 202–203. A special letter was sent to Day of Chichester, ordering him not only to substitute tables for altars, but to explain in a sermon the reasons for the change.

[5] Dixon *op. cit.*, III, 203.

[6] *Norfolk Archaeology*, VII, 73. Cranmer had made a visitation of the diocese before Thirlby's arrival and it was by his orders that the altars had been removed. Thirlby had been Bishop of Westminster from 1540 to 1550.

[7] Alberi, *Relazioni degli Ambasciatori Veneti*, Series I, Vol. II, 247.

[8] The altars have been made into pigsties. Ulmer wrote this in 1548, when the chantries were abolished. (*Zurich Original Letters* I, 48). But it was in 1550 that the campaign against altars became universal.

people lost all reverence for the churches, which were regarded as no more sacred than stables or taverns.[1] They were often the scene of violent brawls, bloody fights and murders.[2]   Goods were bought and sold and games played in them even during service time.[3]   Mules and pigeons were allowed entrance,[4] and men indulged in pigeon shooting.[5]   It is from contemporary chronicles that we learn these facts.

Encouraged by Warwick, Ridley made further changes. Since in Catholic churches the altar faces the east, he placed the table, which took its place, in any other position.   On Holy Saturday, 1551, March 28, we learn from the *Grey Friars' Chronicle*, the position of the table in Saint Paul's was changed, and it was placed below the curtain facing north and south.   Next day the Dean officiated, standing on the south side of the table.[6] "When your table was constituted," Ridley was charged at his trial four years later, "you could never be content in placing the same, now east, now north, now one way, now another, until it pleased God of His goodness to place it clean out of the church."[7]

To make it even more plain that the Eucharist was no longer a sacrifice in whose offering those present took part, but a simple Communion which benefited only those who received it, Ridley had the gate leading into the choir closed, and a curtain drawn before it to prevent

[1] "Making the same" (the churches) "like a stable or common inn or rather a den or sink of all unchristianness." Royal Injunction of 1552 quoted by Strype, *Memorials of Cranmer*, II, 89. Cf. Strype, *Eccles. Mem.*, II, 524. In his *Censura*, Bucer complains that people walk about the church and converse during the time of service and that young ragamuffins make a deafening din.

[2] *Grey Friars' Chronicle*, Camden Society, 67, 68, 73 and the injunction just mentioned.

[3] A royal injunction was found necessary (Art. 13) commanding the churchwardens to see that no one bought or sold in the churches, or played games especially during service or the sermon, and that no talking or brawling should be permitted during service. Cf. Blunt, *op. cit.*, II, 160.

[4] Injunction of 1552, *loc. cit.*, *Grey Friars' Chronicle*, 68.

[5] *Grey Friars' Chronicle*, p. 68 and injunction of 1552.

[6] *Grey Friars' Chronicle*, p. 69; Wriothesley, *Chronicle*, II, 47.

[7] J. Gairdner, *The English Church in the XVIth Century.* 1904, 293.

non-communicants following the service (March 24, 1551).[1] All this harvest of innovations, all this agitation against the 1549 Prayer Book produced their effect. They exercised a powerful influence on the young king's mind. He had received his entire religious education from Protestant teachers, who thus acquired an ascendancy over him, and having moulded his mind and heart, flattered him unceasingly. They were loud in their praises of his "perfect grace, virtue, godly zeal . . . of passing high estimation."[2] Henceforward he heard nothing but denunciations of the abuses which still clung to his Church, and the remnants of idolatry which defiled it. Only the most fiery reformers preached before him. From Geneva Calvin urged him to advance more zealously along the path of salvation and eradicate to the last fibre the remains of Antichrist.[3] Bucer, Peter Martyr, Bourgoyne and Knox visited him in turn and further inflamed his ardour.

Edward was convinced that to hold out any longer against these repeated exhortations would endanger the Church. He pressed for a more thorough-going reform, and said he was prepared to take action himself, if the clergy showed themselves lukewarm. "The Archbishop" (Cranmer), Peter Martyr wrote from Lambeth on January 10, 1551, "has informed me that many changes have been determined upon. What they are I

[1] *Grey Friars' Chronicle*, Camden Society, 69; Wriothesley, *Chronicle*, I, 47. It was in Holy Week and at Easter that Ridley introduced the practice. Gairdner (*op. cit.*, 293) even says that he walled up the entrance of the choir with bricks and mortar. But the chronicles do not bear out his statement.
[2] Strype, *Memorials of Cranmer*, Book II, Chapter XXXIV, ed. 1848, Vol II, 424 *sq.*; Davey, *Lady Jane Grey*, 1909, 126 *sq.*
[3] Calvin to Edward VI, January, 1551. *Zurich Original Letters*, ed. Parker Soc., I, 707. Cranmer pressed Calvin to write frequently to Edward. Calvin to Farel, June 15, 1551. *Opera*, ed. Baum, Vol. XIV, Col. 133. Calvin also wrote to the Protector that "God's people should not be deprived of their spiritual food or the Churches of their pastors". (Strype, *Memorials of Cranmer*, App. LVIII, ed. 1848, II, 654; cf. ibid, 298.) Cf. J. T. Tomlinson, *Why was the First Prayer-book of Edward VI Rejected?* (London Church Association.)

dared not enquire. But Sir John Cheke[1] delighted me by saying that if Convocation should refuse to make them, the King himself would take the matter in hand and employ his royal authority in Parliament."[2] That is to say Edward himself was insisting that the 1549 Prayer Book should be revised and altered. A Committee had in fact just been appointed for the purpose.[3]

The Prayer Book had already been submitted to two famous continental reformers, one German, the other Italian, who were respectively the Regius Professors of Divinity at Cambridge and Oxford, namely Martin Bucer[4] and Peter Martyr.[5] Neither knew English. For Bucer's benefit the book was translated orally into Latin. Peter Martyr employed for the most important passages a translation sent him by the king's tutor, Sir John Cheke.[6] He gave his opinion in a memorandum now lost, and concluded by appealing to the judgment of Bucer, who had composed on the Prayer Book a treatise of twenty-eight chapters, known as the *Censura*. "As to the corrections you think necessary," he wrote to Bucer on January 10, 1551, "I am in entire agreement with you,

---

[1] Sir John Cheke, rector of St. John's College, Cambridge, and an intimate friend of Cranmer's, was the king's tutor. Cf. Strype, *Memorials of Cranmer*, 74 *sq.*, 425 and ibid., 657.

[2] Peter Martyr to Bucer, January 10, 1551. Strype, *Memorials of Cranmer*, App. LXI.

[3] The committee consisted of Cranmer, Holgate of York, Goodrich of Ely, Cox the Chancellor of Oxford, Skinner, a person unknown, a friend of Jean Ulmer's and some other doctors. It does not seem to have been a committee in the strict sense. Its members, it would appear, were charged with two tasks at the same time, to revise the Prayer Book and Canon Law. Skinner to Bullinger, Oxford, January 5, 1551. *Zurich Original Letters*, 314. Jean Ulmer to the same, Oxford, January 10, 1551. Ibid., 444.

[4] Bucer had been professor at Cambridge since the summer of 1549. He began his lectures in January, 1550. Cf. Strype, *Memorials of Cranmer*, Book II, Chapter II, 16.

[5] He was appointed professor in 1547. His lectures on the Lord's Supper, delivered in May, 1549, caused a great sensation and occasioned a debate which lasted for several days. Cf. Foxe, VI, 97-121. On January 20, 1550, he was appointed a Canon of Oxford. For Peter Martyr and his influence upon the English Reformation, see Strype, *Memorials of Cranmer*, Book II, Chapters X, XIII, XIV, XVI, XVII, XXIV, XXV.

[6] Strype, *Memorials of Cranmer*, Book II, Chapter XVI, ed. 1848, II, 203.

and I thank God for having given us this opportunity of advising the bishops, who, as the Archbishop (Cranmer) has told me, decided at their meeting to make many changes."[1]

A few weeks later Bucer died.[2] He had just completed his *De Regno Christi*, written in three months at the king's request, in which he repeated his suggestions for further reform.[3] His *Censura*, finished on January 5, 1551, was addressed not, as is often said, to Cranmer, but to his Cambridge diocesan, Goodrich of Ely.[4] A very considerable part of the alterations made in the Prayer Book were inspired by it. Indeed one of the models of the first Prayer Book had been another of Bucer's works, the *Pia Consultatio*.

Martin Bucer[5] was an Alsatian from Schlestadt[6], who had spent most of his life at Strasbourg, where he introduced the reformation.[7] After the Interim, whose

[1] Peter Martyr to Bucer, Lambeth, January 10, 1551. Strype, *Memorials of Cranmer*, App. LXI (*Censura libri communium precum*, ed. 1848, II, 661). Martyr expresses his regret that he had not had before him a complete translation on which to base his criticisms. He has completed them after reading Bucer's *Censura*. All we know of Peter Martyr's work is derived from this letter, which proves the important part played by these foreign divines in the revision of the Prayer Book (Strype, I, 200 *sq.*), though some authors, particularly Archbishop Lawrence in his *Bampton Lectures*, 254, have denied it.

[2] Strype, *Memorials*, II, 149 *sq.* Bucer's health suffered from the outset from the English climate. His companion, the Hebraist Fagius, died at Cambridge in November 1549. Fagius' death Strype calls "the extraordinary loss of that university, and the grief of all pious men that wished well to religion". It was also at Cambridge that Bucer died on February 28, 1551. On Bucer's death see Sir John Cheke's letter to Dr. Parker, of March 19, 1551. (Strype, *op. cit.*, App. LIX, ed. 1848, II, 657.)

[3] The book made a great impression on the young king and inspired his *Discourse about the Reformation of Many Abuses*. Cf. Burnet, *op. cit.*, V, 96. The *De Regno Christi* was published by Bucer's children at Basle in 1557. (Strype, *Memorials*, II, 551.)

[4] Peter Martyr says so explicitly in the above-mentioned letter of January 10, 1551. (Strype, *op. cit.*, ed. 1848, II, 662.) Cf. Gasquet and Bishop, *op. cit.*, 288, Note I.

[5] Butzer, in Latin Bucerus. Hence the French and English Bucer.

[6] He was born on St. Martin's Day, 1491.

[7] At thirteen he entered the Dominican Order. When he embraced the reformation he was a priest. He married a former nun by whom he had thirteen children. He married a second time, a woman three times widowed, by whom he had three children.

rejection by Strasbourg, in the teeth of the Emperor's threats he did his utmost to secure, he accepted, in April 1549, Cranmer's invitation and came to England.[1] All his life Bucer loved compromise. At the conferences of Hagenau and Worms in 1540, and later at the discussion held at Ratisbon in January 1546, he strove to reconcile the Protestants and Catholics. The latter much preferred him to Melanchthon, regarded him as the most learned of the Protestants and even entertained hopes of his return to the Church.[2] When in 1548 he attended the Diet of Augsburg, it was believed that he had been converted.[3] But it was above all between the Lutherans and the Reformed that Bucer sought to effect a union. His pliant views and expert theological diplomacy marked him out for this role of mediator, which he played almost to the end of his life, but always without success. For he was attempting to unite irreconcilable opinions. The sacramental doctrines, and in particular the doctrine of the Eucharist, held respectively by Luther and the Swiss Protestants differed too widely. Bucer offended both parties. But his efforts to effect a reconciliation led him to devise formulas of concord which considerably influenced his personal views. Setting out from Zwingli's position, he gradually drew closer to Luther's, and in 1538 an attempt undertaken in conjunction with Capito, to bring about an agreement between Luther and the Swiss churches, was on the verge of success, when the opposition of Zurich and Bienne made the negotiations

---

[1] The invitation was pressing. See Cranmer's letter to Bucer, London, October 2, 1548. (Strype, *Memorials of Cranmer*, App. XLIII; cf. E. Schmidt, *Peter Martyr*, 100 *sq.*) ·

[2] "This Bucer is the most learned man they (the Protestants) possess. Melanchthon does not preach but writes execrably." Letter of Negri, Ratisbon, April 16, 1541 (*Brieger's Zeitschrift*, Vol. III, 1879, 632). The same year Morone wrote that, if he were permitted to keep his wife, Bucer would return to Catholicism. Morone's memorandum on Church reform, 1541. (L. Cardauns *Zur Geschiche-der Kirklichen Unions-und Reformbestrebungen, von 1538 bis 1542*; Rome, 1910, 208.)

[3] *Concilium Tridentinum*, ed. by the Gürresgesellschaft, XI, XII, 407; cf. *Nuntiaturberichte aus Deutschland*, X., 295, and Note 2.

break down. Let no one contend for a verbal formula, he had pleaded on that occasion. Rather, let all profess and teach "the true presence and reception of Christ in the Supper". His desire for agreement at any price led him to sign at Cassel on May 21, 1536, the formula of Concord known as that of Wittenberg, which substantially contradicted the Eucharistic doctrine of the Swiss reformers. And later, he partly retracted his own opinions about the Eucharist, in his *Retractations*, in which he recognised the undefinable mystery in the Lord's Supper, though always rejecting a carnal and substantial (*carnalis*, *substantialis*) Presence of Christ. With one consent the Swiss repudiated his new teaching, and he broke with them. In his final work, the *De Regno Christi*, dedicated to Edward VI, his thought has developed along such lines that Catholics found in it "evidence that he disavowed and retracted his former errors", and at the Council of Trent the book was employed to provide "arguments against the heretics and in defence of the authority of the Church".

Bucer, therefore, especially towards the close of his life, represented a compromise between Luther and Zwingli, the combination of two contradictory doctrinal professions. Luther admitted a real Presence in the Eucharist. Zwingli saw in the Supper nothing but a memorial service uniting the assembly of Christian worshippers with the spirit of Christ. Christ who remains in heaven is not *really* given to the communicants. With Luther, Bucer professed that "along with the bread and wine Christ's Body and Blood are truly and essentially received".[1] "The true Body and the true Blood of Christ," he declared, "that is Christ Himself, God and man, is given and received, so that we may have our

---

[1] Article I of the "Wittenberger Konkordie" of 1536. Bucer consistently refused to use the terms "substantially", "really", "carnally", against which he never ceased to protest. "I should wish these words *realiter* and *substantialiter* banished. Never will I admit or tolerate the expressions 'carnally' and 'naturally.'" Bucer's sentences on the Lord's Supper in Strype, *Memorials of Cranmer*, App. XLVI, Arts. 38, 40; cf. Arts. 36, 38, 39.

being and live more fully in Him and He in us.[1] Christ
truly given and received,[2] so that we become His
members, flesh of His flesh, bone of His bone.[3] We
receive Him in accordance with His own words: 'Take,
eat', and in such sort that in the bread and the wine His
Body and Blood are given.[4] To the senses it is bread,
but to the spirit and mind it is the Lord's Body.''[5]
On June 20, 1550, he wrote to Peter Martyr, "People
will believe, I fear, that you hold that Christ is wholly
absent from the Supper, and that the sole presence is that
of His power and spirit''.[6] Accordingly, Bucer is prepared
to retain the practice sanctioned by the first Prayer Book,
of taking the reserved Sacrament to the sick after the
Supper. Peter Martyr was astounded at this opinion
of Bucer's. For since he did not admit any presence of
Christ in the sacrament, he regarded it as essential to
a sacramental communion that the sick man should hear
the words of consecration, whereas he held their repetition
in church to consecrate more wine when the number of
communicants required it, unnecessary, since those
present had already heard them.[7] When the Duke of
Northumberland questioned him about "the real Presence
of Christ's Body in the Blessed Sacrament", Bucer
frankly replied that he could not doubt of the true
Presence of Christ's Body, since he did not doubt the
Evangelist's veracity.

Bucer, however, approached the position of the Swiss

---

[1] *Confessio de Eucharistia*, 543; cf. 551.

[2] Bucer's sentences on the Lord's Supper in Strype, *Memorials of Cranmer*,
App. XLVI, Art. 42. "I profess," he says further (Art. 43), "that Christ,
that is to say participation in His redemption, is given and received in the
Lord's Supper."

[3] Ibid., Art. 47.

[4] Ibid., Art. 54.

[5] Ibid., Art. 50.

[6] Bucer, *Scripta Anglicana*, Basle, 549. Peter Martyr held "Christ is in
the Supper for those who approach His table, and truly feeds believers
with His blood". Manuscript treatise by Peter Martyr "of the Sacrament
of Thanksgiving". Preserved in the British Museum, (Royal MS., 17
C: V., and quoted by Gasquet and Bishop, *op. cit.*, 158–159).

[7] Peter Martyr to Bucer, January 10, 1551. Strype, *op. cit.*, App. LXI.

by maintaining that the union of Christ's Body and Blood with the bread and wine is exclusively sacramental, and does not exist apart from the reception of the sacrament which is spiritual. Christ is and remains in heaven.[1] "The signs of bread and wine are *purely figurative*. They are not united in any way with the Body and Blood of Christ. They are simply a figure, attesting that by them Our Lord truly communicates Himself to the recipient to be seen and eaten by faith. They serve only to raise the mind up and assure us that Christ has indeed communicated Himself to us."[2] There is no difference between the Eucharist and the other sacraments. "By these signs the Lord gives Himself—just as He gave the Holy Ghost to His disciples, by breathing upon them . . . and as He gave sight to the blind man by clay mixed with spittle . . . and as He bestows regeneration by the water of baptism.[3] The Lord has been pleased to employ the signs of food and drink to give us His flesh to eat *spiritually* under the sign of the bread which we eat *substantially*, and His Blood to drink *spiritually* under the sign of the wine which we drink *substantially*.[4] The bread is the figurative sign of the Lord's Body. He gives the thing signified by it. But it is no more than a sign."[5]

The following language, used by Bucer writing to Peter Martyr, is an excellent statement of his two-edged formula: "Confess if you can with a good conscience that Christ is certainly *present* in His Sacrament, not absent. But you can always add that we feed on Him by faith."[6] Bucer's belief is equally well stated in the following

---

[1] Strype, *loc. cit.;* Art. 25, also Arts. 19, 20 and 27.

[2] *Definitio Plenior (Scripta Anglicana*, Basle, 1577, 552–553; cf. ibid., 473). Cf. Strype, *loc. cit.,* Art. 45.

[3] Strype, *loc. cit.,* Art. 45; ibid., Art. 53.

[4] Strype, *loc. cit.,* Arts. 46 and 47.

[5] Ibid., Art. 54. Peter Martyr also said there is no transubstantiation, nor any mixture of the substances of bread and wine with Christ's Body and Blood; but the nature of communion is such that it suffices to receive the former with faith really to receive the latter. Gasquet and Bishop, *op. cit.,* 159.

[6] Bucer, *Scripta Anglicana,* 549.

words:[1] "Christ is received *truly and indeed by faith* and *His substance is given us* in the Sacrament . . . but I deny His earthly presence, since He has left this world."

That is to say the Body and Blood of Christ are truly received by faith, but the bread and wine do not contain them.[2] Therefore there is no permanent presence either in virtue of transubstantiation or by concomitance.[3] These doctrines, in Bucer's opinion, are "a common source of impiety and superstition";[4] "they cause men to fall into heinous wrath and madness and cast them headlong into idolatry".[5] The adoration of the Sacrament, which he regarded as bound up with a permanent presence, is therefore unlawful.[6]

It was in accordance with these doctrinal standards that the Anglican Mass of 1549 was remodelled. Care was taken to leave nothing susceptible of a Catholic interpretation.[7] "Those who could not endure that at least by this ceremony the figure and representation of Christ's death should be honoured according to ancient use, brought it about no long while after that all such ceremonies should be abrogated and the Canon entirely removed, and a new form of service was put forth."

The prayer immediately preceding the consecration

[1] Strype, *loc. cit.*, Art. 39. The words in italics are underlined in the original. In all this there is great metaphysical subtlety.

[2] Strype, *loc. cit.*, Art 52; cf. Art. 5.

[3] Strype, *loc. cit.*, Art. 24; ibid., Arts. 21, 51, 10.

[4] *Explicatio de vi et usu S. Mysterii (Scripta Anglicana*, 610–612). These are his Cambridge lectures, interrupted by his death.

[5] Strype, *loc. cit.*, Art. 48. Like his friend, Peter Martyr held that at no time whatsoever "is Christ present, but only in the use of the Supper" (the moment of reception) and "that the remains of the sacrament after the communion should not be reserved, as they are in the churches of the papists". Gasquet and Bishop, *op. cit.*, 159.

[6] *Explicatio de vi et usu S. Mysterii, loc. cit.* On receiving the Sacrament, said Peter Martyr, the communicant "who has faith" should "adore in his soul Christ Himself and not the signs" of bread and wine. Gasquet and Bishop, *loc. cit.*

[7] According to Strype, *Memorials of Cranmer*, such was the deference paid to Bucer's judgment that most of the things he found fault with were corrected, as he advised. (Book II, Chapter XVI, ed. 1848, II, 203.) Cf. Cardwell, *The Two Books of Common Prayer . . . Compared*, Oxford, 1841.

invoked upon the bread and wine the power of the Holy
Ghost as though to change them: "Hear us, O merciful
Father, we beseech Thee, and with Thy Holy Spirit and
Word vouchsafe to bless and sanctify[1] these Thy creatures
of bread and wine that they may be unto us the Body
and Blood of thy most dearly-beloved Son Jesus Christ."
According to Gardiner this prayer implied the doctrine
of transubstantiation.[2] Bucer found fault with it and
suggested in its place another which substitutes for the
notion of a change in the bread and wine that of receiving Christ by faith.[3] His advice was followed:
"Grant," says the Prayer Book of 1552, "that we,
receiving these Thy creatures of bread and wine, according
to Thy Son our Saviour Jesus Christ's holy institution,
in remembrance of His death and passion, may be partakers of His most blessed Body and Blood."[4]

Bucer particularly disliked the gesture which up
to the present preceded or accompanied the consecration, and whose meaning implied the belief in transubstantiation. "The priests," he wrote, "make the same
inclinations as before over the bread and wine, so that
they seem to intend rather to change by their words the
bread and wine into Our Lord's Body and Blood, than
to prepare the congregation to communicate. I could
wish that the little black crosses[5] and the rubric which

---

[1] A sign of the cross was, in fact, attached to each of these words. They
were the only two in the Communion Service of the 1549 Prayer Book.

[2] *An Explication and Assertion of the True Catholique Fayth touching the Most
Blessed Sacrament of the Aulter with Confutation of a Book Written Against the
same* (1551), Parker Society's edition of Cranmer's works, 79.

[3] "The prayer blessing and sanctifying the bread and wine must be cut
out of the book." (*Censura*, 472.) No precept of Christ's, Bucer argues, no
word or example of the Apostles, commands us to bless and hallow the
bread and wine, that they may be Christ's Body and Blood. In its place
he suggests the prayer: "Bless and sanctify us by Thy Word and Holy
Spirit, that with true faith we may in these mysteries receive the Body
and Blood of Thy Son for meat and drink of life everlasting."

[4] *Second Prayer Book*, above-mentioned ed., 169; Elizabeth's *Prayer Book*,
103. This prayer expresses Bucer's doctrine very clearly. We receive only
bread and wine, but at the same time truly partake of Christ's Body
and Blood.

[5] Which indicate that the priest is to bless the bread and wine.

bids the priest take the bread and wine in his hands,
might be taken out of the book." This was done. The
general rubric of 1549 permitting the priest to make
whatever gestures his devotion might suggest, was removed,[1] and even before 1552 all these gestures were
forbidden by a royal injunction.[2]

The prayer, now called the prayer "of humble access",[3]
which was then placed immediately after the Consecration, was said kneeling before the altar. In Gardiner's
view this constituted a genuine adoration of the Blessed.
Sacrament. "The adoration of Christ's flesh in the
Sacrament", he wrote, "is in my judgment well set forth
in the Book of Common Prayer, where the priest is
ordered to kneel and make a prayer in his own and in
the name of all that shall communicate, conforming"
(confirming) "therein that is prepared there."[4]

In 1552 the position of the prayer was changed and
placed before the consecration, that no one might see in
it the adoration which Bucer condemned.[5] For the same
reason the *Agnus Dei*, which both in the Lutheran and
Catholic liturgy is said at the moment of Communion
as a sign of belief in the Real Presence, was abolished.
According to Gardiner the rubric which declared the
entire Body of Christ contained in each particle of the
consecrated bread[6] also taught the Catholic doctrine.
"In the Book of Common Prayer . . . it is ordered
to teach the people that in each part of the bread
consecrate broken, is the whole Body of our Saviour
Christ, which is agreeable to the Catholic doctrine."[7]

---

[1] *First Prayer Book*, 268.
[2] Cardwell, *Documentary Annals*, 63.
[3] *First Prayer Book*, 203, *Second Prayer Book*, 168.
[4] Gardiner, *op. cit.*, Parker Society, 229.
[5] Bucer disliked the allusion to the ministry of Angels charged to bring
the prayers and acts of the faithful before God. (*First Prayer Book*, 294.)
He proposed to substitute the words: "Mercifully receive these prayers
for the sake of Thy Son, our Mediator." The passage to which he took
exception was omitted from the new book.
[6] *First Prayer Book*, 210.
[7] Gardiner, *op. cit.*, 62.

The rubric did in fact affirm that the bread is more than a sign, that it actually contains Christ's Body, which is opposed to Bucer's opinion. On his advice it was removed.[1]

Another rubric ordered the minister to take only so much bread and wine as was required for the communion of the people.[2] It also disappeared from the new Prayer Book. For Bucer saw in it the belief in the permanent presence of Christ's Body, His presence apart from Communion. "It is," he said,[3] "a cause of superstition, making the people think that if any of the bread and wine used for Communion remains over, it must not be employed for common uses, as though the bread and wine contained something divine or holy apart from their use for Communion." Accordingly the rubric of 1552 prescribes that "if any of the bread and wine remain over, the Curate shall have it to his own use"[4].

The prayer for the living and the dead from the old Canon was still said in the Mass of 1549 at the moment of the commemoration of Our Lord's Death. This, according to Gardiner, proved that the new Mass was still a propitiatory sacrifice.[5] To render Gardiner's Catholic interpretation impossible the prayer for the King, Church, clergy and people was placed before the Preface.[6]

The Memento of the Dead, censured by Bucer, was

---

[1] "I would cut out," he said, "the words which say that no one should suppose he receives less in a fragment of the Host than in the whole." The opening of this rubric ordered the use of unleavened wafers. Bucer asked that ordinary bread should be used. The change was made. *Second Prayer Book*, 172.

[2] *First Prayer Book*. 200.

[3] *Censura*, 552-553.

[4] *Second Prayer Book*, 172. Reservation for the sick, to which Peter Martyr, though not Bucer, had objected, was discontinued and a private celebration substituted. See *First Prayer Book*, 247; *Second Prayer Book*, 201 *sq*; and Peter Martyr to Bucer, January 10, 1551, in Strype, *Memorials of Cranmer*, App. LXI.

[5] Gardiner, *op. cit.*, Parker Society, 84.

[6] Between the collection and the exhortation to Communion. This is its place in the *Second Prayer Book* (p. 162) and in Elizabeth's (96-97).

abolished, and the Communion service was no longer to be celebrated at funerals, because it suggested Mass for the dead.[1] The verses taken from Scripture (Job 1, xxi. 2; xiv. 1-3; xix. 25-27; John xi. 25-26; 1 Tim. vi. 7) and read at the opening of the funeral service, the Epistle (1 Cor. xv. 20-58) and the prayers, all speak of the future life and the Resurrection. But nothing even implies a prayer for the dead, or belief in Purgatory. Every prayer is for the living. When the body has been lowered into the grave, the officiant says: "In the midst of life we are in death; of whom may we seek for succour, but of Thee, O Lord, who for our sins art justly displeased? Yet O Lord God most holy, O Lord most mighty, O holy and most merciful Saviour, deliver us not into the bitter pains of eternal death. Thou knowest Lord, the secrets of our hearts; shut not Thy merciful ears to our prayers; but spare us, Lord most holy, O God most mighty, O holy and merciful Saviour, Thou most worthy Judge eternal, suffer us not, at our last hour, for any pains of death, to fall from Thee". "Have mercy upon us,"— not have mercy upon him—the clergyman prays after the Epistle. And while earth is cast upon the body, he says: "Forasmuch as it hath pleased Almighty God of his great mercy to take unto Himself the soul of our dear brother here departed, we therefore commit his body to the ground; earth to earth, ashes to ashes, dust to dust; in sure and certain hope of the resurrection to eternal life through our Lord Jesus Christ; who shall change our vile body that it may be like unto His glorious body, according to the mighty working whereby He is able

[1] (106) Bucer objected to any commemoration of the dead, not only in his *Censura* but also in a letter to his colleagues at Strasbourg, of April 26, 1549, in which he speaks of the Prayer Book (*Zurich Original Letters*, 536). He proposed to replace the *Memento* of the dead by the following prayer, in which the departed are not prayed for: "that together with these and all who have departed hence in the faith of Thy Name we may at the advent of thy Son, come forth in glory unto the resurrection of life, and may be set at thy Son's right hand and hear His glad words: 'Come ye blessed'."

to subdue all things to Himself." Though a funeral service is still performed, its significance has been changed.[1]

In Bucer's opinion a common table is preferable to an altar, which is too suggestive of sacrifice, and better instructs the people in the true meaning of the service.[2] To prove that the Mass of 1549 still taught the old doctrine, Gardiner had relied upon the use of the altars which the Prayer Book had not abolished[3]. The new Prayer Book no longer mentions altars. In future a table would be used placed on the floor, to the north of which the minister stands.[4]

Hitherto the priest had continued to wear the sacerdotal vestments.[5] Bucer disapproved of their use. Now the alb, chasuble and cope are expressly forbidden.[6] If the Royal Commission of 1551 leaves a chasuble or cope in any church, it orders that it is to be used to cover the communion table, and must not be worn by the minister.[7] "The minister at the time of the Com-

[1] Already in 1551 Hooper had ordered his clergy to choose for funerals psalms thanking God for having delivered the departed from this world of misery, in place of mournful chants praying for them. (Hooper, *Later Writings*, Parker Society, 166) compare *First Prayer Book*, 256, with *Second Prayer Book*, 205–206 and *Elizabeth's Prayer Book*, 138.

[2] Undated letter of Bucer's in MS. 113 in the library of Corpus Christi College, Cambridge, quoted by Gasquet, *op. cit.*, 267.

[3] He is refuting Hooper, who wished to substitute an ordinary table for the altar. *State Papers Domestic*, Vol. XII, Fols. 64–65, quoted by Gasquet and Bishop, *op. cit.*, 285.

[4] *Second Prayer Book*, 157; *Prayer Book of Elizabeth*, 62.

[5] *First Prayer Book*, 1549, 193, 268. "They use the priestly vestments," the Venetian Ambassador wrote in 1551. Alberi, *Relazioni degli Ambasciatori Veneti*, Series I, Vol. II, 249.

[6] Bucer's Letter of April 26, 1549, *Zurich Original Letters*, Parker Soc., 536. In his *Censura* he urges the disuse of the vestments, not as being sinful in themselves, but in order to have nothing in common with the Romish antichrists. Hooper and John Butler also censured these ornaments and their pomp. Hooper to Bullinger, December 27, 1549. (Ibid. 72) and Butler to Thomas Blaurer, February 16, 1550 (ibid. 635).

See *Second Prayer Book*, 29.

[7] Cf. Surrey, *Archaeological Collection*, Vol. IV. On the subject of ornaments see: *Liturgies of Edward VI*, Parker Soc., ed. Ketley, Cambridge, 1844; Peacock, *English Church Furniture, Ornaments and Decorations at the Period of the Reformation*, London, 1866; Micklethwaite, *The Ornaments of the Rubric*, Alcuin Club Tracts, London, 1897.

munion," the new rubric ran, "and all other times in
his ministration shall use neither alb, vestment, nor cope:
but being archbishop or bishop, he shall have and wear
a rochet; and being a priest or deacon, he shall have and
wear a surplice only."[1]

Bucer considered that the practice of receiving the
sacrament in the mouth and not in the hands, implied
the belief of the Romish anti-christs that the priest's
anointed hands are holier than the hands of a layman.
The rubric which retained it[2] disappeared in 1552.[3]
Thus everything which seemed to Bucer a relic of the
Catholic Mass was abolished.[4]

That is to say, Bucer's *Censura* had a considerable
influence upon the revision of the Prayer Book. This
was recognised even by contemporaries.[5] But his was not
the sole inspiration. Bucer, as we have seen, occupied
a middle position between Luther and the Swiss. When he
advised the adoption of Swiss formularies, his advice was

[1] *Second Prayer Book*, 29, Cf. *Grey Friars' Chronicle*, 76. Ridley was the
first to celebrate in this attire at St. Paul's. The chroniclers remark upon
it. (Strype, *Memorials of Cranmer*, Book II, 406 *sqq.*) Cranmer had already
attempted the innovation in 1549 (*Grey Friars' Chronicle*, 60).

[2] *First Prayer Book*, 211.

[3] "Then shall the minister deliver it (the communion) to the people in
their handes." *Second Prayer Book*, 169.

[4] The better to distinguish the Holy Communion from the Mass, the
Eucharist was celebrated only once a day in each parish. After 1552 there
were celebrations only on Sunday. *Grey Friars' Chronicle*, 78.

[5] The Venetian Ambassador, Barbaro, had already reported that "anything which the English believe to have been ordered by the Pope, they
at once abolish, and this at the persuasion of Bucer, who was in the utmost
repute with them, but is now dead." Report on England, 1551, Alberi,
Relazioni Degli Ambasciatori Veneti, Series I, Vol. II, 245.
"In England," wrote the Catholic controversialist Cornelius Schulting,
"the Supper is celebrated according to the rite and fashion of Bucer,
which is completely different from the rite used by the Lutherans in
Saxony." *Hierarchica Anacrisis Adversus Varios Calvinistorum Libros* (1604).
Part III, 87; cf. the same author's, *Bibliotheca Ecclesiastica* (1609), Vol. IV, I,
133.
Procter's statement (*History of the Book of Common Prayer*, 38 *sq.*) that the
work of revision had been completed before Bucer finished his *Censura*,
and was substantially the independent production of the Anglican clergy,
is hardly borne out by the facts. For as early as January 1551, Bucer's
book was in the hands of Peter Martyr (Strype, *Memorials of Cranmer*,
App. LXI) and a month later (February 28) Bucer died, whereas the
Prayer Book was not submitted to Parliament until January 23, 1552.

followed; when he advised the retention of Luther's, it was
neglected. In 1549 the doctrine of the Eucharistic sacrifice
had been attacked in agreement with Luther. In 1552
Luther was left behind, and the Real Presence, denied by
Zwingli and Calvin, became the object of attack. Already
the doctrine had been vigorously denounced by the van-
guard of the Episcopate in the Parliament of 1549, which
passed the First Act of Uniformity. Cranmer had ceased
to believe it in 1548. Concessions had, however, been
made to win the Henricians over. But with Warwick
the period of compromise was at an end. The orthodox
must no longer be permitted to read their own interpretation into the new service book. No channel was left
open through which the old doctrine might insinuate
itself.[1] Even Bucer was not thought sufficiently radical.

He pressed for the retention, in the prayer following the
Consecration, of the words: "Humbly beseeching Thee
. . . that whosoever shall be partakers of this holy
Communion may worthily receive the most precious
Body and Blood of Thy Son Jesus Christ."[2]

To cut them out would, he said, cast doubt upon the
reality of the act of receiving communion. Even if Catholics read their own meaning into them, they should be
retained.[3] Nowhere else in his treatise does he argue
at such length or so earnestly. "I beseech our Saviour,"
he concludes, "that these words may be kept as they stand
at present. For they are in truth pure and in conformity
with the words of the Holy Ghost uttered by Christ
Himself. I am, therefore, confident that the formula will
be retained. . . . You are not unaware that all men's
eyes are to-day fixed upon this realm, to which God has
granted a king, bishops and nobles who will not permit
any irreligious or excessive novelty. I am sure my
beloved colleague Peter Martyr, and all who are well

[1] Gasquet and Bishop, *op. cit.*, 289.
[2] *First Prayer Book*, 204.
[3] *Censura* (*Scripta Anglicana*, 473-476). Bucer suggested various definitions
to obviate any confusion with the Catholic doctrine.

instructed in what pertains to Christ's kingdom, share my judgment, my thought and my desire."[1] In spite of Bucer's insistence the words he desired to retain were cut out. They were too suggestive of belief in the Real Presence.

On this point the English reformers departed from the Lutherans because they were too Catholic. The pure doctrine of the Swiss was alone true. Communion was feeding upon Christ spiritually by faith, not, as Bucer still taught, the real reception of His Body and Blood.

Accordingly, the words "the body and blood of Christ" were removed from the formula of administration;[2] words which Gardiner argued proved that "the Church of England teacheth" the Real Presence "at this day, in the distribution of the holy communion, in that it is there said, the Body and Blood of Christ to be under the form of bread and wine".[3]

"The priest must simply say: 'Take and eat *This*—Drink *This*'."[4]

Any allusion to the Real Presence was carefully avoided. The words, "Blessed is He that cometh in the name of the Lord" were removed from the *Sanctus*, though they were taken from Scripture.[5] In the exhortation to the Communicants which precedes the general confession, the minister is to say: "we spiritually eat the flesh of Christ and drink His blood."[6] The *Agnus Dei* which by Lutherans and Catholics alike is said at the time of Communion as a profession of faith in the Real Presence, was also removed.

Thus any conception either of sacrifice or of bodily Presence, conceptions in which every word and gesture of the old Eucharistic liturgy had been steeped, were

---

[1] *Censura, loc. cit.*
[2] *First Prayer Book,* 206.
[3] Gardiner, *op. cit.*, Parker Soc., 51.
[4] *Second Prayer Book,* 169.   Elizabeth's *Prayer Book* combined the formulas of 1549 and 1552. (Ed. Farran Browne, 103.)
[5] *Second Prayer Book,* 168.
[6] *Second Prayer Book,* ed. *cit.*, 165.

excluded with an uncompromising thoroughness. The reformers' aim was to make the Eucharist a pure memorial service, nothing more than a rite of remembrance and thanksgiving. By thus refashioning the Communion service, "the Zwinglians abolished the sacrifice of Christ's body and blood, which sacrifice had from antiquity received the name and appellation of the Mass". "The priest," Froude remarks, "was converted absolutely into a minister, the altar into a table, the Eucharist into a commemoration, and a commemoration only."[1]

The prudent moderation which Bucer had advised was not observed.[2] He had died in 1551 (February 28) and the final revision of the Prayer Book was influenced by Peter Martyr, more radical than his friend,[3] by Bullinger,[4] whose disciples surrounded Cranmer, secured seats on the episcopal bench and possessed the ear of the government, and by Bishop Hooper, "whose sole occupation at this time, was to combat alike the Lutherans and Bucer's disciples."[5]

Cranmer even was almost carried further than he wished to go. Warwick favoured the extreme left of the reformers. In their opinion, to receive Communion kneeling

---

[1] *The Reign of Edward the Sixth*, Chapter V, Everyman, 237.

[2] Bucer had warned Cranmer not to go too fast—to reform persons rather than external ritual practices, and preach essential truths, rather than destroy the old usages at a single blow. (MS. 123 Corpus Christi College, Cambridge, quoted by Gasquet and Bishop, *op. cit.*, 267, Note 1.) He even urged the king to moderate his zeal for reform, to effect reforms prudently, moderately and gradually. Solid instruction must prepare the people for religious changes, and minds must be reformed before customs. *De Regno Christi*, Book II, cap. V, 60–61.

[3] Strype, *Memorials of Cranmer*, Book II, Chapter XVI, ed. 1848, Vol. II, 203.

[4] Bullinger was Zwingli's successor. He modified Zwingli's doctrine of the sacraments. According to Zwingli, the Lord's Supper was a pure, figurative symbol, a simple commemoration of Christ's death. Bullinger admitted a certain presence of Our Saviour in the act of Communion. This was the principal point in the Zurich agreement (*Consensus Tigurinus*) reached in 1549 between Calvin and himself. The latter could repeat what he had already written in 1540. "We know, therefore, in what respect Luther has erred on one side, Zwingli and Œcolampadius have erred on the other." *Œuvres Françaises Recueillies par L. P. Jacob*, 208.

[5] *Zurich Original Letters*, Parker Soc., 659; cf. 662.

amounted to an act of adoration, and expressed faith
in the Real Presence. In a sermon preached before the
King, Hooper denounced the practice as superstitious.
"The outward behaviour," he argued, "and gesture of
the receiver should want all kind of suspicion, shew, or
inclination of idolatry. Wherefore seeing kneeling is a
shew and external sign of honouring and worshipping,
and heretofore hath grievous and damnable idolatry
been committed by the honouring of the Sacrament,
I would wish it were commanded by the magistrates
that the communicators and receivers should do it
standing or sitting. But sitting in mine opinion were best
for many considerations"[1]

The Polish reformer Laski, who possessed great influence
in England, supported their attitude. At Berwick, Knox
on his own authority had discontinued the practice of
kneeling to receive Communion. To put an end to this
abuse, the Prayer Book of 1552 ordered kneeling.[2] Some
of the reformers vigorously protested,[3] and Knox permitted himself an outburst of invective in the King's
presence.[4] The book had been approved and printed,
when Warwick ordered the printer Grafton to withdraw
it from sale.[5] At the same time he wrote to Cranmer
bidding him take counsel with Ridley and Peter Martyr
as to the advisability of removing the rubric which
ordered kneeling[6]. The Archbishop was averse to the
alteration. After an exchange of letters and lengthy
discussions it was decided to insert into the book an

[1] *Hooper's Works*, 576.
[2] *Second Prayer Book*, 169.
[3] In a letter to the Council entitled a "Confession" and attributed by
Lorimer to Knox, several reformers protest against the 38th of the XLII
articles, namely the article declaring the ceremonies of the New Prayer
Book in conformity with Scripture, because, they say, the rubric which
orders communion to be received kneeling seems to sanction idolatry.
[4] Letter from Utenhove of October 12, 1552. *Zurich Original Letters*,
Parker Soc., 591.
[5] September 26, 1552. *Acts of the Privy Council*, ed. Dasent (1892), IV,
131. The sale of copies is strictly prohibited "until certain faults have been
amended".
[6] Cranmer to the Privy Council. October 6, 1552. Blunt, *op. cit.*, II, 169.

additional leaf containing what was termed the "Black Rubric", which explained that the act of kneeling, though still retained, did not imply any superstitious belief (October 27, 1552).[1] Three days later the new *Book of Common Prayer* came into use.

Henceforward Cranmer was regarded as a moderate man. For he had been outstripped by men more radical than himself.

He wrote to the Council, "The book being read and approved by the whole state of the realm in the High Court of Parliament, with the King's Majesty's his royal assent that this should now be altered without Parliament, of what importance this matter is, I refer to your lordships' wisdom to consider. I know your lordships' wisdom to be such, that I trust ye will not be moved with these glorious" (conceited) "and unquiet spirits, which can like nothing but that is after their own fancy; and cease not to make trouble when things be most quiet and in good order. If such men should be heard— although the book were made every year anew, yet it should not lack faults in their opinion. 'But,' say they, 'it is not commanded in the Scripture to kneel, and whatsoever is not commanded in the Scripture is against the Scripture and utterly unlawful and ungodly.' But this saying is the chief foundation of the Anabaptists and of divers other sects. This saying is a subversion of all order, as well in religion as in common policy. If this saying be true, take away the whole book of service; for what should men travail to set in order in the form of service, if no order can be got but that is already

---

[1] The result of the discussions recorded in the minutes of the Council October 27, 1552. *Acts of the Privy Council*, ed. Dasent, IV, 154. Cf. Burnet *op. cit.* III, 368; Perry, *Historical consideration on the Declaration on Kneeling* The advanced reformers were satisfied with the declaration, and Knox in an apostolical letter to his community at Berwick, explained his acceptance of it. (Lorimer, *op. cit.*, 251 *sq.*) Though his language was violent, Knox was moderate in his actions. For the later history of the Black Rubric, see Rev. N. Dimock, *On the Doctrine of the Church of England, Concerning the Eucharistic Presence*, London, 1911.

prescribed by Scripture? . . . 'But it is not expressly
contained in the Scripture' (say they) 'that Christ
ministered the Sacrament to His Apostles kneeling.
Nor they find it not expressly in Scripture that He
ministered it standing or sitting. But if we will follow
the plain words of the Scripture, we should rather receive
it lying down on the ground—as the custom of the
world at that time almost everywhere, and as the Tartars
and Turks use yet at this day to eat their meat lying
upon the ground".[1] The reply to this letter was a
command to leave London on the pretext that the
Archbishop's presence was required in Kent, to combat
the Anabaptists, and two of his manors were seized.
The Imperial Ambassador wondered whether this was
the beginning of Divine vengeance upon the Archbishop.[2]

Though the notion of sacrifice had been expunged,
the Mass of 1549 was substantially the same as the
old. Its parts corresponded with those of the Catholic
Mass. The prayers and their order had been, generally
speaking, preserved. Even the Canon was retained. It
was still possible for the people to believe that they
were taking part in the same service as before. By con-
tinuing the old ritual gestures, the priests gave the new
service the appearance of "The popish Mass". With the
liturgy of 1552 this was no longer possible. Of the Canon,
the centre of the old Liturgy, there remained only a
few lines, and the remainder of the service was so revolutionised that the Mass could be no longer recognised in it.

The Introit had disappeared. The celebrant, standing
on the floor of the church[3] in front of a table covered
with a white cloth, began with the Our Father and a

---

[1] This letter of Cranmer's of October 7, 1552, from which I have quoted
only a few phrases, is printed in Perry. *Op. cit.*, 77; also in Lorimer, *Knox
in England*, 103, and Blunt, *op. cit.*, Vol. II (ed. 1896), 103–105.
[2] Cf. Scheyfve to Granvelle, November 20, 1552. *Spanish Calendar*,
X, 593.
[3] Bucer did not want the celebrant to be in the Chancel separated from
the people. As a result of his criticism the words of the First Prayer Book,
"The priest being in the chancel" were replaced by a lengthy rubric.

Collect,[1] followed in accordance with a Calvinist practice by the ten Commandments. [2]After each commandment the congregation asked forgiveness for any transgressions of it they might have committed and grace to keep it faithfully. This was the sole vestige remaining of the Kyrie Eleison. The Collects, Epistle, Gospel, and the Creed which the sermon or reading of a homily follows are the only parts of the service whose order was left unchanged. After some verses of Scripture from which the minister might select, urging charity to the poor, there was a prayer for the king, church, clergy and people, a relic of the Memento for the living said in the Canon. After this, the exhortation to Communion, the general confession, and the absolution followed, all of which in 1549 immediately preceded the Communion. Then the celebrant recited the Preface with the Sanctus, the prayer of humble access, the solitary and deformed survival of the old Canon, and the words of consecration. The Communion of the people followed immediately. The service concluded with the Our Father,[3] a prayer of thanksgiving, which also prayed that the communicants might receive the fruits of the passion and death of Christ, whose body and blood had just fed them spiritually, the *Gloria in Excelsis* thus transferred from the beginning to the end, and the minister's blessing. In all essentials this is still the Communion Service of the Anglican Church.

The Divine Office was little changed.[4] But whatever

---

[1] It was followed by a short prayer to ask the illumination of the Holy Spirit, which was already in the 1549 Book.

[2] This practice was followed by the French Colony at Glastonbury, of which Valérand Poullain was minister, and in the Strasbourg liturgy. Its introduction into the Prayer Book was probably due to Hooper, who during the visitation of his diocese in 1551, had ordered his clergy to read the decalogue to all communicants. (Cf. Hooper, *Later Writings*, Parker Soc., 132–133.) (*Second Prayer Book*, 158–9).

[3] The *Pater noster*, said at the close of the Canon, was thus placed after the Communion, and the *Pax Domini* was suppressed.

[4] At Matins the Athanasian creed was to be recited thirteen times a year instead of six as before. (*Second Prayer Book*, 31). The Apostles' creed was added to Morning and Evening Prayer. (Ibid., 35). Both offices

of the old rites had hitherto been retained in the administration of the Sacraments, was almost completely suppressed on the advice of Bucer or to imitate the Swiss liturgies. In Baptism the white robe, the anointing of the forehead,[1] and the exorcisms,[2] were abolished. The priest no longer blessed the water of the font,[3] and no longer addressed the child when signing him with the cross.[4] Thus almost every survival of the old ritual disappeared[5]—with the exception of a prayer common to the Sarum ritual and Luther's liturgy, which, however, was mutilated.[6] The introductory rubrics, after pointing out that in the primitive Church baptism was administered only twice a year, namely at Easter and Whitsunday, advised parents not to delay it longer than the Sunday or festival following the birth. Baptism was to be administered on Sundays or feasts after Matins or Evensong, that it might be witnessed by a larger number, who would thus be reminded of the promises they made to God at their baptism.[7]

---

began, no longer with the "Our Father" and "Lord, open Thou my lips", but with Scripture verses on the forgiveness of sin, an exhortation to repentance, and the general confession and absolution. (Ibid., 29–31). The addition would seem to have been inspired by Calvin (Dixon, *op. cit.*, III, 493, Note, Valérand Poullain) (Lawrence, *Bampton Lectures*, 207; Procter, *History of the Book of Common Prayer*, 45) and Laski (Cardwell, *Two Liturgies*, p. xxxii). All these changes were retained in the later Prayer Books.

[1] These ancient customs, Bucer had said in his *Censura*, are pious testimonies of gratitude towards God, but the Roman antichrists have perverted them into play-acting.

[2] Are they all born then in diabolic sin, Bucer had asked, that you retain the exorcism?

[3] Hitherto the rubric had ordered the water to be renewed every month, and blessed according to the prescribed form. (*First Prayer Book*, 226–227). Bucer regarded this as superstition, an expression of belief in some magic change of the water.

[4] Bucer did not object to the sign of the cross, but to addressing the baby, who is unable to understand what is said to it.

[5] A careful examination proves that the parts omitted from the new baptismal service are precisely those which the First Prayer Book had retained from the Catholic office.

[6] Cf. *First Prayer Book*, 118 and *Second Prayer Book*, 174.

[7] *Second Prayer Book*, 172 and 179. Also ibid., 173–178. Without very grave reason children must not be baptised at home. For such cases of

For Confirmation, in accordance with Bucer's suggestion, a fuller catechetical instruction was now required.[1]
The short catechism to be learned by candidates com-
prised the baptismal vows, for one of the purposes of
Confirmation is that the child shall ratify the promises
previously made in his name,[2] the articles of the Creed,
the ten commandments, and an explanation of the
Lord's Prayer. When they have thoroughly learned
these things, they are to be presented to the bishop for
Confirmation as soon as possible. For they require the
sacrament to strengthen their will, and enable them to
keep their baptismal vows, also in order to be admitted
to Communion. Nevertheless, we must believe that
children being baptised but not confirmed "have all
things necessary for their salvation, and be undoubtedly
saved."[3] The form of 1549 which had remained partly
the same as the Sarum form, was replaced by another
entirely different. In 1549 the bishop made the sign of
the cross on the candidate's forehead, and laid his hands
upon him with the words, "N. I sign thee with the sign
of the Cross, and lay my hand upon thee. In the name
of the Father, and of the Son, and of the Holy Ghost".
The form in the Roman Pontifical runs, "I sign thee
with the sign of the cross, and I confirm thee with the
chrism of salvation. In the name of the Father, and of the
Son and of the Holy Ghost". Since 1552 the Anglican
bishop, laying his hand on the candidate, but not making
the sign of the cross, says: "Defend O Lord this Thy
child with Thy heavenly grace, that he may continue
Thine for ever; and daily increase in Thy Holy Spirit,

---

need the Prayer Book prescribed the essential sacramental form. If the
infant lived, it must be brought to church. The priest was to enquire
carefully into the manner of its baptism in order that, if he thought its
validity dubious, he might rebaptise it conditionally. In any case the
ceremonies omitted must be supplied. (Ibid., 179–183).

[1] *Second Prayer Book*, 188. See also Elizabeth's Prayer Book, 120–121.
[2] *Second Prayer Book*, 184 and the second rubric on p. 183.
[3] Ibid., 183–186, 188; cf. 178.

more and more, until he come unto Thy everlasting kingdom. Amen." The signing of the cross upon the forehead was thus abolished together with the invocation which by its mention of "the inward unction of thy Holy Ghost", preserved a memory of the anointing.[1] The Confirmation service of the new Prayer Book was extremely short. Two invocations, each but a few lines in length, praying for the Holy Spirit and His gifts, frame the imposition of hands. Then the bishop leaves the Church after the traditional blessing: "The Blessing of God Almighty, the Father, the Son and the Holy Ghost, be upon you and remain with you for ever. Amen."

As regards the visitation of the sick, Bucer had advised the abolition of Extreme Unction. His advice was followed. The anointings were abolished, the remainder of the rite retained. There are many exhortations and prayers, some of them derived from the Catholic ritual. The priest reminds the sick man of his baptismal vows, his duties towards his neighbour, to forgive injuries, make restitution for wrongs, make his will and give alms to the poor, and if he feels his conscience troubled, the priest hears his confession and absolves him.[2] He reminds him that "Almighty God, the Lord of life and death" sends illness only for our good, to increase "our glory and endless felicity", or "to correct and amend" our sins, and that He is a loving Father who chasteneth His beloved sons "for our profit that we may be partakers of His holiness". Therefore "you should bear your sickness patiently, trusting in God's mercy, . . . and render unto Him humble thanks" "whatsoever your sickness is", and for what cause soever

---

[1] *First Prayer Book*, 252.

[2] The Prayer Book form of Absolution is as follows: "Our Lord Jesus Christ who hath left power to His Church to absolve all sinners who truly repent and believe in Him, of His great mercy forgive thee thine offences; And by His authority committed to me, I absolve thee from all Thy sins. In the name of the Father, and of the Son, and of the Holy Ghost, Amen."

"it is sent unto you". Christians have no greater consolation than to resemble Christ by patiently suffering adversities, afflictions, and sickness. For Christ did not come into the world to enjoy Himself but to suffer, and it was through crucifixion that He entered into His glory. The visitation concludes with the Psalm *In te Domine speravi* in English and the following prayer: "O Saviour of the world, who by Thy cross and Precious Blood hast redeemed us, save us and help us we humbly beseech Thee, O Lord. The Almighty Lord, who is a most strong tower to all them that put their trust in Him, to whom all things in heaven, in earth and under the earth, do bow and obey, be now and evermore thy defence; and make thee know and feel that there is none other Name under heaven given to man, in whom and through whom, thou mayest receive health and salvation, but only the Name of our Lord Jesus Christ. Amen."[1] The sick man may also receive communion by having Holy Communion celebrated in his home.[2]

Although the long general confession said daily at Matins, tended to replace individual and private confession, and nothing was said directly about the latter,[3] it was not abolished.[4]

---

[1] See *Second Prayer Book*, 201–202; *Prayer Book of Elisabeth*, 129–135.

[2] In "Extremity of sickness," or when it was difficult to celebrate Communion at the dying man's house, the priest was to invite him to make a spiritual communion. This was already advised by a rubric in the First Prayer Book (249) but, whereas it was then stated that in such case the sick man received Christ's Body and Blood *spiritually*, the qualification was now removed.

[3] An explicit statement in the First Prayer Book that the form of absolution provided in the visitation of the sick, was to be employed in every private confession, was omitted.

[4] It continued to exist if not as a Sacrament—its sacramental character is denied by the 35th of Elizabeth's XXXIX Articles—at least as a laudable practice. The Prayer Books of 1552 and 1563 and also the present Prayer Book speak of "a special confession" in the Visitation of the Sick, and both there and at Morning and Evening Prayer affirm the power of Christ's ministers to absolve penitents, (*Second Prayer Book*, 30, 198. *Prayer Book of Elisabeth*, 42, 131), and in the Anglican Ordinal the Bishop confers on a priest authority to remit sin. See further, a declaration of the Lambeth Conference, July 1878. Hall, *Confession and the Lambeth Conference,* Boston, 1879; Carter, *The Doctrine of Confession in the Church of England.* Also the

Of all the services marriage seems to have undergone the least change. Holy Communion is still to be celebrated at weddings, and the bridal pair are expected to receive Communion. After the Gospel a sermon is to be preached dealing with the duties of married people, or failing this the homily in the Prayer Book read. Before the communion service begins, the marriage has taken place.

All these liturgical alterations delighted the continental reformers. "They praised their God that having had mercy on the world, He had at last flung the door wide open for the propagation and publication of the Gospel throughout the world. They all jumped for joy that such a great kingdom had embraced and received their sect, not only in a certain number of scattered provinces, as in Germany, but as a whole from one end to another. From every quarter their congratulations poured in that the English had a monarch of such promise and they dedicated books to him and called him a modern Josiah and David."[1]

On June 14, Peter Martyr wrote to Bullinger from Oxford that everything which could possibly encourage superstition had been carefully excised from the new Prayer Book.[2] Bullinger and Calvin, officially consulted,[3] found nothing to object to except a few details which did not affect the substance of the services.[4] With the Communion Service they were perfectly satisfied. That is to say the Anglican liturgy agreed in substance with

Book of *Homelies*, (*Cranmer's Works*, IV, 282, 285) the Canons of 1603 (Canon CXIII). See also the opinions of Hooker (*Ecc. Polity*, 1600, Book VI, Chapter IV, 7), Bishop Andrewes (1625) and Bishop Jeremy Taylor (1667). From these authorities it is clear that the Anglican doctrine is that auricular confession is optional, not as the Church teaches, obligatory.

[1] Sanders. *Op. cit.*
[2] Goode, *Unpublished Letter of Peter Martyr*, 15.
[3] In 1554 by the English refugees at Strasbourg.
[4] Bullinger objected to the surplice, private baptism, the churching of women, and the wedding ring (*A Brief Discourse of the Troubles begun at Frankfort about the Book of Common Prayer* (1575), ed. Peterham, 1846, 50).

those of Zwingli[1] and Calvin, and was in conformity with their doctrine. Nevertheless, an even more radical reform was, it would seem, projected. Bullinger speaks of a draft of Cranmer's a hundred times better than the Prayer Book of 1552,[2] and shortly before the end of the reign the Council sent the bishops "fifty-four articles concerning the uniform order to be observed in every church of this realm".[3]

Edward's death put an end to a transformation which would have led to an even more rigid Puritanism, a Puritanism whose excesses many Anglican writers deplore to-day.[4]

The new Book of Common Prayer was imposed upon the kingdom by the Second Act of Uniformity,[5] which declared it to be simply an improvement and explanation of the previous book, which was "agreable to the Word of God and the primitive Church". But the new book had been issued "for the more perfection of the said order of Common Service in some places where it is necessary to make the said prayers and fashion of service more earnest and fit to stir Christian people to the true knowing of Almighty God".[6]

The Bill introduced into the Lords on March 9, 1552, was passed by both Houses on April 14.[7] Next day, Good Friday, Parliament adjourned. The majority of the Henrician bishops were in prison or had been

---

[1] As represented and toned down by his successor, Bullinger.

[2] *A Brief Discourse of the Troubles, &c.* ed. above-mentioned, 50; Strype, *Memorials of Cranmer*, Book II, Chapter XXVI, ed. 1848, 347. Cf. Pollard, *Cranmer*, London, 1904, 334.

[3] Warrant Book. British Museum, Royal Ins., 18 c. xxiv, fol. 352, quoted by Gasquet and Bishop, *op. cit.*, 304. Strype, (*Eccles. Memorials*, II, 369) has confused these articles with the XLII articles of 1553.

[4] Dixon, *History of the Church of England*, 282, 292, &c.; Blunt, *The Reformation of the Church*, ed. 1892–1896, II, 95–107; Moreton, *op cit.*, Chapter VIII.

[5] "An act for the uniformity of Common Prayer and administration of the Sacraments." *Statutes of the Realm* (Vol. IV, 1819), 5 and 6. Edward VI. cap. 1. The New Prayer Book was presented as an authorised revision of the 1549 Prayer Book.

[6] *Statutes of the Realm*, loc. cit.

[7] *Lords' Journal; Commons' Journal.*

deprived of their sees. The only opposition to the Bill came from the Bishops of Carlisle and Norwich, Aldrich and Thirlby, the Earl of Derby, Lord Windsor and Lord Stourton.[1] For the first time a penalty was imposed on laymen. To stay away from church on a Sunday or festival rendered the offender liable to ecclesiastical censure, and to be present at an unauthorised service was a criminal offence. For the first offence the penalty was six months' imprisonment, for the second, twelve months', for the third, imprisonment for life.[2] The Second Prayer Book came into use on November 1, 1552. It remained in use barely a year. For in the following July, Edward VI died, and in October Parliament abolished his service book. But Elizabeth restored it. Her Book of Common Prayer is, practically speaking, a reissue of the Prayer Book of 1552. The attempt of the Scottish Prayer Book of 1637 to return in some respects to the liturgy of 1549 failed. Thus apart from a few details, the Second Book of Common Prayer has been used in the Church of England for more than three centuries and a half.[3]

The Parliament which had imposed the first Book of Common Prayer upon the country, appointed a Committee of twelve[4] to draw up before the following April 1 an Ordinal or "form and manner of making, ordaining, and consecrating of archbishops, bishops, priests, deacons, and other ministers of the church" (1549).[5] The Henricians, Tunstall, Aldrich, Thirlby, Heath and Day had voted against the measure. By the appointed day the committee had accomplished their task.[6] Two years

[1] *Lords' Journal*, April 6.
[2] *Statutes of the Realm*, loc. cit.
[3] It is not therefore true to maintain, as its editor does in the Griffith Farran Browne reprint (p. viii) that its interest is merely historical. Cf. Pollard, *Cranmer*, 274: *Political History of England*, VI, 69.
[4] Six bishops were to be of the number. With the exception of Cranmer and Heath whose place was soon taken by Day, their names are not known.
[5] *Statutes of the Realm* (Vol. IV, 1819), 3 and 4, Edward VI, cap. 12.
[6] It was entitled: "The Forme and Manner of makyng and consecratyng of Archbischoppes, Bischoppes, Priestes and Deacons." It did not form

later the Ordinal was revised and incorporated into the
Prayer Book of 1552 by the Second Act of Uniformity.
The revision consisted simply in removing from the
ordination of priests the delivery of the chalice and paten,[1]
and from the consecration of bishops the delivery of the
pastoral staff.[2] Henceforward the Anglican Ordinal
has remained practically unchanged.[3]

The same spirit which had inspired the expurgation
of the liturgy presided over the remodelling of the
Ordinal. A return, it was claimed, was made to primitive
usage.[4]

The four minor orders, doorkeeper, reader, exorcist,
acolyte, disappeared completely, also the subdiaconate,
though the Statute had allowed for their retention.[5]
The ecclesiastical hierarchy had in fact originally
consisted only of three degrees, the diaconate, the
priesthood, and the episcopate.[6]

In the primitive church the ritual employed for ordaining deacons, priests, and bishops, was extremely simple,
both in the Western and in the Oriental Churches.[7]

To return to the ancient simplicity, the new Ordinal
abolished the imposing ceremonies with which ordination
had been surrounded. In particular the consecration of
bishops was stripped of all the solemn and extremely

---

part of the Prayer Book, but it was proposed to bind it up with it. *First
Prayer Book*, ed. Griffith Farran, 271. Lindsay reprinted it in 1734. The
bill was introduced in the Lords, January 8, 1550. *Lords' Journal*, I, 377.
See Dom W. Raynal, O.S.B., *The Ordinal of King Edward VI : Its History,
Theology, and Liturgy.* 1871.

[1] *First Prayer Book*, 290.
[2] Ibid., 295. The accompanying prayer, however, was left unchanged.
[3] Under Elizabeth the oath of supremacy against the Bishop of Rome
(*First Prayer Book*, 223) was replaced by an oath of fidelity to the sovereign,
in which the Pope was designated in more veiled and less offensive language.
(*Prayer Book of Elisabeth*, ed. above-mentioned, 165).
[4] Cf. *Responsio ad Litteras Leonis Papae XIII de Ordinationibus Anglicanis*,
February 18, 1897, Note 18.
[5] As in fact Collier remarks (*Ecclesiastical History*, II, 290).
[6] Duchesne, *Origines du Culte Chrétien*, 329, 330, 332.
[7] Duchesne, *op. cit.*, 340, 345.

significant rites with which in the course of ages the Church had enriched it. [1]

In every liturgy during the earliest centuries of the Church, the ceremony of ordination consisted in a consecratory prayer said over the ordinand at a public and solemn gathering of the Church, and accompanied by the imposition of hands. [2] The English bishops knew, it would appear, that this was in fact the essential rite of conferring orders. [3] According to the new Ordinal, hands were laid upon the candidate for the priesthood by the bishop and the priests present, upon the priest to be consecrated bishop by the consecrating bishop and his assistant bishops. And except in the case of the diaconate, this imposition of hands was preceded by the consecratory prayer, more or less refashioned, and was accompanied by an imperative formula. For a deacon the formula ran: "Take thou authority to execute the office of a deacon in the Church of God committed unto thee; in the Name of the Father and of the Son and of the Holy Ghost. Amen." [4] In the case of a priest it ran: "Receive the Holy Ghost. Whose sins thou dost forgive they are forgiven: and whose sins thou dost retain they are retained. [5] And be thou a faithful dispenser of the

[1] The length of the two other ordinations remained roughly the same, and the number of prayers was not diminished.

[2] Duchesne, *op. cit.*, 363.

[3] The Committee of 1543 declared in fact "that from the beginning of Christ's Church . . . orders were transmitted by the laying on of hands with prayer." (Burnet, *op. cit.*, ed. Pocock, 1865, IV, 485, and to Cranmer's questions had replied: "Bishops, priests, deacons are expressly ordained by the laying on of hands with prayer." (Strype, *Memorials of Cranmer*, ed. 1848, I, 426. Cf. answer to the 14th question. Ibid., 425, 427). The Henricians themselves, therefore, did not regard the tradition of the instruments as an essential rite.

[4] *Second Prayer Book*, ed. above-mentioned, 224.

[5] The formula differs completely from that of Bucer's *Ratio Ordinandi*, which seems to have very largely inspired the remaining prayers in the ordination of priests. Bucer had in fact suggested: "May the hand of God Almighty, Father, Son and Holy Ghost, be with you, protect and govern you, that the fruit of your ministry may abound unto life everlasting. Amen." This proves that in respect of the ceremonies and prayers regarded as essential the Committee of 1550 plainly departed from Bucer. The same is true of the rest of this prayer with the delivery of the chalice

Word of God and of his holy Sacraments; in the Name
of the Father and of the Son and of the Holy Ghost.
Amen."[1] and in the case of a bishop: "Receive the Holy
Ghost. And remember that thou stir up the grace of
God which is given thee by this imposition of our hands:
for God hath not given us the spirit of fear but of power
and love and soberness."[2] Prayers partly taken from
Scripture preceded and followed this ceremony. They
are substantially in harmony with the traditional prayers,
of which they even contain echoes.[3] The Litany, the
Veni Creator,[4] and the examination of the candidate[5] are
all retained in the Anglican Ordinal. And the ordination
still takes place during the Eucharist, with a special
epistle and gospel in harmony with the rite publicly
performed.

At first sight, therefore, Edward VI's Ordinal seems to
conform to primitive usage. On this ground the validity
of Anglican orders has been defended; and until the
publication of Leo XIII's Bull, this was substantially the
argument advanced by those Catholics who, though
not maintaining in principle the validity of Anglican
orders, sought to reach a precise theological conclusion
on this knotty question, particularly as regards the rite
employed.

The ordination of deacons lacks the consecratory
prayer. This renders it invalid in the opinion of those
who regard this prayer as the essential form of their

---

and paten. Dr. Messenger in his book, *The Lutheran Origin of the Anglican
Ordinal*, 1934, fails to notice this important point, which is incompatible
with his thesis.

[1] *Second Prayer Book*, 233–234. In 1662 the formula was rendered more
precise and the order conferred mentioned.

[2] *Second Prayer Book*, 238. In 1662 the formula was also rendered more
explicit and the order mentioned.

[3] See Appendix IV.

[4] The verse translation, somewhat free, of the *Veni Creator* would seem
to have been Cranmer's work, as also the Litany.

[5] In the Roman Liturgy only the candidate for the Episcopate is still
questioned. In the Anglican Ordinal the interrogatory is retained for
all three orders.

ordination.[1] But the imperative formula: "take thou authority to execute the office of a deacon, etc.," is a sufficient form in the opinion of theologians who regard the imperative formula as the sacramental form.

In the case of the Anglican presbyterate and episcopate there is a consecratory prayer. The *minimum* content of this prayer, as it results from a comparison of different liturgies, amounts to this: "*Deus qui . . . respice propitius super hunc famulum tuum quem ad diaconatum vel presbyteratum vel episcopatum vocare dignatus es; da ei gratiam tuam, ut munera hujus ordinis digne et utiliter adimplere valeat.*" (*God who . . . look mercifully upon this thy servant whom Thou hast deigned to call to the diaconate or priesthood or episcopate. Grant him grace worthily and profitably to perform the functions of this Order*). Does the Anglican Ordinal contain this minimum?

As far as the priesthood is concerned, in the view of Boudinhon[2] and Gasparri,[3] it does not contain it. For they argue that the prayer "Almighty God" which precedes the imposition of hands, is not a prayer *for the ordinand*, asking Divine grace for the future priest in the performance of his priestly functions. It is rather a thanksgiving concluded by a prayer for all men. The prayer, however, does not exclude intercession for the new priests. While thanking God for having furnished His Church with ministers, it asks Him that "by these Thy ministers . . . Thy holy Name may be for ever glorified and Thy blessed kingdom enlarged". This certainly seems a prayer that they may receive the graces of their order. And this is made still clearer in the short prayer which precedes the prayer just discussed and must be taken in conjunction with it. The bishop, who has just examined the ordinands on the duties of the priesthood and their purpose to fulfil them, prays:

[1] Boudinhon, *De la Validité des Ordres Anglicans*, Paris, 1896, 52, 57.
[2] Ibid., 50, 53–55, 57.
[3] *De la Valeur des Ordinations Anglicanes*, 47.

"Almighty God who hath given you the will to do all these things; grant also unto you strength and power to perform the same; that he may accomplish His work which He hath begun in you, through Jesus Christ our Lord."[1] After this prayer a short silence is kept for the bishop and congregation to pray privately for these graces. In any case the consecratory prayer used at the consecration of bishops, whose phraseology slightly abbreviated has been taken from the Sarum Pontifical, seems to contain all the necessary constituents. It refers to the consecration, and is a prayer for *the man about to be consecrated*.[2] Though it does not explicitly mention the episcopate, its meaning is sufficiently determined by the rite as a whole.[3]

It would therefore seem as though the Anglican form of episcopal consecration were valid. But according to a theological opinion solidly founded upon the study of Christian antiquity,[4] the episcopate is not simply the completion of the presbyterate but *the fullness of priesthood*, and therefore an episcopal consecration is valid, though unlawful, if the subject has not first received the priesthood.[5] Therefore if the rite alone is taken into consideration, it follows that a valid episcopate has been handed down in the Church of England and that Anglican bishops are validly ordained. Gasparri in fact concluded his study by saying: "In my humble opinion, it would perhaps be advisable to modify the practice hitherto followed and reordain only conditionally

---

[1] *Second Prayer Book*, ed. above-mentioned, 233.

[2] Boudinhon, *op. cit.*, 55–57; Gasparri, *op. cit.*, 49; cf. Dalbus, *Les Ordinations Anglicanes*.

[3] Boudinhon, *op. cit.* See also my Appendix IV.

[4] Thomassin, *De Veteri et Nova Ecclesiastica Disciplina*, Vol. I, Book I, Cap. I, Note 5; Mabillon, *Commentarium Praevium in Ordines Romanos*, Sec. 12; Martène, *De Antiquis Ecclesiae Ritibus*, Cap. VIII, Art. 3, Note 9 *sq.*; Bingham, *Origines Ecclesiasticae*, Book II, Chapter X, Note 5; Riganti, *Regula XXIV Cancellariae Apostolicae*, Sec. I, Note 12; Phillipps, *Du Droit Ecclésiastique*, I, Sec. 36; Duchesne, *Liber Pontificalis Passim* and *Bulletin Critique*, July 15, 1894.

[5] Gasparri, *Tractatus de Sacra Ordinatione*, Paris, 1893, Note 23 *sq.*, and *De la Nature de L'Episcopat*, in *Le Canoniste Contemporain*, February 1895.

(*sub conditione*) Anglican clergymen who return to the Catholic Church, bishops at any rate."[1]

But just as the Prayer Book had deprived the Eucharist of its sacrificial character, so the Ordinal was at pains to present the priest not as one who offers sacrifice but as a minister of God's word. Every reference in the Ordination service to the office of teaching and preaching was carefully preserved and even amplified. Not only does the ordaining bishop deliver to the deacon the New Testament[2] and to the bishop the Bible,[3] but he also delivers it to the priest,[4] insisting in each instance upon the ministry of preaching. On the contrary, all the rites which, though not of apostolic origin, implied the traditional doctrine of the Mass were abolished. The delivery for example of the chalice and paten was discontinued, a ceremony which had signified the power to change bread and wine into Christ's Body and Blood and to offer the Eucharistic sacrifice. "Receive power," the bishop had said as he delivered them, "to offer sacrifice to God and celebrate Mass for the living and the dead," *in nomine Domini*.[5] The anointing of the hands bore a similar meaning. It was accompanied by the following words of the bishop: "Vouchsafe, O Lord, to consecrate and hallow these hands by this anointing and our blessing, that whatsoever they bless shall be blessed and whatsoever they consecrate shall be consecrated, in the Name of Our Lord Jesus Christ." The ceremony was suppressed. For it was primarily to celebrate Mass that the priest's hands were hallowed, and Bucer condemned the unction as superstitious.

The prayer *Deus sanctificationum omnium Auctor*, which

[1] *Op. cit.*, 5. Cf. Denny and Lacey, *op. cit.*, 68 *sq.*; *De Materia et Forma in Ritu Anglicano*.
[2] *Second Prayer Book*, 225.
[3] *Second Prayer Book*, 238.
[4] *Second Prayer Book*, 234.
[5] So long as the Prayer Book did not exclude belief in the Real Presence, the delivery of the chalice and paten continued. It was the Ordinal of 1552 that abolished it.

at the ordination of priests follows the Preface of the Mass, was refashioned and placed at the conclusion of the ceremony. Every allusion to the Mass was excised, and in particular the petition "*et in obsequium plebis tuae panem et vinum in corpus et sanguinem filii Tui immaculata benedictione transforment;*" (and for thy people's service may they change bread and wine by their pure blessing into thy Son's Body and Blood).

The consecratory prayer itself, though retained in its usual place,[1] was altered. Every allusion to the Old Testament priesthood whose essential function was to offer sacrifice was removed. To the Deacon no longer did the consecrating prelate speak of the tribe of Levi attached to the ministry of the altar. Neither did he remind the priest of the saving victim offered so frequently to the Lord by the sons of Aaron, nor explain to the bishop the mystical meaning of the high priest's vestments. And he made no mention of "their ministry of supreme priesthood". The sacerdotal character of the old prayer had vanished.

Taken together all these changes[2] reveal a preoccupation, we might call it an obsession, the same in fact under whose influence, as we have seen, the Prayer Book of 1549 was composed. Just as that book carefully excluded from its Holy Communion the notion of sacrifice, so the Ordinal removed from the ritual of ordination "all notion of a priestly or sacrificial function".[3] The priest remained the dispenser of the sacraments and

---

[1] Instead of accompanying, it preceded the imposition of hands. But it may be regarded as forming a moral unity with the latter.

[2] The significance of each of these suppressions and alterations taken individually would be dubious. But taken together they reveal the intention and purpose of those responsible for them.

[3] Cardinal Vaughan in his letter of December 2, 1894. Fr. Mason, theologian and chaplain to King James I, who is regarded by Anglicans as the protagonist in defence of their orders, says that the formula "Receive the Holy Ghost" fully expresses all the functions of a priest and excludes "the offering of any sacrifice, which does not pertain to any man on earth". *De Ministerio Anglicano*, 1625, Book V, Chapter 14. In 1613 the first edition was published of his book *of the Consecration of Bishops in the Church of England against Bellarmine, Sanders, Stapleton and other Romanists.*

above all of God's word[1]. But of his former Eucharistic power not a word was said. This is the chief ground on which the conclusion has been reached that Anglican orders are invalid.[2] The Reformers, of whose views the Ordinal is a mouthpiece, had no intention, it is argued, of doing what the Church does when she ordains her ministers.[3]

If they have preserved the sacerdotal power of jurisdiction, namely the priest's authority to teach, preach, and preside over public worship, as the lawful representative of the Church, they have deprived the priest of one part at least of his power of order, namely the power to offer Christ's body in sacrifice.[4] The Bishop no longer ordained sacrificing priests.[5] And had it rested entirely with Cranmer and his supporters, the Ordinal would have made no mention whatsoever of the power of order, that is to say of the power to communicate the grace of each sacrament to the soul of the recipients.[6]

[1] Second Prayer Book, 234.

[2] See Sydney Smith, Reasons for Rejecting Anglican Orders, Chapter III: "The Anglican Ordinal certainly insufficient"; Dom. Bede Camm, Revue Bénédictine for December 1894. Cf. E. E. Estcourt, The Question of Anglican Ordinations Discussed, App. XXXVI; Rome's Witness against Anglican Orders, Historical series No. 14, Catholic Truth Society.

[3] The Church intends to create priests in the true sense, who do not merely commemorate the sacrifice of the Cross but offer on the altar the true though unbloody sacrifice of Christ's Body and Blood. For this sacrifice her ministers are ordained. It is the function of priests to offer the Eucharistic Sacrifice, of bishops to offer it also and to ordain sacrificing priests. Denny and Lacey anticipate the objection. They devote an entire chapter to the subject of intention and another to the Anglican doctrine of the Eucharist, the sacrifice of the Mass, and the power to offer it.

[4] See Bull of Leo XIII of September 13, 1896, Acta S. Sedis, Vol. XXIX, 193 sq.

[5] See Bull above-mentioned.

[6] The formulas mentioned above: "Receive the Holy Ghost", "Take thou authority to minister the Holy Sacraments", though indeterminate, may signify that in virtue of orders a special grace is bestowed upon the ordinand, empowering him to convey sacramental grace to souls. The formulas were in fact drawn up at a time of compromise, when vague expressions still left a Catholic interpretation open. It would have been different had Bucer's formula (see above note) been accepted. (Bucer De Ordinatione Legitima Ministrorum Ecclesiae Revocanda). Under Edward

No

As early as 1543 in fact, the Archbishop had denied the sacramental character of Ordination. According to him it was not a rite which conferred a distinctive grace, but simply the official transmission of the ecclesiastical jurisdiction of which the king was the fountain-head. "All Christian princes", he affirmed, "have committed unto them immediately of God the whole care of all their subjects, as well concerning the administration of God's word, for the care of souls, as concerning the ministration of things political and civil governance". Since, however, the monarch cannot perform all his functions in person, he appoints ministers to act for him in various capacities. All these owe their appointment and commission to the law and the royal command. It is customary to observe certain ceremonies in their admission to office, but their omission could not invalidate their authority, for "there is no more promise of God that grace is given in the committing of the ecclesiastical office, than it is in the committing of the civil."[1] It could not have been more plainly stated that order confers no special grace, and that the liturgical ministers are merely the official representatives in the religious sphere, of the secular government. This was the Lutheran conception of the ecclesiastical ministry.

Contemporary observers seem hardly to have been aware of the changes introduced into the new Ordinal. "They have issued," wrote the Venetian Ambassador Barbaro, "and have given it Parliamentary sanction,

---

VI, order was not explicitly excluded from the number of sacraments. Article 26 of the XLII Articles of 1552 refrained from enumerating the sacraments. It was content to affirm they were very few. It was Elizabeth's XXXIX Articles which definitely stated that there were only two sacraments. (Art. 25) The composers of the Ordinal were dead by that time. We cannot therefore affirm that by this article 25 they rejected the sacrament of order.

[1] This view seemed to have been derived from Marsilius of Padua, whose *Defensor Pacis* was printed in England in 1536. (Cf. Dunning, *Ancient and Medieval Political Theory*, 242–243).

a book containing the rite of conferring Holy Orders.
Between their Ordinal and ours, the only difference
is that those ordained by them take an oath denying
the Pope's teaching and authority."[1]

Until Leo XIII issued his Bull,[2] the briefs of Julius III
(March 8, 1554)[3] and Paul IV (June 20 and October
30, 1555)[4] were not universally regarded as an un-
qualified condemnation of the orders conferred by the
new Ordinal.[5] From the beginning the validity of their
orders has been an article of faith for Anglicans. The
articles of religion issued respectively under Edward
VI and Elizabeth pronounce the Ordinal free from all
doctrinal defect, and declare that all ordained by it
are "rightly, orderly, and lawfully consecrated and
ordained."[6] The Church of England claims to have
preserved unbroken the ministerial succession of the
Apostles as well as their teaching. "In this country,
however, as the old episcopal succession was preserved
inviolate, the succession of ministers was also unin-
terrupted. . . . Parker was felt to occupy substantially
the same position as Warham, and hierarchical ideas

---

[1] Albèri, *Relazioni Degli Ambasciatori Veneti*, Series I, Vol. II, 249.
Barbaro's statement is the more remarkable, because in other respects
he was fully aware of the difference between the Anglican and the Catholic
forms of worship. His remark is made about the Ordinal of 1550 which,
as we have seen, apart from the delivery of the instruments, was the same
as that of 1552.

[2] The Bull is partly based upon the decisions of Julius III and Paul
IV (*Acta Apostolicae Sedis*, Vol. XXIX, 193).

[3] Wilkins, *Concilia Magnae Britanniae*, IV, 91; Burnet, *op. cit.*, VI, 322;
Denny and Lacey, *op. cit.*, 258.

[4] The Bull of June 20 and the brief of October 30 published in part
for the first time by Dom Gasquet in the *Civiltà Cattolica* (June 1, 1895)
are to be found in full in Boudinhon, *De la Validité des Ordres Anglicans*,
78 and 82.

[5] Cf. Boudinhon, *op. cit.*, 73–87; Gasparri, *De la Valeur des Ordinations
Anglicanes*, 10–15.
A number of reordinations under Queen Mary are now known. (Frere,
Marian Reaction, 1896; Dom. Norbert Birt *The Line of Cleavage under Elizabeth*,
76–79; E. C. Messenger, *The Reformation, the Mass and the Priesthood*, 1936–
1937, Vol. II, Chapters V and VI.) They clearly prove the opinion of the
1552 Ordinal held by the Henrician bishops, the Queen and Cardinal
Pole.

[6] Article 35 of the XLII, and Article 36 of the XXXIX Articles.

were thus transmitted with few modifications from the Mediaeval to the Modern Church of England."[1]

Denny and Lacey conclude their monograph *De Hierarchia Anglicana* with the following passage:

"We are not defending ourselves so much as the treasure entrusted to us, the Eucharists we celebrate, the graces conferred upon us, the pardon of sins, the tears of penitents, the joys of holy souls, in short all the benefits obtained by a valid reception of the Sacraments. Nor are we defending only what is our own. For the entire body of the faithful benefits by the grace of the Holy Spirit bestowed on each part. We are defending not the Anglican Church alone but the Universal Church."

In a speech delivered on February 14, 1895, Lord Halifax pointed out that priests who had received Roman orders could officiate, members of the Roman church communicate, at Anglican altars. With all their hearts, he said, Anglicans desired to be allowed when abroad to confess to the Roman clergy and receive Communion from their hands. But they could not surrender in any point what they knew to be truth and justice, could not, for example, admit even in practice, that they had no priests or sacraments. The Anglican reply was clear, their episcopate was in every respect the true and direct descendant of the mission which had evangelised England.[2]

The Bull *Apostolicae Curae*, published by Leo XIII on September 13, 1896, disappointed the hopes of those who shared the view of Lord Halifax, and closed for Catholics the discussion as to the validity or otherwise of Anglican Orders.[3]

The axiom *Lex Orandi, Lex Credendi* is verified in the period we are studying. It was in her liturgy that the new Anglican faith found its first expression. It was not

---

[1] Hardwick, *A History of the Christian Church*, ed. 1856, 356.
[2] Speech by Lord Halifax at Bristol, February 14, 1895.
[3] For the arguments put forward in the Bull, and the controversy on the subject of Anglican orders, see my Appendix V.

until the very end of Edward's reign that an official
statement of doctrine was issued.[1] But no reign in the
history of Christian England witnessed a more radical
or a more rapid doctrinal change. Within a few years
Anglican dogma traversed in successive stages the
entire distance dividing Catholicism from the most
thorough-going Protestantism. If it halted a short while
with Luther, it soon followed the inspiration of Zwingli
and Calvin. The transformation is reflected in the
liturgy, the two books of Common Prayer and the
Ordinal, which put into practice what the reformers
already believed in their hearts. These books are
obviously manuals of devotion, devout formulas of
prayer, and a collection of rules prescribing the order
of public worship. But they are also the expression of
a novel religious belief, and a denial of the old sacramental doctrine. The transformation of worship was
but the effect of a doctrinal transformation. *Lex Orandi,
Lex Credendi.*[2]

[1] The XLII Articles were signed by Edward VI on June 12, 1553.
On July 6 he died.
[2] For the Anglican liturgy from the beginning of the Reformation to
modern times see *Hierurgia Anglicana: Documents and Extracts illustrative of
the Ceremonial of the Anglican Church after the Reformation* compiled by the
members of the Ecclesiological Society, revised and considerably enlarged
by Vernon Staley, Provost of St. Andrew's, Inverness, 1902–04.

CHAPTER VII

THE MODERATE BISHOPS AND THE RELIGIOUS REVOLUTION

The Henrician bishops: Gardiner of Winchester, Tunstall of Durham, Bonner of London, Heath of Worcester, Day of Chichester. Their attitude towards the religious innovations under Edward—Their treatment by Somerset and by Warwick.

ONE of the two religious parties between whom Henry VIII's personal authority had kept the balance, namely the Reformers, had possessed the upper hand since Edward's accession. Through its action Protestantism had made its way into the Church of England under Somerset, and had finally taken complete possession of it under Warwick. What attitude then was adopted by the other party, that of the Henricians or orthodox, when confronted by their adversaries and the religious revolution they effected?

The leader of this party, Gardiner, Bishop of Winchester, was sixty-four years of age and had been a bishop for sixteen years. He was a prelate of keen intellect, "of learning, virtue, and wit,"[1] a learned and shrewd lawyer,[2] a clever diplomat, and a man accustomed to struggle with enemies and defeat them. Under Henry VIII he had overthrown Cromwell and seriously endangered Cranmer's position.[3] Few

[1] Said by Dr. Weston as reported in Foxe, *Acts and Monuments*, VI, 222.
[2] Though hostile to Gardiner, Foxe admits his eminence as a lawyer, *op. cit.*, VI, 266.
[3] He shewed his capacity by the extreme skill with which he handled the matter of Henry's divorce as in dealing with Pope Clement. After Wolsey's fall he served the King as a diplomatist both in France and Germany.

felt themselves capable of opposing him.[1] His was a strong character that could bear with equanimity favour and disgrace, and in Henry's stern school he had learned to fear no man. More than once in Edward's reign, he had found himself compelled to oppose the plans of his enemies, who could not endure him. One of them, Bishop Ponet, who usurped his see of Winchester, drew the following unflattering portrait of him. "This doctor had a swart colour, an hanging look, frowning brows, eyes an inch within the head, a nose hooked like a bustard, wide nostrils like a horse, ever snuffing into the wind, a sparrow mouth, great paws like the devil, talons on his feet, like a grype" (griffin) "two inches longer than natural toes, and so tied to with sinews that he could not abide to be touched nor scarce suffer them to touch the stones."[2] Gardiner, who had not been mentioned in Henry's will, and was excluded from the Council of which he had hitherto been a member, saw clearly from the very outset of the new reign, that the Reformers would rule henceforward and revolutionise the doctrine and discipline of the Anglican Church, and that the religious edifice erected by the late king would be demolished by the very men entrusted with the office of preserving it intact.[3] Prepared to resist, he took his stand upon the constitutional ground: the king, he argued, is *personally* the supreme head of the Church. Therefore during his minority his spiritual authority is in abeyance, and cannot be exercised in his name either by the Council or by the Protector. Therefore no religious change can lawfully be made until the king is old enough to give his consent to it. The Act of 1536 which empowered Edward on attaining his twenty-fourth year to annul whatever had been done

[1] According to Paget, Henry VIII said that he was the only one capable of doing so. Cf. Maitland, *Essays on the Reformation*, Chapter XVI.

[2] Ponet, *Treatise of the Politik Power*. Cf. Maitland, *op. cit.*, 71. Foxe (*Acts and Monuments*, VII, 586) half believes this caricature.

[3] Cf. Chapter I and Pollard, *England under Protector Somerset*, 21-23.

before his majority, lent no slight support to this argument, plausible in itself. The Henricians therefore, Gardiner himself for example, appealed to it to justify their resistance. They could not, they maintained, be bound by any change made in the conduct of public worship, whereby it departed from the order prescribed by Henry VIII.[1]

When at Henry's death the bishops were obliged to ask the king to renew their spiritual jurisdiction, Gardiner raised objections,[2] which were curtly and peremptorily answered by Paget, the Secretary of State.[3] But it was when Barlow preached against images and ceremonies[4] that he put forward for the first time his theory of the *status quo*. Barlow and others[5] urged the government to proceed with the Reformation. "If my Lord of Saint David's or such others," Gardiner wrote to Somerset on February 28, 1547, "have their head encumbered with any new platform I would wish they were commanded, between this and the King's Majesty's full age to draw the plat, diligently to hew the stones, dig the sand and chop the chalk in the unseasonable time of building; and when the King's Majesty cometh to full age, to present their labours to him: and in the mean time, not to disturb the state of the realm, whereof Your Grace is protector, but that you may in every part of religion, laws, lands and decrees (which four contain the state) deliver the same unto our Sovereign Lord, according unto the trust you be put in; which shall be much to your honour and as all honest men wish and desire."[6]

---

[1] Van der Delft to Charles V, October 18, 1547. *Spanish Calendar*, IX, 178.

[2] Gardiner to Paget, Southwark, March 1, 1547. J. A. Muller, *The Letters of Stephen Gardiner*, Cambridge, 1933, 268. Paget was entrusted with the execution of these episcopal commissions.

[3] Paget to Gardiner, March 24, 1547. Tytler, *op. cit.*, I, 24.

[4] Bishop of St. David's.

[5] Nicholas Ridley, the future Bishop of London, and Dr. Glazier, Cranmer's commissary, preached at Paul's Cross in the early part of 1547 to the same effect as Barlow.

[6] Foxe, *op. cit.*, VI, 25; J. A. Muller, *op. cit.*, 265. See Strype (*Cranmer*, ed. 1848, II, 127 *sq.*) who treats the Henricians, who employed this argument, as papists.

Gardiner's thesis found many supporters. Throughout Edward's reign the Emperor and his ambassadors in London never ceased to urge that the religion of England as it had been established in Henry's reign should be restored. "When you speak to the Protector and the other members of the government," Charles V instructed Van der Delft on September 2, 1549,[1] "you are to attempt to persuade them, as tactfully as you can, to restore religion if not to its old form, as it is with us, at least such as it was left by the late king, that they may not be liable to censure hereafter for having made changes during the minority of the present monarch, or refer the matter to the General Council and meanwhile observe the Interim, though in our opinion there is more likelihood of persuading them to restore the position as it was under the late king."

The following November 26, the ambassador replied that he had had a long interview with Warwick and had found him "extremely obstinate". He had pointed out to him "that the late king had never intended to go so far. On the contrary, for all his hostility to the Pope, he had kept the old faith to the end and had left them as councillors to his son, not kings of the country with power at their arbitrary whim to make changes, such as no king or other ruler in the world had ever attempted without thereby occasioning his ruin. Moreover, since God has appointed princes to govern this world to His glory, it does not befit subjects of a monarch to usurp his authority of which that king himself, when he came of age, would not make such wanton use. . . . I therefore besought him, as one who desired the prosperity of this realm and moreover the welfare and honour of himself and his house to whom I bore no less affection than he

---

[1] Staats Archiv of Vienna, *England*, Fasc. 18. In his letters of May 10 and 28, June 8 and July 26, *Spanish Calendar*, IX, 373 *sq.*, 385, 419, the Emperor had insisted that these representations should be made to the Protector. Somerset had replied (Van der Delft to Charles V, ibid, IX, 381) that it was not in his power to quash acts of parliament" and "that I was asking what was dangerous to the realm."

has always displayed towards myself, that he would consider well all that I had said and would take the surest path to surrender a good account of all when the need should arise. And, I added, this would have been easier had they left things as they were at the late king's death."[1]

Writing of the new English Mass which the government sought to impose upon her, Princess Mary reminded the Council on June 22, 1549[2] that the executors of Henry's will had sworn to maintain the laws then in force, and had no authority to pass new legislation until the King was old enough to give his free assent. "When her royal brother was of age to decide these matters in person, she would obey his orders about religion".

The Government could scarcely admit this theory of the *status quo* without tying its own hands and indeed committing suicide, the more since it could be applied to secular politics as well as religion. "Let the Scots," Gardiner did in fact say, "remain Scottish until the king comes of age. If he then decides to conquer them, the honour will be his."[3] According to this argument no statute passed during Edward's minority would have the force of law. If, however, the authority of the crown were diminished by the fact that the king is a minor or mad, government would be brought to a standstill, when it was most required. The question was vital for the Council. It was thus compelled to do its utmost to extort from its opponent the admission that the King's authority was as great during his minority, as it would have been had he been of age.[4]

Even if Gardiner's argument had been admitted, it

[1] Staats-Archiv of Vienna, *England*, Fasc. 17.
[2] Foxe, VI, 7 sq.
[3] He disapproved of Somerset's project of conquering Scotland. Cf. Blunt, *op. cit.*, II, 127; Dixon, *op. cit.*, II, 440.
[4] The Council therefore required Gardiner and Bonner to admit this; and in a letter to Mary (June 22, 1549) answered her objection by asserting that the King acting by his councillors' advice was entitled to the same obedience as though he had attained his majority, as was proved by one "of Solomon's Proverbs in the sixth chapter of the Book of Wisdom". (Foxe, *Acts and Monuments*, VI, 7-10.)

could have preserved England only for a time from a change of religion. It was clever and specious. But the bishop had given his case away by accepting royal instead of papal supremacy.[1]

The first bishop to come into open conflict with the government was Bonner of London. On September 12, 1547, he was summoned before the Privy Council to answer for his action in opposing the royal visitation in his diocese,[2] and for having accepted the injunctions of July 31 and the homilies only with the reservation "If they are not contrary to God's law and the laws and rules of the Church". These injunctions and homilies were the first step towards reform taken under Edward. The former were directed against images[3] and certain ceremonies. The latter taught in several places Lutheran doctrine. Bonner was reprimanded for "a protestation . . . to the evil example of all such as should hear of it, and to the contempt of the authority which his Majesty hath justly on earth of this Church of England and Ireland."[4] The Bishop made a rather evasive defence, and his explanations were regarded by the Council as mere hair-splitting. An unconditional retractation was demanded. He made it in the following terms: "I have thought it my bounden duty not only

---

[1] It would seem that on the brink of a religious revolution he was powerless to avert, Gardiner dreamed of a reconciliation with Rome which without detriment to the Royal Supremacy, would have kept England in the old faith. In certain cases, he said in his sermon of June 29, 1548, the King might send an ambassador to Rome and, if the Bishop of Rome were able by his wisdom, virtue and knowledge, to establish unity in the Church of England, the King might well ask his aid and counsel. This would not give the Bishop of Rome any authority superior to the King's.

[2] It was carried out by Sir Anthony Cook and several other laymen. Bonner required them to show him their commission from the King. They refused and complained to the Council. For the royal visitation of 1547, see chapter II of Book II of Strype's *Cranmer*.

[3] Nevertheless a distinction was made between superstitious images and those which were not thus abused. The injunction ordered the destruction only of the former. In October 1547, the Imperial Ambassador wrote that the crucifix and the image of the Blessed Virgin were still retained. *Span. Cal.*, IX, 182.

[4] *Acts of the Privy Council*, II, 125.

to declare before your Lordships that I do now, upon better consideration of my duty, renounce and revoke my said protestation, but also most humbly beseech your Lordships that this my revocation of the same may be likewise put in the same records" (the visitors' report) "for a perpetual memory of the truth".[1] This humiliating repudiation of his action did not save Bonner from imprisonment and he remained several weeks in prison.[2]

Gardiner's opposition on the same occasion was both cleverer and bolder. He had first attempted to stop the innovations by pointing out to the Protector the danger of hurrying them through.[3] Somerset had replied that his fear was exaggerated. When they had been decided upon, Gardiner declared that he would frankly state his views to the royal visitors, but would not offer any resistance to them. He even prepared to give them an honourable reception, and instructed his secretary to meet them at Chichester and conduct them to Winchester with every mark of respect. In his absence one of his chaplains was to act in his name, and take the oath of royal supremacy.[4] But before the Commissioners' arrival,[5] he was summoned to London by the Council (September 21, 1547).[6] He was accused of having spoken against the Homilies.[7] Cranmer had in fact attempted to gain his assent to them by pointing out that the book of Homilies had been presented to

---

[1] *Acts of the Privy Council*, II, 126–7. Cf. ibid., 517.

[2] Cf. *Spanish Calendar*, IX, 153, 169, 188, 453, 458.

[3] He wrote to Somerset to this effect (Somerset's reply is in Foxe, *op. cit.*, VI, 28). About the destruction of images in his diocese, about attacks upon the observance of Lent, and the public sale of a treatise by Bale entitled, *Elucidation of Anne Askew's Martyrdom*. (Gardiner to Somerset, May 21 and June 6, 1547. Foxe, *op. cit.*, VI, 30 *sqq.* Strype, *Eccles. Memorials*, III, 53 *sqq.*; J. A. Muller, *op. cit.*, 276, 286).

[4] Blunt, *op. cit.*, II, 129.

[5] The visitation was not held until October.

[6] *Acts of the Privy Council*, II, 517.

[7] A certain Philip Paris, as is shown by the minutes of the Council, had declared that the Bishop of Winchester told him that His Majesty's Homilies contained both heresy and treason. Paris, however, confessed that he, not Gardiner, had said this. *Acts of the Privy Council*, II, 130.

Convocation,[1] and by offering him a share in their composition. Henry VIII, he added, had been "seduced" when he laid down the doctrine contained in the King's Book, the final confession of his reign. Gardiner rounded upon the unfortunate word. "Your Grace hath four year continually lived in agreement of that doctrine under our late Sovereign Lord. Now, so suddenly after his death, to write to me that His Highness was seduced, it is, I assure you, a very strange speech. In the truth there can be no seducing to it, but from it."[2] "My Lord of Canterbury," he wrote to Somerset, "will needs maintain that our late sovereign Lord was seduced; and then it is possible that Your Grace may be seduced also".[3] To avoid all occasion of dissension, Gardiner refused to take part in drawing up the Homilies which he regarded as useless. The people had done quite well without them hitherto, and would continue to go to heaven without their assistance. It was probably to avenge himself on Gardiner that Cranmer had him summoned before the Council.

Gardiner appeared "laden with books" to maintain against the Archbishop the heterodoxy of his Homilies.[4] But the Council was in no mood for a theological debate. It offered Gardiner the choice between unquestioning obedience and imprisonment. That very evening Gardiner joined Bonner in the Fleet, for "having written to the Lords of the Council, and besides that spoken to others, impertinent things of the King's Majesty's visitation, and refused to set forth and receive the injunctions and homilies, for that, as he said, being examined by their Lordships thereupon, they contained things dissident

---

[1] But it had not approved them. Cf. Foxe, VI, 41.

[2] Gardiner to Cranmer, shortly after June 12, 1547. Strype, *Cranmer*, App. XXXV; J. A. Muller, *op. cit.*, 299, cf. his letter of the following July. Ibid., 316.

[3] Gardiner to the Protector, Foxe, VI, 54. J. A. Muller, 425.

[4] Gardiner to Somerset, October 14, 1547. Strype, *Cranmer*, App. XXXVI and Foxe, VI, 42–46. Strype gives the first part of the letter, Foxe the second. J. A. Muller. Note 130.

with the Word of God, so as his conscience could not suffer him to accept them"[1]

Gardiner, a more skilful diplomat than Bonner, far from admitting that he had been guilty of disobedience, attacked the government's religious policy as unconstitutional. The royal authority over the Church, he argued, ought to be and is subject to the restrictions imposed by the common law upon the king's secular prerogative.[2] The injunctions, however, are merely royal decrees without legal authority. They cannot therefore possess the force of law. To obey them would render him liable to the same penalty as Wolsey, who although expressly authorised by the king to exercise his legatine functions, could not thereby escape the statute of Praemunire.[3] This argument was reinforced by that which Gardiner had already put forward. If the king has no right to make any religious changes without the assent of Parliament, Parliament is equally incapable of enacting any before the king attains his majority. Therefore the final confession of faith imposed by Henry VIII[4] must be the sole doctrinal standard of the Anglican Church so long as the king is a minor. The King's Book, Gardiner wrote to Cranmer,[5] has been recognised, imposed, and sanctioned by Parliament. Like his colleagues, the Archbishop issued and read and enforced it.[6] We

[1] *Acts of the Privy Council*, II, 131–132. Cf. 208. *Spanish Cal.*, IX, 169, 182, 197, 230. In October 1547, the report was also current that Gardiner had been imprisoned on account of his opposition to the injunctions against images. Ibid., IX, 182, 188.

[2] Gardiner to Somerset, Foxe, VI, 42 *sqq.* J. A. Muller, 380. The royal supremacy, it was replied, was strictly royal, not parliamentary. The king did not share with Parliament his spiritual, as he shared his temporal authority. The Act of Supremacy and the subsequent statutes of Henry VIII gave the king the right to reform ecclesiastical abuses at his discretion. *Statutes of the realm*, Henry VIII, cap. 1.

[3] See Gardiner's letters to Somerset, Foxe, *Acts and Monuments*, VI, 42–53. J. A. Muller, *op. cit.*, 380–410.

[4] The King's Book or Necessary Erudition of a Christian Man.

[5] Strype, *Cranmer*, App. XXXV. J. A. Muller, 299.

[6] Cranmer had forbidden a certain John Joseph a former monk of Canterbury to attack the King's Book. This John Joseph was one of the preachers at the royal visitation of 1547.

must, therefore, adhere to it and no alteration must be made.

The Council took this action against Bonner and Gardiner in the absence of Somerset, who on August 22, had left London for Scotland.[1] It was probably inspired by Cranmer, who regarded these two bishops as the chief obstacle to the projected reforms and had not forgiven Gardiner's attempt to destroy him in the closing years of Henry's reign. Somerset had scarcely returned when Bonner was released. He took his seat in Parliament from the opening of the session (November 4, 1547), and voted against several measures of religious reform.[2] Gardiner, included in the general pardon, left prison on January 8, 1548, having first received from the Council a severe admonition. He simply replied that he did not refuse the King's pardon for which he humbly thanked His Majesty.[3] The rumour spread that he would be appointed ambassador to Charles V.[4]

But the Bishop of Winchester was not at the end of his troubles. His haughty character and biting replies made him detested by his opponents. Whereas Bonner had recanted, Gardiner continued to maintain that he was in the right. During his imprisonment Cranmer had left no stone unturned to overcome his opposition. He had engaged in a lengthy discussion with him in the presence of bishops,[5] and doctors of divinity,[6] had pointed

[1] The fact that Somerset's name is to be found in the minutes of the Council on the occasion of Gardiner's summons to appear before it, does not prove that he was present. It was his custom to sign on his return whatever had been done during his absence.

[2] In particular against the bill for Communion under both kinds (December 10) and the bill abolishing the chantries (December 15). Lords' Journal, 308. Gairdner (*A History of the English Church in the XVIth Century*, 248) is therefore mistaken when he says that Bonner was not released until the general amnesty of January 1548.

[3] Foxe, *Acts and Monuments*, VI, 65, *Span. Cal.*, IX, 242.

[4] De Selve to the Constable, January 21, 1548. *Correspondance Politique de Odet de Selve*, p. 247.

[5] Ridley, Bishop of Rochester, and Holbeach, Bishop of Lincoln.

[6] Dr. Cox, and May the Dean of St. Paul's, at whose house the interview took place.

out that he was the only man in the kingdom who refused to accept the Homilies and even promised him a seat in the Council if he yielded. "My Lord of Canterbury's homely of salvation hath as many faults as I have been weeks in prison", was Gardiner's reply.[1] He proceeded to contrast their teaching with that of Erasmus' Paraphrases imposed upon the clergy by the same injunction. "The injunctions", he wrote, "contain a commandment to see taught and learned two books, one of homelies, another of Erasmus' Paraphrases. . . . These books strive one against another directly."[2] He took particular delight in attacking the Homily on Justification, composed by Cranmer himself. "I offered to yield," he wrote to Somerset, "if he" (the Archbishop) "could shew me one Scripture affirming faith to exclude charity in justification, or, Scripture failing, as it doth indeed, but one ancient writer that writeth so. . . ."[3]

When he left the Fleet he was asked to conform to the Royal Injunctions and accept the Homilies, particularly that on Justification, a demand which reveals the quarter from which the insistence and the animosity proceeded. He asked a few days for reflection. The following Thursday, January 12, 1548, he gave his opinion in writing. On the 19th he was confined to his house for refusal to subscribe the Homily on Justification. It was

---

[1] Gardiner to Somerset, October 14, 1547 (Strype, *Cranmer*, App. XXVI. J. A. Muller, *op. cit.*, 380).

[2] "The book of Homelies teacheth faith to exclude charity in justification, Erasmus' Paraphrases teacheth faith to have charity joined with him in justification. The Book of Homelies teacheth how men may swear. The Paraphrase teacheth the contrary very extremely. The Book of Homelies teacheth how subjects owe tribute to their prince and obedience very well. The Book of Paraphrases knitteth up the matter untruly that between Christian men there should be no debt or right but mutual charity." Gardiner to Somerset, October 14, 1547, in Strype and Muller, loc. cit., Foxe, VI, 42–46, gives only the latter part of this letter.

[3] Letter to Somerset of October 14, 1547. Cf. Strype, *Cranmer*, Book II, Chapter III. The Imperial Ambassador praised Gardiner's firmness. Van der Delft to the Emperor, February 23 and April 23, 1548, *Spanish Calendar*, IX, 253, 263.

in vain that Bishop Ridley of Rochester attempted to convert him.[1] Somerset sent to him the two secretaries of state, Sir Thomas Smith and Cecil, and accepted the declaration on Justification which Gardiner sent him through them.

At the approach of Lent, the Bishop was allowed to retire to his diocese. On his way at Farnham, he spoke of the duty of obedience to authority.[2] At Winchester he was living quietly, practising the submission he preached to others, when the Council summoned him to appear before them at Greenwich.[3] He was accused of having secretly armed his servants on his return to his diocese, who were stirring up the people against the religious measures taken by the Government. Gardiner excused himself from coming on the plea of his health. But when the summons was repeated twice, he was obliged to set out about Whitsun and make the journey in a litter.[4]

He was charged with retaining the ceremonies which had been abolished, and having preached on the Real Presence, though an injunction expressly forbade any controversial questions regarding the Eucharist to be ventilated,[5] of having forbidden two royal chaplains sent down by the Council to preach, and of having preached in their place and warned the people against novelties. The chaplains, he replied, had received every courtesy. To the second charge he replied that he had not used the term "real" which was unnecessary, and to the first that he had retained only the ceremonies authorised by law. He was confined to his London house to keep him away from his diocese for a time.[6] Thus Gardiner was repeatedly

---

[1] Strype, *Ecclesiastical Memorials*, III, 107.
[2] Foxe, *op. cit.*, VI, 206, 208, 211, 213–214.
[3] Ibid., 208–210, 212, 216.
[4] *Acts of the Privy Council*, II, 209. *Span. Cal.*, IX, 263, 266.
[5] Royal injunction of December 27, 1547.
[6] *Acts of the Privy Council*, II, 209.

charged with failure to conform and disobedience to the Council.[1]

To clear himself from these charges, the Bishop agreed to preach (indeed he made the proposal himself, promising that they would be satisfied as to his conformity) at Saint Paul's Cross on the subjects prescribed to him. He refused, however, to submit his sermon in writing for the Council's approval. This, he said, would amount to treating him as guilty, though nothing could be proved against him. After some negotiation Somerset took his part, and allowed him to omit a few unimportant topics and choose his own day. But he expressly forbade him to deal with the Eucharist and the Mass, subjects of heated controversy, about which the royal injunction of December 27, 1547, had commanded silence to be kept until further orders. Probably the Protector desired to prevent him contradicting Cranmer and the advanced Reformers, who would not fail to reply by a fresh accusation. Gardiner decided to disobey. The day before his sermon he spent in great disquiet. He would neither drink, eat, nor sleep. But he was perfectly self-possessed when he made his appearance in the pulpit before the King, the heads of the Council and a congregation so large that its like was seldom seen.[2]

It was June 29, 1548, the Feast of Saint Peter and Saint Paul. Taking for his text the Confession of the Prince of the Apostles, "Thou art the Christ, the Son of the Living God" (Matthew xvi, 16), he proceeded to maintain the supremacy of the king and deny the papal supremacy. "Saint Peter," he preached, "might be

[1] He was accused of being the only bishop who did not accept and carry out the injunctions and, in spite of his promise to obey, of having caused more disputes and dissensions in his small city and diocese than his colleagues throughout the entire kingdom. (June 1548). He was also charged with having meddled, immediately after his exclusion from the Council, with matters which were no concern of his or of any bishop but of the crown alone. *Acts of the Privy Council*, II, 208, 209. Cf. *Span. Cal.*, 272.

[2] *Acts of the Privy Council*, II, 209.

called the head of the Church as the head of the river
is called the head; because he was the first that made
this confession of Christ: which is not an argument for
dignity, but for the quality, that was in the man—for
the first man is not evermore the best. The only foundation of the Church is Christ, for none can put 'aliud funda-
mentum nisi quod positum est, qui est Christus Jesus'".
Gardiner accepted the new Statute suppressing the
chantries, if they had become the occasion of abuses,
also the Statute imposing Communion under both kinds
as being in conformity with the ancient practice of the
Church and even with certain English usages. "It was
well done of the Parliament for moving the people more
and more with devotion to ordain that the Sacrament
should be received in both kinds. . . . I said also
that the proclamation which was made that no man
should unreverently speak of the Sacrament was well
made: for the proclamation stoppeth the mouths of all
such as will unreverently speak of the Sacrament. . . .
I like well the rest of the King's Majesty's proceedings
concerning the Sacrament. If an order be set by such
as have power, we must follow it, and we must obey
the rulers . . . because it is so appointed by the
rulers. I have ever been of this opinion."

That is to say, Gardiner professed his obedience and
conformity in everything which was not plainly inconsistent with orthodoxy. But in spite of Somerset's
prohibition, he spoke of the Mass and upheld the doctrine of the Church, saying that it is a "daily sacrifice
Christ instituted to be continued among Christian men,
not for the need of another Redemption or satisfaction
for the sins of the world (for that was sufficiently performed by his sacrifice of his Body and Blood, done upon
the cross) . . . but to continue us in the remembrance
of his Passion suffered for us; to make us strong in believ-
ing the fruit of his Passion." Though accepting the suppression of the monasteries and the removal of images,

in so far as they were the occasion of superstitious abuse, he defended the veneration of the latter and the binding force of vows. He denounced the marriage of priests. And instead of upholding the authority of the Council, as he had been required to do, he restricted it by saying that the King alone should be obeyed.[1]

"The Bishop of Winchester remains firm in the old religion," the Imperial Ambassador wrote a few days later,[2] "but some consider that he opposes too vehemently those who hold the reins of government, which perhaps is the source of his troubles."

The following day (June 30) Gardiner was committed to the Tower "because he did most arrogantly and disobediently, and that in the presence of His Majesty, their Graces, and Lordships, speak of certain matters contrary to an express commandment given to him on his Majesty's behalf".[3] Though he still possessed many friends, and the Chancellor Wriothesley remained devoted to his cause, the Bishop was to remain in prison until he had entered his seventieth year.[4]

Bonner joined him in prison a year later under similar circumstances and for similar reasons. Since his release from the Fleet, though keeping his opinions and beliefs, he had been careful not to leave an opening for his enemies to accuse him. He had abolished the forbidden ceremonies, and he accepted the new Anglican Prayer Book of 1549. The Council forbade the Mass of the Apostles, and the Mass of Our Lady, which were still said at Saint Paul's under the name of the Communion of the Apostles, and the Communion of the Blessed Virgin. In order to abolish private Masses, the celebration of Holy

---

[1] Foxe (VI, 87–93) prints Gardiner's entire sermon. The eighth and ninth articles of the charge brought against him in December 1550 relate to this sermon. Ibid., 70–76. Cf. V, 763; VII, 594.

[2] Van der Delft to Charles V, July 7, 1548. *Span. Cal.*, IX, 278. Cf. ibid., 279 and 469.

[3] *Acts of the Privy Council*, II, 209–210.

[4] Van der Delft to Charles V, July 24, 1548; November 7, 1549. *Span. Cal.*, IX, 279, 469. Cf. Foxe, V, 704; VI, 46, 69, 71, 106.

Communion, other than at the High altar, was forbidden.[1] Without a word Bonner passed on these orders to the Dean to be carried out by him. But his opposition to the Reformation was well known. It was sufficiently proved by his long absences from the pulpit, his readiness to wink at breaches of the Act of Uniformity, his reluctance to make changes, and his purely passive obedience. His example in the capital of the kingdom was not without effect and hampered the Reformers in their programme.

When the revolt of the West broke out, the cause of which was predominantly religious, he was ordered to preach against the rebels and, moreover, on four points intimated to him in writing (August 1549). He was commanded to say that by their disobedience to authority the rebels merited damnation, that they could not be saved from it by the Mass and Holy Water, that the ceremonial of public worship should not be placed before the obedience due to lawful authority, and that the king, like Josiah,—should be obeyed as though he were thirty or forty.[2]

The final point, which amounted to recognising as legitimate every act of the government during Edward's minority, was the most important, and the Council, if they would establish their authority, must get it admitted by the recalcitrant Henricians. Whether intentionally or not, Bonner forgot to mention it. "The principal charge against him," wrote the Imperial Ambassador,[3] "is that of the four articles sent to him in writing to preach to the people he omitted the first, namely, that whatever has been done and ordained in this realm since the late king's decease has been lawfully

[1] Letters of the Council, June 24, and July 23, 1549. *Grey Friars' Chronicle*, 59. Wilkins, III, 34. Foxe, V, 723, 726 *sq.* Heylyn, I, 154 *sq.* Cardwell, *Documentary Annals of the Reformed Church of England*, I, 76–80. Cf. Burnet, II, 219.

[2] Collier, V, 335 *sq.* Cf. Foxe, V, 728 *sqq.*; Burnet, II, 219.

[3] Van der Delft to Charles V, September 23, 1549. Haus-Hof-und Staats-Archiv, Vienna, England, fasc. 17. *Span. Cal.*, IX, 453.

done, the king's minority notwithstanding." He aggravated his offence by speaking of the Real Presence (September 1, 1549). Two priests of his diocese, John Hooper and William Latimer, whom Bonner had forbidden to preach, denounced him to the Council. A week later, September 8, a commission was appointed to examine him. It consisted of Cranmer, Ridley of Rochester, the Dean of St. Paul's, Dr. W. May, and the secretaries, William Petre and Sir Thomas Smith.[1] Bonner appeared in his episcopal dress and rochet.[2] Well acquainted with the law, he did not fail to call attention to the legal flaws in the procedure: the incompetence of those who claimed to be his judges one of whom was not present at the first sitting and some of whom were laymen—the King was in fact obliged to confer special powers upon them[3]—and the incompetence of his accusers as belonging to his own clergy, of evil repute and known as heretics and as such excommunicated. To the charge of having omitted the principal point in his sermon, he replied that he had carefully prepared it, noting the many kings of Judah, who had reigned before their majority, also the English monarchs, Henry III, Edward III, Richard II, Henry VI, and Edward V, but that he had lost his notes and had appealed in vain to the memory of his two secretaries, Bourne and Harpsfield. That he regarded obedience to the King as a duty was proved by the fact that in his sermon he had denounced those who disobeyed him as rebels, and had himself obeyed the royal injunctions. He was, therefore, guiltless. "It must have been plain to all who heard him," the Imperial Ambassador wrote on September 23, "that the charges were inspired by

[1] Rymer, XV, 191 *sq.* Foxe, V, 748. Cardwell, *Documentary Annals*, I, 80 *sqq.* Foxe (V, 747 *sq.*, 781) gives Hooper and Latimer's denunciation, at length, also the Bishop's protest against it and his judges' competence.
[2] *Grey Friars' Chronicle*, 63.
[3] This *Alia Commissio*, of September 17, empowering them to act *Ex Officio Mero*, is in Rymer, XV, 192, Cardwell, *Documentary Annals*, I, 83, cf. Strype, *Whitgift*, II, 28 *sqq.*, III, 232.

pure malice and were brought in order to deprive him
of his bishopric."[1]

His demeanour was resolute and firm. He took
advantage of the opportunity to proclaim once more his
faith in the Real Presence, and from the accused became
the accuser. "Now I see," he said, "that the cause of my
trouble is not the matter that you pretend against me,
but it is for that I did preach and set forth in my late
sermon the true Presence of the most blessed Body and
Blood of our Saviour Jesus Christ to be in the Sacrament
of the Altar. For (Hooper) the same day at afternoon
. . . openly in the pulpit within my diocese did preach
erroneously to the people against it; and maliciously in-
veighing against my sermon, denied the verity and presence of Christ's true Body and Blood to be in the same
Sacrament, and also falsely and untruly interpreted and
expounded my words".[2] He had, he told his judges, a
few goods, his old carcass, and his soul. The two former
they could take from him, the latter "is always in mine
hands". But Cranmer saw in him an invincible champion
of the Catholic doctrine of the Eucharist, a doctrine which
he himself treated with such contumely as to provoke
from Bonner, during the trial, the repartee "I am truly
grieved to hear your Grace speak so." Moreover, the
Council considered that he had disregarded and flouted
its authority. Therefore his clever defence availed nothing.
Moreover, he damaged it by his insulting language,
freely bestowing such epithets as daws, woodcocks,
asses, ignoramuses and fools. "He gave them a good
dressing down," reported Charles's ambassador,[3] "and

---

[1] *Spanish Calendar*, IX, 453.

[2] Punning on the words 'ass' and 'as' he called his opponent an ass.
"Where I preached and affirmed the very true Body and Blood of Our
Saviour Jesus Christ to be in the said Sacrament, the selfsame in substance
that was hanged and shed upon the cross, he like an ass (as he is an ass
indeed) falsely changed and turned the word 'that' into 'as', like an ass,
saying that I had said *as* it hanged and *as* it was shed upon the cross".
Foxe V, 752.

[3] Letter mentioned above of September 23, 1549. Cf. Burnet, II,
220 *sqq.*

in his own mind he "sent them to the devil."[1] When the secretary Smith spoke of him as a robber and a traitor, he charged him with a partiality which made him incapable of acting as a judge. He was "an incompetent and suspect judge". As a Privy Councillor Bonner professed his respect for Smith, but as a man he held him a liar and defied his malice. It was in vain that Bonner appealed "to the most high and mighty Prince our Sovereign Lord against 'the evil men' who had 'belied' him." On October 3 he was sent to the Marshalsea. It was just at this time that the Council was plotting against the Protector, who fell from power four days later.[2]

"I am ready to suffer death," Bonner had told one of his chaplains during the trial, "to defend the truth and presence of Christ's Body and Blood in the Sacrament." This was indeed the centre of the struggle between the Reformers and the orthodox. It was for upholding the Catholic doctrine of the Blessed Sacrament that Gardiner and Bonner were in prison. All the Henricians defended it; and on that account they were imprisoned and deprived by Warwick of their sees.

When at the end of 1548, Cranmer asked the bishops a number of questions about the Mass, whose character he sought to change, the Henricians returned Catholic replies, maintaining that the Mass was a sacrifice and not, as the Reformers held, a mere Communion. In particular, Day of Chichester, Heath of Worcester, Skip of Hereford, and Rugg of Norwich, pronounced very plainly in this sense. It was in vain that Cranmer

---

[1] Burnet, II, 228. Burnet, who was no friend to Bonner, quotes private letters written in prison in which he asks for pears and puddings. Burnet excuses himself for publishing what was intended for the secrecy of private friendship. "But he was a man so brutal and so bloody that I am not displeased to exhibit him to the world in his true character."

[2] For all this see Foxe, op. cit., V, 747–800. This is the source of Heylyn, I, 162 sq., Burnet, II, 218–229; Collier, V, 335, 338, 340–350; Dixon, III, 128, 130 sqq., 143 sq.; Fr. Lee, King Edward VI Supreme Head, ed. II, 1889.

submitted to them a new interrogatory couched in a tone of insulting scorn, they held their ground and the insolence of the questions only brought out the orthodoxy of their replies.[1]

It was above all in the Parliament which met in December 1548 that the Henricians displayed their true sentiments. As has been said above, it was proposed to approve the Book of Common Prayer, the first attempt to get rid of the Mass and the Blessed Sacrament as Catholics understand it.[2] The entire debate turned on this issue. The Breviary and the Ritual were left in the shade. Attention was concentrated upon the Missal. The Henricians unmasked the secret doctrine of the Reformers which Cranmer had attempted to conceal beneath vague formulas and the general outline of the old Mass. The attack was opened by Tunstall, the Bishop of Durham. "Adoration", he said, "is left out of the book because there is nothing in the Sacrament but bread and wine", yet he believed "that there is the very Body and Blood of Christ both spiritual and carnal". When Cranmer contradicted him, he replied "Our Lord's Body is in the bread and wine because God hath spoken it which is able to do it, saying: 'This is my Body; and This is my Blood'." Bonner said: "This doctrine of the Prayer Book is not decent because it hath been condemned abroad as an heresy; and in this realm, example of Lambert".[3] The new book was heretical because it called the Blessed Sacrament "bread".

Day of Chichester expounded the Catholic doctrine that the Body of Christ is present after consecration. "Christ gave the Sacrament that the form and accidents of the bread should remain but not very bread. . . . It is that Body by which hell was broken and heaven

[1] Strype, *Memorials of Cranmer*. App. XXXVI, 475-479. Jenkyns, *The Remains of Cranmer*, II, 178-185.

[2] Chapter III.

[3] John Lambert had been burned under Henry VIII for denying transubstantiation (1538).

opened, the selfsame Body that was wounded with the spear and gushed out blood".

Skip of Hereford refuted Cranmer's objection that since Christ's Body is in heaven it cannot be on the altar, and concluded that "the very Body that is in heaven," is present in the Eucharist. "Lanfranc," he added, "understood it so, who was your predecessor."[1]

All the Henricians, with the exception of Gardiner who was in prison, voted against the Prayer Book of 1549. So determined was their opposition that four weeks elapsed between the debate and the final passage of the bill. The interval was spent in making alterations in the book to satisfy the orthodox party and win their vote. Somerset, who wanted an agreement rather than the forcible imposition of the book, insisted upon this. Therefore some modifications were made to appease the hostility of the Henricians. One of the most important of these was to substitute the words "Sacrament of the Body and Blood" for the words "Sacrament of the bread—sacrament of the wine" in the final rubric of the Communion service. In spite of these changes Day of Chichester refused his assent. The remainder gave their approval to the Prayer Book in the interest of public tranquillity, and for fear of disturbances, not because they were completely satisfied with it. Their signature was, as it were, a *nolens volo*, a reluctant assent to avoid worse evils.[2]

When the Book of Common Prayer was imposed by statute in 1549, the Henricians conformed to it. Though its tendency was Lutheran, it was, as it has been already shown, patient of a Catholic interpretation.[3] And the

---

[1] This debate on the Eucharist was recorded at the time. It is to be found in MS. Reg. 17, B XXXIX in the British Museum (fol. 1 *sq.*). "Certain notes touching the disputations of the bishops in this last Parliament assembled of the Lord's Supper." Gasquet and Bishop printed it in Appendix V of their *Edward VI and the Book of Common Prayer*.

[2] Cf. *Span. Cal.*, IX, 261, 345. Burnet, II, 168 *sq.*, 176, 281; V, 7, 287 591. Strype, *Memorials of Cranmer*, ed. 1848, 137 *sqq.* Dixon, II, 554 *sqq.* Gasquet and Bishop, 171 *sqq.*

[3] Chapter III.

strategy of the orthodox party was to dispute every inch of ground with the innovators, and to put a Catholic interpretation upon whatever the law, in spite of their efforts, forced upon the Church. It was in pursuance of this policy that Gardiner declared the book, as he interpreted it, "godly and Christian".[1] So long as Somerset remained in power this strategy was possible. It was indeed favoured by the Protector himself, who desired to keep the support of the Henricians and avoid any serious dissension in the Church. Under his successor it became impossible.

The Reformation was now frankly Calvinist. The Reformers were so bent upon uprooting the Catholic doctrine of the Mass and the Real Presence, that the Henricians were driven from the ground they had hitherto defended with equal skill and firmness. For the first time they were persecuted. The action taken against Bonner and Gardiner during the Protectorate was, as it has been said, the work of Cranmer and the Council rather than of Somerset. The Duke refused to ratify the sentence of deposition pronounced against Bonner. It was on February 7, 1550, four months after Somerset's fall, that the Bishop's appeal to the Council was refused, that he was deprived of his see, which was given to Ridley, and condemned to imprisonment for life. And the conditions of his imprisonment were made harsher. For a time he was even deprived of his bed and compelled to sleep on the straw which covered the floor.[2]

Not a single Bishop had been deprived of his see by Somerset. Warwick deposed and imprisoned all the prominent Henricians.

Gardiner had hoped that the change of government would restore him to liberty. The contrary happened.

[1] Gasquet and Bishop, 278.
[2] *Acts of the Privy Council*, II, 385 *sq.*, 400. Foxe, V, 750–799. Strype, *Memorials of Cranmer*, II, 123 *sq.*, 175 *sq.* John Todd, *Life of Arch. Cranmer*, London, 1831, II, 140 *sqq.* Dixon, III, 132 *sqq.*, 143 *sq.*, 164, 203. J. Gairdner, *Lollardy*, 102 *sq.*, 125, 185–189, 249 *sq.*, 257, 259, 311.

His repeated protests against his illegal imprisonment went unanswered for months. Finally on May 15, 1550, certain articles were presented for his signature. One of them recognised the powers exercised by the Council during the king's minority, another the justice of his own punishment. He was also required to declare that the Mass was an invention of the Bishop of Rome, private Masses a device of men, and that the consecrated Host should not be shown to the people and worshipped. That is to say he was called upon to deny the Blessed Sacrament, which he had always defended. He was further asked to express his approval of the new Ordinal and the changes it had made in the rite of ordination. Gardiner refused to sign so humiliating a recantation. The goods of his see were confiscated, his vicar general, who had dared to defend him, was imprisoned and a Commission was appointed to try him.

The Commission consisted of six laymen and four bishops, Goodrich of Ely, Cranmer, Holbeach of Lincoln, and Ridley, the new Bishop of London. Gardiner objected to the three latter, who were leaders of the reforming party and had been his opponents in the debate on the Real Presence. His objection was over-ruled. The Commissioners heard the evidence of numerous witnesses on their way to a sentence decided beforehand. As usual Gardiner made a very able defence, and the trial assumed the appearance of a comprehensive enquiry into the origins of the English Reformation. One of the principal charges against the Bishop was the sermon he had preached on June 29, 1548, on the Mass and the Real Presence. His colleagues Heath and Tunstall deposed that at that date no learned man in the country questioned this dogma. Gardiner called Cranmer a heretic and a sacramentary, and reproached him for being the first English Archbishop to deny the Real Presence. Throughout the trial he did not cease to declare his obedience to the King and the law, but only in so far

as he was bound by the latter. Like Bonner he appealed
to the King. Nevertheless he was deprived on February
14, 1551. The sentence pronounced him guilty of opposing the reforms ordered by the King and disobeying his
orders. The brave bishop was sent back to the Tower—
where he remained until the accession of Mary—and his
imprisonment became more rigorous. Under Somerset
he had been permitted to take exercise outside his cell,
to write, and have the use of books. Now he was kept in
close confinement and completely deprived of the means to
study and write. His bishopric of Winchester was given to
Ponet, a convinced Calvinist who, as will be remembered,
had married a butcher's wife.[1] "The Bishop of Winchester," the Venetian ambassador wrote, "a man of
great learning and exemplary life, has been condemned
and deprived of his see, which brought him a yearly
income of 12,000 crowns, which in truth was his worst
offence. For the same reasons any other bishops who
will not bow to the views of their present masters are
doomed to the same sacrifice."[2]

In fact the other Henricians were treated by Warwick
with equal severity. Had not John Ponet denounced
them to the king as patrons of Popery for clinging to the
creed of their fathers and desiring to keep the nation
faithful to it?[3]

Tunstall of Durham was Somerset's personal friend.
Thanks to this friendship and his extreme caution he
had been left in peace during the earlier part of the reign.
His difficulties began with the Protector's fall. In September 1550 he was accused by a Scotsman, Ninian

---

[1] *Spanish Cal.*, X, 168 *sq.*, 213 *sq.*, 220 Note, 225 *sq.*, 244, 262, 381;
Foxe, V, 704; VI, 46, 64–266. Burnet, II, 245, 261 *sq.*, 263, 284 *sqq.*;
III, 334, 337, 338, 344; V, 21, 23, 31. J. Todd, *Life of Archbishop Cranmer*,
1831, II, 237 *sqq.*, 259 *sqq.*, Gasquet and Bishop, *op. cit.*, 57, 62, 113, 117,
277–285. Dixon, III, 220, 223, 226 *sqq.*, 228, 257 *sqq.*, 260, 263, 265 *sq.*,
270 *sqq.*, 273, 275. J. Gairdner, *Lollardy*, III, 209–223, 231–243, 245,
249, 273.

[2] Report by Daniel Barbaro, 1551. Alberi, *op. cit.*, Series I, II, 230.

[3] *A Notable Sermon*, printed by G. Lynne, 1550, fol. 2. Ponet preached
it before Edward on March 14, 1550.

Mainvil, of having encouraged the rebellion of the North and the Scottish invasion. Probably the charge was brought for no other reason than Tunstall's sympathy for Somerset and Warwick's desire to seize the Bishopric of Durham. Tunstall was summoned to London on May 15, 1551, and on the 20th confined to his own house. It was at this time that in retirement and silence he wrote his treatise *De Veritate Corporis et Sanguinis D. N. J. Christi in Eucharistia*, the best contemporary explanation of Catholic sacramental doctrine. It was printed at Paris in 1554, in Mary's reign. His views about the Mass and the Real Presence no doubt contributed very largely to the result of his trial. In December 1551, he was sent to the Tower and on October 3, 1552, a Commission entirely composed of laymen pronounced a sentence of deprivation.

Warwick even attempted to bring him to the block. He had a bill of attainder for high treason brought in against him. But the House of Commons for once showed independence and refused to pass it. In March 1553, his see was suppressed, and Warwick was on the point of seizing its lands and revenues, when he himself fell.[1]

Heath of Worcester had been placed in 1550 on the Commission appointed to draw up the new Ordinal. He refused to subscribe to the draft which Cranmer presented to him. Summoned before the Council, he persisted in his refusal and was sent to the Fleet, March 4, 1551.

Five months later, September 21, he was once more asked to express his approval. This time, he replied that it was against his conscience, and further that he

---

[1] *Spanish Cal.*, 166, 214 *sq.*, 300, 425, 582, 591, 593. Foxe, V, 704, 827; VI, 124, 126, 137, 188, 240, 257, 389, 412, 505. Burnet, II, 176, 248, 250, 328 *sq.*, 360; III, 356 *sq.*; V, 59, 89. Strype, *Memorials of Cranmer,* II, 403-405. J. Todd, *op. cit.*, II, 260 *sqq.* Dixon, III, 272, 320, 324, 331, 441 *sq.*, 467. Gasquet and Bishop, *op. cit.*, 29, 161 *sq.*, 302, J. Gairdner, *Lollardy*, 46, 249 *sq.*, 250.

could not consent to demolish the altars in his diocese and replace them by tables. He was ready to accept deposition or any other penalty it might please the King to inflict. A Commission of laymen deprived him on October 8. But he was allowed to share Bishop Ridley's palace.[1] On the same grounds Day of Chichester was brought to trial. On November 8, 1550, Dr. Cox, to whom had been entrusted the task of keeping watch upon the bishop, accused him of holding the old doctrine of the Eucharist. He was ordered to demolish all the altars in his diocese and personally justify the order in a sermon to be preached in his cathedral. He refused. The Council then summoned him to appear before them. From Scripture and the Fathers he defended the use of altars, while Cranmer and Ridley attempted to refute him. As always the theological debate ended with imprisonment. On December 9, 1550, he was imprisoned in the Fleet, and the following October was deprived of his see for having contemned the King's command.[2]

Bishop Thirlby, who had been despatched as ambassador to Francis I (1538), and had later been ambassador at the Imperial Court (1542-1545) was, say his Anglican biographers, "a Catholic at heart". In Parliament he consistently opposed the religious changes, the destruction of images, the Prayer Books of 1549 and 1552, the Ordinal, and the Act of Uniformity of 1552. In the royal presence he praised Charles V's interim (1548), which forbade any religious change or controversy pending the decision of a general council, and he would gladly have supported a bill to preserve the realm from

---

[1] *Acts of the Privy Council*, II, 208. Foxe, VI, 240 *sq.* Burnet, 168, 173, 203, 248, 250 *sq.*, 341; III, 339, 343; V, 49 *sq.*, 197-215. Dixon, III, 111, 159, 161, 196, 203, 258, 268, 322, 324. Gasquet and Bishop, *op. cit.*, 80, 161, 168, 170, 262 *sq.* J. Gairdner, *Lollardy*, III, 174, 177-180, 187, 189, 249, 259, 266, 288.

[2] *Spanish Cal.*, X, 381. Foxe VI, 126, 137, 240, 389, 412. *Acts of the Privy Council*, 1550-1552, 168, 170 *sq.* Strype, *Memorials of Cranmer*, I, 298, 301, 432; II, 245, 250-256, 259 *sq.* Burnet, II, 168, 176, 248, 250, 281; III, 341, 343, 362; V, 14, 49 *sq.* Gasquet and Bishop, *op. cit.*, 268. Dixon, III, 203 *sqq.*

the heresies introduced by the foreigners living in England. Warwick deprived him of his see of Westminster, which was suppressed, and translated him to Norwich. His talents as a diplomatist, which the government desired to employ, preserved him from more serious trouble. Mary gave him the see of Ely.[1] The Henricians thus combated the religious revolution which was making the Church of England a Protestant body. They did so cautiously and without quitting the ground of legality so long as Somerset was in power. Warwick's advent compelled them to fight in the open. The reformation he imposed was too obviously Protestant and anti-Catholic for any other course. Their consciences no longer permitted subtle interpretations. Without further shifts they refused to obey laws which their consciences rejected. Nothing could overcome their constancy, neither a prison cell, nor privations, nor the loss of their sees and possessions. Until Mary's accession the majority of them remained in prison or at least without freedom of movement.

[1] *Spanish Cal.*, IX, 270, 279, 562; X, 43, 265, 282, 292, 592. Thomas Fuller, *Worthies of England*, ed. 1840, 230. Dixon, III, 111, 159, 161, 196 *sq.*, 434, 439, 441. Turba, *Venetianische Depeschen Vom Kaiserhofe*, Vienna, 1889–1895, Vol. II, p. xvii, 30, 175, 178, 320, 418, 657.

CHAPTER VIII

CRANMER AND THE REFORMATION

Thomas Cranmer, Archbishop of Canterbury and Primate of England—
The development of his theological opinions—His share in the religious
revolution under Edward—The works which have entitled him to be
regarded as one of the principal Fathers of the Anglican Church.

FROM the day when his pronouncement of Henry VIII's
divorce had broken the last links binding England to
the Holy See, Cranmer had always been the soul of the
Reformation.[1] Under Henry he represented together
with Cromwell the advanced party, which sought to bring
the Church of England close to the Lutheran Churches
of Germany and seal their alliance by a doctrinal agreement.[2] Under Edward VI he carried into execution
plans of reformation he had thought out and prepared
during the closing years of the previous reign.[3] Archbishop of Canterbury and Primate of all England, he
took his place as the official leader of a movement which
at times he followed rather than led. In company with
him the Church of England became Lutheran, and when
he was converted to the doctrines of the Swiss reformers,
the Church also embraced the latter. Therefore to study
Cranmer's theological development is to study that of
the Anglican Church and to analyse one of its principal
causes. Cranmer's theological views underwent surprising
changes within a few years. The Reformers congratulated

[1] See my *The Reformation in England,* Henry VIII, Chapters II and VI.
[2] Strype, *Memorials of Cranmer,* (ed. 1848-1852, Book II, Chapter XXXI).
The chapter is entitled "His kindness for Germany". Cranmer had a
sister a nun. On November 11, 1534, she was elected prioress of the
Benedictines of Minster in Sheppey. Cf. G. Baskerville, *A Sister of Archbishop
Cranmer* in *The English Historical Review,* April 1936.
[3] Strype, *Memorials,* Book III, Chapter XXXII.

him on his conversion, whereas his opponents reproached him for his flagrant self-contradiction. It was an easy task for Bishop Gardiner[1] and Richard Smith[2] to point out the changes in his teaching.

He himself admitted them: "This I confess of myself," he wrote in 1551, "that not long before I wrote the said Catechism, I was in that error of the Real Presence, as I was many years past in divers other errors: as of transubstantiation, of the Sacrifice propitiatory of the priests in the Mass, of pilgrimages, purgatory, pardons and many other superstitions and errors that came from Rome. . . . For the which and other mine offences in youth, I do daily pray God for mercy and pardon saying: Delicta juventutis meae et ignorantias meas ne memineris, Domine. Good Lord remember not mine ignorances and offences of my youth".[3]

In his lifetime Cranmer was accused of being in turn Papist, Lutheran, and Zwinglian.[4] This triple charge describes in fact the successive stages of his doctrinal evolution and the beliefs he held at different periods of his life. While Henry was on the throne, Cranmer, though at heart a thorough-going Protestant, subscribed confessions of faith which were obviously Catholic, particularly the last, *The Necessary Erudition of a Christian Man*, 1543. He issued them, read them, saw that they were followed in his diocese, and forbade preachers to attack them. Gardiner reminded him that so long as Henry lived, he had conformed to the established doc-

---

[1] Particularly in his treatise: *An Explanation and Assertion of the True Catholique Fayth touchyng the Moost Blessed Sacrament of the Aulter with a Confutation of a Booke written agaynst the Same.* Rouen, 1551.

[2] *A Confutation of a Certain Booke called a Defence of the True and Catholike Doctrine of the Sacrament . . . sette fourth of late in the Name of Thomas Archebysshope of Canterburye* (1550), by Richard Smith, doctor of divinite and some tyme reader of the same in Oxforde, s.l. n.a.

[3] Cranmer, *Works on the Lord's Supper*, ed. Parker Society, Cambridge, 1844, I, 374; ed. Jenkyns, *Remains*, Oxford, 1833, III, 13. It replies to the preface of the book just mentioned. Smith had accused Cranmer of no longer teaching the same doctrine about the Eucharist that he used to teach.

[4] R. Laurence, *Bampton Lectures*, London, 1805, 211.

trine.[1] This contrast between Cranmer's practice and
his personal convictions constitutes a serious difficulty
for many sincere Anglicans. It does not seem to have
troubled the Archbishop. The profession of his private
views should, he held, be subordinated to the King's
will and judgement. He taught that Christian princes
are God's direct delegates for all their subjects' needs
spiritual as well as temporal, that the administration of
God's word and the care of their peoples' souls has been
committed to them as well as their civil and political
government.[2] Therefore in his eyes the authority of the
supreme head of the Church is absolute in matters of
faith and discipline alike. The king is the *summus epis-
copus*. From him the bishops receive their jurisdiction
and the doctrine they are to teach. Hence their duty is
not so much to secure the victory of their own beliefs
as to make their practice conform with the rule of faith
he imposes. At every discussion which preceded the
issue of Henry's Confessions of Faith, Cranmer gave his
opinion freely, but accompanied it by the reservation,
even on questions of the utmost moment: "this is
mine opinion and sentence at this present, which I
do not temerariously define but do remit the judgement thereof wholly unto your Majesty".[3] For Cranmer
the authority of the crown had replaced that of the
Pope.

Cranmer early adopted the opinions of the Lutherans.
During his embassy to Charles V in 1532, he entered
into relations with them. The conferences of Wittenberg
(1536) and London (1538) between German and English
theologians did but draw them closer.[4] Osiander, whose

[1] Letter from Gardiner to Cranmer, Strype, *Memorials of Cranmer*, II,
App. XXXV. Muller, *Letters of S. Gardiner*, No. 124.
[2] Reply to a series of questions addressed to the Bishops about 1537.
Burnet, *History of the Reformation*, ed. Pocock, Oxford, 1845, IV,
467 *sqq.*
[3] Reply mentioned in the previous note. Burnet, IV, 494. Jenkyns ,
Cranmer's Remains, Oxford, 1833, II, 103.
[4] See my earlier volume, Chapter VIII.

niece he had wedded,[1] maintained a long and cordial correspondence with him,[2] which did not fail to influence his beliefs. As early as 1536 he was regarded as the English bishop most favourable to the new opinions. The same year Bucer dedicated to him his *Commentary on the Epistle of the Romans*, in which in a long preface, he exhorted him to reform the Church of England and praised him in language which shows the hope which the German Protestants entertained of him.[3] The following year Osiander also dedicated to him his *Concordance of the Four Gospels*, with a complimentary letter.[4] At this period (1537) Cranmer rejected as superstitions "purgatory, pilgrimages, praying to saints, images, holy bread, holy water, holy days, merits, works, ceremony, and such other."[5] Henry VIII, who always protected him against his enemies, greeted him one day in 1541 with the words, "O my chaplain, now I know who is the greatest heretic in Kent." And at the same time he put into his hands a list of accusations signed by many of his own clergy and chapter and several magistrates of Kent.[6] The Lutheran theologians who attended the London conference of 1538 found in Cranmer their strongest support, and it is probable that he took the chair at their meetings. On several occasions he pressed Bucer to visit England, and three times he invited Melanchthon. "I have invited Melanchthon for the third time," he wrote to Laski in 1548.[7] And this was not the last invitation.[8] He had read all the

[1] When on an embassy to the Emperor (1532). Cf. Strype, *Memorials of Cranmer*, II, 115.

[2] Ibid., loc. cit.

[3] Strype, *Memorials of Cranmer*, I, 103.

[4] Cranmer had encouraged Osiander to persevere with this work whose difficulties had almost made him lose heart. Strype, *op. cit.*, I, 15.

[5] Cranmer, *Works*. Ed. Parker Soc., Cambridge, 1846, II, 351.

[6] See my *Reformation in England under Henry VIII*, p. 336.

[7] *Zurich Original Letters*, 1531–1558, Parker Soc., 1846–1847, I, 17.

[8] On February 10, 1549, he renewed the invitation and sent John Laski to persuade him to come. *Zurich Original Letters*, I, 22. In 1552 he made a further attempt. Cranmer to Laski. Cranmer's *Letters*, No. cclxxii. Jenkyns, *Cranmer's Remains*, I, 329 *sqq.*; cf. Preface, CV.

most important works by Lutheran authors, and when he was compiling the Book of Common Prayer, he consulted the missals and rituals of the German Reformers.[1] The library of Corpus Christi College, Cambridge, possesses a copy of the first two volumes of Luther's works bearing the Archbishop's signature.

At the beginning of Edward's reign he was still under Lutheran influence. Justus Jonas the Younger, an intimate friend of Luther's, was his guest at Lambeth palace and on most intimate terms with him. Jonas had accompanied Melanchthon and Bucer on their journey to Cologne, where they had attempted to introduce the Reformation with the aid of the *Pia Consultatio*.[2] At this period the advanced Reformers remarked that the Archbishop preferred the society of the Lutherans to theirs and complained that he was drugged by Luther's teaching.[3]

Hence his writings composed at this epoch are Lutheran. The Homilies which he had begun as early as 1539[4] and which were imposed upon the Church in the first year of Edward VI (1547) reflect the views of the German reformers. In particular the Homily on Justification teaches that man is justified by faith alone, that to obtain sanctifying grace it is sufficient to believe, without the necessity to prepare for it by a movement of the will, and that hope and charity are not required for justification.[5] According to Luther man has been totally

---

[1] Cf. Strype, *Memorials of Cranmer*, Book III, Chapter XXXI.

[2] Strype, *op. cit.*, I, 227.

[3] Traheron and Jean Ulmer to Bullinger. August 1 and November 27, 1548. *Zurich Original Letters*, I, 320, 383 &c. Cf. R. Laurence, *Bampton Lectures*, 1805, 16 Note.

[4] *Letters and Papers*, XIV, Part I, 446. They were not laid before Convocation before 1543. Ibid., Part I, 167. *The First Book of Homilies* was published in 1547. (J. Ames, *Hist. of Printing in England*, 1471–1600, London, 1749, 196). The following year the complete book was published. It was re-issued under Elizabeth. On the *Homilies* see Strype, *Mem. of Cranmer*, Book II, Chapter III; Hardwick, *Hist. of the Christian Church*, 194; Dixon, II, 314; III, 106, 225, 285.

[5] The Homily printed in his works, II, 128–134 (ed. Jenkyns, II, 138–151) is certainly Cranmer's. His *Notes on Justification*, a selection of passages from Scripture, the Fathers, and the schoolmen, are to be found in his works, ed. Parker Society, II, 203–211, and Jenkyns, II, 121 *sqq.*

corrupted by original sin, and therefore any effort to attain salvation is vain, and the will is not free. God justifies us by faith and trust in Jesus Christ. Man remains a sinner, and his justice, which is that of God Himself, is wholly external to him. Nothing can deprive him of it, not even relapses into sin, so long as he believes and trusts in God. Cramner therefore follows Luther when he says: "Faith does not exclude repentance, hope, love, dread, and the fear of God, to be joined with faith in every man that is justified, but it excludeth therefrom the office of justifying."[1] In other words: faith alone justifies. And in fact Gardiner charged him with excluding charity from the work of justification.[2] In another passage he says: "Nor that faith also doth not exclude the justice of our good works, necessarily to be done afterwards of duty towards God . . . but it excludeth them, so that we may not do them to this intent, to be made good by doing of them". That is to say good works have no part in our justification. It is useless to attempt to dispose ourselves for it. Everything man does before justification is sinful, as Article 12 of the XLII Articles of 1552 was to pronounce.[3]

A year after the Homilies, in the summer of 1548, the Catechism appeared which bears the Archbishop's name, Cranmer's Catechism. It was at the suggestion of his Lutheran friends and of Peter Martyr, Burcher wrote to

---

[1] Cranmer, as is his wont, expresses himself in ambiguous and quibbling language. "It is so but all the same it is not so. Faith does not exclude charity but it does exclude it." He almost always argues in this fashion.

[2] See Gardiner's entire letter to Cranmer printed in Strype, *Memorials of Cranmer*, II, 780–785. Gardiner also censures Cranmer for excluding charity and the other virtues from the work of justification in his letter to Somerset (ibid., 785, Muller, *Letters of Gardiner*, Nos. 130, 131).

[3] *Of Works Before Justification.* "Works done before justification . . . for that they are not done as God hath willed and commanded them to be done, we doubt not, but they have the nature of sin." Cranmer, however does not seem to have held. like Luther, that free will has been completely destroyed by original sin. See article 9 of the XLII Articles, *De Libero Arbitrio*, which simply speaks of prevenient grace, as Catholic theology understands it.

Bullinger, that Cranmer published it.[1] It was in fact simply a translation of the Wittenberg catechism. In the copy in the Cambridge University Library, the following note is written on the first page: "This catechism is simply a translation of the Lutheran catechism printed at Wittenberg in 1539." It had been compiled for the Church of Nuremberg. Justus K. Jonas the Younger, the friend of Luther and Cranmer, had translated the German original into Latin. And it was this Latin version which the Archbishop translated. It is entitled, *A Short Instruction into the Christian Religion for the Singular Commodity and Profit of Children and Young People, Set Forth by the Most Reverend Father In God, Thomas Archbishop of Canterbury, London,* 1548.[2] Though there are a few differences—hardly noticeable at first reading—between the two books,[3] as a whole the doctrine is Luther's. The Real Presence in the Eucharist is maintained,[4] the value of auricular confession and absolution, the reality of the priestly vocation,[5]

[1] Burcher to Bullinger, October 29, 1548. *Zurich Original Letters*, I, 642. It has been held that the catechism is not the work of Cranmer himself, but of a subordinate acting by his instructions (*Cranmer's Works*, ed. Parker Society. 188). But in his *Defence of the True and Catholic Doctrine of the Sacrament*, of 1550, the Archbishop admits that the translation was his work, and he repeats this in his reply to Gardiner of 1551. (Jenkyns, II, 440; III, 13, 42, 297).

[2] *A Short Instruction into the Christian Religion for the Singular Commodity and profit of Children and Young People, set forth by the Most Reverend Father in God, Thomas Archbishop of Canterbury.* It was reprinted at Oxford, in 1829, with the title: *A Short Instruction into Christian Religion, being a Catechism set forth by Th. Cranmer in* 1548: *together with the same in Latin translated from the German by Justus Jonas in* 1539.

[3] Burton has collected them in *Cranmer's Short Instruction into Christian Religion*, 1829, XIII–XVI.

[4] Gardiner will not fail to call attention to it. (See the counts of his trial in 1551 in Foxe, *Acts and Monuments*, VI, 126). In his *Explication and Assertion* of 1551, Gardiner brings out the discrepancies between the Eucharistic doctrine of the Catechism of 1548, and Cranmer's Treatise on the Eucharist of 1550. For Cranmer's changing views on the Real Presence see Strype, *Cranmer*, I, chapter XVIII and Appendix XXV; II, 321 *sqq.*; Cranmer's trial in 1555 in Foxe, VIII, 56, and Jenkyns, I, 380 *sqq.*; his *Reformatio Legum Ecclesiast.*, cap. 19, ed. Cardwell, 18; Pollard, *Cranmer*, 215 *sqq.*; 234 *sqq.*; Gasquet and Bishop, *The Book of Common Prayer* 129, 246; Dixon, III, 372; J. A. Muller, *Stephen Gardiner*, 197, 209, 374 Note 11.

[5] Cf. Article XIV of the Confession of Augsburg and Article X of the XIII Articles of London of 1538.

and canonical jurisdiction, all which the Zwinglians and Calvinists rejected and abominated.

Accordingly they greeted the Catechism with an indignant outcry. "At the instigation no doubt of Peter Martyr and other Lutherans," Burcher wrote to Bullinger in October, 1548, "the Archbishop of Canterbury has translated and published in our tongue a Catechism teaching Lutheran opinions. The little book has provoked serious dissensions." "He has published a catechism," John Ulmer adds (August 18, 1548), "in which he not only upholds the mad and sacrilegious transubstantiation of the Papists in the Lord's Supper, but all Luther's delusions seem to him well founded, clear, and lucid." [1] All the advanced Reformers complained of Cranmer's slackness, of the Lutheran lethargy into which he had sunk. "Our Thomas," John Ulmer proceeds to lament in the same letter to Bullinger, "has fallen into a slumber so deep that we have little hope that even your learned letter will rouse him from it." An English disciple of Bullinger's wrote to him on August 1, 1548, "All our compatriots who favour the restoration of the truth share your (Zwinglian) opinions with the exception of Cranmer and Latimer . . . Canterbury's conduct is such . . . that the people do not know what to think of him and the nobility regard him as lukewarm." [2] Shortly however Bullinger and his disciples would have occasion to rejoice at the favourable turn Cranmer's thought had taken and the change in his views which soon became obvious to all.

The origin of this change is somewhat mysterious. To what influence was it due? It has been variously attributed

---

[1] Both letters are in the *Zurich Original Letters*, II, 380, 642. Cf. R. Soames, *The History of the Reformation of the Church of England*, London, 1826–1828, III, 69; Jenkyns, *Cranmer's Remains*, I, pref., p. lxxix.

Jean Ulmer confuses transubstantiation with consubstantiation, the Lutheran doctrine. What he means by the term is the Real Presence.

[2] Bartholomew Traheron to Bullinger, August 1, 1548. *Zurich Original Letters*, ed. Parker Society, I, 320. Bullinger's correspondent is far more hopeful of Latimer's conversion than of Cranmer's.

to Latimer, Ridley and the Pole Laski. It was probably the joint effect of several influences. "A great patron of exiled reformers," the Archbishop had given hospitality since 1547 to Peter Martyr and Bernardino Ochino, "his spoiled children."[1] For a long while past the eyes of the Zwinglians had been fixed on Cranmer, and for many years he had entertained relations with them and corresponded with them, particularly with Joachim de Watt (Vadianus).[2] They had desired his conversion and worked for it, especially Bullinger who had succeeded Zwingli at Zurich, when he was killed at the battle of Cappel, (1531).

Bullinger had always opposed the Lutheran doctrines. He put obstacles in the way of the infant church of Berne because it was semi-lutheran. He refused to accept the Wittenberg Concordia of 1536, and to avenge his master Zwingli he embarked in 1544 upon a literary war against Luther which continued until the German Reformer's death.[3] Bullinger therefore was most decidedly not the "moderate Lutheran" that Dixon calls him in his *History of the Church of England*.[4] Throughout his life he stood for the beliefs of his father-in-law, Zwingli. In 1549 he concluded an agreement with Calvin, the *Consensus Tigurinus* (the agreement of Zurich) which

[1] The Imperial Ambassador to the Council of Flanders, December 27, 1547, and his secretary to the President of the Council, October 15, 1548. *Spanish Cal.*, IX, 238, 299. "Peter Martyr," the Ambassador wrote on February 23, 1548 (ibid., 253) "preaches in Latin to the university of Oxford, and Ochino in Latin in London. Ochino, who in Italy was in high repute as a preacher, seems by God's punishment to have been deprived of his gifts. His audience diminishes daily, and I most sincerely hope he will end by finding himself without a congregation, though the Duchess of Suffolk" (Charles Brandon's widow) "and the Marquis of Northampton, Catherine Parr's brother, are faithful to him."

[2] He was in correspondence with him from 1547 at the latest. See a letter of that year from Cranmer to Joachim Watt in Cranmer's *Works*, ed. Parker Society, II, 343.

[3] Cf. Pestalozzi, *Heinrich Bullinger Leben und Ausgewaehlte Schriften*, Elberfeld, 1857, 194 *sqq.*

[4] Dixon was perhaps misled by his belief that Bullinger had accepted the Wittenberg *Concordia* of 1536, which was not the case. Cf. Pestalozzi, *op. cit.*, 194 *sq.*

definitely laid down the sacramental doctrine of the Swiss churches. This confession of faith, while maintaining man's subjective part in the Eucharist, taught by Zwingli, also affirmed that the sacrament is efficacious in virtue of God's action, Calvin's view. This efficacy however is confined, as Calvin taught, to the elect. Bullinger considered with truth that, if Cranmer's adherence could be secured, he and his friends would hold the key to the religion of England, that if England were to be won for Zwinglianism, the Archbishop must first be converted to it. The entire weight of his supreme authority would thus be transferred from Lutheranism to the Swiss Reformation. Victory would lie with those who gave definite shape to Cranmer's views on the Eucharist. There ensued therefore what we may term a skilful and prolonged investment of the Archbishop, of whose details we possess no information. All we can now know is its result.

In June 1548, Bullinger was anxiously waiting to hear news of the conversion so eagerly desired. He has, he says, sent Cranmer a book accompanied by a letter in which, on the pretext of exhorting him to fulfil the duties of his office, he expounds the doctrine of the Eucharist, which is the vital point. The publication during the summer of the Lutheran catechism revives his anxiety. In August and again in November he is anxious to learn the effect produced upon the Archbishop by his book and letter. At the same time he urges the Pole Laski to accept Cranmer's invitation and go to England. On several occasions he inquires of Richard Hilles and Bucer at Strasbourg what has become of Laski and what are his plans.[1] For he was well aware of the influence which the Polish reformer could exercise upon a mind so supple and malleable as the Archbishop's.

[1] This second Helvetic confession approached Calvinism, as the first of 1536 had approached Lutheranism. It was drawn up by Bullinger and Calvin in the strictest secrecy.

He hoped through Laski to arouse Cranmer from the "dangerous lethargy" of his Lutheranism.[1] Laski arrived in England at the end of September, 1548.

He was a man of great learning and noble birth. His family was not, as he stated in a letter to King Sigismund in 1548, of English origin but genuinely Polish and had been raised from obscurity by one of its members towards the close of the fourteenth century.[2] Born in 1496 at his ancestral castle in the government of *Piotrkov*, John Laski studied at the University of Bologna. Still a student, he was made a Canon of Cracow at the age of 21 (1517) and later of Leczyc and Plock. Immediately on his ordination to the priesthood he became Dean and later Provost of the Chapter of Gniésno (1531) of which his uncle was Archbishop. In 1538 King Sigismund appointed him Archdeacon of Warsaw. On three occasions he was on the verge of the Episcopate. In 1524 his uncle attempted to have him chosen co-adjutor bishop of Plock (Cujavie). About 1530 Zapolya, whose cause he and his brother Jaroslav had espoused, selected him for the Hungarian see of Vesprim. Finally in 1539 he was put forward as a candidate for the bishopric of Posnan. He was early attracted by the new religious doctrines. Already in 1524 he came into contact with Erasmus and Pellican at Basle, and with Zwingli and Œcolampadius at Zurich.[3] It was at this time, he tells us, that he received his "first lessons in the true religion." Gradually he was won over

---

[1] Cf. *Zurich Original Letters*, I, 262, 560.

[2] Dalton, *Lasciana*. Berlin, 1898, 296. P. David in *Revue d'Histoire Ecclésiastique*, October 1936, 1057.

In Latin John Laski signed himself Joannes a Lasco. If, as some writers do, we use the form Lasco, we must therefore place an a before it. English writers often write Alasco, which is a distortion of the correct form.

[3] At this period he lived with Erasmus whose library he purchased. He left Erasmus the use of it during his life and took delivery of it in October 1536 by the intermediary of Andrew Frycz Modrzewski (St. Kot, *Andrzy Frycz Modrzewski*, Cracow 1923, 38). The subsequent fate of the library is unknown. But one of the books which belonged to it, *Diogenis Laertii Vitae Philosophorum*, Basle, 1534, was discovered in 1936 in a second-hand bookshop at Cracow by M. Rosenblatt, professor of mathematics at the University of Lima. *Revue d'Histoire Ecclésiastique*, October 1936, 1057.

to the views of the Swiss Reformers, and he finally embraced them unreservedly. In 1539 after his failure to
obtain the see of Posnan, he openly adhered to the
Reformation. He went to Frankfort, where he converted
the Lutheran Hardenberg to the doctrines of Zwingli,
to Mainz where he married, and to Louvain where he
joined a Protestant community and won the friendship
of the Spanish Protestant Enzinas. When this became
known, he was deprived of his Polish benefices. Three
years later, on his brother's death, he returned to his native
country and was reconciled to the Catholic Church,
February 6, 1542. But shortly afterwards he once more
left her communion.[1] He returned to Louvain and
resigned his benefices, February 16, 1543. From Louvain
he went first to Emden in East Friesland, where he became
the superintendent of the reformed Churches. The
doctrine of these Churches was explicitly anti-Lutheran.
He gave them an organisation and a confession of faith
after the Swiss model. It was from Emden that he
came to England in the autumn of 1548.[2]

He became Cranmer's guest at Lambeth, where he
spent six months with the Archbishop on terms of the
closest intimacy. Cranmer esteemed him highly, and
gave him his full confidence, communicating all his
thoughts to him and, as a letter to Melanchthon of
February 10, 1549, proves, accepting what he said without
question.[3] Laski's words, inspired by a powerful con-

---

[1] Cf. *Stan Hosii Epistolae*, ed. Hopler and Zarkrzewski, Cracow, 1879–
1888, I, 416 *sq.*

[2] For Laski, see G. Pascal, *Jean de Lasco, Baron de Pologne, Évêque Catholique,
Réformateur Protestant, 1499–1560; Son Temps, sa vie, ses Œuvres*, Paris 1894.
Dalton has published several writings about him, in particular *Johannes
a Lasco. Beitrag zur Reformationsgeschichte Polens, Deutschlands und England*,
1881, the first part of which was translated into English by H. J. Evans
in 1886 with the title *John a Lasco : His Earlier Life and Labours*. See also
Dictionary of National Biography, XXXII, 158; Strype, *Eccl. Mem.*, I, 341
and *Mem. of Cranmer*, Vol. II, Chapter XXII; C. H. Smyth, *Cranmer and
the Reformation under Edward VI*, Cambridge 1926, Chapter VI. For Laski's
works, see *Opera tam Edita quam Inedita de Laski*, edited by A. Kuyper, 1866.

[3] Pestalozzi, *op. cit.*, 22.

viction, and his daily conversations with the Archbishop, produced more effect upon the latter than Bullinger's letters. It was not long before Bullinger received from London news which delighted him, "Latimer," Traheron wrote to him, "has come over to our view of the true sacramental doctrine, as also have the Archbishop of Canterbury and other bishops who up to the present have been regarded as Lutheran." "Thomas himself," John Ulmer informed him, "owing to the intervention of John Laski, a man of great skill and wisdom, has largely awoken from his dangerous lethargy."[1]

It was Laski therefore who was credited by the foreign reformers with Cranmer's conversion. And Bishop Hooper himself thought that the Archbishop's perseverance in the right road depended on the presence of the Polish Protestant.[2] It is certain that from the moment of Laski's arrival Cranmer began to profess doctrine ever more closely in agreement with Bullinger's.[3] His thought had, however, already for some time taken that direction, and it is probable that Laski merely settled his conviction, confirming him in his new opinions and strengthening his determination. He has indeed told us himself that, shortly before the publication of his Catechism in the summer of 1548, he had abandoned the error of the Real Presence.

Indeed, an expression in this very Cathechism proves that he had begun to depart from the Lutheran doctrine of the Eucharist.[4]

[1] Traheron's letter is dated September 28, 1548. *Zurich Original Letters* I, 321 *sq.* Jean Ulmer's is of November 27 the same year, ibid., 383.
[2] *Zurich Original Letters*, I, 61.
[3] Ibid., 380, 383. Cf. Hardwick, *A History of the Church during the Reformation*, 197, 207 *sqq.*
[4] *Cranmer's Works*, I, 374. The original catechism (1539: p. 131) said, "God is almighty. He can therefore do whatever He wills. *When He calls and names a thing what it was not before, it becomes in truth what He calls it. When He takes bread and says 'This is my Body,' then His Body is immediately present.*" Cranmer cut out the sentence in italics and translated the rest as follows: "Therefore when He says 'Take eat this, we must not doubt, etc." The Lutheran text and Cranmer's teach two conflicting doctrines. The former makes the Real Presence depend on the conse-

It was during the session of Parliament which lasted from November 1548 until January 1549 that Cranmer revealed to the public his new opinions. The Book of Common Prayer was being debated. The orthodox Bishops attacked its Eucharistic doctrine as suspect of heresy. Cranmer did not conceal his opinion which he expounded at length. He distinguished between Christ's *Spiritual* and His *Material* Body. "They be two things," he said, "to eat the Sacrament and to eat the Body of Christ. The eating of the Body is to dwell in Christ, and this may be though a man never taste the Sacrament." It would be impossible to state more explicitly that the Sacramental Presence of Christ is spiritual and not, as the Catholic and the Lutheran doctrines teach, corporeal. The Archbishop developed this view in a long speech in which he dwelt on two points (1) that "When the evil eateth the Sacrament bread and wine, he neither hath Christ's Body nor eateth it. The eating with the mouth cannot give life. For then shall a sinner have life. If the evil man eat this Body, he hath life everlasting: Qui edit me habet vitam eternam". and (2) that the true Christian faith is not that Jesus Christ is present in the bread and wine but in heaven. This, he argued, is proved by Scripture and the Fathers who wrote before the usurped power of the Bishop of Rome introduced the opposite belief.[1]

---

cration, the latter on communion. According to the former Christ is present on the altar independently of communion, according to the latter is present only to the communicant. The later opinion is that expressed by Cranmer's translation. That is to say the Archbishop held a different view from Luther's even before Laski's arrival, who after his first interview remarked that Cranmer inclined to his opinion. Cf. Hardwick, *op. cit.*, 93, Note 2; Todd, *Life of Archb. Cranmer*, London, 1831, II, 53 *sq.*; *Cranmer's Works*, II, 43 *sq.*

Cranmer's Catechism has been reprinted by Ed. Burton (Oxford 1829). who believed it was by one of his chaplains: R. Taylor, G. Poinet, or The. Bacon. Cf. Todd, *op. cit.*, II, 43 *sq.*

[1] See Gasquet and Bishop, *op. cit.*, Chapter XI and App. V, also *Lords' Journal*. Bucer, whose influence on Cranmer is discernible, expressed the same views. (Strype, *Mem. of Cranmer*, App. XLVI, especially Nos. 19, 20, 25, 27.

At the close of the second sitting he summed up his sacramental belief. "Christ," he said, "is eaten with the heart. Eating with the mouth cannot give life. The righteous alone can eat the Body of Christ. If the evil man eats the Sacrament, he eats only bread and wine, not Christ's Body. . . . The righteous has the Word and His Godhead in him in virtue of its indissoluble union with the humanity. Eating with the mouth gives a man nothing. For the Body is not in the bread".[1]

On December 19, Cranmer concluded the debate by repeating his profession of Zwinglian doctrine: "The bread and wine," he declared, "are not changed outwardly but inwardly, just as we remain men when changed by grace into new men. The righteous communicant is made a son of God, and Christ dwells in his soul. The change is interior not external, not in the bread but in him who receives it. It is not required for my sanctification that I should believe Christ is really present in the Sacrament since I can receive Him by faith. Christ is on earth by His Godhead not by or with His humanity. It is the nature of His Godhead to be everywhere. But His humanity is in one place alone."

Pressed with questions by the Bishops of Durham and Worcester, Tunstall and Heath, he replied that if the word *hoc* signified this bread, then the bread would be the Body. But if it does not signify the bread, Christ did not say the bread is His body. What was ordinary bread, is so no longer, since it has been set apart for another use, in virtue of which it should be called bread of life.[2]

That is to say Cranmer's sacramental belief had completely changed. Formerly with Luther he had affirmed the Real Presence, in particular in a letter to the Zwinglian J. de Watt (1537) and he admitted the fact himself in

[1] Gasquet and Bishop, *op. cit.*, 418 *sq.* Ridley, though his language was more guarded, supported Cranmer. Gasquet and Bishop, 169, 414-418, cf. 443.

[2] Ibid., 440 *sq.* Cf. Bucer's opinion in Strype, *Mem. of Cranmer*, App. XLVI, Nos. 20, 39.

1551 when he attempted to refute Richard Smith.[1] Now he shared the views of the Swiss reformers. Their delight knew no bounds. "The detestable error," John Ulmer exclaimed, "and foolish opinion of a carnal eating has been at last banished and completely overthrown."[2] Never, they declared, had there been a greater theologian than Cranmer. On December 26, Peter Martyr wrote to his friend Bucer:[3] "The Popish party has been defeated and the credit of their defeat is due to our friends, in particular the Archbishop of Canterbury. Hitherto he has been regarded as ignorant of theology and exclusively occupied with matters of Church government. But, believe me, he has proved himself so excellent a theologian in his contest with the Papists, that they have been compelled in spite of themselves to recognise his knowledge, his power and skill in debate. Transubstantiation is now, I believe, banished, and as to the Real Presence, that is the issue being debated at the present time." "The Archbishop of Canterbury," Traheron wrote in the same strain to Bullinger, on December 31,[4] "contrary to the general expectation, has defended your opinion on the Eucharist openly, firmly and learnedly. His arguments were these: Christ's Body has been removed from earth to heaven. Christ has left this world. Never has truth won such a splendid triumph among us. Lutheranism has received its death-blow. For those who were regarded as its firmest supporters have come over to our side."

Cranmer had indeed been converted to the ideas of the Swiss reformers and would never turn back. He had finally abandoned both the Catholic and the Lutheran doctrines of the Eucharist. Moreover, Bullinger and Calvin kept him under observation. They fed his

[1] *Answer to Smythe's Preface*, ed. Jenkyns, III, 13; ed. Parker Society, I, 374; Strype, *Cranmer's Mem.*, II, 321.
[2] Letter of November 27, 1548, *Zurich Original Letters*, 383.
[3] Ibid., 469 *sq.* Gasquet and Bishop, 174 *sq.*; Pollard, *op. cit*, 217 *sq.*
[4] *Zurich Original Letters*, I, 323; Gasquet and Bishop, 175 *sq.* According to Pollard, *op. cit.*, 217, Note 3, Traheron as a member of the House of Commons attended the debate in the Lords.

zeal and took care he did not stray from the path on which they had set him. The former maintained a correspondence with him, the latter sent him books, which Cranmer had translated by Laski and circulated throughout the kingdom.

After defending the Eucharistic doctrine of the Swiss Calvinists in Parliament, Cranmer expounded it in two writings which he published during the last years of this reign, and which fixed the Anglican doctrine on the most important point at issue in the sixteenth century between the Protestant and the Catholic religions.

The Eucharistic teaching of the 1549 Prayer Book was a compromise between Cranmer's views and those of the orthodox bishops. The language used was deliberately chosen so as to be susceptible of a Catholic as well as a Protestant interpretation, and either party was able to argue that its own interpretation was the true one. But the events of 1549 had substituted for Somerset's moderate rule the aggressive policy of Warwick. And it was with the approval, if not at the instigation of the Government, that Cranmer launched his assault against the doctrine of the Real Presence, hitherto the doctrine of the Church of England. At his trial in 1551 Gardiner declared, as also did Tunstall and the other Henrician bishops, that "the truth of Christ's most precious Body and Blood in the Sacrament of the Altar hath not been nor was impugned by any famous clerk . . . and in England no learned man named had or yet did openly defend or favour that error".[1]

In 1550 Cranmer published a treatise entitled: *A Defence of the True and Catholic Doctrine of the Sacrament of the Body and Blood of Our Saviour Christ*. It was divided into five parts: (1) An exposition of the Reformers' doctrine; (2) A denial of transubstantiation; (3) The mode of Christ's presence; (4) What we should understand by the words "eat the flesh and drink the blood of Christ";

[1] Foxe, ed. Pratt, VI, 126, 240 *sq.*

(5) A violent diatribe against the Mass. The Archbishop takes Gardiner to task, attacking what the bishop had said about the Blessed Sacrament and the Mass in the famous sermon preached before the King on June 29, 1548. Gardiner took up the challenge and though imprisoned found means to publish abroad a refutation of Cranmer's book entitled: *An Explication and Assertion of the True Catholic Faith Touching the Most Blessed Sacrament of the Altar with Confutation of a Book written against the same.* It was calculated to enrage Cranmer. For Gardiner pretended to believe that the Archbishop's treatise, though bearing his name, was not written by him, since it formally contradicted what he had earlier held and taught. Beneath the shelter of this supposition, he exposed with a bitter and pitiless pen all the Archbishop's contradictions in the course of his doctrinal evolution. To his latest treatise he opposed his Catechism of 1548 and the Prayer Book of 1549, to which, like his fellow Henricians, he gave the most Catholic interpretation possible.[1] At the same time Dr. Richard Smith, Peter Martyr's predecessor as Regius Professor of Divinity at Oxford, attacked Cranmer in another treatise: *A Confutation of the True and Catholic Doctrine of the Sacrament.*[2] Cranmer replied to both attacks in 1551, by a second treatise of 530 pages octavo entitled: *An Answer by the Reverend Father in God Thomas Archbishop of Canterbury unto a Crafty and Sophistical Cavillation Devised by Stephen Gardiner, Doctor of Law, Late Bishop of Winchester, against the True and Godly Doctrine of the Most Holy Sacrament of the*

---

[1] It was perhaps Tunstall's evidence at Gardiner's trial which suggested to the latter the idea of attacking Cranmer indirectly. "I have seen," Tunstall said, "a book defending the same error against the Sacrament of the altar. Its title affirms that the Archbishop of Canterbury is its author, but whether it was really written by him, I know not". Cf. ed., Jenkyns, III, 35, 37, 42 &c.

[2] *A Confutation of the True and Catholike Doctrine of the Sacrament.* Cf. Strype, *Mem. of Cranmer*, II, 308, 312, 315n, 321, 325; Jenkyns, II, 140; III, 34, 75 *sq.*, 80, 87, 96, 128, 131, 143, 149, 174, 181 *sq.*, 237, 253, 475, 503, 507, 545, 550; IV, 48, 69; Todd, II, 245, 253 *sq.* Smith had written in 1546 an *Assertion and Defence of the Sacrament of the Aulter.*

Body and Blood of Our Saviour Christ. Wherein is also, As Occasion Serveth, Answered Such Places of the Book of Dr. Richard Smith as May Seem Anything Worth the Answering, and by another treatise (far shorter, 23 pages): *The Answer of Thomas Archbishop of Canterbury against the False Conclusions of Dr. Richard Smith who hath Taken upon him to Confute the Defence of the True and Catholic Doctrine of the Sacrament of the Body and Blood of Our Saviour Christ.*[1] His easiest reply to his enemies would have been to admit that the 1549 Prayer Book was but a temporary phase of the Reformation, a step on the road to its final form. But the Archbishop, dealing with every point individually, strove to prove that the teaching of the Catechism and the Prayer Book was in every respect in conformity with his new opinions: "Nor I," he wrote, "in no point improve" (blame) "that godly book nor vary from it".[2] It was a difficult task, and it involved him in more subtleties, hair-splitting and sophistry than any other work of his composition. Gardiner had objected that "in the Sacrament we receive the Body of Christ with our mouth", and that this was in fact asserted in Cranmer's own Catechism and Prayer Book. The Archbishop had no better reply than to say that in every case the word "spiritually" must be understood. All the Prayer Book formularies, Gardiner had argued, imply belief in the Real Presence. Cranmer attempted to place another interpretation upon them. They signified nothing, he said, save Christ's *spiritual* presence in communion and for the communicant. It is not the consecration but the communion that makes Him present.

[1] The two treatises compose volume III of Jenkyns' *Remains of Th. Cranmer*. The second is a reply to Smith's preface. Cf. Todd, *op. cit.*, II, 237 *sqq.*

[2] Ed. Jenkyns, III, 60 *sqq.*; 297 *sqq.*; ed. Parker Soc., *Cranmer's Works*, II, 55. Cf. Gasquet and Bishop, 281; Strype, *Mem. of Cranmer*, Vol.III, Chapters V and XXV; Todd, *op. cit.*, II, 53 *sqq.* "As for the expressions, he thought that we in the sacrament do receive the Body and Blood of Christ spiritually; and that the words *really* and *substantially* were not used, but *truly*." (Strype, *Mem. of Cranmer*, II, 47.)

Cranmer plays with words. He uses the expression "Real Presence" but gives it a different sense to that given to it by the Catholics and the Lutherans. A spiritual object is real. And it was in this sense that he affirmed the real presence. Bucer also said: "I would defend the terms *realiter* and *substantialiter*, if by Our Saviour's real and substantial presence, it were meant that He is *truly and really received by faith*."[1] Cranmer admitted a real presence but of a spiritual nature. "Christ's Body and Blood be given to us *indeed*, yet not corporally and carnally but *spiritually* and effectually." "Surely", Gardiner objected, "a real presence implies a bodily presence." To which Cranmer replied: "Doth not God's Word teach a true presence of Christ in spirit where He is not present in His corporal substance? As when He saith: 'Where two or three are gathered together in my name, there am I in the midst of them.' And also where He saith: 'I shall be with you unto the end of the world.' Was it not a true presence that Christ in these places promised?"[2]

The thesis maintained by the Archbishop against Gardiner was that neither the Bible nor the ancient Fathers mention or approve of transubstantiation, that Christ's Body and Blood are not present really, corporally and naturally under the appearances of bread and wine, that the wicked do not eat the true Body nor drink the true Blood of Christ, that Christ is not daily offered by the priest as a propitiatory sacrifice for sins. All this, he says, is the doctrine of Antichrist and his heir, Pope Nicholas II.

The Real Presence, such as Luther affirmed it, has no existence. His own (Cranmer's) belief was that "Christ is not received with the mouth but with the heart and

---

[1] See Cranmer's reply to Gardiner, ed. Jenkyns, 93 *sqq.*: *The Confutation of the Third Book* and n. 39 of App. XLVI of the *Mem. of Cranmer: The Sententious Sayings of Master Martin Bucer upon the Lord's Supper*.

[2] Bucer said (App. XLVI, No. 34): "What we know by faith is more certain than what we know by the senses or reason. How then can we do otherwise than affirm that Christ our Head is present with His members, since we know by faith that He lives and dwells in us?"

entereth by faith".[1] Such was Cranmer's doctrine. It was not original. It was in all points the doctrine of Bucer, Theodore Beza, and Calvin.

It became the doctrine of the Anglican Church. For it made its way into the XLII Articles of 1553, of which I shall soon be speaking (Article 29) and into the XXXIX Articles of Elizabeth, which remain the official Anglican creed. The 28th of these Articles runs: "Transubstantiation (or the change of the substance of bread and wine) in the Supper of the Lord, cannot be proved by Holy Writ; but is repugnant to the plain words of Scripture, overthroweth the nature of a Sacrament and hath given occasion to many superstitions.

"The Body of Christ is given, taken and eaten in the Supper, only after a heavenly and spiritual manner. And the means whereby the Body of Christ is received and eaten in the Supper is Faith." And the title of the next Article is couched in language dear to Cranmer: " Of the Wicked which eat not the Body of Christ in the use of the Lord's Supper."

Cranmer had the principal share in compiling the Prayer Books of 1549 and 1552. The XLII Articles are also to a considerable extent his composition and they reflect his beliefs. His *Homilies* and his treatises on the Eucharist officially teach for the first time in England the doctrine of Zwingli and Calvin.

Cranmer had also compiled a new code of canon law, the *Reformatio Legum Ecclesiasticarum*, in which he adapted the old canon law, the legal code of the Roman Church, to the requirements of the new religion. This

[1] In all this, as before, Cranmer simply adopts Bucer's views. See Appendix XLVI of *Mem. of Cranmer*, Nos. 20, 28–41, 43, 45, 46–8; cf. 12, 13, 16, 50 and 51. In the *Reformatio Legum Ecclesiasticarum* (ed. Cardwell, 1850, 18 *sqq.*, 31 *sq.*), Cranmer combats transubstantiation, impanation, and the real presence, as Catholics understand it, whereas in his first draft of 1538 he had explicitly affirmed the real and substantial presence of Christ's Body and Blood. Dixon, (III, 373 n.) points out the Archbishop's self-contradictions and changes of belief. See also for Cranmer's varying opinions, Ch. Hardwick, *History of the Christian Church*, ed. Stubbs, 1872, 196 *sqq.*, 207.

important work was published after his death under Elizabeth by John Day, chiefly owing to John Foxe, who wrote a preface. But it was never approved either by Convocation or Parliament, nor put into force. It contained too many survivals of Catholicism to please the advanced Protestants, and too many novelties to satisfy those whose tendencies were Catholic. Its interest is purely historical.[1]

That is to say Cranmer's writings embrace dogma, liturgy, and canon law, in fact every branch of religious knowledge. He revolutionised them all, infusing into them the spirit of the Reformation.[2] Under Queen Mary the Southern Convocation officially condemned "the pestilential books of Thomas Cranmer, late Archbishop of Canterbury".[3] Anglicans of Protestant views regard him as the first Father of their Church, the man to whom they owe their creed and service-book.

[1] The *Reformatio Legum Ecclesiasticarum, ex Auctoritate Primum regis Henrici VIII Inchoata, Deinde per Regem Edouardum VI Provecta, Adauctaque in hunc Modum, atque nunc ad Pleniorem Ipsarum Reformationem in Lucem Edita* was reprinted in 1640, and again from the edition of 1571 by Edward Cardwell, Oxford, 1850. On three occasions Parliament asked Henry VIII to appoint a committee composed half of clergy, half of laymen, to revise the canon law. In Edward's reign this committee, consisting of 32 members whose names are recorded in Edward's *Journal*, was actually appointed after another motion to that effect had been made by Parliament (1549). Cranmer's work was already completed and the committee had, practically speaking, only to revise it. The Archbishop made several changes chiefly suggested by Peter Martyr and Laski, who were members of the committee. Cf. Strype, *Mem. of Cranmer*, I, Chapter, XXX; Burnet, V, 64; Fuller, V, 469–488; J. Todd, *op. cit.*, 99 II, 325 *sqq.*; Dixon, III, 366–382; Blunt, II, 13 *sqq.*, 164, 166, 169–170; Gairdner, *Lollardy*, III, 363, 400; also my *Reformation under Henry VIII*, 648, and *Spanish Cal.*, XI, 33.

[2] Strype, *Memorials of Cranmer*, Vol. II, Chapter. V, ascribes to him the authorship of the *Confutation of Unwritten Verities*, printed abroad in Queen Mary's reign by an English exile, who signed himself E. P. If the materials, a collection of notes preserved in the British Museum, are Cranmer's, the treatise is anonymous. It was with this reservation that Jenkyns reprinted it in his fourth volume (143–273). The author is hostile to tradition, the fathers and the general councils. "God's written word in Scripture is a true, deep and complete doctrine containing in itself everything necessary for salvation." The *Reformatio Legum Ecclesiasticarum* says: "The authority of the fathers is not to be despised. But we do not allow that the sacred text is to be submitted to their judgment. Let them therefore keep their authority and the reverence due to them; but these must be subject and yield to the teaching, truth and authority of the sacred books."

[3] Wilkins, IV, 96. Cf. the proclamation prohibiting all books and other writings against the Pope. Ibid., 128–129.

CHAPTER IX

ENGLAND PROTESTANT

The influence of foreign Protestants upon the religious revolution in England—The effect of the religious changes under Edward VI—The XLII Articles of 1553—A comparison between them and Elizabeth's XXXIX Articles, still imposed to-day.

THERE was nothing original about the English Reformation under Edward VI, nor even anything peculiar to itself. It was the work of men who were disciples of the continental Reformers, and the changes it effected resemble those which overthrew the old religious order in Germany and Switzerland. The Prayer Book of 1549 reflected the Lutheran liturgy and doctrine, that of 1552 was inspired by the Swiss Reformation. Cranmer was in turn the disciple of Luther, Zwingli and Calvin. Like him, the other bishops of his party, such as Ridley, Ponet, Bale, Hooper and Coverdale, derived their creed from some continental Reformer. It was not the profession of any doctrine peculiar to herself that separated the Anglican Church from orthodoxy. Nor did she later invent any such. Her sole originality consisted in preserving traces of the diverse confessions and liturgies which marked the stages of her doctrinal evolution. The insularity and majestic isolation which were the boast and pride of the English in the nineteenth century, were not sentiments of the sixteenth nor of the Renaissance. Neither Cranmer nor the Government ever thought of setting up a Church national in her doctrine or ritual, but a Church national only in her jurisdiction and hierarchy. They still believed that the Church of Christ is Catholic. They desired to remain in communion with the Churches which had been cleansed from what they called the papal corruption. All the changes effected between 1549 and 1552 were intended to facilitate agreement with these continental Churches. This new catholicity was to be established by means of what may be termed a free general council which would unite in the unity of Scripture the scattered members of reformed Christendom. Such was Cranmer's dream, as it had been Melanchthon's before him, and would still be a few years later the dream of Calvin, Farel and Laski.[1]

The Archbishop wanted to gather in England an assembly of Protestant divines whose influence would counterbalance that of the Fathers then assembled at Trent. It was particularly in the years 1548, 1549 and 1552, that he cherished the project and sought to carry it into execution. "Our adversaries," he wrote to Calvin,[2] "are holding their Council at Trent to establish error. Shall we then neglect to assemble a pious synod to confute these errors and purify and propagate sound doctrine?" Calvin replied that there could be no more profitable remedy for the Churches divided by mutual dissension than this assembly projected by Cranmer, "which would transmit to posterity, on every article of faith, a definite formulation of doctrine in conformity with the opinion of all".[3] Cranmer urged the leading reformers of Germany and Switzerland to lend their assistance to "an undertaking so necessary and so profitable to the Christian commonwealth". Some had already responded to his appeal. "Bucer is expected," Laski announced, "Francis Dryander is already here,

---

[1] It was Melanchthon who first broached the project to Henry VIII in a letter of March 26, 1539. In 1542 he repeated the proposal, and again to Edward VI in January 1548. See Strype, *Mem. of Cranmer*, III, 292; Jenkyns, *Cranmer Remains*, I, 337, n.f.; Archbishop R. Laurence, *Bampton Lectures*, 223; C. H. Smyth, *Cranmer and the Reformation under Edward VI*, 36 *sqq.*

[2] Letter of March 20, 1552. Jenkyns, *op. cit.*, I, 346. When the German Protestants sent delegates to Trent (1552) Cranmer exerted all his influence to prevent the King sending any. Ibid., 344.

[3] *Zurich Original Letters*, XII, 711 *sqq.*

and there is even talk of Calvin's coming." Soon only Melanchthon will be lacking, the peacemaker, and the Archbishop will address repeated appeals to him.[1] Cranmer was delighted by the prospect and unfolded his design in the following terms: "We desire," he says, "to lay before our Churches the true and evident teaching of God in conformity with Scripture, not adapting it to any man's taste, nor cloaking it with ambiguities. We all wish carefully to eschew carnal prudence and to give the nations an illustrious testimony of our doctrines, based on the authority of pious and erudite men, that posterity may have a model to imitate. For this end we have deemed it necessary to have the assistance of learned men who can compare their doctrine with our own, put an end to all doctrinal controversy, and construct a complete system of true doctrine. We have invited many. Almost all have arrived, and the others, we hope, will arrive shortly."[2] They have come from Italy and Germany, he wrote a little later to Melanchthon[3] pressing him to join them, "to give the greater lustre to God's glory". "You have often I know desired that pious and holy men should take council together, to communicate their ideas one to another and execute a work of great authority, which should embrace the chief articles of doctrine and transmit to future generations the truth pure from any admixture of error. This at present is the object of all our efforts. I beseech God to guide us and unite us in a Church which shall abide for ever, and not ourselves alone but also those still without. And this He has already begun to do."

---

[1] "Bring Melanchthon with you," he wrote to Laski on July 4, 1548 (Jenkyns, I, 330 *sqq.*). "This is the third time that I have pressed him to come." It would not be the last. He even offered Melanchthon the chair at Cambridge made vacant by Bucer's death. Strype, *Eccl. Mem.*, IV, 76; Todd, *Cranmer's Life*, II, 214; Dixon, III, 470 *sq.* Cf. Todd, II, 196.

[2] Cranmer to Laski July 4, 1548; to Albert Hardenberg at this time in charge of the reformed Church of Bremen, July 28, 1548; to Bucer, October 2, 1548. Jenkyns, I, 329 *sqq.*

[3] Letter to Melanchthon of February 10, 1549, Jenkyns, I, 337.

In his sturdy optimism Cranmer believed that he could provide a remedy for the doctrinal dissension with which Catholics did not fail to reproach the Protestants and which shocked the most sincere among them. For a long time he had lamented the internal strife which was corroding the Reformation, and had begged the Protestant leaders not to tear each other to pieces but to come together in a sincere agreement.[1] He deplored the profound differences which kept them apart, both about the Eucharist, predestination and ecclesiastical government, not to speak of other questions.[2] Where does the truth lie? Can truth dwell in a body whose members are irreconcilable foes?

The first point was to agree upon a common doctrine of the Eucharist, the "Symbol of unity and charity whereby Jesus Christ willed all Christians to be brethren".[3] Was not the agreement of Zurich concluded between Bullinger and Calvin, the *Consensus Tigurinus* of 1549, of good augury for its attainment? By putting an end to the "dissension about the Sacrament" the assembly would achieve its principal purpose. But all the most controversial questions would be discussed in order to reach a genuine agreement, a universal pacification among Protestants. "All questions of ecclesiastical doctrine," Cranmer declared, "will be discussed, and not only the doctrines themselves but the way of stating them."[4]

Was the agreement between England and Germany, several times attempted, really likely, and would some great doctrinal League unite the Protestants of every country? The three surviving leaders of the Reformation

[1] See his letter written to the Swiss reformer Joachim von Watt (Vadianus), as early as 1537. Q. Reuter, *Andreae Dudithii de Horehoviza. . . . Orationes in Concilio Tridentino Habitae*. Offenbach, 1610, 230; Strype *Cranmer*, I, 409.

[2] Cf. Strype, *Cranmer*, Book III, Chapter XXIV: Todd, Book II, Chapter IX, Dixon, III, 96 *sqq*.

[3] Council of Trent, *Decretum de Sanctissimo Eucharistiae Sacramento*, October 11, 1551.

[4] Cranmer to Bullinger, Calvin and Melanchthon, March 20 and 27, 1552, Jenkyns, I, 344 *sqq*.

must meet in London and establish a lasting union. "I have written to Calvin and Bullinger," the Archbishop writes to Melanchthon, "pressing them to come.[1] I have urged them to participate in a work so necessary and so useful to the Christian commonwealth."

But although the invitation was several times repeated, Melanchthon never crossed the Channel. His abstention rendered impossible an agreement which at this late date he probably regarded as chimerical. But in 1539 he had broached it to Henry VIII and had returned to the project in 1542 and even in 1548. Bucer himself had, throughout his life, sought to achieve an impossible accord between Zwingli and Luther. He alone by his supple and ambiguous formulas might have succeeded. Cranmer however had declared that he would have "no more actors' boots" fitting the right and left, feet alike, that is to say no more ambiguous formulas which could provide only an artificial link between Churches of conflicting belief. Melanchthon inspired by the Adages of Erasmus had already employed this simile to prove that ambiguity must prove a new source of disagreement: *Cothurnos facit qui novas discordias excitabunt*—"Such a one makes actors' boots which will arouse fresh strife". In the Church, Melanchthon added, "we must call a spade a spade instead of employing vague language that will prove an apple of discord to posterity".[2] But this surely was to attempt to square the circle and to aim at something which contradicts the fundamental principle of the Reformation, free private judgment whose effects are as certain as they are inevitable.

The difficulties inherent in Cranmer's scheme condemned it to be nothing more than a splendid dream. It was impossible to unite Lutherans, Zwinglians and Calvinists in a common creed. Cleverer men than

---

[1] Letter of March 27, 1552, in Jenkyns, I, 348. The letters to Bullinger and Calvin were written on March 20. Ibid., 344, 346.
[2] Letter to Cranmer of May 1, 1548. Cf. Strype, *Cranmer*, III, 302 *sq.*

Cranmer had failed. The strife between the Germans and the Swiss was destined to continue with the utmost bitterness on either side until the end of the century. And England in place of the unity for which the Archbishop longed so passionately, would herself witness before long the multiplication of warring sects.

Cranmer's pressing invitations and the welcome given in London to the foreign Protestants did not fail, however, to influence the future of the Anglican Church. Many accepted the Archbishop's invitation. They escaped thus the disturbed conditions in Germany, the Interim to which they would not submit, and the vengeance of the victorious Emperor. The gates of Lambeth Palace were opened wide to them. "Yesterday," Bucer and Fagius wrote on April 26, 1549,[1] "we called upon the Archbishop of Canterbury, that excellent and most benevolent father of the Churches and of godly men. He received us and welcomed us not as inferiors but as brothers. We met at his palace—a meeting most joyful for us—our dear friend, Doctor Peter Martyr, with his wife and his friend Giulio, Master Emanuele (Tremellio) and his wife, Dryander, and several good Frenchmen, whom we had sent on ahead." The Archbishop offered them all hospitality. "His palace," Tremellio tells us later, "was a hostel open to all learned and godly people. Host, Maecenas, and father in one, he knew how to welcome strangers, and could speak their language. *Homo* φιλόξένος *nec minus* φιλολόγος." Lambeth palace was never empty. Men of all nations mingled there. Italians, Germans, Spaniards, and Frenchmen fraternised around Cranmer who could thus cherish the illusion that he had bound them all together in a common bond.[2]

In 1547, the Florentine Peter Martyr Vermigli had arrived in England. He was "the most learned" of the

---

[1] *Zurich Original Letters*, I, 535 *sq.*
[2] See Strype, *Cranmer*, Book II, Chapters XIII and XXII; Todd, Book II, Chapter VIII.

Italian Protestants of the sixteenth century, and is best known by his Christian name, Peter Martyr, the name of the Saint to whom his father had vowed him. Like Luther he had been an Augustinian friar. In succession prior of Spoleto, where he had been sent to restore discipline, of the friary of San Pietro ad Aram at Naples, and of San Frediano at Lucca, and visitor of the Order, he was denounced by Cardinal Guiddicione and summoned to Genoa by his Master General in 1542, as suspect of heresy. He thereupon left for Bologna and Ferrara, where he was a guest of Duchess Renée. From there he went on to Verona, Zurich, Basle and Strasbourg, where he married a former nun and taught theology for four years. It was from Strasbourg that he proceeded to England (December 1547). He was given the Regius Professorship of Divinity at Oxford, and made a Canon of Christ Church. The King had defrayed the bulk of his expenses since he left Strasbourg and at Cranmer's suggestion increased his emoluments as Professor and Canon.[1]

A compatriot and friend, Emanuele Tremellio, followed him to London. He also came from Strasbourg, where together with Vermigli he had taught Hebrew. He was a Jew of Ferrara. Converted to Catholicism in 1540 by

[1] *Archaeologia*, Vol. XXI, 470. See Latimer's sermon preached before the King on March 22, 1549. (Ed. Parker Soc., I, 141; ed. J. Watkins, I, 127). "I could wish," added Latimer, "the King would give him £1,000 and the same to Ochino." Cf. Todd, II, 190, 196.

No life of Peter Martyr has been written since the life published at Elberfeld in 1858. It is the work of E. Schmidt, Professor of Protestant theology at Strasbourg: *Peter Martyr Vermigli. Leben und Ausgewaehlte Schriften, nach Handschriften und Gleichzeitigen Quellen*. Benrath's article in the *Realencyclopedie Fuer Prot. Theologie und Kirche*, ed. 3, Vol. XX, 550 *sqq.* is short but accompanied by a good bibliography. Strype and Todd treat of Martyr's relations with Cranmer in Chapters XXIV and IX of Books III and II of their respective works. Wood (*Athenae Oxonienses*, ed. 1641, col. 108) gives a list of his writings available in English which, therefore, influenced in some degree the English reformation. *The Italian Reformers*, 1534-1564. By Frederick C. Church, New York and London, 1932, studies the influence of the Italian exiles on the Protestant Churches north of the Alps. It is, therefore, of interest from the present point of view.

Cardinal Pole, he very soon embraced Protestantism. He was appointed Professor of Hebrew at Cambridge in 1549 and three years later was made a Canon of Carlisle. At Cambridge he became a friend of the future Archbishop Parker, who put him into communication with Elizabeth.[1] A third Italian, a Siennese, Bernardino Ochino, answered Cranmer's invitation from Augsburg. He also was a friend of Peter Martyr, whom he had known at Naples. Formerly a Capuchin Vicar-general, he was famous for his pulpit eloquence after the style of Savonarola. Having embraced the new ideas, he was obliged to go into exile at the age of fifty-six (1542).[2] He went in turn to Zurich, Geneva, Basle and Augsburg, where he settled as preacher to the "Welsch" or foreigners. In 1548 Cranmer gave him a prebend in his cathedral of Canterbury. The following year he dedicated to the young King his *Tragœdiae*, a violent diatribe against the Papacy, which was translated by Bishop Ponet.[3] Already his works had been translated into English (1548) and spread throughout the realm.

In 1548 the Pole, Laski, became Cranmer's guest and, as we have seen, converted him definitely to the Eucharistic doctrine of Zwingli and Bullinger.[4]

The following year Bucer and Fagius reached Cambridge, where both taught and died before the close of the reign. "Thomas Cranmer," Sleidan wrote, "a man of excellent learning, in frequent letters entreated Bucer and Paul Fagius, a very learned Hebraist, to come to

---

[1] M. Becker's *Immanuel Tremellius*, Breslau 1887, contains a good bibliography and is the latest work on the subject. See further Ney's article in the *Realencyclopedie*, Vol. XX, 95–98; and *Spanish Cal.*, IX, 238, 253, 266; X, 170, 349.

[2] Cf. E. Solmi, *Fuga di Bernardino Ochino*.

[3] *Tragoedie or Dialoge of the Injuste usurped Primacie of the Bishop of Rome, and of all the just Abolishing of the Same* made by Master Bernardino Ochino, an Italian, and translated out of Latine into Englishe by Master John Ponet, Dr. of Divinitie, 1549. Benrath, the author of the article on Ochino in the *Realencyclopedie* (ed. 3, XIX, 256–260), is his latest biographer. There is an English translation of his biography: *Bernardino Ochino von Siena. Ein Beitrag zur Geschichte der Reformation in Italien*, 2nd ed. Brunswick, 1892.

[4] Preceding chapter.

England, promising them every kindness and faithful
support. Therefore with the consent of the Senate they
set out on April 1 (1549) to sow in England the seed of the
pure doctrine. Their arrival pleased the King and well
nigh all the nobility and people."[1]

Bucer, Peter Martyr, Laski, Tremellio, and Ochino were
consulted about the revision of the Prayer Book and
exercised a powerful influence upon Cranmer.

Other foreign Protestants were to be met with at Lambeth. There was the Spaniard, Francis Dryander or
Duchesne, whose true name was Francisco Enzinas, who
had translated the New Testament into Castilian and
was a friend of Melanchthon's. He was made a professor
at Cambridge.[2] There were also John Utenhove,
Martin Micronius, Peter Alexander, Jean Véron, Valerand
Poulain, and Michael Angelo Florio. John Utenhove of
Ghent became in Elizabeth's reign "first elder" of the
Flemish Church in London.[3] Martin Micronius (Martin
de Cleyne) was another Fleming from Ghent, a friend of
Bullinger's, who with Utenhove, took charge of the
Flemish colony in London and in 1552 brought out
(for the use of his compatriots in England)[4] a short

---

[1] *Commentarium de Statu Religionis et Reipublicae. Carolo Quinto Caesare.
Libri XXVI.* Cf. *Span. Cal.*, 383.

[2] Besides Cooper, *Athenae Cantabrigienses*, Foxe, IV, 449, 458, 741; **VI**,
139, Menendez y Pelayo, *Historia de Los heterodoxos Espanoles* (Madrid 1880)
the *Bibliotheca Wiffeniana : Spanish Reformers of Two Centuries* (Strasbourg—
London, 1874-1904) by Ed. Boehmer. The following may also be consulted:
Merle d'Aubigné, *Histoire de la Réformation en Europe au Temps de Calvin*,
Paris, 1864-1878; L. Linnhoff, *Spanische Protestanten und England*, Emsdetter,
1934; A. Hoermann, *Francisco de Enzinas und Sein Krels*, 1902; A. Sanve,
La Chasse aux Luthériens des Pays Bas, Souvenirs de Fr. d'Enzinas, annotés etc.,
Paris, 1910; M. Bataillon, *Érasme et l'Espagne*, thèse, Paris, 1937, 552-554,
590 *sq.*, 666. Fifty Letters written by Enzinas were published in the
Zeitschrift Für die Historische Theologie, Leipzig, 1870. He died on December
30, 1552.

[3] See article in Dictionary of *Nat. Biog.* Also *J. Utenhovii, Simplex et
Fidelis Narratio de Instituta ac Demum Dissidata Belgarum Aliorumque Pere-
grinorum in Angliae Ecclesia*, Basle, 1560: and Fr. Pijper, *Jan Utenhove. Zijn
Leven en Zijne Werken*, 1883.

[4] *The Christlicke Ordinarien Enz.*, 1554, German translation, Heidelberg,
1565, gives information about the religious organisation of the Flemish
Protestants in England.

catechism, which went through many editions, and a *Treatise on the Lord's Supper*. Peter Alexander of Arles had been a chaplain of Charles V's sister, Mary of Hungary. He received several English benefices.[1] Jean Véron was a Frenchman, who wrote blasphemous attacks upon the Mass, for example, *Cinq abominables Blasphèmes Contenus dans la Messe* (London, 1548).[2] Valerand Poulain was the head of a Protestant colony of Walloon, Flemish, and French weavers, which Somerset had established in the former Abbey of Glastonbury. He published in London a translation of the liturgy used at Strasbourg.[3] Michael Angelo Florio was a Florentine, who thundered against the Pope and denounced to the Council any of his compatriots, the Italian mercenaries, who dared hear Mass, though the immorality of his private life nearly led to his expulsion from the kingdom.[4]

Around these well-known Reformers communities of foreign Protestants gathered, who like them, had fled from persecution at home, Italians, Dalmatians, Frenchmen, Germans and Flemings.

By a patent of July 24, 1550, Laski was appointed superintendent of all these foreign churches. He had been naturalised a month earlier. Assisted by four ministers for the communities of different languages, he organised these Protestant groups, as he had formerly organised them in East Friesland. He obtained for them from Warwick the right to worship in freedom without

---

[1] When on Mary's accession Gardiner summoned him, he fled back to the Continent. *Span. Cal.*, XI, 217. He had been condemned in the Netherlands by the Inquisition in 1545.

[2] Without knowing the writer's name, Pocock (*English Historical Review*, X, 419 *sqq.*) published a study of the *Five Abominable Blasphemies contained in the Mass*.

[3] Though there is nothing about him in the *Dict. of Nat. Biog.* Strype (*Cranmer*, Book II, Chapter XXIII) devotes an entire chapter to him and his church at Glastonbury, also Nos. LV–LVIII of the Appendix. After Somerset's fall the colony, unpopular with the natives of the district, underwent great hardships. On Mary's accession its members sought refuge at Frankfort.

[4] Strype, *Mem. of Cranmer*, II, 280 *sq.*, also Appendix LII, LIII; III, 699; Dixon, III, 425 *sq.*; C. H. Smyth, *op. cit.*, 221 *sq.*

interference by the Bishop of London, who had sought
to force the Prayer Book upon them. Calvin thanked
the King for this privilege: "Sire, all good souls praise
God and feel themselves much bound in gratitude to
you that it has pleased your Grace to grant churches to
your French and German speaking subjects."[1] Henceforward, the foreign Churches enjoyed their independent
existence protected by the state. To unite them the
more closely, Laski gave them a common profession of
faith, the *Confessio Londinensis*, which children were to
learn as a catechism. He also wrote for their use his
treatise on the sacraments: *Brevis et Dilucida de Sacramentis
Ecclesiae Christi Tractatio*, which he dedicated to Edward
VI, as Calvin had dedicated to Francis I his *Institutio
Christiana*. The pastors and elders were to digest it
thoroughly and teach it to every member of the community.[2]

By these means it was sought to remedy the evils,
arising out of this invasion by continental sects seeking an
asylum in England, which had aroused the anxiety of
more than one observer. "This influx of all the French
and German apostates," the Venetian Ambassador wrote
in 1551, "is bringing with it confusion of tongues and
unbridled licence; it is a veritable chastisement of God."[3]
"It is not good that England should be termed to-day

[1] Letter of January 1, 1551. *J. Calvini, Opera*, ed. Baum, and Vol. XIV,
col. 38; *Zurich Original Letters*, I, 710.

[2] The letters patent of July 24, 1550, granting the foreign Protestants
an independent organisation, are in Burnet, *History of the Reformation*,
ed. Pocock, V, 305–309 and Collier, *Ecclesiastical History* ed. Lathbury
IX, 276–279, in Latin in the former, in French in the latter case. Utenhove
describes this new organisation at length in a letter to Calvin of August 23,
1550 (*J. Calvini Opera*, ed. Baum, etc., Vol. XIII, col. 625 *sqq.*). Cf.
Strype, *Cranmer*, Book II, Chapter XXII; Kuyper, *Jo. A Lasco Opera tam
Edita quam Inedita*, Amsterdam, 1866, 2 vols.: C. H. Smyth, *op. cit.*, Chapter
VI.

For the foreign churches in England at this period see Baron F. de
Schickleer, *Les Églises du Refuge en Angleterre*, Paris, 1892, 4 vols.; Van
Schelven, *Églises Néerlandaises du Refuge au XVIe Siècle, en Angleterre et en
Allemagne*; Dixon, III, 96 *sq.*, 424 *sqq.*

[3] Report by Daniel Barbaro in Albèri, *Reliazoni degli Ambasciatori
Veneti al Senato*, Series I, Vol. II, Florence, 1840, 250.

the refuge of every form of infidelity," the English Ambassador to the Empèror wrote to the Council (June 7, 1551).[1] Towards the close of the reign it was ordered that to obtain naturalisation a foreigner must have made his profession of faith to a minister of one of the Reformed Churches.[2] All these diverse elements, all these more or less conflicting beliefs cannot fail to have affected the future religion of the country.

Already under the influence of these foreigners, the theological teaching at the Universities was being transformed. At Oxford, Peter Martyr replaced Richard Smith, who had taught the Catholic doctrine of the Eucharist. At Cambridge, Bucer occupied the corresponding chair of Divinity. Thus both the Regius Professorships at the English Universities were held by continental reformers.

In May 1549 Oxford and Cambridge were subjected to a rigorous visitation, intended to change their spirit. The visitors, selected from the adherents of the Reformation, were equipped with extraordinary powers. At Oxford the visitation was inaugurated by a sermon from Peter Martyr, who on May 17 challenged a public disputation on the Eucharist which lasted several days. The impression generally received was apparently that Martyr would have been worsted, had he not been supported by the visitors' authority and if Dr. Cox, the Dean of Christ Church, had not more than once come to his assistance.[3] Oxford was regarded as the stronghold of orthodoxy. A correspondent wrote to Bullinger that the university "was crammed with those savage brutes the Roman Catholics," and that the members of the University "remain obstinately fixed in the mire of Popery."[4] Therefore the visitation concluded by the issue of

---

[1] Tytler, *op. cit.*, I, 380.
[2] Micronius to Bullinger, February 1553. *Zurich Original Letters*, I, 581.
[3] Strype, *Cranmer*, Book II, Chapter XIV; Burnet, II, 195 *sqq.*, and III, 360; J. Collier, ed. Lathbury, V, 324 *sqq.*; Gasquet and Bishop, *op. cit.*, 159.
[4] *Zurich Original Letters*, I, 464.

"Edward's Statutes," which, as the historian of the university[1] informs us, "changed the entire organisation of its government." The works of the schoolmen both printed and in manuscript were destroyed. Orthodox preachers and professors were expelled and replaced by Protestants.

It was the same at Cambridge. Ridley and his colleague challenged a public disputation in which the thesis was maintained that the dogma of transubstantiation is not taught or proved by Scripture or the Fathers, and the Lord's Supper is a simple memorial of Christ and not a sacrifice. As at Oxford, the visitors imposed ordinances whose essential purport was to implant and propagate the doctrines of Zwingli and Calvin.[2]

By the end of the reign England seemed a doctrinal province of continental Protestantism. From Geneva Calvin addressed exhortations and remonstrances. "The King must persevere in the right way and combat Antichrist. Cranmer must eradicate the last traces of error."[3] From Zurich Bullinger encouraged the English reformers, and through his friends took possession of the Archbishop's mind. No Popish ceremony must be left, he insisted.[4] From Basle translations of Zwingli's Confession, diatribes against the Mass, and similar literature, arrived in bundles. (Their importation was forbidden in Mary's reign by an order of 1555).[5] From the very beginning of the schism, the continental Protestants had had their eyes fixed upon England and had cherished the unavowed hope of winning it to their cause. Had not Bucer in 1544 projected a doctrinal agreement between

[1] Anthony A. Wood, *Historia et Antiquitates Universitatis Oxoniensis*, 1674, Book I, 267.

[2] See *Ridley's Works*, ed. Parker Society, 169 *sqq.* The account of an eye-witness, Alban Langdale of Trinity College who complains of Ridley's interruptions, attempts at intimidation and mockery is to be found in his *Catholica Confutatio*, Paris, 1556, fol. 5-7; see also Gasquet and Bishop (*op. cit.*, 247 *sqq.*), Cooper, *Annals of Cambridge*, II, 25 *sq.*

[3] *Zurich Original Letters*, 707; cf. 132; Strype, *Cranmer*, III, 308.

[4] Strype, *Eccl. Mem.*, III, 53.

[5] Cf. Foxe, VII, 127.

England and Germany? Henry's death had removed
the sole dam, and the foreign flood inundated the kingdom and Church. Englishmen who had hitherto been
compelled to live in exile on account of their religious
beliefs and had become members of continental Protestant
communities returned to their native country, where their
influence was very powerful. Some of them became bishops.
Hooper, Bishop of Gloucester, Bullinger's friend and
disciple, Miles Coverdale, Bishop of Exeter, Bale, Bishop
of Ossory, John Rogers, Bartholomew Traheron spread
the foreign doctrines among the people far more effectively
than the immigrants who knew very little English. As a
result of these combined influences the Church of England
was transformed. One who had known her as she was
when Henry died would hardly have recognised her in
1553. Within those few years she had changed from
orthodoxy to Protestantism.

I have described the change in her worship and liturgy.
We shall now study her new creed, namely the XLII
Articles of 1553.

Cranmer had given the Church of England an English
translation of the Bible, and a liturgy, namely the Prayer
Books of 1549 and 1552. He had attempted to lay down
her code of law in his *Reformatio Legum Ecclesiasticarum*.
He desired to define her faith, so that it should reflect
his own.[1] Had not Bucer in his *Censura* reproached the
Church of England with her lack "of a confession or
creed stating the dogmas and precepts of the Christian
religion, in particular those which have been the object
of recent controversy?"

In 1549 the Archbishop had exacted from every cleric
who asked for a licence to preach or teach theology the

---

[1] According to Foxe, whom some of the older historians have followed,
Cranmer when questioned at his trial under Queen Mary admitted that
he was the author of the articles. In fact he merely admitted that he had
advised their compilation. Todd (*op. cit.*, II, 286) thinks that he employed
the services of Ridley and Latimer. In any case the Council submitted
Cranmer's text to the royal chaplains: Harley, Bill, Horne, Grindal,
Perne and Knox. Cf. Strype, *Cranmer*, II, 367.

subscription of a series of articles. These were probably the embryo of those imposed by the Government in 1553. "They contain the pure and godly doctrine of the Eucharist in conformity with what you teach in Switzerland," adds John Hooper, to whom we owe our knowledge of these Articles.[1] In 1551 the King and the Privy Council ordered the Archbishop "to frame a book of Articles of Religion for the preserving and maintaining of peace and unity of doctrine in the Church". He submitted them to the advice of several bishops and on May 2 of the following year the Council, without whom no step was now taken, asked him to send them the Articles and to signify whether the same were set forth by any public authority."[2]

Several times the articles were sent back to Cranmer, returned by him to the Council, and submitted to the examination of extremely advanced reformed theologians, such as Knox and Robert Horne, or of the royal chaplains (October 21, 1552). It was not until November 24, 1552, that Cranmer sent them for the last time to the Council, where they were dealt with particularly by Cecil and Sir John Cheke. Cranmer urged that they should be authorised by the crown and approved by the clergy, "and he trusted," he concludes with his incurable optimism, "that such a concord and quietness in religion would soon follow, as otherwise would not be in many years."[3]

They did not in fact receive the royal authorisation until June 12 of the following year, three weeks before the King's death.

In the course of their refashioning, the Articles, originally XLV, were reduced to XLII, the four which dealt with the Eucharist being fused into one, the twenty-ninth.

More than half the articles are in conformity with

---

[1] Letter to Bullinger, December 27, 1549. *Zurich Original Letters*, I, 71.
[2] Strype, *op. cit.*, Vol. II, Chapter XXVII.
[3] Letter of November 24, 1552. Strype, *Cranmer*, II, 367 *sq.*, Appendix LXVI; Todd, *op. cit.*, 289 *sq.* The royal assent had been obtained on October 21. *Acts of the Privy Council*, ed. Dasent, IV, 148.

Catholic doctrine. Some indeed are concerned with doctrines not in dispute between Catholics and Protestants. These are the opening articles on the Trinity, the Incarnation of the Word, the Descent of Christ to Limbo, His Resurrection, that the Old Testament is not to be rejected, and the Three Creeds. The concluding articles envisage certain sects which had revived heresies of primitive Christianity, namely the Millenarians, the Anabaptists, who forbade private property and oaths, and sectaries who denied the resurrection of the dead or maintained that souls sleep until the resurrection, or that the suffering of the lost will have an end.[1] To these articles we may apply what Bossuet wrote of the Confession of Augsburg in his *Histoire des Variations des églises Protestantes* (Book III): "It is surprising how many important articles are stated in conformity with our beliefs."

The rule of faith is Scripture, of which the Church is the *testis* and *conservatrix* (Arts. 5 and 21) and therefore the interpreter. This statement is directed against the Anabaptists and private interpretation of the Bible, and would prove very obnoxious to the Puritans. By calling the Bible the rule of faith it is meant that every article of faith should be based upon it. Thus expressed, this Article V does not conflict with the Catholic doctrine, which is that every truth of faith is contained in Scripture explicitly or implicitly. Nor was Tradition rejected. Throughout his life Cranmer professed his respect for the Fathers and ancient Doctors as the interpreters of the words of Christ and the apostles.[2] The Council of Trent declared Scripture the foundation of every article of faith and Tradition its authorised commentary.

[1] Articles XXXVII–XLII. See also the articles *De Communitate Bonorum et Uxorum, de Incredulorum et Impiorum Damnatione*, in Cardwell, *Reformatio Legum Ecclesiasticarum*, Oxford, 1850, 13, 15. Elizabeth's articles will retain only those on property and oaths. Presumably the other doctrines condemned were no longer current in England.

[2] Cf. his *Reformatio Legum Ecclesiasticarum*, Title I, Chapter XXXV, ed. Cardwell, 7.

The doctrinal divergences begin with the question of grace. Nevertheless, the definition of grace itself, aimed at certain advanced Reformers, is orthodox. Though its action influences the will, it never supersedes it, and the sinner has only himself to blame (Article X). But justification by *faith only* is affirmed in conformity with Cranmer's teaching, and reference is made to his Homily on Justification.[1] Freedom of the will i not denied, as it was by Luther (Article IX)[2]. But every work done before justification is declared to have the nature of sin (Article XII), which is a Lutheran doctrine.[3] Luther added that even after justification, every work apparently good is a mortal sin. In the Confession of Augsburg, intended for the Emperor (Article XX *De Bonis Operibus*), Melanchthon so whittled this doctrine of despair away, that it became unrecognisable, and he continued to tone it down to such an extent that he was suspected of Catholic tendencies. Cranmer, whose temper was more akin to Melanchthon's than Luther's, would have nothing to do with this harsh opinion. The following article declares that to teach works of supererogation is "arrogance and impiety," "for by them men do declare that they do not only render unto God as much as they are bound to do, but that they do more for His sake than of bounden duty is required: whereas Christ saith plainly, 'When ye have

---

[1] See the previous chapter.
In his Homily on Justification (Jenkyns, *op. cit.*, IV, 143 *sqq.*) Cranmer taught that to be justified by faith does not mean that we can be justified without sincere repentance, hope, charity and fear of God—nor without subsequent good works. But the expression is employed to make it clear that the merit of our works is insufficient to obtain our justification from God, and to express better man's weakness and God's mercy. It would seem that Cranmer's view toned down the Lutheran doctrine.

[2] Of free will "We have no power to do good works pleasant and acceptable to God, without the grace of God by Christ preventing us, that we may have a good will, and working with us, when we have that good will."

[3] "Works done before the grace of Christ" do not "make men meet to receive grace or (as the school-authors say) deserve grace of congruity: yea rather, for that they are not done as God hath willed and commanded them to be done, we doubt not but they have the nature of sin." This was Bucer's doctrine: "Every good work before justification is in reality sin and merits the Divine wrath."

done all that are commanded to you say, we are unprofit-able servants'."[1] In Article XVII "of Predestination and Election" there is not a word which even suggests Calvin's doctrine. There is a warning against presumption and despair, both of which lead to a dissolute life. In the godly the thought of predestination arouses loving gratitude, combined with humility and distrust of self, born of the knowledge that our salvation is the gift of God's free goodness.[2]

The Church is defined as "a congregation of faithful men in the which the pure word of God is preached and the sacraments be duly ministered according to Christ's ordinance" (Article XX)[3] But nothing is said of obedi-ence to the Church's legitimate pastors. For "the King of England is the supreme head under Christ of the Church of England and Ireland, and the Pope of Rome hath no jurisdiction in this realm." (Article XXXVI). Moreover, the article continues, "as the Churches of Jerusalem, Alexandria and Antioch have erred; so also the Church of Rome hath erred, not only in their living and manner of ceremonies, but also in matters of faith."[4] The language of Article XXI "of the Authority of General

[1] Cranmer also attacks works of supererogation in his *Reformatio Legum Ecclesiasticarum*, ed. Cardwell, 12.

[2] Towards the end of the article it is stated: "for curious and carnal persons, lacking the spirit of Christ, to have continually before their eyes the sentence of God's Predestination, is a most dangerous downfall, whereby the Devil doth thrust them either into desperation or into wretchlessness of most unclean living, no less perilous than desperation." This was Cranmer's view which he developed at greater length in his *Reformatio Legum Ecclesiasticarum*, ed. Cardwell, Oxford, 1850, 21 *sq.*.

Bucer held predestination in the Calvinist sense: mankind is divided into the predestined and the reprobate, and after justification we can do only good works (cf. Blunt, *op. cit.*, II, 167). Traheron was of the same opinion, though Bullinger attempted to tone down a doctrine which shocked him. See Traheron to Bullinger, September 10, 1552, and June 3, 1553. *Zurich Original Letters*, I, 325-328.

[3] This is practically the definition of the Council of Augsburg (article 7) "The church is the congregation of saints in which the Gospel is truly preached and the sacraments duly administered."

[4] The *Reformatio Legum Ecclesiasticarum* (ed. Cardwell, 20), uses similar language treating as insane persons "Who should be silenced by law," those who think the Church of Rome rests on so firm a foundation that it has not erred and cannot err.

Councils" is no less explicit: "General Councils may not be gathered together without the commandment and will of Princes. And when they be gathered together (for as much as they be an assembly of men whereof all be not governed with the Spirit and Word of God), they may err, and sometimes have erred, even in things pertaining unto God. Wherefore things ordained by them as necessary to salvation have neither strength nor authority, unless it may be declared" (i.e. made clear, proved) "that they be taken out of Holy Scripture."[1]

"The doctrine of the schoolmen[2] concerning Purgatory, Pardons, Worshipping and Adoration, as well as of Images as of Reliques, and also invocation of Saints, is a fond thing vainly invented and grounded upon no warrant of Scripture, but rather repugnant to the Word of God."[3] Long before the Council of Trent in its fifteenth session (December 4, 1563), the Confessions of Faith issued by Henry VIII, and approved and signed by Cranmer himself, had condemned this Article XXIII of Edward VI, by praising the Catholic doctrine on Purgatory and the veneration of the Saints. Images, they stated, those, above all, which represent Christ and Our Lady, are a means of raising our souls to spiritual things. To invoke the saints is a most laudable practice, which must be followed without superstition. To give alms and say Masses or have them said for the souls in Purgatory is a duty of charity.[4]

To blame Catholic theologians for abuses which have occurred among the ignorant and illiterate, but of which even a child instructed in his catechism is not guilty, is a Lutheran procedure as facile as it is unfair. It is also a

[1] The article is plainly aimed at the Council of Trent, which towards the close of 1545 had defined the Catholic doctrine against the Protestants.

[2] Elizabeth's articles will say "The Romish doctrine."

[3] "There is not a syllable about Purgatory in the Bible," *Reformatio Legum Ecclesiasticarum*, ed. Cardwell, 13.

[4] Articles 6, 7, 8, 10 of the Articles of 1536 (Cardwell, *Formularies of Faith . . . during the Reign of Henry VIII*, Oxford, 1856, 13–17. *The Institution of a Christian Man*, 1543, ibid., 299 *sqq.*, 375).

mark of narrow minds to abolish a good thing because of its possible abuse. Judged by that criterion the very best and most valuable things, even health and life itself, must be condemned. And to make the schoolmen or the "Romish" responsible for devotion to the saints proves the authors of this Article ignorant of history and of the Eastern Churches, in which this devotion has never ceased, and is even more prominent than in the Roman Church. Was it not the Second Council of Nicea (787) which defined the doctrine and practice?

The Sacramental doctrine of the Articles is in conformity with the Augsburg Confession, rejecting both the Zwinglian doctrine and the doctrine of Catholic theologians, misunderstood however, on the efficacy of a sacrament *ex opere operato*. On this point Cranmer had not adopted the Zwinglian view. According to the latter, God gives grace directly and does not use the sacraments as a means. The latter are mere external signs of grace, not its channel. They do not confer grace. On this point a lengthy discussion took place in 1552 between Cranmer and Hooper, who was a sacramentarian. The Archbishop won the victory. Article XXVI of the Sacraments runs: "The Sacraments ordained by the Word of God be not only badges or tokens of Christian men's profession; but rather they be certain sure witnesses, effectual signs of grace and God's goodwill towards us, by which He doth work invisibly in us; and doth not only quicken, but also strengthen and confirm our faith in Him."[1] The Confession of Augsburg did not contain these most significant words "effectual signs of grace"; but they occur twice in the XIII Articles of 1538, debated between the English and the Lutheran theologians.[2]

[1] The passage is modelled upon Article 9 of the XIII Articles of 1538 (Jenkyns, *op. cit.*, V, 285) itself inspired by the Confession of Augsburg (Art. 13).

[2] Article 9, *De Sacramentorum Usu* and Art. 14, *De Missa Privata*, the latter of which was dropped. Jenkyns, *op. cit.*, IV, 285 and 295. The latter Article calls the sacraments "Visible signs certain and efficacious through which God works invisibly in those that rightly use them."

Even if the minister is unworthy, "the grace of God's gifts" is not "diminished from such as by faith and rightly do receive the sacraments ministered unto them, which be effectual because of Christ's institution and promise, although they be ministered by evil men."[1] This agrees with the teaching of Trent, which requires only that "the minister shall have the intention of doing what the Church does" (Session VII. *Can.* ii., 12). "The sacraments in such only as worthily receive the same," Edward's Article XVI adds, "have a wholesome effect or operation; not, however, as some say, *ex opere operato*, which terms, as they are strange and utterly unknown to the Holy Scripture, so do they yield a sense which savoureth of little piety but of much superstition". This clause, which does not appear in Elizabeth's Articles, attributes to the phrase *ex opere operato* a meaning entirely false, as though it signified some magical operation as Calvin and Chemnitz affirmed, or in the case of adults rendered the indispensable dispositions, faith and repentance, superfluous. It was indeed in this sense that Protestants understood the Catholic doctrine. "Some say the sacraments confer grace *ex opere operato* apart from the good will of the recipient."[2]

The original draft of the Articles declared Baptism and the Lord's Supper to be the only sacraments. But the final text was content to affirm (Article XXVI) that the sacraments ordained by Christ for the new people are "very few in number, most easy to be kept and of much excellent signification: that is to say Baptism and the Supper of the Lord". And in fact the Articles that follow speak only of these two sacraments. Eliza-

---

[1] Article XXVII of Edward and Article XXVI of Elizabeth. These articles are derived from the XIII Articles of 1538 (Art. 7 and 10, Jenkyns, IV, 279, 286), in which not only the same doctrine but the same terminology is to be found.

[2] Article 9 of the XIII Articles (Jenkyns, IV, 286). To the same effect Article 13 of the Confession of Augsburg said: "They condemn those who teach that the sacraments justify *ex opere operato* and that in their use faith that our sins are remitted is not required."

beth's Articles explicitly state that "there are two sacraments ordained of Christ our Lord in the Gospel, that is to say, Baptism and the Supper of the Lord," and that "those five commonly called sacraments . . . are not to be counted for sacraments of the Gospel," for they "have not like nature of sacraments with Baptism and the Lord's Supper, for that they have not any visible sign or ceremony ordained of God." Nevertheless the *Homily on Common Prayer and Sacraments* does not refuse them the name of sacraments and, with the exception of Extreme Unction, disused in the Church of England until in the nineteenth century the ritualists revived it on their private initiative, the Prayer Book prescribes forms for their administration.[1] The Council of Trent in its Sixth Session defined that there are seven sacraments instituted by Our Saviour and that these are diverse in dignity. This also had been affirmed by the second and third Confessions of Faith in Henry's reign (1537 and 1543).

The definition of baptism is Catholic. The Article adds that "the Baptism of young children is in any wise to be retained in the Church" since, as Elizabeth's Articles added, it is "most agreeable with the institution of Christ." This, however, is incompatible with the denial in Article XXVI that any sacrament is effective *ex opere operato*.

Article XXIX, of the Lord's Supper, has an unexceptionable opening, as also has Elizabeth's XXVIIIth Article: "The Supper of the Lord is not only a sign of the love that Christians ought to have among themselves one to another;[2] but rather is a Sacrament of our Redemption by Christ's death; insomuch that to such as

---

[1] See E. H. Browne, *op. cit.*, 580–590; E. C. Gibson, *op. cit.*, ed. 1910, 602–610; cf. 593 *sqq.*; H. A. Moreton, *op. cit.*, 284 *sqq.*; F. W. Puller, *The Anointing of the Sick in Scripture and Tradition*, 1904.

[2] The Articles of 1552 and 1563 affirm that the Eucharist is *not only* a sign of the love that Christians ought to have one to one another, because some Protestants sought to reduce it to this, seeing in the Lord's Supper nothing more than a symbol of brotherly communion.

rightly, worthily and with faith receive the same, the Bread which we break is a partaking of the Body of Christ; and likewise the Cup of Blessing is a partaking of the Blood of Christ." But it proceeds to deny transubstantiation and to affirm that "since the being of human nature doth require that the body of one and the same man cannot be at one and the same time in many places, but of necessity must be in some certain and determinate place: therefore the Body of Christ cannot be present in many different places at the same time. And since . . . Christ hath been taken up into heaven and there is to abide till the end of the world; it becometh not any of the faithful to believe or profess that there is a real or corporal presence . . . of the Body and Blood of Christ in the Holy Eucharist." This is a statement of Cranmer's Calvinist view which we have already explained.[1] The Council of Trent (Session XIII, Cap. i) replies to the objection raised, by denying that the fact that Our Lord "is seated on His Father's right hand according to the natural mode of a body's existence" is incompatible "with His substantial Presence in many places in a sacramental fashion by a mode of existence in no wise impossible to God which no language can explain, but which the intellect can apprehend by faith and in which we must firmly believe." Elizabeth's Articles, though removing Cranmer's argument, were even more emphatic: "Transubstantiation (or the change of the substance of Bread and Wine) in the Supper of the Lord cannot be proved by Holy Writ; but is repugnant to the plain words of Scripture, overthroweth the nature of a Sacrament, and hath given occasion to many superstitions. The Body of Christ is given, taken, and eaten, in the Supper only after a heavenly and spiritual manner. And the means whereby the Body of Christ is received and eaten in the Supper is Faith."

[1] Previous chapter.

In the reign of Charles II in 1673, Parliament, to debar Catholics from every public office, passed the Test Act, which was not repealed until 1828. The terms of the oath it prescribed were as follows: "I, A.B., do declare that I do believe that there is not any transubstantiation in the Sacrament of the Lord's Supper or in the elements of bread and wine at or after the consecration thereof by any person whatsoever."[1] Five years later, as a result of the imaginary Popish plot, Parliament in an anti-Catholic frenzy, imposed an oath declaring transubstantiation and the invocation of Saints idolatrous.[2]

The Articles of Edward and Elizabeth proceed to say: "The Sacrament of the Lord's Supper was not by Christ's ordinance reserved, carried about, lifted up or worshipped." Already the Article on the Sacraments had declared, with the Sacrament of the Altar in view: "The Sacraments were not ordained of Christ to be gazed upon or to be carried about, but that we should duly use them." This declaration, though its language is moderate, denied and challenged the worship of the Blessed Sacrament, which as a corollary of transubstantiation, had been most vigorously attacked by the sacramentarians. In opposition to their attack the Council of Trent in the sixth canon of Session XIII declared: "If anyone says that in the Holy Sacrament of the Eucharist we should not adore Christ the only Son of God with a worship of latria, even external, and therefore should not honour Him by a special solemnity, bear Him in procession according to the ritual and the laudable

---

[1] *Statutes of the Realm*, 25, Charles II, cap. 2. Gee and Hardy, *Documents Illustrative of English Church History*, ed. 1921, 637; Stephen Liberty, *The Manual Acts as Witness to the Anglican Theory of Eucharistic Consecration* in *The Church Quarterly Review*, Vol. 121, January 1936.

[2] Edward's Articles and the Articles of 1563 say nothing about the communion of the wicked. But the revision of 1571 added a supplementary Article, the XXIXth: "The wicked and such as be void of a lively faith, although they do carnally and visibly press with their teeth (as Saint Augustine saith) the Sacrament of the Body and Blood of Christ, yet in no wise are they partakers of Christ; but rather to their condemnation do eat and drink the sign or sacrament of so great a thing."

and universal custom of the Church, and expose Him publicly to the adoration of the people, and that those who adore Him are idolaters, let him be anathema." For, in fact, the Council adds in the eighth chapter of the same Session, since Christ is God, His person present in the Eucharist has a right to the worship of latria, which the Church has always paid to this Sacrament. Therefore manifestations of devotion to the Blessed Sacrament are perfectly "pious, religious," and an opportune reply to heresy.

The Article which treats of the Mass widens still further the gulf between the Catholic and Anglican doctrines: "The offering of Christ once made is that perfect redemption, propitiation and satisfaction for all the sins of the whole world, both original and actual,[1] and there is none other satisfaction for sin, but that alone. Wherefore the sacrifices of Masses, in the which it was commonly said that the Priest did offer Christ for the quick and the dead, to have remission of pain or guilt, were fables and dangerous deceits."[2] Elizabeth's Articles even said "*blasphemous* fables." To this, which is but a repetition of the Lutheran and Calvinist doctrine,[3] the Council of

---

[1] The Confession of Augsburg, Part II, Article 3, on no better ground than some wholly unauthoritative legend or theologian (see Vasquez *in* 3m, *Partem S. Thomae*, qu. 83, Art. I, c, 4, Vol. VIII of his *Commentarii et Disputationes*, Lyons, 1631, writing against Ambrosius Catharinus, a theologian of singular views, who on several occasions was attacked by Bellarmine. Cf. *Church Quarterly Review*, Vol. XLII, p. 41; Vacant, *Histoire de la Conception du Sacrifice de la Messe*, 40) wantonly charges Catholicism with restricting the Redemption accomplished by Christ to the pardon of original sin, the remission of actual sins being reserved to the sacrifice of the altar. On this point Edward's and Elizabeth's Articles have followed the Confession of Augsburg, as Denny and Lacey plainly state in their *De Hierarchia Anglicana Dissertatio Apologetica* (London, 1895, 126 *sqq.*). Cf. Gibson, *op. cit.*, 692. The definition of Trent in its session XXII of September 17, 1562, was clear enough to make any misunderstanding impossible, so that the language of this Article should have been modified at the revision of 1571.

[2] These are Hooper's actual words in his *Brief and Clear Confession of the Christian Creed*, of 1550. Cf. Messenger, *The Reformation, the Mass and the Priesthood*, London, 1936. I, 548 *sq.*

[3] In his *Institutio Christiana*, Calvin said that to call the Mass a sacrifice is a blasphemy against Christ in as much as it denies the eternity of his priesthood which renders "successors and vicars" superfluous.

Trent replied by anathematising whosoever terms the Sacrifice of the Mass "blasphemy and imposture" (Canons 4 and 5 of Session XXII). The Council also affirms that "Our God and Lord offered Himself *once* to God His Father by His death on the altar of the Cross to accomplish there an everlasting redemption." But this unique sacrifice is perpetuated in the Church by a visible and unbloody rite instituted at the Last Supper, which was the first offering of the Eucharistic sacrifice, when the Divine Priest provided successors throughout the ages to come (Chapter i.). The Supper in union with the Cross constitutes in its integrity the sacrifice of our Redemption. Truly propitiatory, the Mass applies to the living and dead the saving virtue of the Sacrifice of the Cross, whence it derives all its efficacy, while it is at the same time its memorial. Though it does not dispense either with Baptism or Penance, it obtains from "the Lord, appeased by this oblation, the grace and gift of penance." (Chapter ii.).

The Articles of 1553 say nothing of communion under two kinds.

But Elizabeth's Articles declared that: "both the parts of the Lord's sacrament by Christ's ordinance and commandment ought to be administered to all Christian men alike." Like the Council of Constance, the Council of Trent affirmed that communion under both kinds is not necessary *ex Dei praecepto vel necessitate salutis* and that Christ is received whole and entire under either species (Session xxi, ch, 3; *Can.* i, 2, 3). But it left it to the Pope's judgment to grant, if he thought fit, Communion *sub utraque* to those countries of the Empire that asked for it, which Pius IV did in 1564.[1]

The thirty-first of Edward's Articles declared the law of clerical celibacy abolished, saying that it is not a law of God, but not adding with the Wittenberg

[1] See my book: *La Concession à L'Allemagne de la Communion sous les Deux Espèces*, Paris, 1923.

Articles that "the papal prohibition of marriage is unlawful."[1]

Articles XXXIV and XXXV declare that Cranmer's Homilies teach sound doctrine and should be read on Sundays to the people,[2] and that the Prayer Book and Ordinal of 1552 "are very pious, as to truth of doctrine, in nothing contrary but agreeable to the wholesome doctrine of the Gospel." Since under Queen Mary the legate received special instructions for dealing with those who had been ordained under Edward VI,[3] Elizabeth's thirty-sixth article adds that bishops, priests and deacons ordained according to this ordinal of 1552 are lawfully and validly ordained.[4]

There is no doubt that the Confession of Augsburg, through the intermediary of the Articles of Wittenberg (1536) and above all the XIII Articles of 1538, influenced the Anglican Articles.[5] Nevertheless those passages which reproduce them most literally, are not Lutheran but profess Catholic doctrine in opposition to the Anabaptists or other sectaries. "There are," Bishop Hooper wrote to Bullinger,[6] "a large number of Anabaptist groups which cause me considerable trouble by their opinions about Our Lord's Incarnation. They deny His birth according to the flesh of the Virgin Mary. They maintain that after justification man is without sin or concupiscence, that he is incapable of sin, and that there is no hope of pardon for those who having received the Holy Ghost

[1] Art. 14, *De Conjugio Sacerdotum*, Mentz, *op. cit.*, p. 66 *sqq.*
[2] The corresponding Article in the XXXIX Articles added other homilies and gave a complete list of them.
[3] For the brief conferring these faculties upon the legate, March 8, 1554, see Wilkins, *Concilia Magnae Britanniae et Hiberniae*, IV, 91; Burnet, *op. cit.*, ed. Pocock, VI, 322; Denny and Lacey, *op. cit.*, App. VII.
[4] Nothing is said any longer about the Prayer Book against whose rites Knox had formerly protested. Cf. P. Lorimer, *John Knox and the Church of England*, London, 1875, 121.
[5] See my *Reformation in England under Henry VIII*, English trans., pp. 397-404, 412-417.
[6] Letter to Bullinger, June 25, 1549, *Zurich Original Letters*, I, 65. In 1559 Archbishop Parker will still lament that "the realm is full of Anabaptists, Arians, Libertines, &c."

continue to sin, and that there is an ineluctable necessity. . .
to which God Himself is partly subject." And two years
and a half later, Martin Micronius[1] wrote to Bullinger
from London that the "old errors about the Incarnation
of Christ, the authority of magistrates, the lawfulness
of an oath and community of goods are reviving, and we
are obliged to combat them daily."

Hence a score of Articles which entirely or in part are
unmistakably directed against these errors and sometimes mention them by name.[2] It is where there is no
verbal identity that the Anglican Articles are most
Protestant, for example, the Articles on Justification, works
of supererogation, the Mass, ecclesiastical discipline,
marriage of the clergy, use of the vulgar tongue in the
services and administration of the sacraments. Sometimes
the XLII Articles stop short on the slope. Treating of
Justification they are silent about good works and refrain
from denying free will. At other times they go beyond
Lutheranism and are Calvinist (on the Eucharist and
Veneration of the Saints).[3] Nevertheless, they avoid
Calvinism on the delicate question of Predestination,
an example perhaps of the Englishman's practical
temper. Whereas the Confession of Augsburg and the
XIII Articles affirm the real Presence of Christ's Body
and Blood beneath the species of bread and wine,
Edward's Articles deny it. The confession of Augsburg
and the XIII Articles retain auricular confession "because
of the great benefit of absolution, that is to say the remission of sins by the power of the keys." The Anglican
Articles are silent about it. The Doctrine of these XLII
Articles of Edward VI is already that of Elizabeth's

[1] Letter of August 14, 1551. Ibid., 574.
[2] Articles 2, 3, 4, 8, 14, 15, 18, 24, 27, 28 (infant baptism), 32 (excommunication), 33 (the concluding part), 36, 37, 38, 39, 40, 41, 42.
[3] The influence of Bishop Hooper is evident. More than one passage in
the XLII Articles verbally reproduce articles he had drawn up for his
diocese of Worcester. Hooper, however, had been strongly influenced by
the Swiss reformers with whom he was in regular correspondence. Cf.
Messenger, op. cit., I, 534 sq.

XXXIX Articles, which remains the official doctrine of the Anglican Church.[1] The text of the earlier confession of faith was largely reproduced either verbally or for the sense by Elizabeth's. In some places the latter renders more explicit and exaggerates the heterodoxy of the XLII Articles by restoring passages from the original draft of 1552, which had been removed during the subsequent modifications. In others on the contrary it attempts to tone it down, for example as regards the Lord's Supper.

Anglican theologians have attempted with more or less ingenuity to reconcile the Articles with Catholic doctrine. "They are not Protestant," Mr. Moreton affirms.[2] It is not the doctrine of the Catholic church but the opinions of certain schoolmen which a particular article attacks. It was also under the pretext of correcting certain of these theological opinions that the Confession of Augsburg had attacked the Catholic faith. There can be no doubt that, as we have just seen, many passages teach Lutheran or Calvinist doctrine. It is no less certain that their meaning would shock any instructed Catholic, and that it has satisfied Low Church Anglicans for centuries. That is a simple matter of history. A Profession of Faith is not a polemical treatise. It formulates in the clearest

---

[1] Since 1865 a general but not a detailed and literal assent to the XXXIX Articles has been required of every beneficed clergyman.

[2] *Op. cit.*, Chapter XI, 259 *sq.*, cf. 200. Cf. Thomas Rogers, *The Catholic Doctrine of the Church of England. An Exposition of the 39 Articles*, ed. Perowne, Parker Soc., 1854. Thomas Rogers (died 1616) rector of Horningsheath (1581–1616) and a chaplain of Bishop Bancroft, whom he assisted in the composition of his writings, was the author of two works on the Anglican confession of faith. In the XVIIth Century a Franciscan, Christopher Davenport (died 1680), often called Francis a Sancta Clara, chaplain of Queen Henrietta Maria, distinguished himself as the solitary Catholic theologian who has attempted to give the XXXIX Articles an orthodox interpretation. His treatise published in 1646 and reprinted by G. Lee in 1865, is entitled *Paraphrastica Expositio Articulorum Confessionis Anglicanae*. More than once he remarks, "This seems difficult." Of the Article on the Mass he says: "*This entire Article seems extremely difficult.*" He concludes, "*I have laboured*, (Insudavi) (We can well believe it) "to reconcile the articles of the Anglican profession of faith with the definitions of the Catholic church."

and most natural language what those who accept it are bound to believe.[1]

The title page of the XLII Articles declares that they were "approved by the synod of London in 1552." This is untrue. Cranmer complained about the title page to Warwick and the Council. But no notice was taken of his complaint. The new creed was imposed upon the nation solely by the will of a King who was a minor and of the Government. But there was no time to enforce it. It was on June 12, 1553, that Edward signed the Articles. On the following July 6 he died.

[1] This has been plainly stated by the Anglican Bishop Knox (*Times Literary Supplement*, May 4, 1933) "Edward's Articles were a compromise between Lutheranism and Calvinism, but not between Protestantism and Catholicism."

CHAPTER X

EPILOGUE

Death of Edward VI—Warwick's coup d'état to secure the succession to the throne for his family and the Reformation in England (July 1553)—Failure of the plot and sudden check of the Reformation.

IT was on Edward that the Reformers' hopes were fixed. They compared him to the youthful Josiah, Calvin for instance who, when he dedicated to the King his *Explanation of Psalm 87*, held up the Jewish monarch as an example for Edward to imitate by uprooting superstition in his realm.[1] Edward "is full of zeal for the purity of religion and does everything to promote the Reformation", Micronius wrote.[2] Did not the young King say in a short treatise he wrote against the primacy of the Pope that "the Pope and Mahomet were the two eyes of the little horn of Daniel's Beast?"

"The King is firm in his convictions, instructed and pious beyond his years," Traheron had written to Bullinger.[3] "Every day he makes progress in knowledge and piety. If there has ever existed a second Josiah it is he. Have public prayer offered for him that our common Father may long preserve him to us. Believe me, my dear Bullinger, such holy dispositions are unique in our time. By his incredible piety, his saintly life, his prudence and firmness equal to those of a man of mature age, he seems to uphold the Gospel by himself."

[1] Calvin to Edward VI, January 1, 1551; *Zurich Original Letters*, XII. 704 *sqq.*, 714 *sqq.*
[2] Letter of March 9, 1552, *Zurich Orig. Letters*, XII, 580.
[3] Letters of September 10 and 28, 1548. Ibid., I, 321 326.

In his *History of the Reformation*[1] Gilbert Burnet improved, if possible, on contemporary eulogies. After praising the King's character, he continues: "He had above all things a great regard to religion. . . . This made him so set on bringing over his sister Mary to the same persuasions with himself, that, when he was pressed to give way to her having Mass, he said that he would not only hazard the loss of the Emperor's friendship, but of his life and all he had in the world rather than consent to what he knew was a sin: and he cited some passages of Scripture that obliged Kings to root out idolatry, by which, he said, he was bound in conscience not to consent to her Mass; since he believed it was idolatry. . . . Cranmer took Cheke by the hand and said he had reason all the days of his life, to rejoice that God had honoured him to breed such a scholar. All men . . . looked on him as one raised by God for most extraordinary ends. . . . Graver men compared him to Josiah; and long after his death, I find both in letters and printed books they commonly named him Our Josias; others called him *Edward the Saint*."

Burnet also praises Edward's intellectual endowments, his industry, his serious turn of mind, his capacity in argument, his knowledge of languages. At nine Edward wrote in Latin to his father, who would not have overlooked any grammatical fault, to Catherine Parr, his sister Mary, and Archbishop Cranmer. Though the letters published by H. Ellis[2] may perhaps be wholly of his composition, the letter written on September 9, 1547, to the Polish Ambassador contains so many quotations from sacred and profane writers that his tutor must have dictated it. The King was acquainted with Greek, Italian and Spanish. But he chiefly talked English,

---

[1] Ed. N. Pocock, II, 370–375.
[2] *Original Letters Illustrative of English History*, Series I, Vol. II, 130–137. Cf. Strype, *The Life of Sir John Cheke, First Instructor, afterwards Secretary of State to King Edward VI*, ed. Oxford, 1821.

French and Latin. The Italian scientist, Cardano, who was in Scotland from 1552 to 1553, where he had been summoned by the Archbishop of Saint Andrew's, relates a conversation he had with Edward, then aged 15, in which the King expressed himself with perfect ease in Latin. With the charming affability of his age, he combined the gravity of an adult, continues Cardano, who concludes his eulogy with four distichs of which we quote the two following:

Nam regum decus, et juvenum flos, spesque bonorum,
    Delitiae saecli, et gloria gentis erat.
Dignus Apollineis lachrymis, doctaeque Minervae
    Flosculus, heu misere concidis ante diem.[1]

Ornament of monarchs, flower of youths, hope of the
    good,
    Joy of the age was he and the glory of his race.
Worthy the tears of Apollo and learned Minerva
    Frail blossom, woe's me, thou dost untimely fall.[1]

But Edward had reached the age fatal to the Tudors' male heirs, the age at which his uncle Prince Arthur had died, and his brother the Duke of Richmond. Even before his accession his early death had been foretold. In the spring of 1552 an attack of measles followed by smallpox enfeebled a constitution already sickly and consumptive. The cough from which he constantly suffered grew worse during the winter. He was present at the dissolution of Parliament. But immediately after he retired to Greenwich in an alarming state of health. In March 1553 he was unable to go to Westminster to open Parliament. At the end of April the most serious rumours were current about his health. "The King,"

---

[1] G. Cardano, *De Genituris*, Book XII, Vol. V, 503 *sqq.* in the Lyons edition of his works, 1663.; Burnet. II, 34 *sqq.*, V, 125 *sqq.*; J. Foxe, *op. cit.*, V, 702.

wrote the French Ambassador on May 13, is "consumptive and in grave danger."[1]

As fears for Edward's life increased, the rumour spread of secret designs on the part of Warwick. During May and June the Tower of London was filled with prisoners accused of seditious language against the Duke, and two of them lost their ears. But the most carefully kept secrets of rulers cannot be entirely concealed. Warwick, since 1552 Duke of Northumberland, had in fact long entertained the design of securing the crown for himself and his family.

His first plan for getting possession of the crown was, it would seem, a project of marriage between his only unmarried son, Guildford Dudley, and Lady Margaret Clifford, grand-daughter of Henry VIII's sister Mary. But Lady Margaret was, he decided, too remote in the line of succession, and he passed her on to his brother Andrew. He married Guildford Dudley to Lady Jane Grey of the elder branch of the Suffolk line, to which in his will Henry had bequeathed the throne, if all his children should die without posterity. At the same time Lady Jane's sister was affianced to Lord Herbert, son of Northumberland's ally the Earl of Pembroke; and the Duke's daughter married Lord Hastings, who also had a claim to the throne in virtue of his descent from Edward IV's brother Clarence. By this network of marriages, Northumberland had united all interests in the succession, every title and right to the throne against the claims of Mary and Elizabeth, whom he sought to debar from the succession on the alleged ground of illegitimacy.

Lady Jane would be Queen, her husband—Northumberland's son—Prince Consort, and Northumberland

---

[1] Abbé de Vertot, *Ambassades de MM. de Noailles en Angleterre*, Leyden, 1763, II, 24, Frederick Chamberlain (*The Private Character of Henry VIII*, 1932, 234–262 with extracts from works of older writers or *Letters and Papers*) has compiled *The Medical Record of Edward VI* from birth till death, particularly at the age of fifteen and in his final illness.

himself would wield sovereign power behind the throne and exact the obedience of every subject. Such was his project or rather plot.

Never has the madness of ambition conceived a project more illogical, more illegal or more unconstitutional. Edward VI, the Duke argued, was as competent to bequeath the crown by will as was Henry VIII. But Henry had received from Parliament the power to do so, Edward had not. Moreover, the rights of Mary and Elizabeth to succeed did not rest solely upon Henry's will. For a statute passed in 1536 had enacted that, if Edward died childless, Mary and Elizabeth should succeed him, unless Henry determined otherwise. He had not done so. Thus the two sisters' rights of succession were assured both by statute and by Henry's will. Without a new Act of Parliament Edward could not set his father's will aside. And even if Henry's will and the Act of Parliament could have been set aside, and the illegitimacy of Mary and Elizabeth were admitted, the heir to the throne would not be Lady Jane Grey but Mary Queen of Scots. And if she also could be passed over, even then Lady Jane was not next in the line of succession, but her mother, Frances Duchess of Suffolk, so that the Prince Consort would be the Duke of Suffolk, not Northumberland's son. Therefore, she was induced to surrender her right in her daughter's favour.

Northumberland's career had brought him to this fatal impasse. The unbridled ambition which he had displayed since Somerset's death and the fashion in which he had abused his power had created so many enemies that he could be safe from their hostility only by holding the reins of government and thus making it impossible for them to bring him to justice. His own daughter-in-law said that he was hated, that even the common people spoke ill of him and said that "his life was hateful to all." To forestall his fall he had interfered with the last elections to the House of Commons and had

filled the House of Lords with his creatures. Even so
he had been unable to bend Parliament to his will. It
had passed very few of the bills submitted to it, and he
had been obliged to dissolve it a month after it met. A
letter written to Cecil on December 7, 1552,[1] in which
he alludes to his father's execution on August 15, 1510,
proves that he felt the ground crumbling beneath his
feet. "If I should have passed more upon the speech of
the people than upon the service of my master, or gone
about to seek favour of them without respect to His
Highness' surety, I needed not to have had so much
obloquy of some kind of men." And he appeals to "the
living God". The Duke had no hope of escaping his
foes, should they once get him into their hands. Hence
his desperate struggle for life and power.

He had to gain Edward's assent. Since Somerset's
fall and death Northumberland had established a complete ascendancy over the King's mind and made him his
puppet. He employed the argument best calculated to
touch the heart of a youth who had been made a fanatical
Protestant by those who surrounded him. He would later
bid the Council remember that God's cause and the
danger of the Papists coming into power had been the
principal motive of their concurrence with his alteration
of the succession. These were the motives which the Duke
suggested to the King. He depicted the horrors of a
Catholic reaction. The glorious work of Reformation,
which was dearer to Edward than to anyone in his kingdom,
would be undone. The altars of Baal would be re-
erected, and the idolatrous Mass restored. The elect
would be abandoned to the tender mercies of Antichrist's
agents. The dying monarch did not wish to leave his
country a prey to such terrible calamities and made no
opposition to Northumberland's plan.[2] The Council,

[1] Tytler, *op. cit.*, 148–150. See also that of the following January 3,
ibid., I, 154 *sqq.*

[2] Misled, wrote Bossuet (*Histoire des Variations des Églises Protestantes*,
Book VII) by the plausible arguments and authority of his teachers,

of whom the majority were his creatures, was in the Duke's hands and his docile instrument. The legal farce took its course.

On June 12, judges and lawyers assembled at Greenwich palace to give legal shape to what Northumberland called Edward's "plan". When it was broken to them, they said it was an act of treason. When he was informed of their view, the Duke rushed into the Council Chamber, his eyes blazing with wrath and threats on his lips. He called the Lord Chief Justice a traitor and threatened with death anyone who opposed the King's will. The lawyers left the palace trembling for their lives. Two days later the King recalled them. With severe words and angry look he took them to task for their disobedience, and when he dismissed them, the Lords of the Council whispered, as they passed by, "traitors".

The terrorised judges and lawyers assuaged their fears with the King's promise that their act should be ratified by Parliament. Edward, they thought, could not punish them for an offence committed by his order. If Parliament assembled before the King's death, it would legalise what they were about to do, whereas if they refused, it would condemn them to a traitor's death. Accordingly on June 21, 1553, the deed was drawn up and signed by the judges and lawyers, the overwhelming majority of the Council and a hundred and one of the leading persons in the realm.

In virtue of his precedence of rank Cranmer's signature is the first on the list. But the Archbishop was in fact the last member of the Council to sign. The deed was presented to him already covered with the signatures of lawyers and Councillors. He refused to add his own. It would, he said, be an act of perjury, since

---

"the young king saw idolatry everywhere, and his hatred of idolatry easily became hatred of the Church". See in Foxe, *op. cit.*, VI, 352, Edward's dying prayer, "My Lord and God save this realm from popery and maintain in it true religion."

he had already sworn to uphold Mary's right of succession. The other Councillors, they told him, also possessed consciences. He ought not to adopt a singular attitude. Cranmer asked to speak with the King alone. This was refused. For Northumberland feared he might ruin his scheme. It was only in the presence of Northampton and Darcy that he was permitted to see the King. The Duke had already put Edward on his guard against the Archbishop's arguments, which therefore made no impression on his obstinate temper. Edward told Cranmer that the lawyers and the Council were of opinion that his father's will did not bind him, and that, since he was in possession of the Crown, he could dispose of it. The Archbishop declared that he had no competence in legal questions. But he stood firm until the King appealed to his loyalty and asked him not to oppose his will and the wills of the rest of the other Councillors.[1]

The deed was kept secret. The Council occupied the Tower, filled the city with troops and manned the fleet. On July 2, Hodgkin, suffragan Bishop of Bedford, preaching at Paul's Cross omitted to pray for Mary and Elizabeth. The following Sunday Bishop Ridley declared them bastards to the great displeasure of his auditory. Four days later Edward died—"in the 16th year of his age and on the 7th day of the month, the very day on which some years before, his father Henry VIII had caused Thomas More to be beheaded." His death was concealed in order to take possession of Mary's person.[2] She

[1] The Chief Justice, Sir Ed. Montague, when accused under Queen Mary of having drawn up Edward's will, defended himself by relating at length the scene I have described in the text. Fuller, *op. cit.*, IV, 137-147.
    Edward's will and the deed signed by the Council have been reprinted many times. They are in Strype, *Mem. of Cranmer*, ed. 1848, II, 675-677, and again in Vol. III. (Appendix 446-449), a replica of the original documents in the library of the Inner Temple in Burnet, *op. cit.*, VI, 305 and 307, cf. II, 37; and in the *Literary Remains of Edward VI* (1857, I, 561-576), ed. Nichols.
[2] A rumour therefore got abroad that the Duke had poisoned him. *Span. Cal.*, 1553, 70 *sqq.*; *The Diary of Henry Machyn*, (1550-1563), ed. Nichols, Camden Soc., 1847, 35; *Grey Friars' Chronicle;* letters of J. Terentianus of November 20, 1553, and J. Burcher of March 3, 1554,

had in fact been pressed to come to London to be present at her brother's death-bed. She had already reached Hoddesdon in Hertfordshire when on July 7 she received secret news of Edward's death. She immediately mounted her horse and fled to Kenninghall in Norfolk. Northumberland's trick had failed. Lady Jane Grey was proclaimed Queen in London on July 12. But her reign lasted only nine days. Mary, followed by her loyal subjects, entered London and imprisoned the rebel Duke.

The plot was foiled, and the Reformation suddenly checked.

---

in *Zurich Original Letters*, I, 365, 684. For this episode see *The Chronicle of Queen Jane and of Two Years of Queen Mary* (July 1553–October 1554), ed. J. G. Nichols, Camden Soc., 1850; M. A. Florio, *Historia de la Vita e de la Morte de L'Illma Signora Giovanna Graia*, S.L., 1607, which contains an Italian translation of most of the letters and treatises, published, in 1825, by N. H. Nichols; *The Literary Remains of Lady Jane Grey, with a Memoir*; R. Garnett, *The Accession of Queen Mary; being the Contemporary Narrative of Antonio de Guaras, a Spanish Merchant Resident in London*, 1892; R. P. Davey, *The Nine Days' Queen, Lady Jane Grey and Her Times*, 1909.

APPENDIX I

BIBLIOGRAPHY

A. *General*

COMPARED with the reigns of Henry VIII and Elizabeth, for which literature is abundant, though its value certainly is very unequal, the reign of Edward VI has, it would seem, been neglected. Nevertheless, for the history of the English Reformation it is of the first importance. For it was under Edward and thanks to him that the Reformation conquered England.

French books dealing with the period of Edward VI are inadequate, when not actually unreliable. For example H. Prentout (*Histoire de l'Angleterre*, 2nd edition Paris, 1926. I, 296–301), devotes only six pages to the reign. MM. Menaudet (Vol. VIII of *Peuples et Civilisations*, d'Halphen et Sagnac, pp. 493–7) and Maurois (*Histoire d'Angleterre*, Paris, 1937, pp. 324–330) give it no more space. M. Tresal's book, *Les Origines du Schisme Anglican*[1] devotes more space to Edward's reign (225–287). But the few lines in which he speaks of the Holy Communion and the *Prayer Books* of 1549 and 1552 (pp. 243 sqq, 281 sqq.) give no notion of the revolution effected in the liturgy and doctrine of the Eucharist. His paragraph on the Ordinal (p. 262) does not inform us of its nature nor of the grounds on which Rome declared it invalid.

In my first volume[2] I spoke of Sanders's *De Origine et Progressu Schismatis Anglicani*,[3] of the old histories of the

[1] The title is correct only for the reign of Henry VIII. For after his death the Church of England was no longer schismatic simply, but Protestant.

[2] *The Reformation in England*, Henry VIII. Eng. Trs., 1934, 439, 462–465.

[3] Published at Cologne in 1585 it was translated into French two years later. Though Sanders's honesty is beyond doubt, he is at times too credulous, particularly on the subject of Anne Boleyn, the mother of the Queen to whom the English Catholics ascribed all their sufferings.

English Reformation by Fuller, Burnet, Collier and Dodd[1] which contain many valuable pieces of evidence, of Lingard's *History*[2] and the more recent histories by Dixon and James Gairdner, of John Foxe's *Acts and Monuments* and the works of Strype.[3]

Sir John Hayward (died 1627), whose talent as an historian and writer was praised by Lord Bacon, and whom James I chose together with Camden to be the historiographer of his college at Chelsea, gave us the oldest biography of Edward, *The Life and Raigne of King Edward the Sixth*, published after his death in 1630. It was republished by the Bishop of Peterborough, White Kennett, in the second volume of his *Complete History of England* (1706). Though severely judged by Strype, the biography is based upon the King's Journal communicated to the author by Sir Robert Cotton and on several official documents, as has been proved by their subsequent publication. The introduction to G. Nichols' two volumes of which I shall speak shortly, contains a complete monograph on Edward. Sir Clement R. Markham has made copious use of it for his *King Edward VI : His Life and Character*, a defence of the young King in 21 chapters, in which he particularly insists upon his upbringing, character and political capacity, in opposition, he informs us, to those who treat Edward's reign as simply the reigns of Somerset and Northumberland. The little he has to say of the Prayer Books (pp. 72, 126, 128) tells us nothing of the transformation of the Anglican Church at this time.[4]

The best general account of the reign, particularly from the political standpoint, we owe to a former Professor of London University, A. F. Pollard, an expert in

---

[1] Edward's reign is in Book III of the second part; Vol. I, 395-443 of the 1737 edition.

[2] The last English edition in eleven volumes is by Hilaire Belloc.

[3] To these sources we may add two biographies by Strype. *The Life of the learned Sir Thomas Smith, Principal Secretary of State to King Edward the Sixth and Queen Elizabeth*, 1698, and Oxford, 1820; *The Life of the learned Sir John Cheke, First Instructor, afterwards Secretary of State to King Edward VI*, 1705 and Oxford, 1821.

[4] A Review in the *English Historical Review* (Vol. XXIII, 1908, 199) deals very severely with the book, as weak and unfair. Nevertheless, the genealogies, and lists of privy councillors, earls, dukes and other peers appointed and created by Edward VI are useful.

English sixteenth century history. He has written both on its first part (*England Under Protector Somerset*, London 1900) and on the reign as a whole (*The History of England from the Accession of Edward VI to the Death of Elizabeth*, London, 1913. The latter is Volume VI of the *Political History of England*). Hilaire Belloc in Volume IV (1931) of his *History of England* freely acknowledges his debt to the erudition of Professor Pollard, whom he acknowledges to be by far the most valuable authority for the details of this period, though he does not endorse his judgments of men and their motives, since he does not share his religious beliefs (p. 8). Belloc gives a concise and most interesting account of Edward's reign (pp. 176–208) and briefly describes the religious transformation which the government sought to impose upon an unwilling nation, without however having the time to establish it securely. Volume III (1911) of *Lollardy and the Reformation in England* by James Gairdner, the learned editor of *Letters and Papers* (died 1912) imparts in two books and seven chapters a large number of facts and considerable information in a somewhat prolix and unmethodical fashion. The sources and important authorities are indicated, sometimes with a critical estimate, by Conyers Read: *Bibliography of British History*:*Tudor Period*. 1485–1603,[1] and A. F. Pollard in Vol. II of the *Cambridge Modern History* (pp. 795–802) and Vol. VI of the *Political History of England*, in which his headings and subheadings render the bibliography clearer and easier to use. Anything that has appeared since, if of any importance is mentioned in the course of my study of Edward's reign.

Sources long known are: Rymer's *Foedera*; Wilkins's *Concilia Magnae Britanniae et Hiberniae ; The Statutes of the Realm ; The Tudor and Stuart Proclamations*[2]*; The Acts of the Privy Council ; The Journals of the House of Lords* (I, 1509–1572); the chronicles of *Wriothesley, Stow, Holinshed*,

---

[1] pp. 36–37, 141–142 and, for foreign affairs, Nos. 577–585, 598, 620, 685, 689–691, 698, 715.

[2] This collection, which extends from 1485 to 1714, edited by Robert Steele (Oxford, 1910, 2 vols) comprises a useful introduction and a summary of the proclamations or ordinances in chronological order. Volume I is concerned with England and Wales, the second with Scotland and Ireland.

and the *Grey Friars of London ; Original Letters Illustrative of
English History*, edited by Ellis; the publications of the great
English historical societies, such as the Camden Society,
the Parker Society and the Royal Historical Society.[1] To
these must be added Volume I of the *Calendar of State
Papers, Domestic* by Robert Lemon (London, 1856) which
is scarcely more than a catalogue, records of proceedings
in the Court of Chancery during Edward's reign when
the Lord Chancellors were R. Rich (1547–1551) and
Thomas Goodrich, Bishop of Ely: *List of Early Chancery
Proceedings preserved in the Public Records Office*, IX (1544–
1553) by J. B. W. Chapman (London, 1933); Richard
Grafton's chronicle, whose last edition (1572) is brought
down to that date;[2] the diary of H. Machyn, an under-
taker, who carefully records the changes in the church
services;[3] Volume I of the *Somers Tracts*[4] the *Tudor
Tracts* re-edited by A. F. Pollard in 1903; a collection
of documents published in full by P. F. Tytler who has
connected them by a series of introductions and biographical and critical notes;[5] the documents employed
by John Foxe and Strype, but not fully utilised by them,
and published by J. G. Nichols together with two contemporary lives of Cranmer under the title *Narrative of
the Days of the Reformation* (Camden Society, 1859); the
State Papers left by William Cecil, Lord Burghley
published in the eighteenth century by Samuel Haynes
and William Murdin;[6] Vol. I of Edmund Lodge's

[1] For all this see my earlier volume, *The Reformation . . . under Henry
VIII*. Eng. Trs., 465 *sqq.*
[2] *An Abridgement of the Chronicles of England*, London, 1562, 1563, 1564,
1570, 1572.
[3] *The Diary of Henry Machyn, Citizen and Merchant Taylor of London*,
1550–1563. Ed. J. G. Nichols, Camden Society, 1848.
[4] *A Collection of Scarce and Valuable Tracts, Selected from an infinite number
in print and manuscript, in the Royal, Cotton, Sion and other. . . . Libraries,
particularly that of the late Lord Somers*, ed. Walter Scott, 1809–1815,
13 vols.
[5] *England under the Reigns of Edward VI and Mary, illustrated in a series of
Original Letters never before printed, with Historical Introductions and Biographical
and critical notes*, 1839, 2 vols.
[6] *Collection of State Papers relating to affairs in the reigns of Henry VIII,
Edward VI, Mary and Elizabeth*, 1542–1570, *Transcribed from Original Letters
and other authentick Memorials. . . . Left by William Cecil, Lord Burghley*,
1749–1759, 2 vols.

Illustrations of British History;[1] Vol. III of Sir John Harrington's *Nugae Antiquae*;[2] the *Hamilton Papers* purchased in 1889 by the British Museum from the German Government, which had acquired them six years earlier, and edited by Joseph Bain;[3] the diary of Edward VI written in his own hand at the suggestion of his tutor Sir John Cheke, who compared events unrecorded in writing to a flood of words heard but not understood.[4]

The reports and despatches of foreign ambassadors not only inform us of England's relations with foreign powers but also throw light on many domestic events.

In addition to Albèri,[5] Turba,[6] Ribier,[7] Sleidan,[8] and the *Nuntiaturberichte*,[9] valuable sources of information for this reign as for its predecessor, we possess the *Ambassades de MM. de Noailles* (Antoine, Francois, Gilles), 1553–7 and 1559, compiled by the late M. l'abbé Vertot;[10] the *Correspondance Politique d'Odet de Selve* (1546–9) published by Germain Lefèvre-Pontalis (Paris, 1888), which continues the correspondence of Charles de Marillac;

[1] *Biography and Manners in the reigns of Henry VIII, Edward VI, Mary, Elizabeth and James I, exhibited in . . . Original Papers . . . from the manuscripts . . . of Howard, Talbot and Cecil* (1791). Ed. 1838, 3 vols.

[2] *Miscellaneous Collection of Original Papers in prose and verse written in the reigns of Henry VIII, Edward VI, Queen Mary, Elizabeth, King James, etc.* 2nd ed. 1792.

[3] *The Hamilton Papers, Letters and Papers Illustrating the Political Relations of England and Scotland in the Sixteenth Century*, Edinburgh, 1890–1892. Bain also edited the first two vols of the *Calendar of State Papers relating to Scotland and Mary Queen of Scots*, 1547–1603, a compilation begun in 1898, and still in course of publication. Nine vols have appeared.

[4] See Strype's *Life of Sir John Cheke*, and *Literary Remains of King Edward VI*, Roxburghe Club, 1857, 2 vols.

[5] *Relazioni Degli Ambasciatori Veneti al Senato Durante il secolo Decimo Sesto*, Series I, vols II and III, Florence, 1841 and 1853.

[6] *Venetianische Depeschen vom Kaiserhofe*, vol. II, Vienna, 1892.

[7] *Lettres et Mémoires d'Estat des Roys, Princes et Ambassadeurs, sous les Regnes de Francois I et Henri II et Francois II*, 1537–1559, Paris, 1666. 2 vols. Information about Edward's reign is to be found in the latter part of vol. I from p. 614 onwards and in Vol. II.

[8] J. Sleidanus, *Commentariorum de statu religionis, reipublicae, Carolo Quinto Caesare*, Strasbourg, 1555, 1576. Ed. T. G. Boehme, Frankfort, 1785–1786, 3 vols.

[9] *Nuntiaturberichte aus Deutschland*, Erste Abteilung, 1533–1559, Vols. IX, X, XI, XII, Gotha, 1899, Berlin, 1901 and 1907.

[10] Ed. Leyden, 1763 by C. Villaret, 5 vols. The second deals with the reign of Edward VI.

the volume of the *Calendar of State Papers, Foreign*, edited by W. B. Turnbull (1547-1553), (London, 1861); the volume of the *Calendar of State Papers, Venetian* 1534-1554, edited by Rawdon Brown (London 1873); Volume IV (Paris 1843) of the *Papiers D'État du Cardinal de Granvelle*, edited by C. H. Weiss in the " Collection des documents inédits sur l'Histoire de France." Some letters belonging to this last collection are also to be found in the *Calendar of State Papers, Spanish* taken not from Granvella's papers which Weiss studied at Besançon but from those preserved at Simancas. It is at Simancas, Vienna and Paris that the letters are preserved, published by Royall Tyler in Volumes IX, X, XI (1547-1553), (London, 1912-1916). They are primarily the despatches of Francis Van der Delft of Antwerp, Imperial Ambassador in London from 1544 to 1550, an exceedingly conscientious man, but a semi-invalid, and out of sympathy with the English, whose language he was unable to speak, and in touch only with Paget whose information he does little more than repeat. Disgusted at having been duped by Warwick in the latter's struggle with Somerset and seriously ill, he insisted on his recall and returned to Flanders in May 1551, where he died the following month. He was succeeded by Jehan Scheyfve whose instructions are dated May 13, 1550. Besides these letters from London the collection contains letters written by Cardinal Granvella's uncle, Jean de Saint-Maures, Ambassador in Paris until April 1549, and his successor Simon Renard, better informed and of a more active mind, indeed the most brilliant of the Imperial diplomats. At the end of Edward's reign Charles V sent him on a special mission to London together with Jean de Montmorency, Sieur de Courrieres, and Jacques de Marnix, Sieur de Thoulouse. Though these despatches have been faithfully translated or reliable summaries made of them, they have lost the flavour of sixteenth century French. I, therefore, obtained copies of some of them from the *Staatsarchiv* at Vienna.

In my volume on Henry VIII, I mentioned the principal studies of the Reformation from the pen of English writers.[1] N. Pocock's article in Volume I (p. 677) of the *English Historical Review* entitled *The Reformation Settlement of the English Church* should be consulted and even more his *Condition of Morals and Religious Beliefs in the reign of Edward VI* (ibid. vol. x. 1895, p. 417). A year before his death Peter Heylyn (died 1662) chaplain of Charles I (1630) and an Anglican of the High Church school published his *Ecclesia Restaurata* dedicated to Charles II, the first part of which deals with the Reformation under Edward VI.[2] Edward Cardwell's *Documentary Annals of the Reformed Church of England* (Oxford, 2nd Ed., 1844) has superseded a similar collection by Anthony Sparrow, a Bishop of Norwich in the seventeenth century.[3] Frere and Kennedy's three volumes, *Visitation Articles and Injunctions of the Period of the Reformation*, (Alcuin Club collection, 1910) extend from 1536 to 1575. The edition of Calvin's works published by Baum, Cunitz and Reuss contains several letters addressed to Edward VI, Somerset and Warwick.[4] And the correspondence between the Swiss and the English Reformers, contained in the *Zurich Original Letters* is particularly important for this reign.[5] The works of Bishops Cranmer,

[1] My *Reformation . . . under Henry VIII*, Eng. trans., 466 *sqq. The Reformation in England* by L. Elliot Binns (1937) gives a good general account of the social and political factors which favoured the religious revolution of the sixteenth century, and attempts to strike a fair balance between the good and evil results of their operation. But it is hardly more than a popular account and deals only incidentally with doctrinal questions.

[2] *Ecclesia Restaurata or the History of the Reformation of the Church of England, containing the Beginning, Progress and Successes of it*, London, 1661, 1670, 1674, ed. J. C. Robertson, Cambridge, 1849. (For the Ecclesiastical History Society) 2 vols. Edward's reign is in the first of these.

[3] *A Collection of Articles, Injunctions, Canons, Orders, Ordinances, and Constitutions Ecclesiastical, with other Public Records of the Church of England*, 1661, 1675, 1684. Cardwell's, *Documentary Annals*, extend from 1546 to 1716. They are in two volumes, Edward's reign being in the first. Gee and Hardy's, *Documents Illustrative of English Church History*, (ed. 4, 1921) contains (322–373) the Act ordering communion under both kinds, the Acts dissolving the chantries and legalising the marriage of priests, also the first and second Acts of Uniformity.

[4] Calvin was in regular correspondence with Somerset. On August 22, 1548, he wrote to urge him to repress both the Catholics and the Lutherans; "They richly deserve to be repressed by the sword committed to you, for they oppose not only the King, but God." (*Lettres Françaises de J. Calvin*, ed. Bonnet, I, 267).

[5] *Original Letters relative to the English Reformation written during the reign of King Henry VIII, King Edward VI, and Queen Mary, chiefly from the Archives*

Latimer, Ridley, Hooper, John Bale, Myles Coverdale and Thomas Lever, must be mentioned here,[1] also those of their opponents the Henricians, to whom I devoted my seventh chapter.

B. *Protector Somerset* (Chapters II, IV).

The list of sources given above should suffice, the more so that at the end of A. F. Pollard's *England under Protector Somerset*, there is an excellent critical study of the sources for this part of Edward's reign. In his book *The Chief Ministers of England* (920–1720) London, 1923, Clive Bigham has devoted a special study to Protector Somerset (pp. 243–257) as A. D. Innes has also done in his *Ten Tudor Statesmen* (Revised edition, 1934). R. Davey has also concerned himself with Somerset in Chapters VI and XII of *The Nine Days' Queen*, (London, 1909). J. G. Nicholls has written an article on his title of Protector which is amply documented.[2]

For the social disturbances with which Somerset was confronted see *Social Tracts*, edited by A. Lang,[3] and Volume III of *Readings in English Social History from*

---

of Zurich. Parker Society, 1846–1847, 2 vols. The letters were published in the original at Cambridge in 1848 under the title *Epistolae Tigurinae*. (I have translated the extracts in this volume from the French. Translator's note.)

[1] *The remains of Thomas Cranmer, Archbishop of Canterbury*, ed. Henry Jenkyns, Oxford, 1833, 4 vols. A later edition by J. E. Cox for the Parker Society is no improvement, and I have employed the first.

Sermons and Remains of Hugh Latimer, sometime Bishop of Worcester, Martyr, 1555, ed. G. Elwes Corrie (Parker Society, 1844–1845) 2 vols. There is a later edition (1858) by John Watkins: *The Sermons and Life of the Right Reverend Father in God and constant Martyr of Jesus Christ, Hugh Latimer, some time Bishop of Worcester*, 2 vols.

Nicholas Ridley, *Works*, ed. Henry Christmas, Parker Soc., 1841. John Hooper, *Early Writings*, ed. Samuel Carr, Parker Soc., 1852, 2 vols. *Later Writings*, ed. Charles Nevinson, Parker Soc., 1852, 2 vols. John Bale, *Select Works*, ed. Henry Christmas, Parker Soc., 1849. Myles Coverdale, *Writings and Translations, Remains*, ed. George Pearson, Parker Soc., 1844–1846.

Thomas Lever, an advanced reformer who preached before the king in 1550, *Sermons*, ed. Arber, 1871.

[2] *The Second Patent appointing Edward Duke of Somerset Protector Temp. King Edward VI; Introduced by an Historical Review of the various measures connected therewith*, in *Archaeologia*, Vol. XXX, 1884.

[3] Arber's *English Garner*, 1904.

Contemporary Literature (Cambridge, 1921).They furnish contemporary documents. Of these the most important are the *Four Supplications of the Commons* by R. Crowley, (died 1588)[1] and the *Complaynt of Roderych Mors* by Henry Brinkelow,[2] also the Sermons of Latimer and Thomas Lever mentioned above. Crowley also printed, for its application to the contemporary situation, the fourteenth century poem of Langland, *The Vision of Piers Plowman*. For information on the social upheavals, and in particular about the enclosures, a problem so often canvassed since the close of the Middle Ages, and whose aspect was completely changed as a result of the political changes of the sixteenth and eighteenth centuries, the following works may be consulted, bearing on the epoch with which this book is concerned: J. S. Leadam, *The Domesday of Inclosures*, 1517–1518; (Royal Historical Society, 1897, 2 vols.); R. H. Tawney and Eileen Power, *Tudor Economic Documents* (University of London, Historical Series, 1924, 3 vols.); J. E. Thorold Rogers, *A History of Agriculture and Prices in England* (Oxford, 1866–1900, 7 vols.); W. J. Ashley, *An Introduction to English Economic History and Theory* (London, 1888–1892, 2 vols.), several chapters of the second volume relate to the Tudor period; the third edition (1903–1905) of William Cunningham's *The Growth of English Industry and Commerce*, (2 vols. in 3 parts); L. Brentano, *Eine Geschichte der Wirtschaftlichen Entwicklung Englands* (Jena, 1927–8, 3 vols., the second of which deals with the sixteenth century); Vol. II (1931) of Ephraim Lupson's *The Economic History of England*, which furnishes most interesting details about the enclosures; R. Liddesdale Palmer, *English Social History in the Making: the Tudor Revolution*, (1934).[3]

---

[1] See J. M. Cowper's edition. Robert Crowley's *Select Works* for the Early English Text Society, 1872.

[2] Its full title is: "Complaynt of Roderyck Mors somtyme a gray fryre, unto the Parliament house of England his natural cuntry, for the redresse of certen wycked lawes, evel custems and cruel decreys." London, 1548, ed. Early English Text Society, 1874. This edition includes another work of Brinkelow's: *The Lamentacion of a Christen agaynst the Cytye of London*, (1542) which deals with enclosures and other economic problems.

[3] M. F. Moore (*Two Select Bibliographies of Medieval Historical Study*, 1912) has compiled a bibliography of everything printed up to 1910

On the social and religious grievances which by provoking the insurrections of 1549 caused Somerset's fall, documents and some history are to be found in A. Neville, *De furoribus Norfolcensium, Ketto duce* (London, 1575), N. Pocock, *Troubles Connected with the Prayer Book of 1549* (Camden Society, 1884),[1] F. W. Russell, *Kett's Rebellion in Norfolk* (London, 1859), Frances Rose-Troup, *The Western Rebellion of 1549; An Account of the Insurrections in Devonshire and Cornwall against Religious Innovations in the Reign of Edward VI* (London, 1913). The authoress had already studied the rising under Henry VIII, the Pilgrimage of Grace.[2] William Cotton and Henry Woolcombe in their *Gleanings from the Municipal and Cathedral Records relating to the City of Exeter* (Exeter, 1877) furnish many details about the revolt of 1549.

C. *Warwick, Duke of Northumberland* (Chapters V, X).

Though his character, methods of government and tragic end are calculated to attract the historian, there is no good life of John Dudley, Earl of Warwick and Duke of Northumberland. But as he was so closely concerned in Somerset's government and dominated the later part of the reign, to study these periods is to study him. Therefore the documentary sources and the books mentioned above enable us to know him and his method of government. Chapters XII—XVIII of Richard Davey's *Nine Days' Queen; Lady Jane Grey* already mentioned, are largely devoted to him and everything written about Lady Jane necessarily treats of him. Such books are: *The Literary Remains of Lady Jane Grey with a Memoir*, N. H. Nicolas (London, 1825). Most of the documents had already been published in Italian by Michelangelo Florio in 1607: *Historia de la Vita e de la Morte de l'Illma. Signora Giovanna Graia. The Chronicle of Queen Jane and of Two Years of Queen Mary* (July 1553—October 1554),

---

on the history of English agriculture up to 1660. And Conyers Read in his *Bibliography* (1485-1603), gives the principal works and sources on the subject.

[1] Mistakes have been pointed out by Fr. Rose-Troup in an Appendix to the work just mentioned.

[2] See Chapter IV of my *Reformation . . . under Henry VIII*.

Ed. Nichols (Camden Society, 1850). *The Accession of Queen Mary; Being the contemporary narrative of Antonio de Guaras, a Spanish merchant resident in London*, Ed. R. Garnett (London, 1892); *The Life, Death and Actions of Lady Jane Grey . . .* (London 1616, 1829).

D. *Prayer Books of* 1549 *and* 1552 (Chapters III and VI)

I. *Editions.*

The *Order of Communion* of 1548 has been reproduced in facsimile by H. A. Wilson in 1908 among the publications of the Henry Bradshaw Society.

The first Prayer Book of 1549 was published by R. Grafton at the beginning of that year: *The Booke of the Common Prayer and Administration of the Sacramentes, and Other Rites and Ceremonies of the Churche, after the use of the Churche of England* (folio), re-edited in 1844 by the Parker Society. In 1896 three hundred facsimiles were printed: *The Book of the Common Prayer as issued in 1549, in the Reign of Edward VI, being the Original Edition of the Prayer Book, Privately Reproduced in Facsimile* (velum quarto). Vernon Staley, an excellent liturgiologist, reprinted it (*The First Prayer Book of Edward VI*) in 1903 in the "Library of Liturgiology and Ecclesiology for English readers." The Rev. H. B. Walton and P. G. Medd combined in a single volume the *Order of Communion of 1548*, the *Prayer Book of 1549* and the *Ordinal of 1549*: *The First Prayer Book of Edward VI and the Ordinal of 1549, with the Order of Communion 1548* (London, 1883). In 1821 the first Prayer Book was published in eight languages: English, French, Italian, German, Spanish, Ancient and Modern Greek and Latin.[1]

The Second Prayer Book was printed by Ed. Whytchurch in 1552: *The Booke of Common Prayer and Administracion of the Sacramentes and other Rites and Ceremonies in*

---

[1] Attention has often been called to the influence exercised upon the Order of Communion and the First Prayer Book by the *Pia Consultatio* of Hermann von Wied, Archbishop of Cologne. An English translation of the *Consultatio* was, in fact, published at the beginning of Edward's reign: *A Simple Religious consultation, by what means a Christian Reformation of Doctrine, of the Sacraments, of Ceremonies and the whole cure of soules may be begun among us*, London, 1547.

the Churche of England. It was reprinted, like the first, in 1844 by the Parker Society and again in 1883.

The edition of both Prayer Books in two small volumes by Griffith Farran Browne in accordance with the copies of their original editions in the British Museum is convenient to use. I have therefore employed it.[1]

In 1932 D. Cajus Fabricius began to reprint the Prayer Book in his *Corpus Confessionum* (Berlin and Leipzig, W. de Gruyter). It has been recently completed. It is annotated.

Edward Cardwell in 1838 and Joseph Ketley in 1844 published both Prayer Books of Edward, comparing them in the former case, in the latter adding other material.[2] And in 1915 F. E. Brightman published an edition in parallel columns of these Prayer Books, and the Prayer Book of Charles II (1661), which was a revision of the latter, and their sources.[3]

II. *Studies.*

In the century and a half which divides Charles Weathly's book (died 1742)[4] from Fr. Procter's (died 1905),[5] liturgical studies in England made less progress than in the eighty-seven years which passed between Procter's work and the work of nineteen collaborators published in 1932 by Lowther Clarke and C. H. Harris with the title *Liturgy and Worship. A Companion to the*

[1] Both prayer books have also been published together in Everyman's Library with an introduction by the Bishop of Gloucester.

[2] Ed. Cardwell, *The Two Books of Common Prayer set forth by authority of Parliament in the Reign of Edward the Sixth, compared with each other*, Oxford, 1838 and 1841. J. Ketley, *The Two Liturgies, A.D.* 1549 *and A.D.* 1552, *with other documents set forth by authority in the reign of Edward VI, viz. the Order of Communion* 1548 *; the Primer* 1553 *: the Catechism and Articles* 1553 *; Catechismus Brevis* 1553, Parker Society, 1844.

[3] *The English Rite : Being a Synopsis of the Sources and Revisions of the Book of Common Prayer*, London, 1915, 2 vols. There is an introduction of 230 pages and an Appendix. The Ordinals of Edward VI and Charles II have been printed in parallel columns together with their sources, namely the Sarum Pontifical and Bucer's *De Ordinatione Legitima Ministrorum Ecclesiae Revocanda.* The Comparison in parallel columns between the Mass of 1549 and the Sarum Missal in E. E. Estcourt's *The Question of Anglican Orders Discussed* (1873, 292–320) is clear and useful.

[4] *A Rational Illustration of the Book of Common Prayer*, 1710, reprinted Cambridge, 1858.

[5] *History of the Book of Common Prayer with a Rationale of its Offices*, London 1855, revised and corrected several times later.

Prayer Books of the Anglican Communion. There is no country in which, since the middle of last century, such studies have flourished more. Publication has not been at the author's expense. Societies scientifically directed and richly endowed have published and continue to publish, not only works bearing upon the Prayer Book, but many pre-reformation liturgical texts. Such are the Henry Bradshaw Society, the Alcuin Club, and the Surtees Society.

From the historical standpoint Procter's work on the Prayer Book, which has been thoroughly revised by the Bishop of Truro, W. H. Frere, himself well-known as the author of numerous liturgical studies, is considered the "Standard Book."[1] No less important is the work of F. A. Gasquet and Edward Bishop: *Edward VI and the Book of Common Prayer. An Examination into its Origin and Early History with an Appendix of Unpublished Documents* (London, 1890).[2] Both should be supplemented by the book mentioned above, *Liturgy and Worship*, the work of extremely competent liturgical scholars, such as Wickham Legg and F. E. Brightman.[3] Not to speak of writers anterior to the nineteenth century,[4] many have written about Edward's Prayer Books, their work being of very unequal value. Among them are W. Palmer,[5] J. M. Neale,[6] J. H. Blunt,[7] E. Daniel,[8] J. Parker,[9] Morgan

[1] *A New History of the Book of Common Prayer, with a Rationale of its Offices, on the Basis of the former Work by Francis Procter, Revised and Rewritten by W. H. Frere,* 1901, 1914.

[2] A second edition was published in 1926. But the book was not revised. On the contrary the portions dealing with the breviary and the appendices were cut out, though the latter are often of greater value to the historian than the text.

[3] Cf. *Church Quarterly Review,* Vol. 44 (1897), pp. 123-147.

[4] Ant. Sparrow, for example, Bishop of Norwich: *A Rationale upon the Book of Common Prayer of the Church of England,* 1657, reprinted by Newman in 1839.

[5] *Origines Liturgicae or Antiquities of the English Ritual,* ed. 1843, 2 vols.

[6] *Essays on Liturgiology and Church History with an Appendix on Liturgical Quotations from the Apostolic Fathers by G. Moultrie,* 1863.

[7] *Annotated Book of Common Prayer, being an Historical, Ritual and Theological Commentary on the Devotional System of the Church of England,* 1866. Fourth ed. revised and enlarged, 1884.

[8] *The Prayer Book, its History, Language and Contents,* 1877. Revised editions, 1885, 1888, 1913.

[9] *An Introduction to the History of the Successive Revisions of the Book of Common Prayer,* 1877.

Dix,[1] W. M. Myres,[2] J. T. Tomlinson,[3] J. W. Legg,[4] J. Dowden,[5] Leighton Pullan,[6] J. E. Field,[7] and Dyson Hague.[8] I myself published in the *Revue d'Histoire Ecclesiastique*[9] a study on the *Transformation du Culte Anglican sous Edouard VI*.[10] There is even a *Prayer Book Dictionary* (London, 1912), compiled by G. Harford, Morley Stevenson and J. W. Tyred.

The numerous county histories and histories of towns furnish interesting items of information about the liturgical revolution and the amazement, discontent or indifference displayed by clergy and laity towards the Reformation and the Prayer Books. From this point of view the history of the Church of All Hallows, Barking, in Vol. XII of the London County Council Survey of London is of special interest (London, 1929. Part I).

If the language of the Prayer Book, now largely archaic, which delights the English ear is chiefly due to Cranmer,[11] its charm was enhanced by John Merbecke's (died 1585) adaptation of plain chant to the new liturgy and his melodies in unison which have survived the centuries. In 1550 he published an edition of the Prayer

[1] *Lectures on the First Prayer Book of King Edward VI*, New York, 1881.

[2] Introduction to *The Book of Common Prayer, 1886, Compared with the Prayer Book of Edward VI, 1549*, 1887.

[3] *The Prayer Book, Articles and Homilies : some Forgotten Facts in their History*, 1897.

[4] *Some Principles and Services of the Prayer Book Historically Considered*, 1899.

[5] *The Workmanship of the Prayer Book in its Literary and Liturgical aspects*, 1899—*Further Studies in the Prayer Book*, 1908.

[6] *The History of the Book of Common Prayer*, 1909.

[7] *The English Liturgies of 1549 and 1661 Compared with each other and with the Ancient Liturgies*, 1920.

[8] *The Story of the English Prayer Book; its Origin and Developments*, 1926 : *Through the Prayer Book. An Exposition of its Teaching and Language ; The Origins and Contents of its Services*, 1932.

[9] Vol. XII, Louvain, 1911, Nos. 1, 2, 3.

[10] The principal subject of M. le Chanoine Couturier's *Le Book of Common Prayer et l'Eglise Anglicane*, 1928, English trans., with two new appendices (1930), is to write the history of the recent attempt at Prayer Book revision (1927-1928). In his second chapter, however, he treats of the Prayer Books of Edward, Elizabeth, and Charles I. To satisfy the Anglo-Catholics the Archbishop of Canterbury suggested a general permission to make use of the Prayer Book of 1540. Lord Halifax approved the suggestion. *The Good Estate of the Catholic Church*, 1930.

[11] See in *Liturgy and Worship*, above-mentioned, the chapter by its principal editor, Lowther Clarke: "The Prayer Book as Literature" (806-812).

Book "with musical notes," reprinted at Sydney in 1871 by E. F. Rimbault. H. Nicolson has recently produced a facsimile edition based on a copy in the British Museum at the end of his book: *Quires and Places Where They Sing* (London, 1932).[1]

E. *The Henricians and Cranmer* (Chapters VII and VIII).

For the moderate and the advanced parties, of which Gardiner and Cranmer were respectively the most distinguished representatives, I have already mentioned sources and books in my *Anglican Schism* (Chapters VI and VIII),[2] and in the General Bibliography of the present volume I have mentioned the works of Cranmer, Latimer,[3] Ridley, Hooper, John Bale, Myles Coverdale and Thomas Lever.

The introduction to A. F. Pollard's *Cranmer* contains a brief but carefully selected bibliography. The bibliography of the Rev. C. H. Smyth's *Cranmer and the Reformation under Edward VI* (Cambridge, 1926), a controversial work whose theology is sometimes abstruse and vague, enumerates the works of the Reformers who influenced Cranmer and the development of the Reformation in England. Those works which provide information about the Reformers are mentioned in their places in the course of my eighth chapter,[4] and I have already called attention to the importance of the *Zurich Original Letters*. J. Wickham Legg has published with an Introduction, Appendices and Notes *Cranmer's Liturgical Projects, Edited from British Museum MS. Royal 7B IV* (Bradshaw Society, 1915). There are old lives of Cranmer by Strype,[5] and

---

[1] See J. S. Bumpus, *A History of English Cathedral Music, 1549–1889*, 1908, 2 vols, and in particular, P. C. Buck and others, *Tudor Church Music, 1923–1930*, 10 vols.

[2] Eng. Trans., 458 *sqq.*

[3] G. M. Owst (*Literature and Pulpit in Medieval England, a neglected Chapter in the History of English Letters and of the English People*, Cambridge, 1933) has proved that the style and fashion of Latimer's preaching simply continued the tradition of the medieval English pulpit.

[4] For Bucer and Peter Martyr see Chapter VI.

[5] *Memorials of the Most Reverend Father in God, Thomas Cranmer, sometime Lord Archbishop of Canterbury*, 1694, Oxford, 1840, 2 vols.; London, 1853, 2 vols; Oxford Ecclesiastical History Soc., 1848–1854, 3 vols. The last is the edition I have used.

H. J. Todd,[1] more modern ones by C. H. Collette[2] and A. J. Mason,[3] and Hilaire Belloc's *Cranmer* (London, 1931). Belloc tells us that for most of his facts he is indebted to the erudition of Professor Pollard. His book he describes as being not so much a biography as a study of the Archbishop's character, motives, and literary genius, and of the part he played in the Church of England.[4]

There are two lives of Latimer,[5] a sort of autobiography of John Bale,[6] and Hooper's reforming activities are the subject of two studies, the one by James Gairdner,[7] the other by G. Baskerville.[8] In 1564 Myles Coverdale collected and published in London (it was his last work) letters of Cranmer, Ridley, Hooper and others: *The Letters of the Martyrs* (Ed. Edward Bickersteth, London, 1837).

For the Henricians the bibliography of J. A. Muller's *Stephen Gardiner and the Tudor Reaction* (London and New York, 1926) is complete. Appendix II (pp. 309–318) gives a catalogue of the Bishop's printed and manuscript works and Appendix III all his letters not published in the *State Papers of the Reign of Henry VIII*. Since then the same author has published *The Letters of Stephen Gardiner* (Cambridge, 1933). There are 173 letters, a number of which, and not the least important, were written in Edward's reign, twenty in prison.[9] M. P. Janelle in his thesis *L'Angleterre Catholique à la veille du Schisme* (Paris, 1935), deals chiefly with Gardiner, but in the reign of Henry VIII. The same author has published a biblio-

---

[1] *Life of Archbishop Cranmer*, 1831, 2 vols.
[2] *Life and Writings*, 1887.
[3] *Thomas Cranmer*, 1898, 1905.
[4] Chapters XII and XIII deal with Cranmer's action in the reign of Edward VI.
[5] Robert Demaus, *Hugh Latimer*, Religious Tract Society, 1869. R. M. and A. J. Carlyle, *Hugh Latimer*, Boston, 1899.
[6] *The Vocacyon of John Bale to the Bishoprick of Ossorie in Ireland*, Rome [London], 1553; reprinted in the *The Harleian Miscellany*, VI, 437.
[7] *Bishop Hooper's Visitation of Gloucester*, 1551, in vol. XIX (1904) of the *English Historical Review*.
[8] *Elections to Convocation in the Diocese of Gloucester*, ibid., vol. XLIV (1929).
[9] J. A. Muller has divided the 173 letters, of which only 75 had been previously published, and 60 of these only in part, into 13 chronological groups and prefaced each group with a brief *Introduction Note*. Groups 9, 10, 11 and 12 concern our period (Nos. 115–154, pp. 251–455).

graphy of the controversy on ecclesiastical discipline
and other matters between Gardiner and Bucer (*Revue
des sciences religieuses*, Strasbourg, July, 1927), and the
poem written against Gardiner at the beginning of
Edward's reign by a certain William Palmer (*Bulletin of
The Institute of Historical Research*, London, June and
November, 1928). James Gairdner wrote a life of Gardiner
in the second series of *Typical English Churchmen*, edited
by W. E. Collins (Church Historical Society, London,
1902). From this he extracted an article for the eleventh
edition of the *Encyclopaedia Britannica*. The article in the
fourteenth edition, according to J. A. Muller, *The Letters
of S. Gardiner*, p. 36, is very inferior, being "an unin-
telligent résumé of Gairdner's." The *Registra Stephani
Gardiner et Johannis Poynet Episcoporum Vintoniensium* (1531–
1547, 1551–1552), edited by Herbert Chitty (Canterbury
and York Society, V, xxxvii, 1930), is chiefly concerned
with Gardiner's episcopate. Of the treatises composed
by the Bishop—six were written in the Tower—the
most important for our period and subject dealt with the
Blessed Sacrament. Two answer Hooper,[1] two Cranmer,[2]

---

[1] *A discussion of Mr. Hooper's Oversight where he entreateth amonge his other
Sermons the matter of the Sacrament of the Bodye and Bloode of Christ*, 1550, in
manuscript. Cf. Muller, *op. cit.*, 204 *sq.*, 315. Already in 1546 Gardiner
had attacked Hooper in another treatise which was printed: *A Detection
of the Devils Sophistrie, wherewith he Robbeth the unlearned people of the True
Byleef in the Most Blessed Sacrament of the Aulter*, London, 1546. See below,
Appendix VI. In 1552, Gardiner wrote in prison "with an incredible speed"
a refutation of 19 articles imposed by Hooper the previous year upon the
clergy of his diocese. This refutation, together with refutations written by
two of Hooper's priests, was printed at Antwerp in 1564: *Responsio Vener-
abilium Sacerdotum Henrici Joleiffi et Roberti Jonson, sub Protestatione Facta
ad illos Articulos Joannis Hoperi, Episcopi Vigorniae Nomen Gerentis, in Quibus
a Catholica fide Dissentiebat: una cum Confutationibus Eiusdem Hoperi, et
Replicationibus R*mi *in Christo, Bonae Memoriae, Stephani Gardineri, Episcopi
Vintoniensis, tunc Temporis pro Confessione Fidei in Carcere Detenti.* Cf. Muller,
op. cit., 314 *sq.*

[2] *An Explicacion and Assertion of the True Catholique Fayth, touchyng the Most
Blessed Sacrament of the Aulter with Confutacion of a Booke written agaynst the
same*, 1551. The treatise is reprinted in Cranmer's works together with
his reply. Ed. Jenkyns, Vol. III, 33 *sqq.* Gardiner replied to Cranmer's
reply by a general answer to all who attacked the Catholic doctrine of the
Blessed Sacrament: *Confutatio Cavillationum, Quibus Sacrosanctum Eucharistiae
Sacramentum, ab Impiis Capernaitis Impeti Solet Authore Marco Antonio Constantio,
Theologo Lovaniensi.* Paris, 1552. Louvain, 1554. Cf. Muller, *op. cit.*,
207 *sqq.*, 313 *sq.*

a fifth Peter Martyr,[1] and a sixth Œcolampadius.[2]

Among the compositions of the other Henricians, the *De Veritate Corporis et Sanguinis Domini Nostri Jesu Christi in Eucharistia* by Bishop Tunstall of Durham is one of the best, and the *Holsome and Catholyke Doctryne Concerninge the Seven Sacramentes of Chryste's Church* by Thomas Watson, Gardiner's Chaplain, one of the most vigorous.[3] Watson, imprisoned under Edward (1547–8 and 1550), was made Bishop of Lincoln in Mary's reign (1557–9).

The work already mentioned, *Typical English Churchmen*, contains a chapter on Tunstall by G. H. Ross-Levin (Second Series). But Sturge's *Cuthbert Tunstall* (London, 1938) is more recent and fuller and very well documented. George Townsend wrote in 1842 under the title "A Tractarian British Critic," *The Life and Defence of . . . Edmund Bonner, Bishop of London.* S. R. Maitland also wrote on Bonner and Gardiner in his *Essays on Subjects Connected with the Reformation in England* (London, 1849, Chapters XV–XX). E. C. Messenger contributed to the *Dublin Review,* in January 1936, an article on "Bishop Bonner and Anglican Orders."

F. *The, Anglican Profession of Faith or the XLII Articles* (Chapter IX).

In his *Synodalia* (*A Collection of Articles of Religion, Canons . . . from the Year 1547 to the year 1717,* Oxford, 1842) Edward Cardwell republished from Bishop Gibson's (died 1748) *Synodus Anglicana* (1702), the XLII Articles of Edward VI and the XXXIX Articles of Elizabeth (1562 and 1571) in their Latin and English text. They are also to be found in the older histories

---

[1] *In Petrum Martyrem Florentinum Malae Tractacionis Querela Sanctissimae Eucharistiae Novissime Edita, Authore Stephano Vintoniensi,* in manuscript. Cf. J. A. Muller, *op. cit.,* 314, 315.

[2] *Annotaciones in Dialogum Joannis Œcolampadii cum suo Nathanaele de Mysterio Eucharistico Disceptantis.* Written in the Tower and still in manuscript. Cf. Muller, *op. cit.,* 316.

[3] Tunstall's Treatise was not printed until 1554, Paris, Watson's not until 1558, London. T. E. Bridgett reprinted the latter in 1876 with a biographical sketch of Watson.

We also possess visitation articles for his diocese of John Wakeman, Bishop of Gloucester (1541–1549). Wakeman had been Abbot of Tewkesbury (*English Historical Review XXXIX* (1924), 252 *sqq.*).

of the Reformation, such as Collier's (IX, 279 *sqq.*), and in Hardwick's *History of the Articles of Religion*, of which I shall be speaking shortly. In 1811 Dr. Burney published privately and at his own expense a species of concordance in six parallel columns containing Edward's Articles in the original Latin text, the English translation of them, the Articles of 1562 according to the original manuscript in the library of Benet College, Cambridge, the same Articles in accordance with the "Authorised edition" of 1563, and the Articles of 1571 from the original manuscript at Benet College.

In Chapter V of his *History of the Articles of Religion* (London, 1851, 1884, 1904), Charles Hardwick gave an excellent account of the XLII Articles, adding in an Appendix the various Anglican formularies issued between 1536 and 1615.[1] In his book *The Creeds of Christendom* (New York, 1877, 3 vols.) Ph. Schaff discussed them from the historical point of view (1592 *sqq.*) and added to the English the Scottish formularies (III, 437 *sqq.*). There is a copious bibliography.

There are numerous historical and theological explanations of the Articles for the use of the Anglican clergy from Bishop Forbes's *Explanation* and Boultbee's (died 1884) *Theology of the Church of England* to the rather brief *Introduction to the XXXIX Articles* by Maclear and Williams (London, 1908) and the Rev. E. T. Green's *Thirty-nine Articles and the Age of the Reformation* (London, 1896).

To perceive the difference between the interpretation respectively placed upon certain Articles by the Low and the High Church parties it is enough to compare Bishop E. H. Browne's (died 1891) *An Exposition of the Thirty-nine Articles*, which passed through numerous editions since its first publication in 1850, *The Thirty-nine Articles of the Church of England* by Bishop C. S. Gibson

[1] It begins with the Confession of Augsburg (Chapter II) from which the Articles of 1536 and the XIII Articles of 1538 were derived (Chapters III and IV). The author, after studying the Articles of Edward and Elizabeth (Chapters V and VI), studies the Lambeth Articles of 1595 (Chapter VII) and the Irish Articles of 1615 (Chapter VIII). Chapter IX is devoted to the Synod of Dort which condemned the Arminians and the final chapter deals with Puritan objections to several of the Anglican Articles.

of Gloucester (London, 1896, 7th ed., 1910) and the *XXXIX Articles, Their History and Explanation* (London, 1911) by Dr. Kidd, who took part in the Malines Conferences.

In 1699 Gilbert Burnet, Bishop of Salisbury, published *An Exposition of the Thirty-nine Articles of the Church of England* which was censured two years later by the Lower House of Convocation.

Already in Elizabeth's reign Anglican theologians, for example Archbishop Bancroft's chaplain, Thomas Rogers, defended the Catholicity of the Anglican Profession of Faith: *The Catholic Doctrine of the Church of England; An Exposition of the XXXIX Articles.*[1] Some deny that it is in any way Protestant.[2] Others have even attempted to reconcile the Articles with the doctrine of Trent.[3] But with the solitary exception of the Franciscan Christopher Davenport (died 1680), often called Francis a Sancta Clara, I do not think any Catholic theologian has attempted to give a Catholic meaning to the Anglican Articles. Davenport, appealing to the opinion of certain Anglican theologians, who had sought to correct the doctrine of their Church, wrote and dedicated to Charles I his *Paraphrastica Expositio Articulorum Confessionis Anglicanae* (1646). His treatise was reprinted in 1865 (London) by Fr. G. Lee (died 1902), who was converted to the Catholic Church a year before his death.

[1] This book of Thomas Rogers's was reprinted by J. J. S. Perowne at Cambridge, 1854, for the Parker Society.
[2] Rev. H. A. Moreton, *La Réforme Anglicane au XVIᵉ Siècle*, Paris, 1930: "The XXXIX Articles are certainly not Protestant."
[3] H. Edward Symonds, *The Council of Trent and Anglican Formularies*.

APPENDIX II

THE LITURGICAL USE OF THE VERNACULAR

THE ninth question which Cranmer submitted to the
Bishops when the Prayer Book was brought forward—
see Chapter III—asked whether the Mass should not
be celebrated in a language understood by the people.[1]
And an Article in one of Edward's first injunctions
envisaged the abolition of Latin as the liturgical language.[2]
The entire service was shortly to be in English. The
Lutheran *Nova ordinatio Lipsensis* of 1539 retained the
use of Latin for certain liturgical chants, mixing it with
German. The Introit, Gloria, Prose or Sequence,
and the Sanctus were sung in Latin, the Kyrie in Greek.
The Epistle was chanted in German and the Gospel;
and between them a German psalm replaced the Gradual
and Alleluia. The Creed was sung first in Latin, then in
German. The words of consecration were to be said in
German "in a loud and audible voice," the communion
of the people *sub utraque* was accompanied by the *Homo
Quidam* or German canticles.[3] Luther liked to mingle
different languages in the Divine Office; to Latin and
German he would like to have added Greek and Hebrew.
In their letter of August 5, 1538,[4] the German delegates
to the London Conference plead that the vernacular
should be employed for the new Mass: "For Paul commanded that a tongue understood by the people should
be used in the church." The Church has retained one
universal liturgical language as a sign of unity. Neverthe-

[1] Burnet, *op. cit.*, ed. Pocock, V, 212.
[2] Cardwell, *Documentary Annals of the Reformed Church of England*, Oxford,
1844, I, 20.
[3] See W. Friendensburg, *Nuntiaturberichte aus Deutschland*, IV, 566,
Note 1.
[4] Burnet, *op. cit.*, IV, 352.

less to keep those who were attracted to the Reformation by the use of the vernacular in the Protestant services, Ferdinand I and Catherine de Medicis asked the Council of Trent and Pius IV to sanction its employment. One of the Imperial theologians advised a mixture of Latin and the vernacular: "Though the employment of Latin in the Offices and chants of the Church is by no means to be superseded and abolished, but rather retained with the utmost reverence, nevertheless, since the unlearned multitude of both peoples "(Catholic and Protestant)" so insistently demand vernacular chanting and that the mysteries and sacraments of the Church should be made intelligible in their own tongue, if Mother Church . . . would by her supreme authority mercifully sanction or tolerate that in the awful sacrifice of the Mass, at sermons, and at Vespers some German prayers be mingled with the Latin and the holy sacraments be administered in the same tongue . . . according to the regulation of prudent men appointed for the purpose, it would be easier to bring back to the Church of God those who have lapsed or are ill-disposed to her solely on this account." *De Linguae Vernaculae usu in divinis officiis ac ecclesiasticis Sacramentis et canticis permittendo opinio.*[1]

When the French Revolution broke out, a demand for the use of French was raised in the Yonne.[2] And a bull of Pius VI of August 28, 1794, censured two propositions of the Council of Pistoia concerning the abolition of Latin in the Liturgy.

Since the Great War the Holy See has granted Yugoslav Catholics the use of their mother tongue in the chants both at Mass and Benediction and for the Rituale (April, 1921). And the recent Concordat permits old Slavonic to be used for the entire liturgy, including the Mass. Thus the Roman Catholic Church employs the vernacular as a liturgical language. The object of this concession is to promote a better understanding between the Orthodox and Rome, for the former attach great importance to the question of language.

[1] Vienna, Hofbibliothek MS., 5637, fol. 756,vo. Cf. Le Plat, *Monumentorum ad Historiam Concilii Tridentini . . . Collectio*, Louvain, 1781–1787, V, 387.
[2] Archives Nationales, soùs-série Div. 69, No. 2, 110.

APPENDIX III

CRANMER'S PROJECT FOR REFORMING THE BREVIARY

At Matins the introductory prayers "according to the very ancient custom of the Church"—namely the *Pater noster; Domine labia mea aperies; Deus in adjutorium; Gloria Patri* and *Alleluia,* or in Lent *Laus tibi Domine*—[1]are followed by the Invitatory Psalm, a hymn and three psalms each ended by the Gloria. Then after the *Pater* there are to be read outside the choir and in English, so that the people may hear them and be edified, three lessons. The first is taken from the Old Testament, the second from the Epistles, the Prophets, or the Apocalypse, the third from the Gospels or Acts. The *Te Deum* is then recited, followed on Sundays and feasts by a fourth lesson. This is followed by the *Benedictus*, the Collect of the day and the *Benedicamus Domino.* The office concludes with seven versicles and responses (*Ostende nobis Domine misericordiam tuam. Et salutare tuum da nobis. Dignare, Domine, die isto, Sine peccato nos custodire. Miserere nostri, Domine. Miserere nostri. Fiat misericordia tua, Domine, super nos. Quemadmodum speravimus in te. Domine Deus virtutum converte nos. Et ostende faciem tuam et salvi erimus. Domine exaudi orationem nostram. Et clamor noster ad te veniat. Dominus vobiscum. Et cum spiritu tuo*), the Collect of the Day and the Collect for Prime in the Breviary (*Domine, sancte Pater omnipotens, aeterne Deus, Qui nos ad principium hujus diei pervenire fecisti.*) [2]

At Evensong after the same introductory prayers as at Matins a hymn is sung and three psalms, followed by the Pater and two lessons, the first from the Old, the second from the New Testament Epistles "that the people may

[1] See above, p. 79 *sqq.*
[2] Cf. J. W. Legg, *Cranmer's Liturgical Projects,* 20 *sqq.*

return from Church better instructed in God's Word."
They conclude with the Magnificat, the Collect for the
Day and an Evening Collect.

The 150 Psalms—the longer of which (17, 67, 68, 77, 88,
104, 105, 106, 118) are divided into several parts and to
which seven Scripture canticles are added—are arranged
for monthly recitation. The February recitation begins
on January 31 and ends on March 1, and in months of
31 days the psalms for the 30th day are repeated on the
31st.[1] The Gospels and Acts, the third lesson, and the
Epistles, the second lesson, are to be read through three
times during the year; and the remainder of the Bible
(Prophets and Apocalypse for the second lesson, the rest
of the Old Testament for the first) once in the year.
By this means Cranmer believed the people hearing
every day holy lessons from God's Word would progress
in knowledge of Divine Truth, and their devotion would
be nourished.[2]

To appoint the daily lessons Cranmer wrote in his own
hand in the first draft of his Breviary, *Tabulae lectionum*.
These begin on Advent Sunday.[3] He also drew up two
calendars of the lessons to be read every day at Matins
and Evensong. One of these begins on January 2 with
Genesis, first lessons at Matins and Evensong, Isaiah,
second lesson at Matins, St. Matthew, third lesson at
Matins, and the Epistle to the Romans, second lesson at
Evensong. The other begins with Isaiah, the two first
lessons at Matins and the lesson at Evensong, and
St. Luke, third lesson at Matins. On January 4 it be-
gins Genesis, first lesson at Matins, Jeremiah, lesson at
Evensong and St. John, third lesson at Matins.[4] The
Second Prayer Book (1552) begins on January 2 with
Genesis, first lesson at Matins and Evensong, Saint
Matthew, second lesson at Matins, and the Epistle to the
Romans, second lesson at Evensong. The reason for
beginning on the second is that the first, being the Feast
of the Circumcision, has special lessons.

There are two hymns, at Matins and at Evensong,

---

[1] See Calendar I in Legg, *op. cit.*, 30 *sqq.* [3] Ibid., 143–153.
[2] Cf. J. W. Legg, *op. cit.*, 18 *sqq.*, 175. [4] Ibid., 3–14, 154–165.

which vary with the days of the week or in accordance with the season. Passion Week, Holy Week, Easter to Ascension, Ascension to Whitsunday, Whitsunday to Trinity Sunday.[1] They are taken either from the Sarum breviary or from the *Elucidatorium Ecclesiasticum* of Clichtovaeus (Paris 1516), as for example the *O Pater Summe Deitatis Ortus*.[2] Cranmer has merely changed their order either altering the day or putting a hymn of Evensong at Matins or vice versa.

The Collects are taken from the Sarum breviary or the Breviary of Quiñones. As we should expect, Cranmer follows not the Roman arrangement of the Collects after Trinity, but that of Sarum and other non-Roman uses in which they are a fortnight behind the Roman. For example the collect for the Fourth Sunday after Trinity is that of the third after Pentecost.[3]

Cranmer gives some of the fourth lessons to be read on feasts. (Others have merely a title, the remainder of the leaf being left blank—for example those of St. Edward the Confessor, Saint Joseph, Saint Athanasius, Saint Irenaeus, The Assumption, Nativity and Conception of Our Lady, and St. Martin).[4] Some are taken from the Bible, the Vulgate translation being often mixed with Erasmus's (*Novum instrumentum omne, diligenter ab Erasmo Roterodamo recognitum*, Basle 1527) which Cranmer usually prefers to the Vulgate. (Circumcision; Abel; St. Titus; Epiphany; St. Timothy; Conversion of Saint Paul; Ananias; Purification of the Blessed Virgin; St. Matthias; *Anna Uxor Helcanae;* St. Barnabas; the Nativity of St. John Baptist; St. Mary Magdalen; St. James; St. Matthew; *Omnes Sancti Defuncti*, which replaced All Saints; Christmas; St. Stephen; the Holy Innocents).[5] Or they are taken from the Fathers; from St. John Chrysostom (St. Babylas); from St. Jerome (St. Ignatius; St. Mark, a small portion; St. Peter and Paul; the Commemoration of

---

[1] Cf. J. W. Legg, *op. cit.*, 18 *sqq.*, 33–42.
[2] Ibid. 30.
[3] Ibid. 43–48.
[4] Ibid., 71, 75, 77, 87, 95, 98, 107.
[5] Ibid., 48, 49, 51, 52, 54, 57, 59, 64, 68, 75, 81, 86, 93, 94. 102, 106, 108, 109, 111.

Saint Paul; St. Luke; SS. Simon and Jude; St. John,
a portion);[1] from St. Basil (St. Gordius the Martyr)[2];
from St. Gregory Nazianzen (St. Basil);[3] from the
Ecclesiastical History of Socrates (St. John Chrysostom[4]
and St. Basil),[5] and Eusebius (SS. Phileas and Philo-
morus martyrs)[6]; from the *Historia Tripartita* (St. Ben-
jamin martyr; St. Cyprian)[7]; from biographers of the
patristic period, for example Possidius for St. Augustine,
and Paulinus of Milan for St. Ambrose;[8] occasionally from
Quiñones' Breviary (St. Hilary)[9] or Witzel's *Hagiologium*
(Mainz 1541) (St. Mark, the greater portion).[10]

[1] Cf. J. W. Legg, *op. cit.*, 18 *sqq.* 56, 63, 73 *sqq.*, 87, 89, 105, 106, 110.
[2] Ibid., 77.
[3] Ibid., 83.
[4] Ibid., 64.
[5] Ibid., 69.
[6] Ibid., 65.
[7] Ibid., 66, 98.
[8] Ibid., 96, 71.
[9] Ibid., 53.
[10] Ibid., 73.

APPENDIX IV

THE PRAYERS PRECEDING THE IMPOSITION OF HANDS IN THE ORDINAL OF 1552.

IN the form for conferring the Diaconate, the first prayer,[1] it evens mentions St. Stephen (*Cogitate beatum Stephanum* are the words of the Roman Pontifical) is evidently modelled upon the formula of the old liturgy. The idea expressed in the opening words: "Almighty God who by Thy divine Providence hast appointed divers orders of Ministers in Thy Church" echoes the Roman preface: "Pater omnipotens, aeterne Deus, bonorum dator, ordinumque distributor atque officiorum dispositor", also the bishop's exhortation to those about to be ordained priests "Hac certa mira varietate . . . Ecclesia sancta . . . regitur . . . cum alii in ea . . . diversorum ordinum viri consecrantur."

The Prayer which immediately precedes the imposition of hands,[2] in which the Bishop asks God "to make them constant in their ministration, and give them a ready will to observe all spiritual discipline; that, having always the testimony of a good conscience, they may continue ever stable and strong in Thy Son Christ": is directly taken from the portion of the Preface in the Roman *Pontifical* which immediately precedes the imposition of hands: "Abundet in eis totius forma virtutis, auctoritas modesta, innocentiae puritas et spiritualis observantia disciplinae . . . ut bonum conscientiae testimonium praeferentes, in Christo firmi et stabiles perseverantes." Apart from the concluding petitions of the Litany these are the only two prayers in the Anglican form for conferring the Diaconate.

In the form for ordaining priests the first prayer[3] begins like the corresponding prayer for the Diaconate and proceeds "replenish them with the truth of Thy

[1] Second Prayer Book. Ed. above mentioned, 222.   [2] Ibid., 225.
[3] Ibid., 230.

334

doctrine and adorn them with innocency of life that, both by word and good example, they may faithfully serve Thee in this office to the glory of Thy name and the edification of thy Church." It is obviously inspired by the exhortation which in the Roman Pontifical the Bishop addresses to the ordinands; "ut caelestis sapientia, probi mores et diuturna justitiae observatio ad id electos commendent. . . . Vos probi et maturi in scientia similiter et opere eritis. . . . Sit doctrina vestra spiritalis medicina populo Dei; sit odor vitae delectamentum Ecclesiae Christi, ut praedicatione atque exemplo aedificetis domum, id est familiam Dei."

The exhortation addressed by the Bishop to the ordinands is lengthier in the Anglican Ordinal[1] than in the Roman Pontifical. In both it reminds them of the duties of their office. But that of a sacrificing priest has been omitted together with the word "offer" in the Prayer Book form. "And now again we exhort you . . . that you have in remembrance into how high a dignity and to how weighty an office and charge ye are called: that is to say, to be messengers, watchmen, and stewards of the Lord; to teach and to premonish, to feed and provide for the Lord's family; to seek for Christ's sheep that are dispersed abroad. ("Consecrandi, filii dilectissimi" are the words of the Pontifical "in presbyteratus officium, illud digne suscipere ac susceptum laudabiliter exequi studeatis. Sacerdotem enim oportet *Offerre*, benedicere, praeesse, et praedicare et baptizare.") The idea which the Pontifical expresses in the words, "Imitamini quod tractatis, quatenus mortis Dominicae mysterium celebrantes, mortificare membra vestra a vitiis et concupiscentiis omnibus procuretis . . . ut aedificetis domum Dei" reappears in the words, "We have good hope . . . , that, by daily reading and weighing of the Scriptures, ye may wax riper and stronger in your ministry, and that ye may so endeavour yourselves from time to time, to sanctify the lives of you and yours and to fashion them after the rule and doctrine of Christ, that ye may be wholesome and godly examples and patterns for the people to follow."

[1] Second Prayer Book. Ed. above mentioned, 230-232.

The place occupied by the Preface in the Pontifical
is taken by an English preface of equal length, which like
the former immediately precedes the imposition of hands.
It recalls that Jesus Christ, "After He . . . was ascended
into heaven, sent abroad into the world his Apostles,
Prophets, Evangelists, Doctors and Pastors, by whose
labour and ministry He gathered together a great flock
in all the parts of the world." God is thanked that He
has "Vouchsafed to call these" His "servants here
present to the same office and ministry appointed for the
salvation of mankind." And the Bishop prays that
"through them and those whom He shall hereafter
choose, His name may be glorified both here or elsewhere" and his Kingdom enlarged. All sing the creed
at the Communion service and all receive Communion
from the Bishop. (In the Roman Pontifical the *Credo*
precedes the imposition of hands and the *Accipe Spiritum
Sanctum*). The office concludes with the Bishop's blessing
which follows a short prayer, a relic of the *Deus sanctificationum omnium auctor* in which he prays God "to send
upon these Thy servants Thy heavenly blessing, that
they may be clothed with righteousness and that Thy
word spoken by their mouths may have such success
that it may never be spoken in vain."

In the ordination of bishops, the prayers and ceremonies, hitherto more numerous than in the forms for
conferring the other orders, are reduced to a bare minimum, which is nevertheless sufficient since the consecratory prayer accompanies the imposition of hands.
Besides matter common to every order, the Litany, an
interrogatory and the Veni Creator, also an oath of
canonical obedience to the archbishop, which replaces
the former oath of obedience to the Pope, there is simply
the imposition of hands, preceded by the prayer of consecration and the delivery of the Bible (in the Pontifical
it is the Gospel) together with an exhortation to teach
and faithfully observe God's word; "Be to the flock of
Christ a shepherd, not a wolf, feed them, devour them
not. Hold up the weak, heal the sick, bind up the broken,
bring again the outcasts, seek the lost." The Communion

and Consecration conclude with a brief prayer in which
the consecrating bishop asks God to "endue" the new
bishop "with Thy Holy Spirit, that he, preaching Thy
word, may not only be earnest to reprove, beseech and
rebuke with all patience and doctrine; but also may
be to such as believe a wholesome example in word, in
conversation, in love, in faith, in chastity and in purity:
that faithfully fulfilling his course, at the latter day he
may receive the crown of righteousness laid up by the
Lord the righteous Judge." Possibly there is in these
words an echo of the Pontifical "ut tui Spiritus virtus
et interiora ejus repleat et exteriora circumtegat. Abundet
in eo constantia fidei, puritas dilectionis, sinceritas pacis.
. . . Da ei Domine, ministerium reconciliationis in
verbo et in factis." The anointing of head and hands,
the delivery of the crozier, ring and mitre have disappeared. The prayer of consecration runs, "O Lord,
Holy Father, Almighty, Everlasting God: Who of Thine
infinite goodness hast given Thine only and dearly beloved Son Jesus Christ to be our Redeemer and the
author of everlasting life, who after that He had made
perfect our redemption by His death and was ascended
into heaven, poured down His gifts abundantly upon
men, making some Apostles, some Prophets, some Evangelists, some Pastors and Doctors to the edifying and
making perfect His church: Grant, we beseech Thee to
this Thy servant such grace, that he may evermore be
ready to spread abroad Thy Gospel, the glad tidings of
reconciliation with Thee; and use the authority given
him, not to destruction but to salvation; not to hurt
but to help: so that as a wise and faithful servant giving
to Thy family their portion in due season, he may at
last be received into everlasting joy through Jesus Christ
Our Lord."

The conclusion recalls the following passage from the
Preface in the Roman Pontifical. "Sit fidelis servus et
prudens, quem constituas tu, Domine, super familiam
tuam ut det illis cibum in tempore opportuno et exhibeat
omnem hominem perfectum."

APPENDIX V

LEO XIII'S BULL "APOSTOLICAE CURAE" AND THE INVALIDITY OF ANGLICAN ORDINATIONS

THE bull pronounces "Anglican ordinations invalid and null" on account of defective form and intention. They do not ordain *Sacrificing* priests. Therefore, Anglican clergymen, if they are to become Catholic priests, must be *unconditionally* reordained.

As regards the rite itself this bull of September 13, 1896, passes the following judgment upon the Anglican Ordinal. In every sacrament the due matter and form are required. But the words *Accipe Spiritum Sanctum*, which until recent times Anglicans regarded as the form of their orders are insufficient for the priesthood and episcopate. As regards the former they do not sufficiently define the priesthood, its grace and power, in particular the power *Consecrandi et Offerendi Verum Corpus et Sanguinem Domini*, which is the essential priestly power.[1] The Prayer, "Almighty God, giver of all good things"[2] would be a sufficient form were it not too far distant from the imposition of hands.[3] The form for conferring the episcopate makes no allusion to his *summum sacerdotium*, and is therefore insufficient. When more than a century had passed, these formulas were indeed completed. But apart from the fact that the hierarchy had become extinct, the additional words do not possess the meaning required by Catholic doctrine. "The authors of the Ordinal, only too well aware of the

[1] Council of Trent, Session XXIV, *De Sacrificio Missae*, Can. 3.
[2] *Second Prayer Book*, 230.
[3] In 1552 it was the collect of the Litany and it preceded the oath of supremacy, the exhortation to the ordinands and their interrogatory. In 1662 it became the collect of the Holy Communion.

338

necessary relationship between faith and worship, altered
the entire liturgy to bring it into conformity with the
erroneous doctrines of the Reformers under the pretext
of restoring it to its primitive form. Accordingly the
Ordinal not only makes no explicit mention of the
Eucharistic sacrifice, of consecration or of priesthood but,
as we have pointed out above, its compilers were at the
utmost pains to suppress and obliterate any traces of
these institutions, which still remained in the Catholic
prayers partly retained. The adoption of a novel rite
which denies or perverts the sacrament of orders and
rejects every notion of consecration and sacrifice completely deprives the formula, "Receive the Holy Spirit"
of its value. With this defect of form is combined defective
intention. . . . If in fact the rite has been changed with the
manifest intention of introducing another not admitted
by the Church and rejecting the rite she employs, it is
plain that not only is the intention required by the sacrament wanting, but there is a contrary intention opposed
to the sacrament. . . . Undoubtedly the episcopate is
a priesthood of higher rank. Therefore, in view of the
fact that the sacrament of order and the true priesthood
of Christ had been expelled from the Anglican rite and its
episcopal consecration in no way conferred the priesthood, the episcopate could no longer be truly and legiti-
mately conferred, especially since one of a Bishop's
principal functions is to ordain the ministers of the Holy
Eucharist and the Holy Sacrifice." The apostolic succession was therefore broken. It was in vain that a century later "in the time of Charles II certain Anglican
teachers endeavoured to admit to some extent the sacrifice
and priesthood . . . and it was equally in vain that a
few of them thought it possible to give the Ordinal a
satisfactory and Catholic interpretation."

The Tractarian Movement in the nineteenth century,
by reviving the ancient doctrine of priesthood in the
Catholic sense, brought up again the question whether
Anglican orders are valid.[1] But it was not until 1894

[1] P. Rich. Henrick, *The Validity of Anglican Ordinations Examined*, Philadelphia, 1841; Russell, *Anglican Ordination Valid*, London, 1846; J. Oldknow,

that the controversy was really brought to life by an
article of Dalbus (Père Portal), a friend of Lord Halifax,
on "Les ordinations anglicanes."[1] The Abbé Duchesne[2]
supported him. The Jesuit Sydney Smith had hardly
replied to him when a Latin work by Denny and Lacey,[3]
which concluded with the prayer "Pro Ecclesia sancta
Dei; ut eam Deus et Dominus noster pacificare, adunare
et custodire dignetur toto orbe terrarum" and began
with a preface by the Bishop of Salisbury, John Wordsworth, brought to the notice of continental theologians
and canonists arguments which were either new or
unknown to most of them.[4] The discussion conducted
with equal vigour and courtesy made a deep impression
and almost convinced some of the original opponents of
Anglican orders that they were after all valid. (Contrast
Gasparri's judgment of them in his *De Sacra Ordinatione*
and his judgment in the pamphlet *De la valeur des ordinations anglicanes*, Paris, 1895. See also Boudinhon's *Étude
théologique sur les ordinations anglicanes*, Paris, 1895, and his
article "De la validité des ordinations anglicanes"
(Paris, 1896). The story of the irregular consecration at the
Nag's Head Tavern in Cheapside, of Parker, the fountain-
head of the entire Anglican clergy, was now recognised
as a fabrication of Holywood's, forty-five years after the

The Validity of the Holy Orders in the Church of England, London, 1857; W.
Stubbs, *Registrum Sacrum Anglicanum. An Attempt to Exhibit the Course of
Episcopal Succession in the Church of England*, Oxford, 1858; H. W. Haddan,
Apostolical Succession in the Church of England, 1869 (re-issues in 1879 and 1883);
Dr. F. G. Lee, *The Validity of the Holy Orders of the Church of England Vindicated*,
London, 1869; Raynal, *Ordinal of Edward VI*, 1870; Estcourt (Catholic),
The Question of Anglican Orders Discussed, London, 1873; Brun, *Anglican
Orders, Are they Valid?* London 1877; Hutton (Catholic), *The Anglican
Ministry, its Nature and Value in Relation to the Catholic Priesthood*, London,
1879; Meyrick, *Die Bischöfliche Succession in der Anglicanischen Kirche*,
London, 1880.
It was decided not to invite the Anglican bishops to the Vatican Council,
because their orders were not recognised as valid. See Dom C. Butler,
The Vatican Council, 1930, I, 95.

[1] *Science Catholique*, December 15, 1893, January 15 and April 15, 1894.
[2] *Bulletin Critique*, July 1894.
[3] *De Hierarchia Anglicana Dissertatio Apologetica*, published at the expense
of the English Church Union, London, 1895.
[4] See Duchesne's review in the *Bulletin Critique*, July 1894. Denny had
already discussed the question in his *Anglican Orders and Jurisdiction*.

consecration in question[1] spread and embellished by Fitzsimon[2] and A. Champney[3] accepted by theologians such as Perrone, S. J., in his *Praelectionibus theologicis*[4] and for a time by the canonist Gasparri.[5] Besides this fable, the fact that the page recording Parker's consecration is lacking from the episcopal register of Canterbury seemed to justify the contention of those who saw in its absence a proof of the invalidity of his consecration and consequently of Anglican orders, and that the leaf had been destroyed to get rid of its damaging evidence. But the archbishop's register, recognised as undoubtedly authentic by the Catholic historian Lingard and by Canon Estcourt, proves that Parker was consecrated at Lambeth Palace on December 17, 1559, and the fact is no longer questioned.[6]

The *Revue anglo-romaine* in 1895 and 1896[7] took an active part in the controversy which finally engaged to a certain extent the interests of the general public. English Catholics led by Cardinal Vaughan were throughout hostile to Anglican orders and the notion of corporate reunion.[8] Rome took action. A commission was appointed composed both of partisans and opponents of Anglican orders and the bull of September 13, 1896, terminated the controversy. "*Auctoritate Nostra, motu proprio, certa scientia, pronuntiamus et declaramus ordinationes ritu anglicano actas, irritas prorsus fuisse et esse, omninoque nullas.*" The Archbishops of Canterbury and York replied to the bull in the name of the Anglican clergy on February 19, 1897, and defended the validity of their

---

[1] *De Investigatione Verae et Visibilis Christi Ecclesiae*, Antwerp, 1604.
[2] *Britanomachia Ministrorum*, Douai, 1614.
[3] *De Vocatione Ministrorum*, Paris, 1618.
[4] *Tractatus de Ordine*, No. 137, Note 4.
[5] No. 1111 of his *De Sacra Ordinatione*, 1893.
[6] See Bramhall, *Works*, ed. the Anglo-Catholic Library, Vol. III; Denny and Lacey, *op. cit.*, Chapters I and III, Appendices III and IV; Mgr. Barnes, *Bishop Barlow and Anglican Orders*, 1922, Chapters VI, VIII; *Month*, July 1922, also *Dublin Review*, same date. Appendix I of Denny and Lacey deals with Archbishop Laud who was consecrated by a former Bishop of Spalato and with certain Irish bishops consecrated by the Archbishop of Dublin or by Marian Bishops.
[7] See also Mgr. Moyes's Articles in the *Tablet*, 1895.
[8] See letter from Fr. Woodlock, S. J., *Tablet*, January 5, 1924.

orders.[1] To this reply, which was based mainly on Low Church principles, Cardinal Vaughan and the Catholic hierarchy replied in turn by the *Vindication of the Bull "Apostolicae Curae"* (1898). They had been anticipated by Segna: *Breves animadversiones in responsionem Archiepiscoporum anglicanorum ad litteras Apostolicas Leonis P.P. XIII "Apostolicae Curae"* (1897). The Jesuit Brandi commented on the bull and brought arguments in support of its conclusion in his "Condanna Delle Ordinazioni Anglicane",[2] an article translated into French and English[3] under the title "Rome and Canterbury" (1898). The Rev. A. S. Barnes also defended the bull by a collection of documents,[4] while the Anglicans on their part attacked it in a treatise published in 1898 by the Church Historical Society: *Treatise on the Bull Apostolicae Curae.* Finally in 1900 A. Lownes published in New York two volumes maintaining the validity of Anglican Orders: *Vindication of Anglican Orders.*

Leo XIII, who in 1894 had received Lord Halifax twice, followed attentively after the issue of the bull the repercussions of its publication. He personally replied in mild and courteous language to the Anglican archbishops. He pointed out that he was bound to judge Anglican orders by the standards of Catholic doctrine and that on their own admission the views of their Church on Orders, the Priesthood, and the Eucharistic Sacrifice were very remote from the teaching of the Catholic and Roman Church. Then by his command a prelate very well acquainted with English affairs wrote in 1897 a report on the impression produced in England by the letter *Ad Anglos* (April 14, 1895) the encyclical *Satis Cognitum*, and the Apostolic constitution *Apostolicae Curae*. It was published in the *Civiltà Cattolica* on July 6, 1912. After the Pope's death Lord Halifax, who never abandoned

---

[1] *Responsio ad Litteras Apostolicas Leonis Papae XIII de Ordinationibus Anglicanis ;* the English text appeared at the same time and was reprinted in 1912. It is to be found in Vol. III of *Hierurgia Anglicana.* Ed. V. Staley, 269–307.

[2] *Civiltà Cattolica*, Vol. VIII, 1897.

[3] *American Ecclesiastical Review*, XVI, 1897.

[4] *The Popes and the Ordinal. Documents bearing on the Question of Anglican Orders*, London, 1897.

his dream of reunion, reopened the question by a thick volume of 470 pages, in which he strove to prove that Leo's condemnation of Anglican orders had been influenced by a previous decision of 1704 (a Decree of the Sacred Congregation of the Inquisition which declared the ordination of Bishop John Gordon invalid) and that the Commission appointed by him spent the greater part of its time discussing the historical aspect of Anglican ordination and took little account of the essential matter of the rite which for lack of theological competence was treated in a most summary fashion.[1] His book called forth refutations by Dom Gasquet (*The Tablet*, April 13, 1912), and Canon Moyes of Westminster (*Ibid.*, May 25 and June 8, 1912).[2] The Malines Conversations, December 1921 and March 1923, in which Lord Halifax (died 1934) was the protagonist on the Anglican side, as was Cardinal Mercier on the Catholic, revived in another form the project of a corporate reunion of the Anglican with the Catholic Church, a project in which the English Catholics had no more faith in 1923 than in 1895.[3] The Anglicans, however, had not lost hope that the condemnation of their orders might yet be reversed.[4]

---

[1] *Lord Halifax, Leo XIII and Anglican Orders*, London, 1912. In 1910 T. A. Lacey wrote the history of the enquiry which led up to the bull of 1896: *A Roman Diary and other Documents relating to the Papal Enquiry into English Ordinations*, 1896.

An Anglican, Professor Childe of Oxford, in his book on "Church and State under the Tudors," took up the same standpoint as the bull *Apostolicae Curae* and employed the same arguments, about the time when Leo was preparing it.

[2] See *The Month*, April 1912, 337.

[3] Cf. P. Janelle, *Anglicanisme et Catholicisme* in the *Revue Anglo-Américaine*, December 1924, 114–132.

J. G. Lockhart in his life of Lord Halifax (*Charles Lindley, Viscount Halifax*, London, 1935–1936, 2 vols) devotes Chapters IV and XVIII to XXII of Volume 2 to "Leo XIII and Anglican Orders" (38–91) and "The Malines Conversations" (265–343). Lord Halifax had published in 1930; *The Conversations of Malines* (1921–1925). *Original Documents*.

[4] As the bull points out, it is concerned with a point of discipline and not with a definition of doctrine involving infallibility as defined by the Vatican Council (cf. Billot, ed. 4, 631 and the article on Infallibility in the *Dictionnaire de Théologie Catholique*). Nevertheless it was the intention of the Pope, as Cardinal Richard wrote, "to pronounce a final judgment and to settle definitely this very important question", so that "all Catholics are bound to receive the decision with the utmost respect as a matter settled and not subject to appeal."

The Jesuit S. Smith, who had taken part in the original controversy, summed it up in the sixteenth instalment of the *Dictionnaire Apologétique de la foi Catholique* (Ed. 4, 1920). Father E. C. Messenger has discussed the question afresh more extensively and in greater detail in two large volumes.[1] Having first explained the Catholic doctrine on the Mass, Orders and the priesthood, he compares with it the Anglican doctrine on the same subjects in the time of Edward VI, Elizabeth and the Stuarts and proves that the latter was Protestant even in the reigns of James I, Charles I and Charles II, when there was a Catholicising reaction in the Church of England. The final portion of his book, "The Theological Discussion and Final Condemnation of Anglican Orders"[2] recounts the history of the theological discussions of Anglican Orders during the last three centuries, their condemnation by Pope Leo's bull, and the recognition of their validity by the Old Catholics and certain orthodox churches. The concluding theological Essay of seventy pages is devoted to proving that the Anglican rite of ordination to the priesthood has in view "a Protestant ministry evangelical and pastoral in character" which, however, according to Catholic doctrine, "is not the true Christian ministry"; so that Anglican ordination "confers nothing in the sight of God"; and "Anglican clergymen are therefore in God's eyes laymen."

For centuries the Eastern orthodox have regarded Anglican orders in the same light as Catholics regard them. Certain recent orthodox recognitions of their validity are but isolated acts and in many cases have been vehemently contested by the vast majority of the clergy.

Archbishop Wake of Canterbury (died 1737), who cherished hopes of a *rapprochement* with the Gallican Church through the intermediary of Le Courayer,[3] was the first to attempt a similar agreement with the Russian and Greek Churches (1725). His attempt was unsuccessful. It was not until 1841 that negotiations

[1] *The Reformation, the Mass and the Priesthood*, London, 1936–1937.
[2] Vol. II, 464–730.
[3] Cf. P. E. Shaw, *The Early Tractarians and the Eastern Church*, Milwaukee, 1930.

were resumed, equally without success.[1] Since 1863, when an Anglican committee was appointed to study the question of intercommunion with the Greco-Russian church, representatives of the Orthodox Church have regularly taken part in the Lambeth Conferences; and in 1921 for the first time a mixed committee drew up "the terms of a proposed intercommunion between the Church of England and the Orthodox Churches." In the autumn of the following year the Patriarch of Constantinople, Meletios IV Metaxakis, acting in the name of his Church alone and *with reservations*, recognised by an isolated act the validity of Anglican orders. He was followed in 1935 by the heads of the orthodox Churches of Jerusalem, Cyprus and Alexandria which were immediately under English influence.[2] In Roumania in March 1936 the Holy Synod recognised Anglican orders as valid, founding its decision on the agreement concluded in strict secrecy the previous year by a mixed conference of Anglican and Roumanian theologians. This agreement based upon a typically English compromise was not secured without laborious Anglican explanations of their doctrine, which on many points misrepresented the official teaching of the Church of England. The National Church League protested against this agreement of Bucharest (July 30, 1936), the fifteen hundred clerical members of the Anglican Evangelical Group Movement declared it contrary to the doctrine of the Anglican Church (*Record*, August 14, 1936), and in January 1937, the 110th Conference of Evangelical theologians denounced it as a caricature of that doctrine. Nevertheless the Convocation of Canterbury approved it (January 1937). In Roumania, where it was not considered advisable to publish the official texts of the agreement, it met with an extremely hostile reception from well nigh the entire body of clergy, secular and regular, who regarded it as based on "a pure fiction" and "refused to recognise" any compromise with the heretics.[2] Finally the Arch-

---

[1] See in *The Christian East* (London, 1931, pp. 1–3), *Recognition of the Validity of Anglican Ordinations by the Patriarchate of Alexandria, with Translation*.

[2] See Articles by P. Galaction in the Bucharest periodical, *Carentul*, autumn and winter, 1936–1937, and articles by Frs. Gregory Antal and

bishop of Athens, Mgr. Chrysostom Papadopoulos, "The most learned and best informed member of the Orthodox Church," though favourable to an understanding between the Churches, has expressed the view that the question of Anglican Orders is a dogmatic question, which therefore concerns the entire Orthodox Church and can be settled only by a general council, not by the decision of a single patriarch.[1]

Marin Tonescu in the *Glasul Monahilor* of October 11 and 18, 1936, intended for the general public.

[1] See his *Validity of Anglican Ordinations*. Translation with preface by J. A. Douglas, London, 1931.

APPENDIX VI

LETTERS WRITTEN BY GARDINER DURING THE REIGN OF EDWARD VI

THE excellent collection of Bishop Gardiner's letters by J. A. Muller (Cambridge, 1933) of which I spoke above (Appendix I, E) is of particular interest for the period we are studying. Numerous and long, they afford plentiful information on the hopes and illusions entertained, and the tactics employed by the moderate or orthodox party known as the Henricians, and on their treatment first by Somerset, later by Warwick.

When Edward succeeded to the throne, Gardiner thought he could count upon the friendship of the Earl of Hertford, now Lord Protector. Therefore he did not conceal from him his views both political and religious. His friend Paget was now the Protector's right-hand man. Gardiner accordingly expected that through them he would be able, though excluded by Henry's will from all official participation in the administration, to influence to some extent the government of the country. But he soon perceived that Paget had trimmed his sails to the wind and abandoned him. The discovery led him to state his philosophy of life. He opposed to the utmost of his power Cranmer's religious innovations. He appealed to the King's Book, which the Archbishop had approved in 1543, begging him not to contradict himself. But his fears were realised when Cranmer published his Homilies —which were imbued with Protestant doctrine, particularly on the subject of justification—and they were imposed upon the kingdom. In the Protector's absence on his campaign against Scotland (August–September 1547) he protested to the Privy Council against false doctrine, whose effect on the Emperor and the Imperial alliance would be disastrous. He denounced the Act of Parliament as illegal, and in this connection raised the general question of the relation between the Royal Supremacy and Statute Law. Of this letter the historian and Bishop Gilbert Burnet observed that he had never read anything more Christian or more episcopal (Numbers 115–129).

The reply of the Council was to imprison Gardiner in the Fleet (September 25, 1547) on the pretext that he refused to obey the Royal ordinances, in reality because the Council feared he would organise Parliamentary opposition to Cranmer's religious projects. He was still in prison when Somerset returned from Scotland. Gardiner explained his attitude to the Protector, reminding him by the example of Thomas Cromwell, of the danger incurred by unconstitutional action. He criticised the faulty translation of Erasmus's *Paraphrases* and the injunction placing a copy in every Church for the people to read. No other juncture in his life reveals more strikingly the determination of his character than this when, abandoned by all and reduced to complete destitution, he expressed himself happy to suffer for the Commonwealth and the Church (Numbers 130–139).

He was set free on January 7, 1548, as the result of a general amnesty. But the Parliament, whose session concluded two days later, had repealed the Statutes on which Gardiner had based his opposition to the *Book of Homilies*. Therefore the Council called upon him to subscribe the homilies on justification and salvation. He refused, appealing this time to their lack of official sanction. But he wrote to Somerset that he could not approve these homilies, which attributed to the Fathers what they had not taught. He was confined to his own house in Southwark from which he sent a second reply which we no longer possess, but with which the Council, at Somerset's intervention, expressed itself satisfied, and he was sent back to his diocese. There he completed his treatise against Bucer[1] (Numbers 140–144). On the

---

[1] *Exetasis Testimoniorum, Quae Martinus Bucerus ex Sanctis Patribus non Sancte Edidit, ut Patrocinetur Opinioni de Caelibatus Dono, Quam sine dono Spiritus, Contra Ecclesiam Defendit Orthodoxam.* Gardiner sent this treatise to the press in 1548. His imprisonment delayed its publication and it was not printed till 1554 at Louvain.

morrow of his famous sermon on St. Peter's Day, 1548, the
Council sent him to the Tower. Warwick, who he had
hoped would restore orthodoxy after Somerset's fall,
subjected Gardiner to a lengthy trial, deprived him of
his see and kept him in confinement until the end of the
reign. During his imprisonment he wrote six polemical
treatises, in particular the treatise on the Eucharist
against Cranmer[1] (Numbers 145–154).

[1] J. A. Muller (445 *sqq.*) prints the prefaces he wrote at this time to
four of these treatises: the treatise against Peter Martyr, the *Explication of
the True Catholique Fayth* against Cranmer, his reply to Cranmer's reply and
his *Annotaciones* against Œcolampadius.

INDEX

Prepared by DOROTHY E. LYNN *and* EUGENE P. WILLGING, *University of Scranton Library, Scranton, Pennsylvania*

Note: This index differs from that of the preceding volume in that it includes references to subjects, e.g., Mass, supplies modifications where more than five page references are made to a person, and omits names of writers or authors cited in footnotes and in the bibliographical appendices. The following special marks have been used, but sparingly:

* Denoting more than one mention on a page.

n Signifies a note on the page.

q Signifies quoted.

INDEX

INDEX

INDEX

INDEX

INDEX

INDEX

INDEX

INDEX

INDEX

Privy Council, not restrained by Somerset, 40-2; under Henry VIII, 41

Processions, renewed injunction against, 47

Protestantism, growth in Scotland, 99-100; introduced into Church of England, 15; progress under Warwick, 147-70, 220; Western England's rebellion against, 116-7; see also Anabaptists; Calvin; Luther; Lutherans; Zwingli

Protestants, cause espoused by Warwick, 147; denounce return to Catholicism, 145; under Somerset, 44

Psalter, reading of, 80

Purgatory, belief in, claimed superstitious, 157; denied in act against chantries, 64; Lutheran attitude toward, 12; prayers of belief in suppressed, 191; rejected by Cranmer, 250, 287; in Ten Articles of 1536, 12-3

Q

Quiñones, Francisco, O.S.F., General of his Order (1523), Cardinal (1528), breviary revised by, 79-80n

R

Rands, Henry (d. 1551), see Holbeach, or Rands, Henry (d. 1551), bishop of Lincoln

Rationale of Rites and Ceremonies, 67

Real Presence, see Eucharist

Reformatio Legum Ecclesiasticarum, by Cranmer, 20

Reformation, advance toward, 60
Anglican party favors, 18
becomes Calvinist, 241
bishops' material support of, 162-3
Burnet on sacrilegious motives of, 166
checked by Henricians, 17-8, 307
Christian worship and the, 13
Cranmer's contribution, 50-1, 247-68
encouraged in Scotland, 100
favored by Somerset, 37
German, imposed on Anglican liturgy, 84
gradually accepted under Edward VI, 53

Reformation—(Continued)
Henry VIII's attitude toward, 6, 20-1
influence of continental reformers, 269
progress under Warwick, 148-71
rejected by rebels, 119
Somerset's cautious advance, 46-52
See also: Anabaptists; Calvin; Luther; Lutherans; Zwingli

Reformed churches, proposed union of, 270-4

Reformers
chosen by Henry VIII to represent advanced party after his death, 21
complaint against Cranmer, 1, 251
Cranmer's attempt to unite, 270-4
delighted with liturgical changes, 205
demand abolition of clerical celibacy, 51-2
during reign of Edward VI, 22
during reign of Elizabeth, 22
impossibility of union, 273-4
influence during reign of Edward VI, 220
influence on Book of Common Prayer, 251
oppose Six Articles of 1539, 19
opposition to Somerset, 126
position against Catholic Mass, 62, 65
satisfied by Order of Communion, 63-4
weakening of, 19-20
See also Henricians

Religion, repeal of statutes against, 43-4; Articles of, submitted by Cranmer, 283

Reverence, diminution of, 102-3

Rich, Sir Richard (1496?-1567), 30

Ridley, Nicholas, bishop of Rochester (1500?-1555)
abolishes altar at St. Paul's, 177
attempts to convert Gardiner, 231
challenges public disputation of Eucharist at Cambridge, 281
changes position of communion table, 179
changes Prayer Book (First), 176-9
espouses Lutheran doctrine on Mass, 65
influence on Cranmer, 255

INDEX

INDEX

Shaxton, Nicholas, Bishop of Salisbury (1535-39), 17-8, 20

Sick, prayers recited at visitation of, 203-4

Silver, debasement of, 103

Sion Abbey (Middlesex), 4

Skip, John, Bishop of Hereford (d. 1552), 238-9, 240

Slavery, in 16th century England, 109

Smith, Richard, Roman Catholic divine (1500-1563), 65-6, 248, 261-2, 264, 280

Somerset, Duke of, *see* Seymour, Edward

Southwell, Richard, 145, 147

Star Chamber, under Warwick, 42

Strange, Lord, 139

Strozzi, 98

Strype, John, 62

Stukeley, Thomas, adventurer, supporter of Somerset (1525?-1578), 131

Succession, Acts of, 1536 and 1543, 4-5

Suffolk, Duke of, *see* Grey, Henry

Surrey, Earls of, *see:* 1. Howard, Thomas, Earl of Surrey and third Duke of Norfolk (1473-1554); 2. Howard, Henry, Earl of Surrey (by courtesy) (1517?-1547)

Sydney, Henry (1529-1586), 136

T

Taxation, arbitrary, imposed by James I and Charles I, 102; diminishing returns, 102-3

Taylor, John, Bishop of Lincoln (1503?-1554), 65

Ten Commandments, *see* Commandments, Ten

Test Act, against belief in transubstantiation, 292

Thirlby, Thomas, Bishop of Westminster (1540-50), of Norwich (1550-54), and of Ely (1554-58), against Parliament legislating on religious matters, 87; deprived of See, 245-6; finds church at Norwich stripped of altars, 178; opposed Second Prayer Book, 207; opposed to religious change, 245; receives See of Ely from Mary Tudor,

246; voted against formulation of Ordinal, 207

Thomas More, St., execution of, 35; quoted on agrarian crisis, 107-8, 110; quoted on large-scale farming, 104; *Utopia* of, 105

Toleration, anticipated by Somerset's government, 42

Tractarian Movement, and validity of Anglican Orders, 339-40

Tracy, Richard, Gloucestershire gentleman, 18

Tradition, Cranmer's respect for, 284

Traheron, Bartholomew, Protestant writer (1510?-1558?), 172, 259, 262, 282

Transubstantiation, Bucer's refutation of, 187; concomitance substituted for, 77; Cranmer's argument against, 266-7; liturgy on, prepared by Bucer, 188; *see also* Eucharist

Treason, repeal of statute against, 42-3; revived by Warwick, 148; trials under Somerset, 42-3

Tremellius, John Immanuel, Hebraist (1510-1580), background of, 275-6; consulted about revision of Prayer Book, 277; follows Peter Martyr to London, 275; meets with Cranmer at Lambeth on reform of First Prayer Book, 174

Tremillio, Emmanuele, *see* Tremellius

Trent, Council of, Bucer's *De Regno Christi* employed at, 184; on Communion under both kinds, 294; under one kind, 11-12; condemns Cranmer's twenty-third article, 287; defines dogma of Eucharist, 8; on private Masses, 9n; on Scripture, 284; upholds Catholic doctrine of Mass, 293-4

Tunstall, Cuthbert, Bishop of London (1522-30) and of Durham (1530-52; 1553-59), attacks First Prayer Book, 239; chosen by Henry VIII to represent Henricians, 21; Cranmer's reply to, concerning Real Presence, 261; *De Veritate Corporis et Sanguinis* . . . , 244; deposed and imprisoned by Warwick, 243;

INDEX